The METAFONTbook

COMPUTERS & TYPESETTING / C

The METAFONTbook

DONALD E. KNUTH *Stanford University*

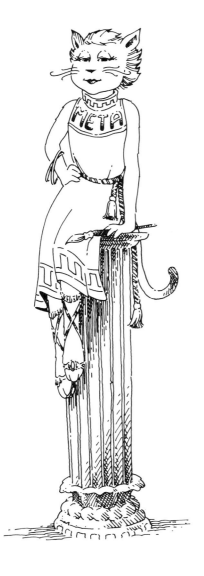

Illustrations by
DUANE BIBBY

**ADDISON–WESLEY
PUBLISHING COMPANY**

Reading, Massachusetts
Menlo Park, California
New York
Don Mills, Ontario
Wokingham, England
Amsterdam · Bonn
Sydney · Singapore · Tokyo
Madrid · San Juan

This manual describes METAFONT Version 2.0. Some of the advanced features mentioned here are absent from earlier versions.

The joke on page 8 is due to Richard S. Palais.

The Wilkins quotation on page 283 was suggested by Georgia K. M. Tobin.

METAFONT is a trademark of Addison–Wesley Publishing Company.

TEX is a trademark of the American Mathematical Society.

Library of Congress cataloging in publication data

```
Knuth, Donald Ervin, 1938-
   The METAFONTbook.

   (Computers & Typesetting ; C)
   Includes index.
   1. METAFONT (Computer system). 2. Type and type-
founding--Data processing. I. Title. II. Series:
Knuth, Donald Ervin, 1938-    . Computers &
typesetting ; C.
Z250.8.M46K58 1986        686.2'24        85-28675
ISBN 0-201-13445-4
ISBN 0-201-13444-6 (soft)
```

Fourth printing, revised, September 1991

ISBN 0-201-13445-4
4 5 6 7 8 9 10 11 12–AL–9594939291

To Hermann Zapf:
Whose strokes are the best

Preface

G ENERATION OF LETTERFORMS by mathematical means was first tried in the fifteenth century; it became popular in the sixteenth and seventeenth centuries; and it was abandoned (for good reasons) during the eighteenth century. Perhaps the twentieth century will turn out to be the right time for this idea to make a comeback, now that mathematics has advanced and computers are able to do the calculations.

Modern printing equipment based on raster lines—in which metal "type" has been replaced by purely combinatorial patterns of zeroes and ones that specify the desired position of ink in a discrete way—makes mathematics and computer science increasingly relevant to printing. We now have the ability to give a completely precise definition of letter shapes that will produce essentially equivalent results on all raster-based machines. Moreover, the shapes can be defined in terms of variable parameters; computers can "draw" new fonts of characters in seconds, making it possible for designers to perform valuable experiments that were previously unthinkable.

METAFONT is a system for the design of alphabets suited to raster-based devices that print or display text. The characters that you are reading were all designed with METAFONT, in a completely precise way; and they were developed rather hastily by the author of the system, who is a rank amateur at such things. It seems clear that further work with METAFONT has the potential of producing typefaces of real beauty. This manual has been written for people who would like to help advance the art of mathematical type design.

A top-notch designer of typefaces needs to have an unusually good eye and a highly developed sensitivity to the nuances of shapes. A top-notch user of computer languages needs to have an unusual talent for abstract reasoning and a highly developed ability to express intuitive ideas in formal terms. Very few people have both of these unusual combinations of skills; hence the best products of METAFONT will probably be collaborative efforts between two people who complement each other's abilities. Indeed, this situation isn't very different from the way types have been created for many generations, except that the rôle of "punch-cutter" is now being played by skilled computer specialists instead of by skilled metalworkers.

A METAFONT user writes a "program" for each letter or symbol of a typeface. These programs are different from ordinary computer programs, because they are essentially *declarative* rather than imperative. In the META-FONT language you explain where the major components of a desired shape are to be located, and how they relate to each other, but you don't have to work out the details of exactly where the lines cross, etc.; the computer takes over the work of solving equations as it deduces the consequences of your specifications. One of the advantages of METAFONT is that it provides a discipline according to which the principles of a particular alphabet design can be stated precisely. The underlying intelligence does not remain hidden in the mind of the designer; it is spelled out in the programs. Thus consistency can readily be obtained where consistency is desirable, and a font can readily be extended to new symbols that are compatible with the existing ones.

It would be nice if a system like METAFONT were to simplify the task of type design to the point where beautiful new alphabets could be created in a few hours. This, alas, is impossible; an enormous amount of subtlety lies behind the seemingly simple letter shapes that we see every day, and the designers of high-quality typefaces have done their work so well that we don't notice the underlying complexity. One of the disadvantages of METAFONT is that a person can easily use it to produce poor alphabets, cheaply and in great quantity. Let us hope that such experiments will have educational value as they reveal why the subtle tricks of the trade are important, but let us also hope that they will not cause bad workmanship to proliferate. Anybody can now produce a book in which all of the type is home-made, but a person or team of persons should expect to spend a year or more on the project if the type is actually supposed to look right. METAFONT won't put today's type designers out of work; on the contrary, it will tend to make them heroes and heroines, as more and more people come to appreciate their skills.

Although there is no royal road to type design, there are some things that can, in fact, be done well with METAFONT in an afternoon. Geometric designs are rather easy; and it doesn't take long to make modifications to letters or symbols that have previously been expressed in METAFONT form. Thus, although comparatively few users of METAFONT will have the courage to do an entire alphabet from scratch, there will be many who will enjoy customizing someone else's design.

This book is not a text about mathematics or about computers. But if you know the rudiments of those subjects (namely, contemporary high school mathematics, together with the knowledge of how to use the text editing or word processing facilities on your computing machine), you should be able to use METAFONT with little difficulty after reading what follows. Some parts of the exposition in the text are more obscure than others, however, since the author has tried to satisfy experienced METAFONTers as well as beginners and casual users with a single manual. Therefore a special symbol has been used to warn about esoterica: When you see the sign

at the beginning of a paragraph, watch out for a "dangerous bend" in the train of thought—don't read such a paragraph unless you need to. You will be able to use METAFONT reasonably well, even to design characters like the dangerous-bend symbol itself, without reading the fine print in such advanced sections.

Some of the paragraphs in this manual are so far out that they are rated

 ;

everything that was said about single dangerous-bend signs goes double for these. You should probably have at least a month's experience with METAFONT before you attempt to fathom such doubly dangerous depths of the system; in fact, most people will never need to know METAFONT in this much detail, even if they use it every day. After all, it's possible to fry an egg without knowing anything about biochemistry. Yet the whole story is here in case you're curious. (About METAFONT, not eggs.)

The reason for such different levels of complexity is that people change as they grow accustomed to any powerful tool. When you first try to use META-FONT, you'll find that some parts of it are very easy, while other things will take some getting used to. At first you'll probably try to control the shapes too rigidly, by overspecifying data that has been copied from some other medium. But later, after you have begun to get a feeling for what the machine can do well, you'll be a different person, and you'll be willing to let METAFONT help contribute to your designs as they are being developed. As you gain more and more experience working with this unusual apprentice, your perspective will continue to change and you will run into different sorts of challenges. That's the way it is with any powerful tool: There's always more to learn, and there are always better ways to do what you've done before. At every stage in the development you'll want a slightly different sort of manual. You may even want to write one yourself. By paying attention to the dangerous bend signs in this book you'll be better able to focus on the level that interests you at a particular time.

Computer system manuals usually make dull reading, but take heart: This one contains JOKES every once in a while. You might actually enjoy reading it. (However, most of the jokes can only be appreciated properly if you understand a technical point that is being made—so read *carefully.*)

Another noteworthy characteristic of this book is that it doesn't always tell the truth. When certain concepts of METAFONT are introduced informally, general rules will be stated; afterwards you will find that the rules aren't strictly true. In general, the later chapters contain more reliable information than the earlier ones do. The author feels that this technique of deliberate lying will actually make it easier for you to learn the ideas. Once you understand a simple but false rule, it will not be hard to supplement that rule with its exceptions.

In order to help you internalize what you're reading, EXERCISES are sprinkled through this manual. It is generally intended that every reader should try every exercise, except for questions that appear in the "dangerous bend" areas. If you can't solve a problem, you can always look up the answer. But please, try first to solve it by yourself; then you'll learn more and you'll learn faster. Furthermore, if you think you do know the solution, you should turn to Appendix A and check it out, just to make sure.

> WARNING: Type design can be hazardous to your other interests. Once you get hooked, you will develop intense feelings about letterforms; the medium will intrude on the messages that you read. And you will perpetually be thinking of improvements to the fonts that you see everywhere, especially those of your own design.

The METAFONT language described here has very little in common with the author's previous attempt at a language for alphabet design, because five years of experience with the old system has made it clear that a completely different approach is preferable. Both languages have been called METAFONT; but henceforth the old language should be called METAFONT79, and its use should rapidly fade away. Let's keep the name METAFONT for the language described here, since it is so much better, and since it will never change again.

I wish to thank the hundreds of people who have helped me to formulate this "definitive edition" of METAFONT, based on their experiences with preliminary versions of the system. In particular, John Hobby discovered many of the algorithms that have made the new language possible. My work at Stanford has been generously supported by the National Science Foundation, the Office of Naval Research, the IBM Corporation, and the System Development Foundation. I also wish to thank the American Mathematical Society for its encouragement and for publishing the *TUGboat* newsletter (see Appendix J). Above all, I deeply thank my wife, Jill, for the inspiration, understanding, comfort, and support she has given me for more than 25 years, especially during the eight years that I have been working intensively on mathematical typography.

Stanford, California   — D. E. K.
September 1985

> It is hoped that Divine Justice may find
> some suitable affliction for the malefactors
> who invent variations upon the alphabet of our fathers. . . .
> The type-founder, worthy mechanic, has asserted himself
> with an overshadowing individuality,
> defacing with his monstrous creations and revivals
> every publication in the land.
> — AMBROSE BIERCE, *The Opinionator. Alphabētes* (1911)

> Can the new process yield a result that, say,
> a Club of Bibliophiles would recognise as a work of art
> comparable to the choice books they have in their cabinets?
> — STANLEY MORISON, *Typographic Design in Relation to
> Photographic Composition* (1958)

Contents

1

The Name of
the Game

This is a book about a computer system called METAFONT, just as *The TEXbook* is about TEX. METAFONT and TEX are good friends who intend to live together for a long time. Between them they take care of the two most fundamental tasks of typesetting: TEX puts characters into the proper positions on a page, while METAFONT determines the shapes of the characters themselves.

Why is the system called METAFONT? The '-FONT' part is easy to understand, because sets of related characters that are used in typesetting are traditionally known as fonts of type. The 'META-' part is more interesting: It indicates that we are interested in making high-level descriptions that transcend any of the individual fonts being described.

Newly coined words beginning with 'meta-' generally reflect our contemporary inclination to view things from outside or above, at a more abstract level than before, with what we feel is a more mature understanding. We now have metapsychology (the study of how the mind relates to its containing body), metahistory (the study of principles that control the course of events), metamathematics (the study of mathematical reasoning), metafiction (literary works that explicitly acknowledge their own forms), and so on. A metamathematician proves metatheorems (theorems about theorems); a computer scientist often works with metalanguages (languages for describing languages). Similarly, a meta-font is a schematic description of the shapes in a family of related fonts; the letterforms change appropriately as their underlying parameters change.

Meta-design is much more difficult than design; it's easier to draw something than to explain how to draw it. One of the problems is that different sets of potential specifications can't easily be envisioned all at once. Another is that a computer has to be told absolutely everything. However, once we have successfully explained how to draw something in a sufficiently general manner, the same explanation will work for related shapes, in different circumstances; so the time spent in formulating a precise explanation turns out to be worth it.

Typefaces intended for text are normally seen small, and our eyes can read them best when the letters have been designed specifically for the size at which they are actually used. Although it is tempting to get 7-point fonts by simply making a 70% reduction from the 10-point size, this shortcut leads to a serious degradation of quality. Much better results can be obtained by incorporating parametric variations into a meta-design. In fact, there are advantages to built-in variability even when you want to produce only one font of type in a single size, because it allows you to postpone making decisions about many aspects of your design. If you leave certain things undefined, treating them as parameters instead of "freezing" the specifications at an early stage, the computer will be able to draw lots of examples with different settings of the parameters, and you will be able to see the results of all those experiments at the final size. This will greatly increase your ability to edit and fine-tune the font.

If meta-fonts are so much better than plain old ordinary fonts, why weren't they developed long ago? The main reason is that computers did not exist until recently. People find it difficult and dull to carry out calculations with a multiplicity of parameters, while today's machines do such tasks with ease. The introduction of parameters is a natural outgrowth of automation.

OK, let's grant that meta-fonts sound good, at least in theory. There's still the practical problem about how to achieve them. How can we actually specify shapes that depend on unspecified parameters?

If only one parameter is varying, it's fairly easy to solve the problem in a visual way, by overlaying a series of drawings that show graphically how the shape changes. For example, if the parameter varies from 0 to 1, we might prepare five sketches, corresponding to the parameter values 0, $\frac{1}{4}$, $\frac{1}{2}$, $\frac{3}{4}$, and 1. If these sketches follow a consistent pattern, we can readily interpolate to find the shape for a value like $\frac{2}{3}$ that lies between two of the given ones. We might even try extrapolating to parameter values like $1\frac{1}{4}$.

But if there are two or more independent parameters, a purely visual solution becomes too cumbersome. We must go to a verbal approach, using some sort of language to describe the desired drawings. Let's imagine, for example, that we want to explain the shape of a certain letter 'a' to a friend in a distant country, using only a telephone for communication; our friend is supposed to be able to reconstruct exactly the shape we have in mind. Once we figure out a sufficiently natural way to do that, for a particular fixed shape, it isn't much of a trick to go further and make our verbal description more general, by including variable parameters instead of restricting ourselves to constants.

An analogy to cooking might make this point clearer. Suppose you have just baked a delicious berry pie, and your friends ask you to tell them the recipe so that they can bake one too. If you have developed your cooking skills entirely by intuition, you might find it difficult to record exactly what you did. But there is a traditional language of recipes in which you could communicate the steps you followed; and if you take careful measurements, you might find that you used, say, $1\frac{1}{4}$ cups of sugar. The next step, if you were instructing a computer-controlled cooking machine, would be to go to a meta-recipe in which you use, say, $.25x$ cups of sugar for x cups of berries; or $.3x + .2y$ cups for x cups of boysenberries and y cups of blackberries.

In other words, going from design to meta-design is essentially like going from arithmetic to elementary algebra. Numbers are replaced by simple formulas that involve unknown quantities. We will see many examples of this.

A METAFONT definition of a complete typeface generally consists of three main parts. First there is a rather mundane set of subroutines that take care of necessary administrative details, such as assigning code numbers to individual characters; each character must also be positioned properly inside an invisible "box," so that typesetting systems will produce the correct spacing. Next comes a more interesting collection of subroutines, designed to draw the basic strokes characteristic of the typeface (e.g., the serifs, bowls, arms, arches, and so on). These subroutines will typically be described in terms of their own special parameters, so that they can produce a variety of related strokes; a serif subroutine will, for example, be able to draw serifs of different lengths, although all of the serifs it draws should have the same "feeling." Finally, there are routines for each of the characters. If the subroutines in the first and second parts have been chosen well, the routines of the third part will be fairly high-level descriptions that don't concern themselves unnecessarily with details; for example, it may be possible to substitute a different serif-drawing subroutine without changing any of the programs that use that subroutine, thereby obtaining a typeface of quite a different flavor. [A particularly striking example of this approach has been worked out by John D. Hobby and Gu Guoan in "A Chinese Meta-Font," *TUGboat* **5** (1984), 119–136. By changing a set of 13 basic stroke subroutines, they were able to draw 128 sample Chinese characters in three different styles (Song, Long Song, and Bold), using the same programs for the characters.]

A well-written METAFONT program will express the designer's intentions more clearly than mere drawings ever can, because the language of algebra has simple "idioms" that make it possible to elucidate many visual relationships. Thus, METAFONT programs can be used to communicate knowledge about type design, just as recipes convey the expertise of a chef. But algebraic formulas are not easy to understand in isolation; METAFONT descriptions are meant to be read with an accompanying illustration, just as the constructions in geometry textbooks are accompanied by diagrams. Nobody is ever expected to read the text of a METAFONT program and say, "Ah, what a beautiful letter!" But with one or more enlarged pictures of the letter, based on one or more settings of the parameters, a reader of the METAFONT program should be able to say, "Ah, I understand how this beautiful letter was drawn!" We shall see that the META-FONT system makes it fairly easy to obtain annotated proof drawings that you can hold in your hand as you are working with a program.

Although METAFONT is intended to provide a relatively painless way to describe meta-fonts, you can, of course, use it also to describe unvarying shapes that have no "meta-ness" at all. Indeed, you need not even use it to produce fonts; the system will happily draw geometric designs that have no relation to the characters or glyphs of any alphabet or script. The author occasionally uses METAFONT simply as a pocket calculator, to do elementary arithmetic in an interactive way. A computer doesn't mind if its programs are put to purposes that don't match their names.

> *[Tinguely] made some large, brightly coloured open reliefs,*
> *juxtaposing stationary and mobile shapes.*
> *He later gave them names like* Meta-Kandinsky *and* Meta-Herbin,
> *to clarify the ideas and attitudes that lay at the root of their conception.*
> — K. G. PONTUS HULTÉN, *Jean Tinguely: Méta* (1972)

> *The idea of a meta-font should now be clear. But what good is it?*
> *The ability to manipulate lots of parameters may be interesting and fun,*
> *but does anybody really need a $6\frac{1}{7}$-point font*
> *that is one fourth of the way between Baskerville and Helvetica?*
> — DONALD E. KNUTH, *The Concept of a Meta-Font* (1982)

2
Coordinates

If we want to tell a computer how to draw a particular shape, we need a way to explain where the key points of that shape are supposed to be. METAFONT uses standard *Cartesian coordinates* for this purpose: The location of a point is defined by specifying its x coordinate, which is the number of units to the right of some reference point, and its y coordinate, which is the number of units upward from the reference point. First we determine the horizontal (left/right) component of a point's position, then we determine the vertical (up/down) component. METAFONT's world is two-dimensional, so two coordinates are enough.

For example, let's consider the following six points:

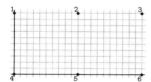

METAFONT's names for the positions of these points are

$$(x_1, y_1) = (0, 100); \qquad (x_2, y_2) = (100, 100); \qquad (x_3, y_3) = (200, 100);$$
$$(x_4, y_4) = (0, \quad 0); \qquad (x_5, y_5) = (100, \quad 0); \qquad (x_6, y_6) = (200, \quad 0).$$

Point 4 is the same as the reference point, since both of its coordinates are zero; to get to point $3 = (200, 100)$, you start at the reference point and go 200 steps right and 100 up; and so on.

▶ **EXERCISE 2.1**
Which of the six example points is closest to the point $(60, 30)$?

▶ **EXERCISE 2.2**
True or false: All points that lie on a given horizontal straight line have the same x coordinate.

▶ **EXERCISE 2.3**
Explain where the point $(-5, 15)$ is located.

▶ **EXERCISE 2.4**
What are the coordinates of a point that lies exactly 60 units below point 6 in the diagram above? ("Below" means "down the page," not "under the page.")

In a typical application of METAFONT, you prepare a rough sketch of the shape you plan to define, on a piece of graph paper, and you label important points on that sketch with any convenient numbers. Then you write a META-FONT program that explains (i) the coordinates of those key points, and (ii) the lines or curves that are supposed to go between them.

METAFONT has its own internal graph paper, which forms a so-called raster or grid consisting of square "pixels." The output of METAFONT will specify that certain of the pixels are "black" and that the others are "white"; thus, the computer essentially converts shapes into binary patterns like the designs a person can make when doing needlepoint with two colors of yarn.

Coordinates are lengths, but we haven't discussed yet what the units of length actually are. It's important to choose convenient units, and METAFONT's coordinates are given in units of pixels. The little squares illustrated on the previous page, which correspond to differences of 10 units in an x coordinate or a y coordinate, therefore represent 10×10 arrays of pixels, and the rectangle enclosed by our six example points contains 20,000 pixels altogether.*

Coordinates don't have to be whole numbers. You can refer, for example, to point $(31.5, 42.5)$, which lies smack in the middle of the pixel whose corners are at $(31, 42)$, $(31, 43)$, $(32, 42)$, and $(32, 43)$. The computer works internally with coordinates that are integer multiples of $\frac{1}{65536} \approx 0.00002$ of the width of a pixel, so it is capable of making very fine distinctions. But METAFONT will never make a pixel half black; it's all or nothing, as far as the output is concerned.

The fineness of a grid is usually called its *resolution*, and resolution is usually expressed in pixel units per inch (in America) or pixel units per millimeter (elsewhere). For example, the type you are now reading was prepared by META-FONT with a resolution of slightly more than 700 pixels to the inch, but with slightly fewer than 30 pixels per mm. For the time being we shall assume that the pixels are so tiny that the operation of rounding to whole pixels is unimportant; later we will consider the important questions that arise when METAFONT is producing low-resolution output.

It's usually desirable to write METAFONT programs that can manufacture fonts at many different resolutions, so that a variety of low-resolution printing devices will be able to make proofs that are compatible with a variety of high-resolution devices. Therefore the key points in METAFONT programs are rarely specified in terms of pure numbers like '100'; we generally make the coordinates relative to some other resolution-dependent quantity, so that changes will be easy to make. For example, it would have been better to use a definition something like the following, for the six points considered earlier:

$$(x_1, y_1) = (0, b); \qquad (x_2, y_2) = (a, b); \qquad (x_3, y_3) = (2a, b);$$
$$(x_4, y_4) = (0, 0); \qquad (x_5, y_5) = (a, 0); \qquad (x_6, y_6) = (2a, 0);$$

then the quantities a and b can be defined in some way appropriate to the desired resolution. We had $a = b = 100$ in our previous example, but such constant values leave us with little or no flexibility.

Notice the quantity '$2a$' in the definitions of x_3 and x_6; METAFONT understands enough algebra to know that this means twice the value of a, whatever a is. We observed in Chapter 1 that simple uses of algebra give METAFONT its meta-ness. Indeed, it is interesting to note from a historical standpoint that Cartesian coordinates are named after René Descartes, not because he invented the idea of coordinates, but because he showed how to get much more out of

---

* We sometimes use the term "pixel" to mean a square picture element, but sometimes we use it to signify a one-dimensional unit of length. A square pixel is one pixel-unit wide and one pixel-unit tall.

that idea by applying algebraic methods. People had long since been using co-ordinates for such things as latitudes and longitudes, but Descartes observed that by putting unknown quantities into the coordinates it became possible to describe infinite sets of related points, and to deduce properties of curves that were extremely difficult to work out using geometrical methods alone.

So far we have specified some points, but we haven't actually done anything with them. Let's suppose that we want to draw a straight line from point 1 to point 6, obtaining

One way to do this with METAFONT is to say

draw $(x_1, y_1) \mathbin{..} (x_6, y_6)$.

The '..' here tells the computer to connect two points.

It turns out that we often want to write formulas like '(x_1, y_1)', so it will be possible to save lots of time if we have a special abbreviation for such things. Henceforth we shall use the notation z_1 to stand for (x_1, y_1); and in general, z_k with an arbitrary subscript will stand for the point (x_k, y_k). The '**draw**' command above can therefore be written more simply as

draw $z_1 \mathbin{..} z_6$.

Adding two more straight lines by saying, '**draw** $z_2 \mathbin{..} z_5$' and '**draw** $z_3 \mathbin{..} z_4$', we obtain a design that is slightly reminiscent of the Union Jack:

We shall call this a hex symbol, because it has six endpoints. Notice that the straight lines here have some thickness, and they are rounded at the ends as if they had been drawn with a felt-tip pen having a circular nib. METAFONT provides many ways to control the thicknesses of lines and to vary the terminal shapes, but we shall discuss such things in later chapters because our main concern right now is to learn about coordinates.

If the hex symbol is scaled down so that its height parameter b is exactly equal to the height of the letters in this paragraph, it looks like this: '✳'. Just for fun, let's try to typeset ten of them in a row:

How easy it is to do this!*

Let's look a bit more closely at this new character. The ✳ is a bit too tall, because it extends above points 1, 2, and 3 when the thickness of the lines is taken into account; similarly, it sinks a bit too much below the baseline (i.e., below the line $y = 0$ that contains points 4, 5, and 6). In order to correct this, we want to move the key points slightly. For example, point z_1 should not be exactly at $(0, b)$; we ought to arrange things so that the top of the pen is at $(0, b)$ when the center of the pen is at z_1. We can express this condition for the top three points as follows:

$$top\ z_1 = (0, b); \qquad top\ z_2 = (a, b); \qquad top\ z_3 = (2a, b);$$

similarly, the remedy for points 4, 5, and 6 is to specify the equations

$$bot\ z_4 = (0, 0); \qquad bot\ z_5 = (a, 0); \qquad bot\ z_6 = (2a, 0).$$

The resulting squashed-in character is

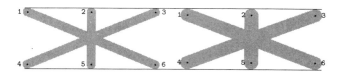

(shown here with the original weight '✳' and also in a bolder version '✳').

▶ **EXERCISE 2.5**
Ten of these bold hexes produce '✳✳✳✳✳✳✳✳✳✳'; notice that adjacent symbols overlap each other. The reason is that each character has width $2a$, hence point 3 of one character coincides with point 1 of the next. Suppose that we actually want the characters to be completely confined to a rectangular box of width $2a$, so that adjacent characters come just shy of touching (✳✳✳✳✳✳✳✳✳✳). Try to guess how the point-defining equations above could be modified to make this happen, assuming that METAFONT has operations '*lft*' and '*rt*' analogous to '*top*' and '*bot*'.

---

* Now that authors have for the first time the power to invent new symbols with great ease, and to have those characters printed in their manuscripts on a wide variety of typesetting devices, we must face the question of how much experimentation is desirable. Will font freaks abuse this toy by overdoing it? Is it wise to introduce new symbols by the thousands? Such questions are beyond the scope of this book; but it is easy to imagine an epidemic of fontomania occurring, once people realize how much fun it is to design their own characters, hence it may be necessary to perform fontal lobotomies.

Pairs of coordinates can be thought of as "vectors" or "displacements" as well as points. For example, $(15, 8)$ can be regarded as a command to go right 15 and up 8; then point $(15, 8)$ is the position we get to after starting at the reference point and obeying the command $(15, 8)$. This interpretation works out nicely when we consider addition of vectors: If we move according to the vector $(15, 8)$ and then move according to $(7, -3)$, the result is the same as if we move $(15, 8) + (7, -3) = (15 + 7, 8 - 3) = (22, 5)$. The sum of two vectors $z_1 = (x_1, y_1)$ and $z_2 = (x_2, y_2)$ is the vector $z_1 + z_2 = (x_1 + x_2, y_1 + y_2)$ obtained by adding x and y components separately. This vector represents the result of moving by vector z_1 and then moving by vector z_2; alternatively, $z_1 + z_2$ represents the point you get to by starting at point z_1 and moving by vector z_2.

▶ **EXERCISE 2.6**
Consider the four fundamental vectors $(0, 1)$, $(1, 0)$, $(0, -1)$, and $(-1, 0)$. Which of them corresponds to moving one pixel unit (a) to the right? (b) to the left? (c) down? (d) up?

Vectors can be subtracted as well as added; the value of $z_1 - z_2$ is simply $(x_1 - x_2, y_1 - y_2)$. Furthermore it is natural to multiply a vector by a single number c: The quantity c times (x, y), which is written $c(x, y)$, equals (cx, cy). Thus, for example, $2z = 2(x, y) = (2x, 2y)$ turns out to be equal to $z + z$. In the special case $c = -1$, we write $-(x, y) = (-x, -y)$.

Now we come to an important notion, based on the fact that subtraction is the opposite of addition. If z_1 and z_2 are *any two points, then $z_2 - z_1$ is the vector that corresponds to moving from z_1 to z_2*. The reason is simply that $z_2 - z_1$ is what we must add to z_1 in order to get z_2: i.e., $z_1 + (z_2 - z_1) = z_2$. We shall call this the *vector subtraction principle*. It is used frequently in METAFONT programs when the designer wants to specify the direction and/or distance of one point from another.

METAFONT programs often use another idea to express relations between points. Suppose we start at point z_1 and travel in a straight line from there in the direction of point z_2, but we don't go all the way. There's a special notation for this, using square brackets:

$\frac{1}{3}[z_1, z_2]$ is the point one-third of the way from z_1 to z_2,

$\frac{1}{2}[z_1, z_2]$ is the point midway between z_1 and z_2,

$.8[z_1, z_2]$ is the point eight-tenths of the way from z_1 to z_2,

and, in general, $t[z_1, z_2]$ stands for the point that lies a fraction t of the way from z_1 to z_2. We call this the operation of *mediation* between points, or (informally) the "of-the-way function." If the fraction t increases from 0 to 1, the expression $t[z_1, z_2]$ traces out a straight line from z_1 to z_2. According to the vector subtraction principle, we must move $z_2 - z_1$ in order to go all the way from z_1 to z_2, hence the point t of the way between them is

$$t[z_1, z_2] \;=\; z_1 + t(z_2 - z_1).$$

This is a general formula by which we can calculate $t[z_1, z_2]$ for any given values of t, z_1, and z_2. But METAFONT has this formula built in, so we can use the bracket notation explicitly.

For example, let's go back to our first six example points, and suppose that we want to refer to the point that's 2/5 of the way from $z_2 = (100, 100)$ to $z_6 = (200, 0)$. In METAFONT we can write this simply as $.4[z_2, z_6]$. And if we need to compute the exact coordinates for some reason, we can always work them out from the general formula, getting $z_2 + .4(z_6 - z_2) = (100, 100) + .4\big((200, 0) - (100, 100)\big) = (100, 100) + .4(100, -100) = (100, 100) + (40, -40) = (140, 60)$.

▸**EXERCISE 2.7**
True or false: The direction vector from $(5, -2)$ to $(2, 3)$ is $(-3, 5)$.

▸**EXERCISE 2.8**
Explain what the notation '$0[z_1, z_2]$' means, if anything. What about '$1[z_1, z_2]$'? And '$2[z_1, z_2]$'? And '$(-.5)[z_1, z_2]$'?

▸**EXERCISE 2.9**
True or false, for mathematicians: (a) $\frac{1}{2}[z_1, z_2] = \frac{1}{2}(z_1 + z_2)$; (b) $\frac{1}{3}[z_1, z_2] = \frac{1}{3}z_1 + \frac{2}{3}z_2$; (c) $t[z_1, z_2] = (1 - t)[z_2, z_1]$.

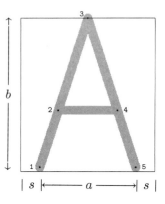

Let's conclude this chapter by using mediation to help specify the five points in the stick-figure 'A' shown enlarged at the right. The distance between points 1 and 5 should be a, and point 3 should be b pixels above the baseline; these values a and b have been predetermined by some method that doesn't concern us here, and so has a "sidebar" parameter s that specifies the horizontal distance of points 1 and 5 from the edges of the type. We shall assume that we don't know for sure what the height of the bar line should be; point 2 should be somewhere on the straight line from point 1 to point 3, and point 4 should be in the corresponding place between 5 and 3, but we want to try several possibilities before we make a decision.

The width of the character will be $s + a + s$, and we can specify points z_1 and z_5 by the equations

$$bot\ z_1 = (s, 0); \qquad z_5 = z_1 + (a, 0).$$

There are other ways to do the job, but these formulas clearly express our intention to have the bottom of the pen at the baseline, s pixels to the right of the reference point, when the pen is at z_1, and to have z_5 exactly a pixels to the right of z_1. Next, we can say

$$z_3 = \big(\tfrac{1}{2}[x_1, x_5], b\big);$$

this means that the x coordinate of point 3 should be halfway between the x coordinates of points 1 and 5, and that $y_3 = b$. Finally, let's say

$$z_2 = alpha[z_1, z_3]; \qquad z_4 = alpha[z_5, z_3];$$

the parameter *alpha* is a number between 0 and 1 that governs the position of the bar line, and it will be supplied later. When *alpha* has indeed received a value, we can say

$$\textbf{draw } z_1 \mathrel{..} z_3; \qquad \textbf{draw } z_3 \mathrel{..} z_5; \qquad \textbf{draw } z_2 \mathrel{..} z_4.$$

METAFONT will draw the characters 'AAAAAAA' when *alpha* varies from 0.2 to 0.5 in steps of 0.05 and when $a = 150$, $b = 250$, $s = 30$. The illustration on the previous page has $alpha = (3 - \sqrt{5})/2 \approx 0.38197$; this value makes the ratio of the area above the bar to the area below it equal to $(\sqrt{5} - 1)/2 \approx 0.61803$, the so-called "golden ratio" of classical Greek mathematics.

> (Are you sure you should be reading this paragraph? The "dangerous bend" sign here is meant to warn you about material that ought to be skipped on first reading. And maybe also on second reading. The reader-beware paragraphs sometimes refer to concepts that aren't explained until later chapters.)

▶ **EXERCISE 2.10**
Why is it better to define z_3 as $(\frac{1}{2}[x_1, x_5], b)$, rather than to work out the explicit coordinates $z_3 = (s + \frac{1}{2}a, b)$ that are implied by the other equations?

▶ **EXERCISE 2.11**
Given z_1, z_3, and z_5 as above, explain how to define z_2 and z_4 so that all of the following conditions hold simultaneously:

- the line from z_2 to z_4 slopes upward at a 20° angle;
- the y coordinate of that line's midpoint is 2/3 of the way from y_3 to y_1;
- z_2 and z_4 are on the respective lines $z_1 \mathrel{..} z_3$ and $z_3 \mathrel{..} z_5$.

(If you solve this exercise, you deserve an 'A'.)

> *Here, where we reach the sphere of mathematics,*
> *we are among processes which seem to some*
> *the most inhuman of all human activities*
> *and the most remote from poetry.*
> *Yet it is here that the artist has the fullest scope for his imagination.*
> — HAVELOCK ELLIS, *The Dance of Life* (1923)

> *To anyone who has lived in a modern American city (except Boston)*
> *at least one of the underlying ideas of Descartes' analytic geometry*
> *will seem ridiculously evident. Yet, as remarked,*
> *it took mathematicians all of two thousand years*
> *to arrive at this simple thing.*
> — ERIC TEMPLE BELL, *Mathematics: Queen and Servant of Science* (1951)

3
Curves

Albrecht Dürer and other Renaissance men attempted to establish mathematical principles of type design, but the letters they came up with were not especially beautiful. Their methods failed because they restricted themselves to "ruler and compass" constructions, which cannot adequately express the nuances of good calligraphy. METAFONT gets around this problem by using more powerful mathematical techniques, which provide the necessary flexibility without really being too complicated. The purpose of the present chapter is to explain the simple principles by which a computer is able to draw "pleasing" curves.

The basic idea is to start with four points (z_1, z_2, z_3, z_4) and to construct the three midpoints $z_{12} = \frac{1}{2}[z_1, z_2]$, $z_{23} = \frac{1}{2}[z_2, z_3]$, $z_{34} = \frac{1}{2}[z_3, z_4]$:

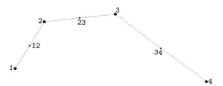

Then take those three midpoints (z_{12}, z_{23}, z_{34}) and construct two second-order midpoints $z_{123} = \frac{1}{2}[z_{12}, z_{23}]$ and $z_{234} = \frac{1}{2}[z_{23}, z_{34}]$; finally, construct the third-order midpoint $z_{1234} = \frac{1}{2}[z_{123}, z_{234}]$:

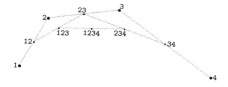

This point z_{1234} is one of the points of the curve determined by (z_1, z_2, z_3, z_4). To get the remaining points of that curve, repeat the same construction on $(z_1, z_{12}, z_{123}, z_{1234})$ and on $(z_{1234}, z_{234}, z_{34}, z_4)$, ad infinitum:

The process converges quickly, and the preliminary scaffolding (which appears above the limiting curve in our example) is ultimately discarded. The limiting curve has the following important properties:

- It begins at z_1, heading in the direction from z_1 to z_2.
- It ends at z_4, heading in the direction from z_3 to z_4.
- It stays entirely within the so-called convex hull of z_1, z_2, z_3, and z_4; i.e., all points of the curve lie "between" the defining points.

The curve defined by these recursive rules can be described algebraically by the remarkably simple formula

$$z(t) = (1-t)^3 z_1 + 3(1-t)^2 t\, z_2 + 3(1-t)t^2 z_3 + t^3 z_4,$$

as the parameter t varies from 0 to 1. This polynomial of degree 3 in t is called a *Bernshteĭn polynomial*, because Sergeĭ N. Bernshteĭn introduced such functions in 1912 as part of his pioneering work on approximation theory. Curves traced out by Bernshteĭn polynomials of degree 3 are often called *Bézier cubics*, after Pierre Bézier who realized their importance for computer-aided design during the 1960s.

 It is interesting to observe that the Bernshteĭn polynomial of degree 1, i.e., the function $z(t) = (1-t)\,z_1 + t\,z_2$, is precisely the mediation operator $t[z_1, z_2]$ that we discussed in the previous chapter. Indeed, if the geometric construction we have just seen is changed to use t-of-the-way points instead of midpoints (i.e., if $z_{12} = t[z_1, z_2]$ and $z_{23} = t[z_2, z_3]$, etc.), then z_{1234} turns out to be precisely $z(t)$ in the formula above.

No matter what four points (z_1, z_2, z_3, z_4) are given, the construction on the previous page defines a curved line that runs from z_1 to z_4. This curve is not always interesting or beautiful; for example, if all four of the given points lie on a straight line, the entire "curve" that they define will also be contained in that same line. We obtain rather different curves from the same four starting points if we number the points differently:

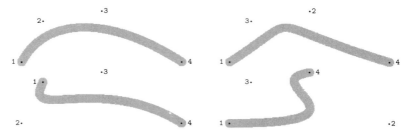

Some discretion is evidently advisable when the z's are chosen. But the four-point method is good enough to obtain satisfactory approximations to any curve we want, provided that we break the desired curve into short enough segments and give four suitable control points for each segment. It turns out, in fact, that we can usually get by with only a few segments. For example, the four-point method can produce an approximate quarter-circle with less than 0.06% error; it never yields an exact circle, but the differences between four such quarter-circles and a true circle are imperceptible.

All of the curves that METAFONT draws are based on four points, as just described. But it isn't necessary for a user to specify all of those points, because the computer is usually able to figure out good values of z_2 and z_3 by itself. Only the endpoints z_1 and z_4, through which the curve is actually supposed to pass, are usually mentioned explicitly in a METAFONT program.

For example, let's return to the six points that were used to introduce the ideas of coordinates in Chapter 2. We said '**draw** $z_1 \ldots z_6$' in that chapter, in order to draw a straight line from point z_1 to point z_6. In general, if three or more points are listed instead of two, METAFONT will draw a smooth curve through all the points. For example, the commands '**draw** $z_4 \ldots z_1 \ldots z_2 \ldots z_6$' and '**draw** $z_5 \ldots z_4 \ldots z_1 \ldots z_3 \ldots z_6 \ldots z_5$' will produce the respective results

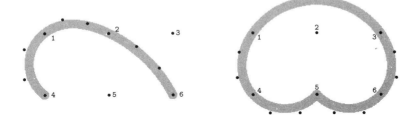

(Unlabeled points in these diagrams are control points that METAFONT has supplied automatically so that it can use the four-point scheme to draw curves between each pair of adjacent points on the specified paths.)

Notice that the curve is not smooth at z_5 in the right-hand example, because z_5 appears at both ends of that particular path. In order to get a completely smooth curve that returns to its starting point, you can say '**draw** $z_5 \ldots z_4 \ldots z_1 \ldots z_3 \ldots z_6 \ldots$ cycle' instead:

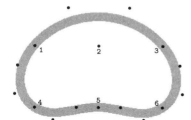

The word 'cycle' at the end of a path refers to the starting point of that path. METAFONT believes that this bean-like shape is the nicest way to connect the given points in the given cyclic order; but of course there are many decent curves that satisfy the specifications, and you may have another one in mind. You can obtain finer control by giving hints to the machine in various ways. For example, the bean curve can be "pulled tighter" between z_1 and z_3 if you say

> **draw** $z_5 \ldots z_4 \ldots z_1 \ldots$ tension $1.2 \ldots z_3 \ldots z_6 \ldots$ cycle;

the so-called tension between points is normally 1, and an increase to 1.2 yields

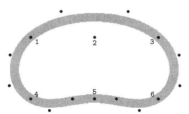

An asymmetric effect can be obtained by increasing the tension only at point 1 but not at points 3 or 4; the shape

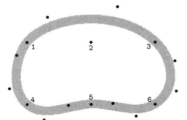

comes from '**draw** z_5 .. z_4 .. tension 1 and 1.5 .. z_1 .. tension 1.5 and 1 .. z_3 .. z_6 .. cycle'. The effect of tension has been achieved in this example by moving two of the anonymous control points closer to point 1.

It's possible to control a curve in another way, by telling METAFONT what direction to travel at some or all of the points. Such directions are given inside curly braces; for example,

$$\textbf{draw } z_5 \; .. \; z_4\{\textit{left}\} \; .. \; z_1 \; .. \; z_3 \; .. \; z_6\{\textit{left}\} \; .. \; \text{cycle}$$

says that the curve should be traveling leftward at points 4 and 6. The resulting curve is perfectly straight from z_6 to z_5 to z_4:

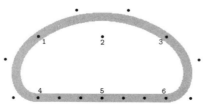

We will see later that '*left*' is an abbreviation for the vector $(-1, 0)$, which stands for one unit of travel in a leftward direction. Any desired direction can be specified by enclosing a vector in $\{\dots\}$'s; for example, the command '**draw** z_4 .. $z_2\{z_3 - z_4\}$ .. z_3' will draw a curve from z_4 to z_2 to z_3 such that the tangent direction at z_2 is parallel to the line z_4 .. z_3, because $z_3 - z_4$ is the vector that represents travel from z_4 to z_3:

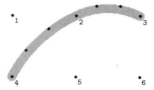

The same result would have been obtained from a command such as '**draw** z_4 .. $z_2\{10(z_3 - z_4)\}$ .. z_3', because the vector $10(z_3 - z_4)$ has the same direction as $z_3 - z_4$. METAFONT ignores the magnitudes of vectors when they are simply being used to specify directions.

▶**EXERCISE 3.1**
What do you think will be the result of '**draw** z_4 .. $z_2\{z_4 - z_3\}$ .. z_3', when
points z_2, z_3, z_4 are the same as they have been in the last several examples?

▶**EXERCISE 3.2**
Explain how to get METAFONT to draw the wiggly shape

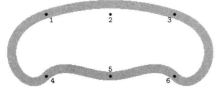

in which the curve aims directly at point 2 when it's at point 6, but directly
away from point 2 when it's at point 4. [*Hint:* No tension changes are needed;
it's merely necessary to specify directions at z_4 and z_6.]

METAFONT allows you to change the shape of a curve at its endpoints
by specifying different amounts of "curl." For example, the two commands

> **draw** $z_4\{\text{curl}\,0\}$ .. $z_2\{z3 - z4\}$ .. $\{\text{curl}\,0\}\,z_3$;
> **draw** $z_4\{\text{curl}\,2\}$ .. $z_2\{z3 - z4\}$ .. $\{\text{curl}\,2\}\,z_3$

give the respective curves

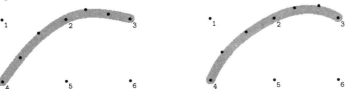

which can be compared with the one shown earlier when no special curl was
requested. (The specification 'curl 1' is assumed at an endpoint if no explicit
curl or direction has been mentioned, just as 'tension 1' is implied between points
when no tension has been explicitly given.) Chapter 14 explains more about this.

It's possible to get curved lines instead of straight lines even when only
two points are named, if a direction has been prescribed at one or both of the
points. For example,

> **draw** $z_4\{z_2 - z_4\}$ .. $\{down\}\,z_6$

asks METAFONT for a curve that starts traveling towards z_2 but finishes in a
downward direction:

Here are some of the curves that METAFONT draws between two points, when it is asked to move outward from the left-hand point at an angle of 60°, and to approach the right-hand point at various angles:

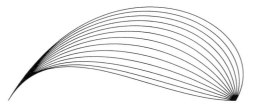

This diagram was produced by the METAFONT program

> **for** $d = 0$ **step** 10 **until** 120:
>   **draw** $(0,0)\{\mathrm{dir}\,60\} \mathbin{..} \{\mathrm{dir}\,-d\}(6cm,0)$; **endfor**;

the 'dir' function specifies a direction measured in degrees counterclockwise from a horizontal rightward line, hence 'dir $-d$' gives a direction that is $d°$ below the horizon. The lowest curves in the illustration correspond to small values of d, and the highest curves correspond to values near 120°.

A car that drives along the upper paths in the diagram above is always turning to the right, but in the lower paths it comes to a point where it needs to turn to the left in order to reach its destination from the specified direction. The place where a path changes its curvature from right to left or vice versa is called an "inflection point." METAFONT introduces inflection points when it seems better to change the curvature than to make a sharp turn; indeed, when d is negative there is no way to avoid points of inflection, and the curves for small positive d ought to be similar to those obtained when d has small negative values. The program

> **for** $d = 0$ **step** -10 **until** -90:
>   **draw** $(0,0)\{\mathrm{dir}\,60\} \mathbin{..} \{\mathrm{dir}\,-d\}(6cm,0)$; **endfor**

shows what METAFONT does when d is negative:

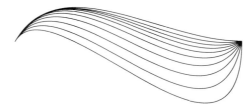

It is sometimes desirable to avoid points of inflection, when d is positive, and to require the curve to remain inside the triangle determined by its initial and final directions. This can be achieved by using three dots instead of two when you specify a curve: The program

> **for** $d = 0$ **step** 10 **until** 120:
>   **draw** $(0,0)\{\mathrm{dir}\,60\} \ldots \{\mathrm{dir}\,-d\}(6cm,0)$; **endfor**

generates the curves

which are the same as before except that inflection points do not occur for the small values of d. The '...' specification keeps the curve "bounded" inside the triangle that is defined by the endpoints and directions; but it has no effect when there is no such triangle. More precisely, suppose that the curve goes from z_0 to z_1; if there's a point z such that the initial direction is from z_0 to z and the final direction is from z to z_1, then the curve specified by '...' will stay entirely within the triangle whose corners are z_0, z_1, and z. But if there's no such triangle (e.g., if $d < 0$ or $d > 120$ in our example program), both '...' and '..' will produce the same curves.

In this chapter we have seen lots of different ways to get METAFONT to draw curves. And there's one more way, which subsumes all of the others. If changes to tensions, curls, directions, and/or boundedness aren't enough to produce the sort of curve that a person wants, it's always possible as a last resort to specify all four of the points in the four-point method. For example, the command

draw z_4 .. controls z_1 and z_2 .. z_6

will draw the following curve from z_4 to z_6:

And so I think I have omitted nothing
that is necessary to an understanding of curved lines.
— RENÉ DESCARTES, *La Géométrie* (1637)

Rules or substitutes for the artist's hand must necessarily be inadequate,
although, when set down by such men as
Dürer, Tory, Da Vinci, Serlio, and others,
they probably do establish canons of proportion and construction
which afford a sound basis upon which to present new expressions.
— FREDERIC W. GOUDY, *Typologia* (1940)

4
Pens

Our examples so far have involved straight lines or curved lines that look as if they were drawn by a felt-tip pen, where the nib of that pen was perfectly round. A mathematical "line" has no thickness, so it's invisible; but when we plot circular dots at each point of an infinitely thin line, we get a visible line that has constant thickness.

Lines of constant thickness have their uses, but METAFONT also provides several other kinds of scrivener's tools, and we shall take a look at some of them in this chapter. We'll see not only that the sizes and shapes of pen nibs can be varied, but also that characters can be built up in such a way that the outlines of each stroke are precisely controlled.

First let's consider the simplest extensions of what we have seen before. The letter 'A' of Chapter 2 and the kidney-bean '◯' of Chapter 3 were drawn with circular pen nibs of diameter 0.4 pt, where 'pt' stands for a printer's point;* 0.4 pt is the standard thickness of a ruled line '——' drawn by TEX. Such a penpoint can be specified by telling METAFONT to

   pickup pencircle scaled $0.4pt$;

METAFONT will use the pen it has most recently picked up whenever it is asked to '**draw**' anything. A **pencircle** is a circular pen whose diameter is the width of one pixel. Scaling it by $0.4pt$ will change it to the size that corresponds to 0.4 pt in the output, because pt is the number of pixels in 1 pt. If the key points $(z_1, z_2, z_3, z_4, z_5, z_6)$ of Chapters 2 and 3 have already been defined, the METAFONT commands

   pickup pencircle scaled $0.8pt$;
   draw $z_5 \mathinner{.\,.} z_4 \mathinner{.\,.} z_1 \mathinner{.\,.} z_3 \mathinner{.\,.} z_6 \mathinner{.\,.}$ cycle

will produce a bean shape twice as thick as before: '◯' instead of '◯'.

More interesting effects arise when we use non-circular pen nibs. For example, the command

   pickup pencircle xscaled $0.8pt$ yscaled $0.2pt$

picks up a pen whose tip has the shape of an ellipse, 0.8 pt wide and 0.2 pt tall; magnified 10 times, it looks like this: '➖'. (The operation of "xscaling" multiplies x coordinates by a specified amount but leaves y coordinates unchanged, and the operation of "yscaling" is similar.) Using such a pen, the '◯' becomes '◯', and 'A' becomes 'A'. Furthermore,

   pickup pencircle xscaled $0.8pt$ yscaled $0.2pt$ rotated 30

takes that ellipse and rotates it 30° counterclockwise, obtaining the nib '✐'; this changes '◯' into '◯' and 'A' into 'A'. An enlarged view of the bean shape shows

---

* 1 in = 2.54 cm = 72.27 pt exactly, as explained in *The TEXbook*.

more clearly what is going on:

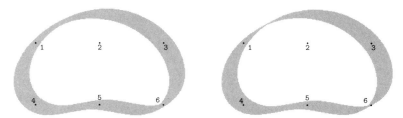

The right-hand example was obtained by eliminating the clause 'yscaled $0.2pt$';
this makes the pen almost razor thin, only one pixel tall before rotation.

▸ **EXERCISE 4.1**
Describe the pen shapes defined by (a) **pencircle** xscaled $0.2pt$ yscaled $0.8pt$;
(b) **pencircle** scaled $0.8pt$ rotated 30; (c) **pencircle** xscaled $.25$ scaled $0.8pt$.

▸ **EXERCISE 4.2**
We've seen many examples of '**draw**' used with two or more points. What do
you think METAFONT will do if you ask it to perform the following commands?

$$\textbf{draw } z_1; \quad \textbf{draw } z_2; \quad \textbf{draw } z_3; \quad \textbf{draw } z_4; \quad \textbf{draw } z_5; \quad \textbf{draw } z_6.$$

Let's turn now to the design of a real letter that has already appeared
many times in this manual, namely the 'T' of 'METAFONT'. All seven of the
distinct letters in 'METAFONT' will be used to illustrate various ideas as we get
into the details of the language; we might as well start with 'T', because it
occurs twice, and (especially) because it's the sim-
plest. An enlarged version of this letter is shown at
the right of this paragraph, including the locations
of its four key points (z_1, z_2, z_3, z_4) and its bounding
box. Typesetting systems like TEX are based on the
assumption that each character fits in a rectangular
box; we shall discuss boxes in detail later, but for
now we will be content simply to know that such
boundaries do exist.* Numbers h and w will have
been computed so that the corners of the box are at
positions $(0,0)$, $(0,h)$, $(w,0)$, and (w,h) as shown.

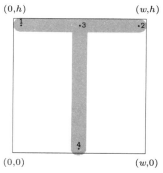

Each of the letters in 'METAFONT' is drawn
with a pen whose nib is an unrotated ellipse, 90% as tall as it is wide. In the
10-point size, which is used for the main text of this book, the pen is $2/3\,pt$ wide,

---

* Strictly speaking, the bounding box doesn't actually have to "bound" the black pixels
of a character; for example, the 'T' protrudes slightly below the baseline at point 4,
and italic letters frequently extend rather far to the right of their boxes. However,
TEX positions all characters by lumping boxes together as if they were pieces of metal
type that contain all of the ink.

so it has been specified by the command

> **pickup pencircle** scaled $\frac{2}{3}pt$ yscaled $\frac{9}{10}$

or something equivalent to this.

We shall assume that a special value 'o' has been computed so that the bottom of the vertical stroke in 'T' should descend exactly o pixels below the baseline; this is called the amount of "overshoot." Given h, w, and o, it is a simple matter to define the four key points and to draw the 'T':

> *top lft* $z_1 = (0, h)$;   *top rt* $z_2 = (w, h)$;
> *top* $z_3 = (.5w, h)$;   *bot* $z_4 = (.5w, -o)$;
> **draw** $z_1 .. z_2$;   **draw** $z_3 .. z_4$.

 Sometimes it is easier and/or clearer to define the x and y coordinates separately. For example, the key points of the 'T' could also be specified thus:

> *lft* $x_1 = 0$; $w - x_2 = x_1$; $x_3 = x_4 = .5w$;
> *top* $y_1 = h$;   *bot* $y_4 = -o$; $y_1 = y_2 = y_3$.

The equation $w - x_2 = x_1$ expresses the fact that x_2 is just as far from the right edge of the bounding box as x_1 is from the left edge.

 What exactly does '*top*' mean in a METAFONT equation? If the currently-picked-up pen extends l pixels to the left of its center, r pixels to the right, t pixels upward and b downward, then

> *top* $z = z + (0, t)$,   *bot* $z = z - (0, b)$,   *lft* $z = z - (l, 0)$,   *rt* $z = z + (r, 0)$,

when z is a pair of coordinates. But—as the previous paragraph shows, if you study it carefully—we also have

> *top* $y = y + t$,   *bot* $y = y - b$,   *lft* $x = x - l$,   *rt* $x = x + r$,

when x and y are single values instead of coordinate pairs. You shouldn't apply '*top*' or '*bot*' to x coordinates, nor '*lft*' or '*rt*' to y coordinates.

 ▶ **EXERCISE 4.3**
True or false: *top bot* $z = z$, whenever z is a pair of coordinates.

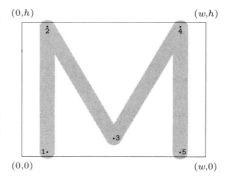

▶ **EXERCISE 4.4**
An enlarged picture of METAFONT's 'M' shows that it has five key points. Assuming that special values ss and $ygap$ have been precomputed and that the equations

$$x_1 = ss = w - x5; \quad y_3 - y_1 = ygap$$

have already been given, what further equations and '**draw**' commands will complete the specification of this letter? (The value of w will be greater for 'M' than it was for 'T'; it stands for the pixel width of whatever character is currently being drawn.)

METAFONT's ability to '**draw**' allows it to produce character shapes that are satisfactory for many applications, but the shapes are inherently limited by the fact that the simulated pen nib must stay the same through an entire stroke. Human penpushers are able to get richer effects by using different amounts of pressure and/or by rotating the pen as they draw.

We can obtain finer control over the characters we produce if we specify their outlines, instead of working only with key points that lie somewhere in the middle. In fact, METAFONT works internally with outlines, and the computer finds it much easier to fill a region with solid black than to figure out what pixels are blackened by a moving pen. There's a '**fill**' command that does region filling; for example, the solid bean shape

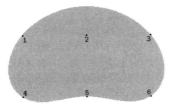

can be obtained from our six famous example points by giving the command

> **fill** $z_5 \mathinner{.\,.} z_4 \mathinner{.\,.} z_1 \mathinner{.\,.} z_3 \mathinner{.\,.} z_6 \mathinner{.\,.}$ cycle.

The filled region is essentially what would be cut out by an infinitely sharp knife blade if it traced over the given curve while cutting a piece of thin film. A **draw** command needs to add thickness to its curve, because the result would otherwise be invisible; but a **fill** command adds no thickness.

The curve in a **fill** command must end with 'cycle', because an entire region must be filled. It wouldn't make sense to say, e.g., '**fill** $z_1 \mathinner{.\,.} z_2$'. The cycle being filled shouldn't cross itself, either; METAFONT would have lots of trouble trying to figure out how to obey a command like '**fill** $z_1 \mathinner{.\,.} z_6 \mathinner{.\,.} z_3 \mathinner{.\,.} z_4 \mathinner{.\,.}$ cycle'.

▶ **EXERCISE 4.5**
Chapter 3 discusses the curve $z_5 \mathinner{.\,.} z_4 \mathinner{.\,.} z_1 \mathinner{.\,.} z_3 \mathinner{.\,.} z_6 \mathinner{.\,.} z_5$, which isn't smooth at z_5. Since this curve doesn't end with 'cycle', you can't use it in a **fill** command. But it does define a closed region. How can METAFONT be instructed to fill that region?

The black triangle '▶' that appears in the statement of exercises in this book was drawn with the command

> **fill** $z_1 \mathbin{-\!\!-} z_2 \mathbin{-\!\!-} z_3 \mathbin{-\!\!-}$ cycle

after appropriate corner points z_1, z_2, and z_3 had been specified. In this case the outline of the region to be filled was specified in terms of the symbol '--' instead of '..'; this is a convention we haven't discussed before. Each '--' introduces a straight line segment, which is independent of the rest of the path that it belongs to; thus it is quite different from '..', which specifies a possibly curved line segment that connects smoothly with neighboring points and lines of a path. In this case '--' was used so that the triangular region would have straight edges and sharp corners. We might say informally that '..' means "Connect the points with a nice curve," while '--' means "Connect the points with a straight line."

The corner points z_1, z_2, and z_3 were defined care- fully so that the triangle would be *equilateral*, i.e., so that all three of its sides would have the same length. Since an equilateral triangle has 60° angles, the following equations did the job:

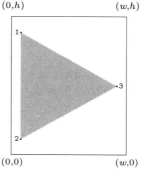

$$x_1 = x_2 = w - x_3 = s;$$
$$y_3 = .5h;$$
$$z_1 - z_2 = (z_3 - z_2) \text{ rotated } 60.$$

Here w and h represent the character's width and height, and s is the distance of the triangle from the left and right edges of the type.

The **fill** command has a companion called **unfill**, which changes pixels from black to white inside a given region. For example, the solid bean shape on the previous page can be changed to

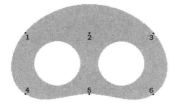

if we say also '**unfill** $\frac{1}{4}[z_4, z_2] .. \frac{3}{4}[z_4, z_2] ..$ cycle; **unfill** $\frac{1}{4}[z_6, z_2] .. \frac{3}{4}[z_6, z_2] ..$ cycle'. This example shows, incidentally, that METAFONT converts a two-point specification like '$z_1 .. z_2 ..$ cycle' into a more-or-less circular path, even though two points by themselves define only a straight line.

▶ **EXERCISE 4.6**
Let z_0 be the point $(.8[x_1, x_2], .5[y_1, y_4])$, and introduce six new points by letting $z'_k = .2[z_k, z_0]$ for $k = 1, 2, \ldots, 6$. Explain how to obtain the shape

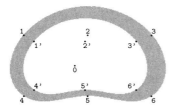

in which the interior region is defined by $z'_1 \ldots z'_6$ instead of by $z_1 \ldots z_6$.

The ability to fill between outlines makes it possible to pretend that we have broad-edge pens that change in direction and pressure as they glide over the paper, if we consider the separate paths traced out by the pen's left edge and right edge. For example, the stroke

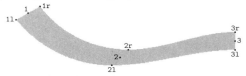

can be regarded as drawn by a pen that starts at the left, inclined at a 30° angle; as the pen moves, it turns gradually until its edge is strictly vertical by the time it reaches the right end. The pen motion was horizontal at positions 2 and 3. This stroke was actually obtained by the command

fill $z_{1l} \ldots z_{2l}\{right\} \ldots \{right\} z_{3l}$
$\phantom{\textbf{fill}}\text{-- } z_{3r}\{left\} \ldots \{left\} z_{2r} \mathrel{.\!.} z_{1r}$
$\phantom{\textbf{fill}}\text{-- cycle;}$

i.e., METAFONT was asked to fill a region bounded by a "left path" from z_{1l} to z_{2l} to z_{3l}, followed by a straight line to z_{3r}, then a reversed "right path" from z_{3r} to z_{2r} to z_{1r}, and finally a straight line back to the starting point z_{1l}.

Key positions of the "pen" are represented in this example by sets of three points, like (z_{1l}, z_1, z_{1r}), which stand for the pen's left edge, its midpoint, and its right edge. The midpoint doesn't actually occur in the specification of the outline, but we'll see examples of its usefulness. The relationships between such triples of points are established by a '*penpos*' command, which states the breadth of the pen and its angle of inclination at a particular position. For example, positions 1, 2, and 3 in the stroke above were established by saying

$$penpos_1(1.2pt, 30); \qquad penpos_2(1.0pt, 45); \qquad penpos_3(0.8pt, 90);$$

this made the pen 1.2 pt broad and tipped 30° with respect to the horizontal at position 1, etc. In general the idea is to specify '$penpos_k(b, d)$', where k is the position number or position name, b is the breadth (in pixels), and d is the angle (in degrees). Pen angles are measured counterclockwise from the horizontal. Thus, an angle of 0 makes the right edge of the pen exactly b pixels to the right of the left edge; an angle of 90 makes the right pen edge exactly b pixels above the left; an angle of −90 makes it exactly b pixels below. An angle of 45 makes the right edge $b/\sqrt{2}$ pixels above and $b/\sqrt{2}$ pixels to the right of the left edge; an angle of −45 makes it $b/\sqrt{2}$ pixels below and $b/\sqrt{2}$ to the right. When the pen angle is between 90° and 180°, the "right" edge actually lies to the left of the "left" edge. In terms of compass directions on a conventional map, an angle of 0° points due East, while 90° points North and −90° points South. The angle corresponding to Southwest is −135°, also known as +225°.

▶ **EXERCISE 4.7**
What angle corresponds to the direction North-Northwest?

▶ **EXERCISE 4.8**
What are the pen angles at positions 1, 2, 3, and 4 in
the circular shape shown here? [*Hint:* Each angle is a
multiple of 30°. Note that z_{3r} lies to the left of z_{3l}.]

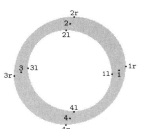

▶ **EXERCISE 4.9**
What are the coordinates of z_{1l} and z_{1r} after the command '$penpos_1(10, -90)$', if $z_1 = (25, 25)$?

The statement '$penpos_k(b, d)$' is simply an abbreviation for two equations,
'$z_k = \frac{1}{2}[z_{kl}, z_{kr}]$' and '$z_{kr} = z_{kl} + (b, 0)$ rotated d'. You might want to use
other equations to define the relationship between z_{kl}, z_k, and z_{kr}, instead of giving a
penpos command, if an alternative formulation turns out to be more convenient.

After '*penpos*' has specified the relations between three points, we still
don't know exactly where they are; we only know their positions relative to each
other. Another equation or two is needed in order to fix the horizontal and
vertical locations of each triple. For example, the three *penpos* commands that
led to the pen stroke on the previous page were accompanied by the equations

$$z_1 = (0, 2pt); \qquad z_2 = (4pt, 0); \qquad x_3 = 9pt; \qquad y_{3l} = y_{2r};$$

these made the information complete. There should be one x equation and one
y equation for each position; or you can use a z equation, which defines both x
and y simultaneously.

It's a nuisance to write long-winded **fill** commands when broad-edge
pens are being simulated in this way, so METAFONT provides a convenient abbreviation: You can write simply

penstroke $z_{1e} \mathinner{.\,.} z_{2e}\{right\} \mathinner{.\,.} \{right\}z_{3e}$

instead of the command '**fill** $z_{1l} \mathinner{.\,.} z_{2l}\{right\} \mathinner{.\,.} \{right\} z_{3l} \mathbin{-\,-} z_{3r}\{left\} \mathinner{.\,.}$
$\{left\} z_{2r} \mathinner{.\,.} z_{1r} \mathbin{-\,-}$ cycle' that was stated earlier. The letter 'e' stands for the
pen's edge. A **penstroke** command fills the region '$p.l \mathbin{-\,-}$ reverse $p.r \mathbin{-\,-}$ cycle',
where $p.l$ and $p.r$ are the left and right paths formed by changing each 'e' into
'l' or 'r', respectively.

The **penstroke** abbreviation can be used to draw cyclic paths as well as
ordinary ones. For example, the circle in exercise 4.8 was created by saying
simply '**penstroke** $z_{1e} \mathinner{.\,.} z_{2e} \mathinner{.\,.} z_{3e} \mathinner{.\,.} z_{4e} \mathinner{.\,.}$ cycle'. This type of penstroke essentially
expands into

fill $z_{1r} \mathinner{.\,.} z_{2r} \mathinner{.\,.} z_{3r} \mathinner{.\,.} z_{4r} \mathinner{.\,.}$ cycle;
unfill $z_{1l} \mathinner{.\,.} z_{2l} \mathinner{.\,.} z_{3l} \mathinner{.\,.} z_{4l} \mathinner{.\,.}$ cycle;

or the operations '**fill**' and '**unfill**' are reversed, if points $(z_{1r}, z_{2r}, z_{3r}, z_{4r})$ are on the
inside and $(z_{1l}, z_{2l}, z_{3l}, z_{4l})$ are on the outside.

▶ **EXERCISE 4.10**
The circle of exercise 4.8 was actually drawn with a slightly more complicated
penstroke command than just claimed: The edges of the curve were forced to be
vertical at positions 1 and 3, horizontal at 2 and 4. How did the author do this?

Here's an example of how this new sort of pen can be used to draw a sans-serif letter 'l'. As usual, we assume that two variables, h and w, have been set up to give the height and width of the character in pixels. We shall also assume that there's a *stem* parameter, which specifies the nominal pen breadth. The breadth decreases to *.9stem* in the middle of the stroke, and the pen angle changes from 15° to 10°:

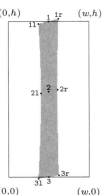

$$penpos_1(stem, 15); \quad penpos_2(.9stem, 12);$$
$$penpos_3(stem, 10); \quad x_1 = x_2 = x_3 = .5w;$$
$$y_1 = h; \quad y_2 = .55h; \quad y_3 = 0;$$
$$x_{2l} := \tfrac{1}{6}[x_{2l}, x_2];$$
$$\textbf{penstroke } z_{1e} \mathbin{..} z_{2e}\{down\} \mathbin{..} z_{3e}.$$

Setting $x_1 = x_2 = x_3 = .5w$ centers the stroke; setting $y_1 = h$ and $y_3 = 0$ makes it sit in the type box, protruding just slightly at the top and bottom.

The second-last line of this program is something that we haven't seen before: It resets x_{2l} to a value 1/6 of the way towards the center of the pen, thereby making the stroke taper a bit at the left. The ':=' operation is called an *assignment*; we shall study the differences between ':=' and '=' in Chapter 10.

It is important to note that these simulated pens have a serious limitation compared to the way a real calligrapher's pen works: The left and right edges of a *penpos*-made pen must never cross, hence it is necessary to turn the pen when going around a curve. Consider, for example, the following two curves:

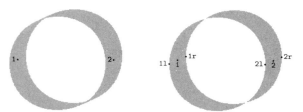

The left-hand circle was drawn with a broad-edge pen of fixed breadth, held at a fixed angle; consequently the left edge of the pen was responsible for the outer boundary on the left, but the inner boundary on the right. (This curve was produced by saying '**pickup pencircle** xscaled 0.8*pt* rotated 25; **draw** $z_1 \mathbin{..} z_2 \mathbin{..}$ cycle'.) The right-hand shape was produced by '*penpos*$_1$(0.8*pt*, 25); *penpos*$_2$(0.8*pt*, 25); **penstroke** $z_{1e} \mathbin{..} z_{2e} \mathbin{..}$ cycle'; important chunks of the shape are missing at the crossover points, because they don't lie on either of the circles $z_{1l} \mathbin{..} z_{2l} \mathbin{..}$ cycle or $z_{1r} \mathbin{..} z_{2r} \mathbin{..}$ cycle.

To conclude this chapter we shall improve the hex character ✖ of Chapter 2, which is too dark in the middle because it has been drawn with a pen of uniform thickness. The main trouble with unvarying pens is that they tend to produce black blotches where two strokes meet, unless the pens are comparatively thin or unless the strokes are nearly perpendicular. We want to thin out the lines at the center just enough to cure the darkness problem, without destroying the illusion that the lines still seem (at first glance) to have uniform thickness.

 It isn't difficult to produce '⟩◇◆◇◆◇◆◇◆◇◆◇◆◇◆◆K' instead of '⟩◇◆◇◆◇◆◇◆◇◆◇◆◇K' when we work with dynamic pens:

pickup pencircle scaled b;
top $z_1 = (0, h)$; *top* $z_2 = (.5w, h)$; *top* $z_3 = (w, h)$;
bot $z_4 = (0, 0)$; *bot* $z_5 = (.5w, 0)$; *bot* $z_6 = (w, 0)$; **draw** $z_2 \mathbin{..} z_5$;
$z_{1'} = .25[z_1, z_6]$; $z_{6'} = .75[z_1, z_6]$; $z_{3'} = .25[z_3, z_4]$; $z_{4'} = .75[z_3, z_4]$;
$theta_1 := \text{angle}(z_6 - z_1) + 90$;
$theta_3 := \text{angle}(z_4 - z_3) + 90$;
$penpos_{1'}(b, theta_1)$; $penpos_{6'}(b, theta_1)$;
$penpos_{3'}(b, theta_3)$; $penpos_{4'}(b, theta_3)$;
$penpos_7(.6b, theta_1)$; $penpos_8(.6b, theta_3)$;
$z_7 = z_8 = .5[z_1, z_6]$;
draw $z_1 \mathbin{..} z_{1'}$; **draw** $z_{6'} \mathbin{..} z_6$;
draw $z_3 \mathbin{..} z_{3'}$; **draw** $z_{4'} \mathbin{..} z_4$;
penstroke $z_{1'e}\{z_{6'} - z_{1'}\} \mathbin{..} z_{7e} \mathbin{..} \{z_{6'} - z_{1'}\}z_{6'e}$;
penstroke $z_{3'e}\{z_{4'} - z_{3'}\} \mathbin{..} z_{8e} \mathbin{..} \{z_{4'} - z_{3'}\}z_{4'e}$;

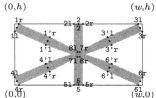

Here b is the diameter of the pen at the terminal points; 'angle' computes the direction angle of a given vector. Adding 90° to a direction angle gives a perpendicular direction (see the definitions of $theta_1$ and $theta_3$). It isn't necessary to take anything off of the vertical stroke $z_2 \mathbin{..} z_5$, because the two diagonal strokes fill more than the width of the vertical stroke at the point where they intersect.

 ▶ **EXERCISE 4.11**
Modify the hex character so that its ends are cut sharply and confined to the bounding box, as shown.

> It is very important that the nib be cut "sharp,"
> and as often as its edge wears blunt it must be resharpened.
> It is impossible to make "clean cut" strokes with a blunt pen.
> — EDWARD JOHNSTON, *Writing & Illuminating, & Lettering* (1906)

> I might compare the high-speed computing machine
> to a remarkably large and awkward pencil
> which takes a long time to sharpen and
> cannot be held in the fingers in the usual manner so that it
> gives the illusion of responding to my thoughts,
> but is fitted with a rather delicate engine
> and will write like a mad thing
> provided I am willing to let it dictate pretty much
> the subjects on which it writes.
> — R. H. BRUCK, *Computational Aspects of Certain Combinatorial Problems* (1956)

5

Running
METAFONT

It's high time now for you to stop reading and to start playing with the computer, since METAFONT is an interactive system that is best learned by trial and error. (In fact, one of the nicest things about computer graphics is that errors are often more interesting and more fun than "successes.")

You probably will have to ask somebody how to deal with the idiosyncrasies of your particular version of the system, even though METAFONT itself works in essentially the same way on all machines; different computer terminals and different hardcopy devices make it necessary to have somewhat different interfaces. In this chapter we shall assume that you have a computer terminal with a reasonably high-resolution graphics display; that you have access to a (possibly low-resolution) output device; and that you can rather easily get that device to work with newly created fonts.

OK, are you ready to run the program? First you need to log in, of course; then start METAFONT, which is usually called mf for short. Once you've figured out how to do it, you'll be welcomed by a message something like

```
This is METAFONT, Version 2.0 (preloaded base=plain 89.11.8)
**
```

The '**' is METAFONT's way of asking you for an input file name.

Now type '\relax'—that's backslash, r, e, l, a, x—and hit ⟨return⟩ (or whatever stands for "end-of-line" on your keyboard). METAFONT is all geared up for action, ready to make a big font; but you're saying that it's all right to take things easy, since this is going to be a real simple run. The backslash means that METAFONT should not read a file, it should get instructions from the keyboard; the 'relax' means "do nothing."

The machine will respond by typing a single asterisk: '*'. This means it's ready to accept instructions (not the name of a file). Type the following, just for fun:

```
drawdot (35,70); showit;
```

and ⟨return⟩—don't forget to type the semicolons along with the other stuff. A more-or-less circular dot should now appear on your screen! And you should also be prompted with another asterisk. Type

```
drawdot (65,70); showit;
```

and ⟨return⟩, to get another dot. (Henceforth we won't keep mentioning the necessity of ⟨return⟩ing after each line of keyboard input.) Finally, type

```
draw (20,40)..(50,25)..(80,40); showit; shipit; end.
```

This draws a curve through three given points, displays the result, ships it to an output file, and stops. METAFONT should respond with '[0]', meaning that it has shipped out a character whose number is zero, in the "font" just made; and it should also tell you that it has created an output file called 'mfput.2602gf'. (The name mfput is used when you haven't specified any better name in response to the ** at the beginning. The suffix 2602gf stands for "generic font at 2602 pixels per inch." The data in mfput.2602gf can be converted into fonts suitable for a wide assortment of typographical output devices; since it doesn't match the font file conventions of any name-brand manufacturer, we call it generic.)

This particular file won't make a very interesting font, because it contains only one character, and because it probably doesn't have the correct resolution for your output device. However, it does have the right resolution for hardcopy proofs of characters; your next step should therefore be to convert the data of mfput.2602gf into a picture, suitable for framing. There should be a program called GFtoDVI on your computer. Apply it to mfput.2602gf, thereby obtaining a file called mfput.dvi that can be printed. Your friendly local computer hackers will tell you how to run GFtoDVI and how to print mfput.dvi; then you'll have a marvelous souvenir of your very first encounter with METAFONT.

Once you have made a complete test run as just described, you will know how to get through the whole cycle, so you'll be ready to tackle a more complex project. Our next experiment will therefore be to work from a file, instead of typing the input online.

Use your favorite text editor to create a file called io.mf that contains the following 23 lines of text (no more, no less):

```
1  mode_setup;
2   em#:=10pt#; cap#:=7pt#;
3   thin#:=1/3pt#; thick#:=5/6pt#;
4   o#:=1/5pt#;
5  define_pixels(em,cap);
6  define_blacker_pixels(thin,thick);
7  define_corrected_pixels(o);
8   curve_sidebar=round 1/18em;
9  beginchar("O",0.8em#,cap#,0); "The letter O";
10   penpos1(thick,10); penpos2(.1[thin,thick],90-10);
11   penpos3(thick,180+10); penpos4(thin,270-10);
12   x1l=w-x3l=curve_sidebar; x2=x4=.5w;
13   y1=.49h; y2l=-o; y3=.51h; y4l=h+o;
14   penstroke z1e{down}..z2e{right}
15              ..z3e{up}..z4e{left}..cycle;
16   penlabels(1,2,3,4); endchar;
17 def test_I(expr code,trial_stem,trial_width) =
18   stem#:=trial_stem*pt#; define_blacker_pixels(stem);
19   beginchar(code,trial_width*em#,cap#,0); "The letter I";
20   penpos1(stem,15); penpos2(stem,12); penpos3(stem,10);
21   x1=x2=x3=.5w; y1=h; y2=.55h; y3=0; x2l:=1/6[x2l,x2];
22   penstroke z1e..z2e{down}..z3e;
23   penlabels(1,2,3); endchar; enddef;
```

(But don't type the numbers at the left of these lines; they're only for reference.)

This example file is dedicated to Io, the Greek goddess of input and output. It's a trifle long, but you'll be able to get worthwhile experience by typing it; so go ahead and type it now. For your own good. And think about what you're typing, as you go; the example introduces several important features of METAFONT that you can learn as you're creating the file.

Here's a brief explanation of what you've just typed: Line 1 contains a command that usually appears near the beginning of every METAFONT file; it tells the computer to get ready to work in whatever "mode" is currently desired. (A file like `io.mf` can be used to generate proofsheets as well as to make fonts for a variety of devices at a variety of magnifications, and '**mode_setup**' is what adapts METAFONT to the task at hand.) Lines 2–8 define parameters that will be used to draw the letters in the font. Lines 9–16 give a complete program for the letter 'O'; and lines 17–23 give a program that will draw the letter 'I' in a number of related ways.

It all looks pretty frightening at first glance, but a closer look shows that Io is not so mysterious once we penetrate her disguise. Let's spend a few minutes studying the file in more detail.

Lines 2–4 define dimensions that are independent of the mode; the '**#**' signs are meant to imply "sharp" or "true" units of measure, which remain the same whether we are making a font at high or low resolution. For example, one '`pt#`' is a true printer's point, one 72.27th of an inch. This is quite different from the '*pt*' we have discussed in previous chapters, because '*pt*' is the number of pixels that happen to correspond to a printer's point when the current resolution is taken into account. The value of '`pt#`' never changes, but **mode_setup** establishes the appropriate value of '*pt*'.

The assignments '`em#:=10pt#`' and '`cap#:=7pt#`' in line 2 mean that the Io font has two parameters, called *em* and *cap*, whose mode-independent values are 10 and 7 points, respectively. The statement '`define_pixels(em,cap)`' on line 5 converts these values into pixel units. For example, if we are working at the comparatively low resolution of 3 pixels per pt, the values of *em* and *cap* after the computer has performed the instructions on line 5 will be *em* = 30 and *cap* = 21. (We will see later that the widths of characters in this font are expressed in terms of ems, and that *cap* is the height of the capital letters. A change to line 2 will therefore affect the widths and/or heights of all the letters.)

Similarly, the Io font has parameters called *thin* and *thick*, defined on line 3 and converted to pixel units in line 6. These are used to control the breadth of a simulated pen when it draws the letter O. Experience has shown that META-FONT produces better results on certain output devices if pixel-oriented pens are made slightly broader than the true dimensions would imply, because black pixels sometimes tend to "burn off" in the process of printing. The command on line 6, '`define_blacker_pixels`', adds a correction based on the device for which the font is being prepared. For example, if the resolution is 3 pixels per point, the value of *thin* when converted from true units to pixels by **define_pixels** would be 1, but **define_blacker_pixels** might set *thin* to a value closer to 2.

The 'o' parameter on line 4 represents the amount by which curves will overshoot their boundaries. This is converted to pixels in yet another way on line 7, so as to avoid yet another problem that arises in low-resolution printing. The author apologizes for letting such real-world considerations intrude into a textbook example; let's not get bogged down in fussy details now, since these refinements will be explained in Chapter 11 after we have mastered the basics.

For now, the important point is simply that a typeface design usually involves parameters that represent physical lengths. The true, "sharped" forms of these parameters need to be converted to "unsharped" pixel-oriented quantities, and best results are obtained when such conversions are done carefully. After METAFONT has obeyed line 7 of the example, the pixel-oriented parameters *em*, *cap*, *thin*, *thick*, and *o* are ready to be used as we draw letters of the font.

Line 8 defines a quantity called *curve_sidebar* that will measure the distance of the left and right edges of the 'O' from the bounding box. It is computed by rounding $\frac{1}{18} em$ to the nearest integer number of pixels. For example, if $em = 30$ then $\frac{30}{18} = \frac{5}{3}$ yields the rounded value *curve_sidebar* = 2; there will be two all-white columns of pixels at the left and right of the 'O', when we work at this particular resolution.

Before we go any further, we ought to discuss the strange collection of words and pseudo-words in the file `io.mf`. Which of the terms '`mode_setup`', '`em`', '`curve_sidebar`' and so forth are part of the METAFONT language, and which of them are made up specifically for the Io example? Well, it turns out that almost *nothing* in this example is written in the pure METAFONT language that the computer understands! METAFONT is really a low-level language that has been designed to allow easy adaptation to many different styles of programming, and `io.mf` illustrates just one of countless ways to use it. Most of the terms in `io.mf` are conventions of "plain METAFONT," which is a collection of subroutines found in Appendix B. METAFONT's primitive capabilities are not meant to be used directly, because that would force a particular style on all users. A "base file" is generally loaded into the computer at the beginning of a run, so that a standard set of conventions is readily available. METAFONT's welcoming message, quoted at the beginning of this chapter, says '`preloaded base=plain`'; it means that the primitive METAFONT language has been extended to include the features of the plain base file. This book is not only about METAFONT; it also explains how to use the conventions of METAFONT's plain base. Similarly, *The TEXbook* describes a standard extension of TEX called "plain TEX format"; the "plain" extensions of TEX and METAFONT are completely analogous to each other.

The notions of **mode_setup**, **define_pixels**, **beginchar**, *penpos*, and many other things found in `io.mf` are aspects of plain METAFONT but they are not hardwired into METAFONT itself. Appendix B defines all of these things, as well as the relations between "sharped" and "unsharped" variables. Even the fact that z_1 stands for (x_1, y_1) is defined in Appendix B; METAFONT does not have this built in. You are free to define even fancier bases as you gain more experience, but the plain base is a suitable starting point for a novice.

If you have important applications that make use of a different base file, it's possible to create a version of METAFONT that has any desired base preloaded. Such a program is generally called by a special name, since the nickname 'mf' is reserved for the version that includes the standard plain base assumed in this book. For example, the author has made a special version called 'cmmf' just for the Computer Modern typefaces he has been developing, so that the Computer Modern base file does not have to be loaded each time he makes a new experiment.

There's a simple way to change the base file from the one that has been preloaded: If the first character you type in response to '******' is an ampersand ('**&**'), METAFONT will replace its memory with a specified base file before proceeding. If, for example, there is a base file called '**cm.base**' but not a special program called '**cmmf**', you can substitute the Computer Modern base for the plain base in **mf** by typing '**&cm**' at the very beginning of a run. If you are working with a program that doesn't have the plain base preloaded, the first experiment in this chapter won't work as described, but you can do it by starting with '**&plain \relax**' instead of just '**\relax**'. These conventions are exactly the same as those of TeX.

Our Ionian example uses the following words that are not part of plain METAFONT: *em*, *cap*, *thin*, *thick*, *o*, *curve_sidebar*, *test_I*, *code*, *trial_stem*, *trial_width*, and *stem*. If you change these to some other words or symbols—for example, if you replace '**thin**' and '**thick**' by '**t**' and 'T' respectively, in lines 3, 6, 10, and 11—the results will be unchanged, unless your substitutions just happen to clash with something that plain METAFONT has already preëmpted. In general, the best policy is to choose descriptive terms for the quantities in your programs, since they are not likely to conflict with reserved pseudo-words like *penpos* and **endchar**.

We have already noted that lines 9–16 of the file represent a program for the letter 'O'. The main part of this program, in lines 10–15, uses the ideas of Chapter 4, but we haven't seen the stuff in lines 9 and 16 before. Plain METAFONT makes it convenient to define letters by starting each one with

$$\textbf{beginchar}\,(\langle\text{code}\rangle,\ \langle\text{width}\rangle,\ \langle\text{height}\rangle,\ \langle\text{depth}\rangle);$$

here ⟨code⟩ is either a quoted single character like "O" or a number that represents the character's position in the final font. The other three quantities ⟨width⟩, ⟨height⟩, and ⟨depth⟩ say how big the bounding box is, so that typesetting systems like TeX will be able to use the character. These three dimensions must be given in device-independent units, i.e., in "sharped" form.

▶ **EXERCISE 5.1**
What are the height and width of the bounding box described in the **beginchar** command on line 9 of **io.mf**, given the parameter values defined on line 2? Give your answer in terms of printer's points.

Each **beginchar** operation assigns values to special variables called w, h, and d, which represent the respective width, height, and depth of the current character's bounding box, rounded to the nearest integer number of pixels. Our example file uses w and h to help establish the locations of several pen positions (see lines 12, 13, and 21 of `io.mf`).

▶ **EXERCISE 5.2**
Continuing the previous exercise, what will be the values of w and h if there are exactly 3.6 pixels per point?

There's a quoted phrase "The letter O" at the end of line 9; this is simply a title that will be used in printouts.

The 'endchar' on line 16 finishes the character that was begun on line 9, by writing it to an output file and possibly displaying it on your screen. We will want to see the positions of the control points z_1, z_2, z_3, and z_4 that are used in its design, together with the auxiliary points $(z_{1l}, z_{2l}, z_{3l}, z_{4l})$ and $(z_{1r}, z_{2r}, z_{3r}, z_{4r})$ that come with the *penpos* conventions; the statement 'penlabels(1,2,3,4)' takes care of labeling these points on the proofsheets.

So much for the letter O. Lines 17–23 are analogous to what we've seen before, except that there's a new wrinkle: They contain a little program enclosed by 'def...enddef', which means that a *subroutine* is being defined. In other words, those lines set up a whole bunch of METAFONT commands that we will want to execute several times with minor variations. The subroutine is called *test_I* and it has three parameters called *code*, *trial_stem*, and *trial_width* (see line 17). The idea is that we'll want to draw several different versions of an 'I', having different stem widths and character widths; but we want to type the program only once. Line 18 defines *stem#* and *stem*, given a value of *trial_stem*; and lines 19–23 complete the program for the letter I (copying it from Chapter 4).

Oops—we've been talking much too long about `io.mf`. It's time to stop rambling and to begin Experiment 2 in earnest, because it will be much more fun to see what the computer actually does with that file.

Are you brave enough to try Experiment 2? Sure. Get METAFONT going again, but this time when the machine says '**' you should say 'io', since that's the name of the file you have prepared so laboriously. (The file could also be specified by giving its full name 'io.mf', but METAFONT automatically adds '.mf' when no suffix has been given explicitly.)

If all goes well, the computer should now flash its lights a bit and—presto—a big 'O' should be drawn on your screen. But if your luck is as good as the author's, something will probably go wrong the first time, most likely because of a typographic error in the file. A METAFONT program contains lots of data with comparatively little redundancy, so a single error can make a drastic change in the meaning. Check that you've typed everything perfectly: Be sure to notice the difference between the letter 'l' and the numeral '1' (especially in line 12, where it says 'x1l', not 'x11 or 'xll'); be sure to distinguish between the letter 'O' and the numeral '0' (especially in line 9); be sure to type the "underline" characters in words like 'mode_setup'. We'll see later that META-FONT can recover gracefully from most errors, but your job for now is to make sure that you've got `io.mf` correct.

Once you have a working file, the computer will draw you an 'O' and it will also say something like this:

```
(io.mf
The letter O [79])
*
```

What does this mean? Well, '(io.mf' means that it has started to read your file, and 'The letter O' was printed when the title was found in line 9. Then when METAFONT got to the endchar on line 16, it said '[79]' to tell you that it had just output character number 79. (This is the ASCII code for the letter O; Appendix C lists all of these codes, if you need to know them.) The ')' after '[79]' means that METAFONT subsequently finished reading the file, and the '*' means that it wants another instruction.

Hmmm. The file contains programs for both I and O; why did we get only an O? Answer: Because lines 17–23 simply define the subroutine *test_I*; they don't actually *do* anything with that subroutine. We need to activate *test_I* if we're going to see what it does. So let's type

```
test_I("I",5/6,1/3);
```

this invokes the subroutine, with *code* = "I", *trial_stem* = $\frac{5}{6}$, and *trial_width* = $\frac{1}{3}$. The computer will now draw an I corresponding to these values,* and it will prompt us for another command.

It's time to type 'end' now, after which METAFONT should tell us that it has completed this run and made an output file called 'io.2602gf'. Running this file through GFtoDVI as in Experiment 1 will produce two proofsheets, showing the 'O' and the 'I' we have created. The output won't be shown here, but you can see the results by doing the experiment personally.

Look at those proofsheets now, because they provide instructive examples of the simulated broad-edge pen constructions introduced in Chapter 4. Compare the 'O' with the program that drew it: Notice that the *penpos*$_2$ in line 10 makes the curve slightly thicker at the bottom than at the top; that the equation '$x_{1l} = w - x_{3l} = curve\_sidebar$' in line 12 makes the right edge of the curve as far from the right of the bounding box as the left edge is from the left; that line 13 places point 1 slightly lower than point 3. The proofsheet for 'I' should look very much like the corresponding illustration near the end of Chapter 4, but it will be somewhat larger.

Your proof copy of the 'O' should show twelve dots for key points; but only ten of them will be labeled, because there isn't room enough to put labels on points 2 and 4. The missing labels usually appear in the upper right corner, where it might say, e.g., '4 = 41 + (-1,-5.9)'; this means that point z_4 is one pixel to the left and 5.9 pixels down from point z_{4l}, which is labeled. (Some implementations omit this information, because there isn't always room for it.)

---

* Unless, of course, there was a typing error in lines 17–23, where *test_I* is defined.

The proofsheets obtained in Experiment 2 show the key points and the bounding boxes, but this extra information can interfere with our perception of the character shape itself. There's a simple way to get proofs that allow a viewer to criticize the results from an aesthetic rather than a logical standpoint; the creation of such proofs will be the goal of our next experiment.

Here's how to do Experiment 3: Start METAFONT as usual, then type

```
\mode=smoke; input io
```

in response to the '******'. This will input file `io.mf` again, after establishing "smoke" mode.   (As in Experiment 1, the command line begins with '\' so that the computer knows you aren't starting with the name of a file.)   Then complete the run exactly as in Experiment 2, by typing '`test_I("I",5/6,1/3);` `end`'; and apply GFtoDVI to the resulting file `io.2602gf`.

This time the proofsheets will contain the same characters as before, but they will be darker and without labeled points. The bounding boxes will be indicated only by small markings at the corners; you can put these boxes next to each other and tack the results up on the wall, then stand back to see how the characters will look when set by a high-resolution typesetter. (This way of working is called *smoke* mode because it's analogous to the "smoke proofs" that punch-cutters traditionally used to test their handiwork. They held the newly cut type over a candle flame so that it would be covered with carbon; then they pressed it on paper to make a clean impression of the character, in order to see whether changes were needed.)

Incidentally, many systems allow you to invoke METAFONT by typing a one-line command like '`mf io`' in the case of Experiment 2; you don't have to wait for the '******' before giving a file name. Similarly, the one-liners '`mf \relax`' and '`mf \mode=smoke; input io`' can be used on many systems at the beginning of Experiments 1 and 3. You might want to try this, to see if it works on your computer; or you might ask somebody if there's a similar shortcut.

Experiments 1, 2, and 3 have demonstrated how to make proof drawings of test characters, but they don't actually produce new fonts that can be used in typesetting. For this, we move onward to Experiment 4, in which we put ourselves in the position of a person who is just starting to design a new typeface. Let's imagine that we're happy with the O of `io.mf`, and that we want a "sans serif" I in the general style produced by *test_I*, but we aren't sure about how thick the stem of the I should be in order to make it blend properly with the O. Moreover, we aren't sure how much white space to leave at the sides of the I. So we want to do some typesetting experiments, using a sequence of different I's.

The ideal way to do this would be to produce a high-resolution test font and to view the output at its true size. But this may be too expensive, because fine printing equipment is usually available only for large production runs. The next-best alternative is to use a low-resolution printer but to magnify the output, so that the resolution is effectively increased. We shall adopt the latter strategy, because it gives us a chance to learn about magnification as well as fontmaking.

After starting METAFONT again, you can begin Experiment 4 by typing

`\mode=localfont; mag=4; input io`

in response to the '******'. The plain base at your installation is supposed to recognize `localfont` as the name of the mode that makes fonts for your "standard" output device. The equation '`mag=4`' means that this run will produce a font that is magnified fourfold; i.e., the results will be 4 times bigger than usual.

The computer will read `io.mf` as before, but this time it won't display an 'O'; characters are normally not displayed in fontmaking modes, because we usually want the computer to run as fast as possible when it's generating a font that has already been designed. All you'll see is '(`io.mf [79]`)', followed by '*****'. Now the fun starts: You should type

```
code=100;
for s=7 upto 10:
 for w=5 upto 8:
  test_I(incr code,s/10,w/20);
endfor endfor end.
```

(Here '`upto`' must be typed as a single word.) We'll learn about repeating things with '`for...endfor`' in Chapter 19. This little program produces 16 versions of the letter I, with stem widths of $\frac{7}{10}$, $\frac{8}{10}$, $\frac{9}{10}$, and $\frac{10}{10}$ pt, and with character widths of $\frac{5}{20}$, $\frac{6}{20}$, $\frac{7}{20}$, and $\frac{8}{20}$ em. The sixteen trial characters will appear in positions 101 through 116 of the font; it turns out that these are the ASCII codes for lower case letters `e` through `t` inclusive. (Other codes would have been used if '`code`' had been started at a value different from 100. The construction '`incr code`' increases the value of `code` by 1 and produces the new value; thus, each use of `test_I` has a different code number.)

This run of METAFONT will not only produce a generic font `io.nnngf`, it will also create a file called `io.tfm`, the "font metric file" that tells typesetting systems like TeX how to make use of the new font. The remaining part of Experiment 4 will be to put TeX to work: We shall make some test patterns from the new font, in order to determine which 'I' is best.

You may need to ask a local system wizard for help at this point, because it may be necessary to move the file `io.tfm` to some special place where TeX and the other typesetting software can find it. Furthermore, you'll need to run a program that converts `io.nnngf` to the font format used by your local output device. But with luck, these will both be fairly simple operations, and a new font called '`io`' will effectively be installed on your system. This font will contain seventeen letters, namely an `O` and sixteen `I`'s, where the `I`'s happen to be in the positions normally occupied by `e`, `f`, ..., `t`. Furthermore, the font will be magnified fourfold.

The magnification of the font will be reflected in its file name. For example, if *localfont* mode is for a device with 200 pixels per inch, the `io` font at $4\times$ magnification will be called '`io.800gf`'.

You can use TEX to typeset from this font like any other, but for the
purposes of Experiment 4 it's best to use a special TEX package that has been
specifically designed for font testing. All you need to do is to run TEX—which
is just like running METAFONT, except that you call it 'tex' instead of 'mf';
and you simply type 'testfont' in reply to TEX's '**'. (The testfont routine
should be available on your system; if not, you or somebody else can type it in,
by copying the relevant material from Appendix H.) You will then be asked for
the name of the font you wish to test. Type

    io scaled 4000

(which means the io font magnified by 4, in TEX's jargon), since this is what
METAFONT just created. The machine will now ask you for a test command,
and you should reply

    \mixture

to get the "mixture" test. (Don't forget the backslash.) You'll be asked for a
background letter, a starting letter, and an ending letter; type 'O', 'e', and 't',
respectively. This will produce sixteen lines of typeset output, in which the first
line contains a mixture of O with e, the second contains a mixture of O with f,
and so on. To complete Experiment 4, type '\end' to TEX, and print the file
testfont.dvi that TEX gives you.

If all goes well, you'll have sixteen lines that say 'OIOOIIOOOIIIOI',
but with a different I on each line. In order to choose the line that looks best,
without being influenced by neighboring lines, it's convenient to take two sheets
of blank paper and use them to mask out all of the lines except the one you're
studying. Caution: These letters are four times larger than the size at which
the final font is meant to be viewed, so you should look at the samples from
afar. Xerographic reductions may introduce distortions that will give misleading
results. Sometimes when you stare at things like this too closely, they all look
wrong, or they all look right; first impressions are usually more significant than
the results of logical reflection. At any rate, you should be able to come up
with an informed judgment about what values to use for the stem width and the
character width of a decent 'I'; these can then be incorporated into the program,
the 'def' and 'enddef' parts of io.mf can be removed, and you can go on to
design other characters that go with your I and O. Furthermore you can always
go back and make editorial changes after you see your letters in more contexts.

▶ EXERCISE 5.3
The goddess Io was known in Egypt as Isis. Design an 'S' for her.

Well, this isn't a book about type design; the example of io.mf is simply
intended to illustrate how a type designer might want to operate, and to provide a
run-through of the complete process from design of type to its use in a document.
We must go back now to the world of computerese, and study a few more practical
details about the use of METAFONT.

This has been a long chapter, but take heart: There's only one more experiment to do, and then you will know enough about METAFONT to run it fearlessly by yourself forever after. The only thing you are still missing is some information about how to cope with error messages. Sometimes METAFONT stops and asks you what to do next. Indeed, this may have already happened, and you may have panicked.

Error messages can be terrifying when you aren't prepared for them; but they can be fun when you have the right attitude. Just remember that you really haven't hurt the computer's feelings, and that nobody will hold the errors against you. Then you'll find that running METAFONT might actually be a creative experience instead of something to dread.

The first step in Experiment 5 is to plant some intentional mistakes in the input file. Make a copy of `io.mf` and call it `badio.mf`; then change line 1 of `badio.mf` to

> `mode setup; % an intentional error!`

(thereby omitting the underline character in `mode_setup`). Also change the first semicolon ('`;`') on line 2 to a colon ('`:`'); change '`thick,10`' to '`thick,l0`' on line 10 (i.e., replace the numeral '`1`' by the letter '`l`'); and change '`thin`' to '`thinn`' on line 11. These four changes introduce typical typographic errors, and it will be instructive to see if they lead to any disastrous consequences.

Now start METAFONT up again; but instead of cooperating with the computer, type '`mumble`' in reply to the '`**`'. (As long as you're going to make intentional mistakes, you might as well make some dillies.) METAFONT will say that it can't find any file called `mumble.mf`, and it will ask you for another name. Just hit ⟨return⟩ this time; you'll see that you had better give the name of a real file. So type '`badio`' and wait for METAFONT to find one of the *faux pas* in that messed-up travesty.

Ah yes, the machine will soon stop, after typing something like this:

```
>> mode.setup
! Isolated expression.
<to be read again>
                        ;
1.1 mode setup;
                   % an intentional error!
?
```

METAFONT begins its error messages with '`!`', and it sometimes precedes them with one or two related mathematical expressions that are displayed on lines starting with '`>>`'. Each error message is also followed by lines of context that show what the computer was reading at the time of the error. Such context lines occur in pairs; the top line of the pair (e.g., '`mode setup;`') shows what META-FONT has looked at so far, and where it came from ('`1.1`', i.e., line number 1); the bottom line (here '`% an intentional error!`') shows what METAFONT has yet to read. In this case there are two pairs of context lines; the top pair refers to a semicolon that METAFONT has read once but will be reading again, because it didn't belong with the preceding material.

You don't have to take out pencil and paper in order to write down the error messages that you get before they disappear from view, since METAFONT always writes a "transcript" or "log file" that records what happened during each session. For example, you should now have a file called io.log containing the transcript of Experiment 4, as well as a file mfput.log that contains the transcript of Experiment 1. (The old transcript of Experiment 2 was probably overwritten when you did Experiment 3, and again when you did Experiment 4, because all three transcripts were called io.log.) At the end of Experiment 5 you'll have a file badio.log that will serve as a helpful reminder of what errors need to be fixed up.

The '?' that appears after the context display means that METAFONT wants advice about what to do next. If you've never seen an error message before, or if you've forgotten what sort of response is expected, you can type '?' now (go ahead and try it!); METAFONT will respond as follows:

```
Type <return> to proceed, S to scroll future error messages,
R to run without stopping, Q to run quietly,
I to insert something, E to edit your file,
1 or ... or 9 to ignore the next 1 to 9 tokens of input,
H for help, X to quit.
```

This is your menu of options. You may choose to continue in various ways:

1. Simply type ⟨return⟩. METAFONT will resume its processing, after attempting to recover from the error as best it can.

2. Type 'S'. METAFONT will proceed without pausing for instructions if further errors arise. Subsequent error messages will flash by on your terminal, possibly faster than you can read them, and they will appear in your log file where you can scrutinize them at your leisure. Thus, 'S' is sort of like typing ⟨return⟩ to every message.

3. Type 'R'. This is like 'S' but even stronger, since it tells METAFONT not to stop for any reason, not even if a file name can't be found.

4. Type 'Q'. This is like 'R' but even more so, since it tells METAFONT not only to proceed without stopping but also to suppress all further output to your terminal. It is a fast, but somewhat reckless, way to proceed (intended for running METAFONT with no operator in attendance).

5. Type 'I', followed by some text that you want to insert. METAFONT will read this text before encountering what it would ordinarily see next.

6. Type a small number (less than 100). METAFONT will delete this many tokens from whatever it is about to read next, and it will pause again to give you another chance to look things over. (A "token" is a name, number, or symbol that METAFONT reads as a unit; e.g., 'mode' and

'setup' and ';' are the first three tokens of `badio.mf`, but 'mode_setup'
is the first token of `io.mf`. Chapter 6 explains this concept precisely.)

7. Type 'H'. This is what you should do now and whenever you are faced
   with an error message that you haven't seen for a while. METAFONT
   has two messages built in for each perceived error: a formal one and
   an informal one. The formal message is printed first (e.g., '`! Isolated
   expression.`'); the informal one is printed if you request more help
   by typing 'H', and it also appears in your log file if you are scrolling
   error messages. The informal message tries to complement the formal
   one by explaining what METAFONT thinks the trouble is, and often by
   suggesting a strategy for recouping your losses.

8. Type 'X'. This stands for "exit." It causes METAFONT to stop working
   on your job, after putting the finishing touches on your `log` file and on
   any characters that have already been output to your `gf` and/or `tfm`
   files. The current (incomplete) character will not be output.

9. Type 'E'. This is like 'X', but it also prepares the computer to edit the
   file that METAFONT is currently reading, at the current position, so that
   you can conveniently make a change before trying again.

After you type 'H' (or 'h', which also works), you'll get a message that tries to
explain the current problem: The mathematical quantity just read by META-
FONT (i.e., `mode.setup`) was not followed by '=' or ':=', so there was nothing for
the computer to do with it. Chapter 6 explains that a space between tokens (e.g.,
'`mode setup`') is equivalent to a period between tokens (e.g., '`mode.setup`'). The
correct spelling '`mode_setup`' would be recognized as a preloaded subroutine of
plain METAFONT, but plain METAFONT doesn't have any built-in meaning for
`mode.setup`. Hence `mode.setup` appears as a sort of orphan, and METAFONT
realizes that something is amiss.

In this case, it's OK to go ahead and type ⟨return⟩, because we really
don't need to do the operations of **mode_setup** when no special mode has been
selected. METAFONT will continue by forgetting the isolated expression, and it
will ignore the rest of line 1 because everything after a '`%`' sign is always ignored.
(This is another thing that will be explained in Chapter 6; it's a handy way to
put comments into your METAFONT programs.) The changes that were made
to line 1 of `badio.mf` therefore have turned out to be relatively harmless. But
METAFONT will almost immediately encounter the mutilated semicolon in line 2:

```
! Extra tokens will be flushed.
<to be read again>
                    :
l.2  em#:=10pt#:
                cap#:=7pt#;
?
```

What does this mean? Type 'H' to find out. METAFONT has no idea what to do with a ':' at this place in the file, so it plans to recover by "flushing" or getting rid of everything it sees, until coming to a semicolon. It would be a bad idea to type ⟨return⟩ now, since you'd lose the important assignment 'cap#:=7pt#', and that would lead to worse errors.

You might type 'X' or 'E' at this point, to exit from METAFONT and to fix the errors in lines 1 and 2 before trying again. But it's usually best to keep going, trying to detect and correct as many mistakes as possible in each run, since that increases your productivity while decreasing your computer bills. An experienced METAFONT user will quit after an error only if the error is unfixable, or if there's almost no chance that additional errors are present.

The solution in this case is to proceed in two steps: First type '1', which tells METAFONT to delete the next token (the unwanted ':'); then type 'I;', which inserts a semicolon. This semicolon protects the rest of line 2 from being flushed away, so all will go well until METAFONT reaches another garbled line.

The next error message is more elaborate, because it is detected while METAFONT is trying to carry out a *penpos* command; *penpos* is not a primitive operation (it is defined in plain METAFONT), hence a lot more context is given:

```
>> 10
! Improper transformation argument.
<to be read again>
                   ;
penpos->...(EXPR3),0)rotated(EXPR4);
                                    x(SUFFIX2)=0.5(x(SUFF...
l.10   penpos1(thick,10)
                        ; penpos2(.1[thin,thick],90-10);
?
```

At first, such error messages will appear to be complete nonsense to you, because much of what you see is low-level METAFONT code that you never wrote. But you can overcome this hangup by getting a feeling for the way METAFONT operates.

The bottom line shows how much progress METAFONT has made so far in the **badio** file: It has read 'penpos1(thick,10)' but not yet the semicolon, on line 10. The *penpos* routine expands into a long list of tokens; indeed, this list is so long that it can't all be shown on two lines, and the appearances of '...' indicate that the definition of *penpos* has been truncated here. Parameter values are often inserted into the expansion of a high-level routine; in this case, for example, '(EXPR3)' and '(EXPR4)' correspond to the respective parameters 'thick' and '10', and '(SUFFIX2)' corresponds to '1'. METAFONT detected an error just after encountering the phrase 'rotated(EXPR4)'; the value of (EXPR4) was an undefined quantity (namely '10', which METAFONT treats as the subscripted variable 'l_0'), and rotation is permitted only when a known numeric value has been supplied. Rotations are particular instances of what METAFONT calls *transformations*; hence METAFONT describes this particular error by saying that an "improper transformation argument" was present.

When you get a multiline error message like this, the best clues about the source of the trouble are usually on the bottom line (since that is what you typed) and on the top line (since that is what triggered the error message). Somewhere in there you can usually spot the problem.

If you type 'H' now, you'll find that METAFONT has simply decided to continue without doing the requested rotation. Thus, if you respond by typing ⟨return⟩, METAFONT will go on as if the program had said 'penpos1(thick,0)'. Comparatively little harm has been done; but there's actually a way to fix the error perfectly before proceeding: Insert the correct rotation by typing

```
I rotated 10
```

and METAFONT will rotate by 10 degrees as if '10' had been '10'.

What happens next in Experiment 5? METAFONT will hiccup on the remaining bug that we planted in the file. This time, however, the typo will not be discovered until much later, because there's nothing wrong with line 11 as it stands. (The variable thinn is not defined, but undefined quantities are no problem unless you're doing something complicated like rotation. Indeed, METAFONT programs typically consist of equations in which there are lots of unknowns; variables get more and more defined as time goes on. Hence spelling errors cannot possibly be detected until the last minute.) Finally comes the moment of truth, when badio tries to draw a path through an unknown point; and you will get an error message that's even scarier than the previous one:

```
>> 0.08682thinn+144
! Undefined x coordinate has been replaced by 0.
<to be read again>
                        {
<for(l)> ...FFIX0){up}..z4(SUFFIX0){
                                      left}..cycle; ENDFOR
penstroke->...ath_.e:=(TEXT0);endfor
                                    .if.cycle.path_.l:cyc...
<to be read again>
                    ;
l.15 ...        ..z3e{up}..z4e{left}..cycle;

?
```

Wow; what's this? The expansion of **penstroke** involves a "**for** loop," and the error was detected in the midst of it. The expression '0.08682thinn+144' just above the error message implies that the culprit in this case was a misspelled 'thin'. If that hadn't been enough information, you could have gleaned another clue from the fact that 'z4(SUFFIX0)' has just been read; (SUFFIX0) is the current loop value and '<for(l)>' indicates that the value in question is 'l', hence z_{4l} is under suspicion. (Sure enough, the undefined x coordinate that provoked this error can be shown to be $x_{4l} = 0.08682thinn + 144$.)

In any event the mistake on line 11 has propagated too far to be fixable, so you're justified in typing 'X' or 'E' at this point. But type 'S' instead, just for fun: This tells METAFONT to plunge ahead, correcting all remaining errors as best it can. (There will be a few more problems, since several variables still depend on 'thinn'.) METAFONT will draw a very strange letter O before it gets to the end of the file. Then you should type 'end' to terminate the run.

If you try to edit `badio.mf` again, you'll notice that line 2 still contains a colon instead of a semicolon. The fact that you told METAFONT to delete the colon and to insert additional material doesn't mean that your file has changed in any way. However, the transcript file `badio.log` has a record of all the errors, so it's a handy reference when you want to correct mistakes. (Why not look at `badio.log` now, and `io.log` too, in order to get familiar with log files?)

▶ **EXERCISE 5.4**
Suppose you were doing Experiment 3 with `badio` instead of `io`, so you began by saying '\mode=smoke; input badio'. Then you would want to recover from the error on line 1 by inserting a correct **mode_setup** command, instead of by simply ⟨return⟩ing, because **mode_setup** is what really establishes *smoke* mode. Unfortunately if you try typing 'I mode_setup' in response to the "isolated expression" error, it doesn't work. What should you type instead?

By doing the five experiments in this chapter you have learned at first hand (1) how to produce proofsheets of various kinds, including "smoke proofs"; (2) how to make a new font and test it; (3) how to keep calm when METAFONT issues stern warnings. Congratulations! You're on the threshold of being able to do lots more. As you read the following chapters, the best strategy will be for you to continue making trial runs, using experiments of your own design.

▶ **EXERCISE 5.5**
However, this has been an extremely long chapter, so you should go outside now and get some *real* exercise.

Let us learn how Io's frenzy came—
She telling her disasters manifold.
— ÆSCHYLUS, *Prometheus Bound* (c. 470 B.C.)

To the student who wishes to use graphical methods as a tool,
it can not be emphasized too strongly that practice in the use of that tool
is as essential as a knowledge of how to use it.
The oft-repeated pedagogical phrase, "we learn by doing," is applicable here.
— THEODORE RUNNING, *Graphical Mathematics* (1927)

6

How METAFONT
Reads What You
Type

So far in this book we've seen lots of things that METAFONT can do, but we haven't discussed what METAFONT can't do. We have looked at many examples of commands that METAFONT can understand, but we haven't dwelt on the fact that the computer will find many phrases unintelligible. It's time now to adopt a more systematic approach and to study the exact rules of METAFONT's language. Then we'll know what makes sense to the machine, and we'll also know how to avoid ungrammatical utterances.

A METAFONT program consists of one or more lines of text, where each line is made up of letters, numbers, punctuation marks, and other symbols that appear on a standard computer keyboard. A total of 95 different characters can be employed, namely a blank space plus the 94 visible symbols of standard ASCII. (Appendix C describes the American Standard Code for Information Interchange, popularly known as "ASCII," under which code numbers 33 through 126 have been assigned to 94 specific symbols. This particular coding scheme is not important to a METAFONT programmer; the only relevant thing is that 94 different nonblank symbols can be used.)

METAFONT converts each line of text into a series of *tokens*, and a programmer should understand exactly how this conversion takes place. Tokens are the individual lexical units that govern the computer's activities. They are the basic building blocks from which meaningful sequences of instructions can be constructed. We discussed tokens briefly at the end of the previous chapter; now we shall consider them in detail. Line 9 of the file `io.mf` in that chapter is a typical example of what the machine might encounter:

```
beginchar("0",0.8em#,cap#,0); "The letter O";
```

When METAFONT reads these ASCII characters it finds sixteen tokens:

beginchar	(	"0"	,	0.8	em	#	,
cap	#	,	0	)	;	"The letter 0"	;

Two of these, `"0"` and `"The letter 0"`, are called *string tokens* because they represent strings of characters. Two of them, '0.8' and '0', are called *numeric tokens* because they represent numbers. The other twelve—'beginchar', '(', etc.—are called *symbolic tokens*; such tokens can change their meaning while a METAFONT program runs, but string tokens and numeric tokens always have a predetermined significance. Notice that clusters of letters like 'beginchar' are treated as a unit; the same holds with respect to letters mixed with underline characters, as in 'mode_setup'. Indeed, the rules we are about to study will explain that clusters of other characters like '0.8' and ':=' are also considered to be indecomposable tokens. METAFONT has a definite way of deciding where one token stops and another one begins.

It's often convenient to discuss grammatical rules by formulating them in a special notation that was introduced about 1960 by John Backus and Peter Naur. Parts of speech are represented by named quantities in angle brackets, and *syntax rules* are used to express the ways in which those quantities can be built up from simpler units. For example, here are three syntax rules that completely describe the possible forms of numeric tokens:

$$\langle\text{decimal digit}\rangle \longrightarrow \texttt{0} \mid \texttt{1} \mid \texttt{2} \mid \texttt{3} \mid \texttt{4} \mid \texttt{5} \mid \texttt{6} \mid \texttt{7} \mid \texttt{8} \mid \texttt{9}$$
$$\langle\text{digit string}\rangle \longrightarrow \langle\text{decimal digit}\rangle \mid \langle\text{digit string}\rangle\langle\text{decimal digit}\rangle$$
$$\langle\text{numeric token}\rangle \longrightarrow \langle\text{digit string}\rangle \mid \texttt{.}\,\langle\text{digit string}\rangle$$
$$\mid \langle\text{digit string}\rangle\,\texttt{.}\,\langle\text{digit string}\rangle$$

The first rule says that a ⟨decimal digit⟩ is either '0' or '1' or ··· or '9'; thus it must be one of the ten numerals. The next rule says that a ⟨digit string⟩ is either a ⟨decimal digit⟩ or a ⟨digit string⟩ followed by a ⟨decimal digit⟩; thus it must be a sequence of one or more digits. Finally, a ⟨numeric token⟩ has one of three forms, exemplified respectively by '15', '.05', and '3.14159'.

Syntax rules explain only the surface structure of a language, not the underlying meanings of things. For example, the rules above tell us that '15' is a ⟨numeric token⟩, but they don't imply that '15' has any connection with the number fifteen. Therefore syntax rules are generally accompanied by rules of *semantics*, which ascribe meanings to the strings of symbols that meet the conditions of the syntax. In the case of numeric tokens, the principles of ordinary decimal notation define the semantics, except that METAFONT deals only with numbers in a limited range: A numeric token must be less than 4096, and its value is always rounded to the nearest multiple of $\frac{1}{65536}$. Thus, for example, '.1' does not mean $\frac{1}{10}$, it means $\frac{6554}{65536}$ (which is slightly greater than $\frac{1}{10}$). It turns out that the tokens '.099999' and '0.10001' both have exactly the same meaning as '.1', because all three tokens represent the value $\frac{6554}{65536}$.

▶ **EXERCISE 6.1**
Are the following pairs of numeric tokens equivalent to each other, when they appear in METAFONT programs? (a) 0 and 0.00001; (b) 0.00001 and 0.00002; (c) 0.00002 and 0.00003; (d) 04095.999999 and 10000?

METAFONT converts each line of text into a sequence of tokens by repeating the following rules until no more characters remain on the line:

1) If the next character is a space, or if it's a period ('.') that isn't followed by a decimal digit or a period, ignore it and move on.
2) If the next character is a percent sign ('%'), ignore it and also ignore everything else that remains on the current line. (Percent signs therefore allow you to write comments that are unseen by METAFONT.)
3) If the next character is a decimal digit or a period that's followed by a decimal digit, the next token is a numeric token, consisting of the longest sequence of contiguous characters starting at the current place that satisfies the syntax for ⟨numeric token⟩ above.
4) If the next character is a double-quote mark ('"'), the next token is a string token, consisting of all characters from the current place to the next double-quote, inclusive. (There must be at least one more double-quote remaining on the line, otherwise METAFONT will complain about

an "incomplete string.") A string token represents the sequence of characters between the double-quotes.

5) If the next character is a parenthesis ('(' or ')'), a comma (','), or a semicolon (';'), the next token is a symbolic token consisting of that single character.

6) Otherwise the next token is a symbolic token consisting of the next character together with all immediately following characters that appear in the same row of the following table:

```
ABCDEFGHIJKLMNOPQRSTUVWXYZ_abcdefghijklmnopqrstuvwxyz
<=>:|
‘’
+-
/*\
!?
#&@$
^~
[
]
{}
```
.   (see rules 1, 3, 6)
,   ;   (   )   (see rule 5; these characters are "loners")
"   (see rule 4 for details about string tokens)
0123456789   (see rule 3 for details about numeric tokens)
%   (see rule 2 for details about comments)

The best way to learn the six rules about tokens is to work the following exercise, after which you'll be able to read any input file just as the computer does.

▶ **EXERCISE 6.2**
What tokens does METAFONT find in the (ridiculous) line

  `xx3.1.6..[[a+-bc_d.e] ]"a %" <|>(($1. 5"+-""" % weird?`

▶ **EXERCISE 6.3**
Criticize the following statement: METAFONT ignores all spaces in the input.

▶ **EXERCISE 6.4**
True or false: If the syntax for ⟨numeric token⟩ were changed to include a fourth alternative, '⟨digit string⟩.', the meaning of METAFONT programs would not change in any way.

> *Yet wee with all our seeking could see no tokens.*
> — PHILEMON HOLLAND, *Camden's Brittania* (1610)

> *Unpropitious tokens interfered.*
> — WILLIAM COWPER, *Homer's Iliad* (1791)

7

Variables

One of METAFONT's most important concepts is the notion of a *variable*—
something that can take on a variety of different values. Indeed, this is one of
the most important concepts in all of mathematics, and variables play a promi-
nent rôle in almost all computer languages. The basic idea is that a program
manipulates data, and the data values are stored in little compartments of a
computer's memory. Each little compartment is a variable, and we refer to an
item of data by giving its compartment a name.

For example, the `io.mf` program for the letter O in Chapter 5 contains
lots of variables. Some of these, like '`x1l`' and '`y1`', represent coordinates. Others,
like '`up`', represent directions. The variables '`em#`' and '`thin#`' stand for physical,
machine-independent distances; the analogous variables '`em`' and '`thin`' stand for
the corresponding machine-dependent distances in units of pixels.

These examples indicate that different variables are often related to each
other. There's an implicit connection between '`em#`' and '`em`', between '`x1`' and
'`y1`'; the '*penpos*' convention sets up relationships between '`x1l`', '`x1`', and '`x1r`'.
By choosing the names of variables carefully, programmers can make their programs much easier to understand, because the relationships between variables
can be made to correspond to the structure of their names.

In the previous chapter we discussed tokens, the atomic elements from
which all METAFONT programs are made. We learned that there are three kinds
of tokens: numeric (representing numbers), string (representing text), and symbolic (representing everything else). Symbolic tokens have no intrinsic meaning;
any symbolic token can stand for whatever a programmer wants it to represent.

Some symbolic tokens do, however, have predefined *primitive* meanings,
when METAFONT begins its operations. For example, '`+`' stands initially for
"plus," and '`;`' stands for "finish the current statement and move on to the next
part of the program." It is customary to let such tokens retain their primitive
meanings, but any symbolic token can actually be assigned a new meaning as a
program is performed. For example, the definition of '`test_I`' in `io.mf` makes
that token stand for a *macro*, i.e., a subroutine. We'll see later that you can
instruct METAFONT to '`let plus=+`', after which '`plus`' will act just like '`+`' did.

METAFONT divides symbolic tokens into two categories, depending on
their current meaning. If the symbolic token currently stands for one of META-
FONT's primitive operations, or if it has been defined to be a macro, it is called a
spark; otherwise it is called a *tag*. Almost all symbolic tokens are tags, because
only a few are defined to be sparks; however, METAFONT programs typically involve lots of sparks, because sparks are what make things happen. The symbolic
tokens on the first five lines of `io.mf` include the following sparks:

```
mode_setup  ;  :=  /  define_pixels  (  ,  )
```

and the following tags:

```
em  #  pt  cap  thin  thick  o
```

(some of which appear several times). Tags are used to designate variables, but sparks cannot be used within a variable's name.

Some variables, like 'em#', have names that are made from more than one token; in fact, the variable 'x11' is named by three tokens, one of which is numeric. METAFONT has been designed so that it is easy to make compound names that correspond to the relations between variables. Conventional programming languages like Pascal would refer to 'x11' by the more cumbersome notation 'x[1].1'; it turns out that 'x[1].1' is an acceptable way to designate the variable x11 in a METAFONT program, but the shorthand form 'x11' is a great convenience because such variables are used frequently.

Here are the formal rules of syntax by which METAFONT understands the names of variables:

⟨variable⟩ ⟶ ⟨tag⟩⟨suffix⟩
⟨suffix⟩ ⟶ ⟨empty⟩ | ⟨suffix⟩⟨subscript⟩ | ⟨suffix⟩⟨tag⟩
⟨subscript⟩ ⟶ ⟨numeric token⟩ | [⟨numeric expression⟩]

First comes a tag, like 'x'; then comes a *suffix* to the tag, like '11'. The suffix might be empty, or it might consist of one or more subscripts or tags that are tacked on to the original tag. A *subscript* is a numeric index that permits you to construct arrays of related variables. The subscript is either a single numeric token, or it is a formula enclosed in square brackets; in the latter case the formula should produce a numeric value. For example, 'x[1]' and 'x[k]' and 'x[3-2k]' all mean the same thing as 'x1', if k is a variable whose value is 1. But 'x.k' is not the same; it is the tag 'x' suffixed by the tag 'k', not the tag 'x' subscripted by the value of variable k.

 The variables 'x1' and 'x01' and 'x1.00' are identical. Since any numeric token can be used as a subscript, fractional indices are possible; for example, 'x1.5' is the same as 'x[3/2]'. Notice, however, that 'B007' and 'B.007' are *not* the same variable, because the latter has a fractional subscript.

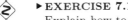 METAFONT makes each ⟨suffix⟩ as long as possible. In other words, a ⟨suffix⟩ is always extended if it is followed by a ⟨subscript⟩ or a ⟨tag⟩.

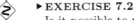 ▶ **EXERCISE 7.1**
Explain how to type a reference to the doubly subscripted variable 'a[1][5]' without using square brackets.

▶ **EXERCISE 7.2**
Is it possible to refer to *any* variable without using square brackets?

▶ **EXERCISE 7.3**
John H. Quick (a student) used 'a.plus1' as the name of a variable at the beginning of his program; later he said 'let plus=+'. How could he refer to the variable 'a.plus1' after that?

METAFONT has several special variables called *internal quantities* that are intimately wired-in to the computer's behavior. For example, there's an internal quantity called '**fontmaking**' that controls whether or not a **tfm** file is produced;

another one called 'tracingtitles' governs whether or not titles like "The letter O" appear on your terminal; still another one called 'smoothing' affects the digitization of curves. (A complete list of METAFONT's internal quantities appears in Chapter 25.) The name of an internal quantity acts like a tag, but internal quantities cannot be suffixed. Thus, the syntax rule for ⟨variable⟩ should actually be replaced by a slightly more complicated pair of rules:

⟨variable⟩ ⟶ ⟨external tag⟩⟨suffix⟩ | ⟨internal quantity⟩
⟨tag⟩ ⟶ ⟨external tag⟩ | ⟨internal quantity⟩

▸**EXERCISE 7.4**
True or false: Every ⟨variable⟩ is a legal ⟨suffix⟩.

The '[' and ']' that appear in the syntax for ⟨subscript⟩ stand for any symbolic tokens whose current meanings are the same as METAFONT's primitive meanings of left and right bracket, respectively; those tokens don't necessarily have to be brackets. Conversely, if the meanings of the tokens '[' and ']' have been changed, brackets cannot be used to delimit subscripts. Similar remarks apply to all of the symbolic tokens in all of the syntax rules from now on. METAFONT doesn't look at the form of a token; it considers only a token's current meaning.

The examples of METAFONT programs in this book have used two different typographic conventions. Sometimes we refer to variables by using italic type and/or genuine subscripts, e.g., 'em' and 'x_{2r}'; but sometimes we refer to those same variables by using a typewriter-like style of type, e.g., 'em' and 'x2r'. In general, the typewriter style is used when we are mainly concerned with the way a programmer is supposed to type something that will appear on the terminal or in a file; but fancier typography is used when we are focusing on the meaning of a program rather than its ASCII representation. It should be clear how to convert the fancier form into tokens that METAFONT can actually understand.

In general, we shall use italic type only for tags (e.g., em, x, r), while boldface and roman type will be used for sparks (e.g., **draw**, **fill**, cycle, rotated, sqrt). Tags that consist of special characters instead of letters will sometimes get special treatment; for example, em# and z2' might be rendered $em\#$ and z_2', respectively.

The variables we've discussed so far have almost always had numbers as their values, but in fact METAFONT's variables are allowed to assume values of eight different types. A variable can be of type

- boolean, representing the values 'true' or 'false';
- string, representing sequences of ASCII characters;
- path, representing a (possibly curved) line;
- pen, representing the shape of a pen nib;
- picture, representing an entire pattern of pixels;
- transform, representing the operations of scaling, rotating, shifting, reflecting, and/or slanting;
- pair, representing two numbers (e.g., a point or a vector);
- numeric, representing a single number.

If you want a variable to represent something besides a number, you must first give a *type declaration* that states what the type will be. But if you refer to a variable whose type has not been declared, METAFONT won't complain, unless you try to use it in a way that demands a value that isn't numeric.

Type declarations are easy. You simply name one of the eight types, then you list the variables that you wish to declare for that type. For example, the declaration

> **pair** *right*, *left*, *a.p*

says that *right* and *left* and *a.p* will be variables of type **pair**, so that equations like

$$right = -left = 2a.p = (1,0)$$

can be given later. These equations, incidentally, define the values $right = (1,0)$, $left = (-1,0)$, and $a.p = (.5,0)$. (Plain METAFONT has the stated values of *right* and *left* already built in.)

The rules for declarations are slightly trickier when subscripts are involved, because METAFONT insists that all variables whose names are identical except for subscript values must have the same type. It's possible to set things up so that, for example, a is numeric, $a.p$ is a pair, $a.q$ is a pen, $a.r$ is a path, and a_1 is a string; but if a_1 is a string, then all other variables a_2, a_3, etc., must also be strings. In order to enforce this restriction, METAFONT allows only "collective" subscripts, represented by empty brackets '[]', to appear in type declarations. For example,

```
path r, r[], x[]arc, f[][]
```

declares r and all variables of the forms $r[i]$, $x[i]arc$, and $f[i][j]$ to be path variables. This declaration doesn't affect the types or values of other variables like $r[]arc$; it affects only the variables that are specifically mentioned.

Declarations destroy all previous values of the variables being defined. For example, the path declaration above makes r and $r[i]$ and $x[i]arc$ and $f[i][j]$ undefined, even if those variables previously had paths as their values. The idea is that all such variables will start out with a clean slate so that they can receive appropriate new values based on subsequent equations.

▶ **EXERCISE 7.5**
Numeric variables don't need to be declared. Therefore is there ever any reason for saying '`numeric x`'?

The formal syntax rules for type declarations explain these grammatical conventions precisely. If the symbolic token that begins a declared variable was previously a spark, it loses its former meaning and immediately becomes a tag.

$\langle$declaration$\rangle$ $\longrightarrow$ $\langle$type$\rangle\langle$declaration list$\rangle$
$\langle$type$\rangle$ $\longrightarrow$ **boolean** | **string** | **path** | **pen**
    | **picture** | **transform** | **pair** | **numeric**

⟨declaration list⟩ ⟶ ⟨declared variable⟩
    | ⟨declaration list⟩ , ⟨declared variable⟩
⟨declared variable⟩ ⟶ ⟨symbolic token⟩⟨declared suffix⟩
⟨declared suffix⟩ ⟶ ⟨empty⟩ | ⟨declared suffix⟩⟨tag⟩
    | ⟨declared suffix⟩ [ ]

▶ **EXERCISE 7.6**
Find three errors in the supposed declaration '`transform t42,24t,,t,path`'.

Beings low in the scale of nature are
more variable than those which are higher.
— CHARLES DARWIN, *On the Origin of Species* (1859)

Among the variables, Beta (β) Persei, or Algol,
is perhaps the most interesting, as its period is short.
— J. NORMAN LOCKYER, *Elements of Astronomy* (1870)

8

Algebraic Expressions

METAFONT programmers express themselves algebraically by writing algebraic formulas called *expressions*. The formulas are algebraic in the sense that they involve variables as well as constants. By combining variables and constants with appropriate mathematical operations, a programmer can specify an amazing variety of things with comparative ease.

We have already seen many examples of expressions; our goal now is to make a more systematic study of what is possible. The general idea is that an expression is either a variable (e.g., 'x_1') or a constant (e.g., '20'), or it consists of an operator (e.g., '+') together with its operands (e.g., '$x_1 + 20$'). The operands are, in turn, expressions built up in the same way, perhaps enclosed in parentheses. For example, '$(x_1+20)/(x_2-20)$' is an expression that stands for the quotient of two subexpressions. It is possible to concoct extremely complicated algebraic expressions, but even the most intricate constructions are built from simple parts in simple ways.

Mathematicians spent hundreds of years developing good ways to write formulas; then computer scientists came along and upset all the time-honored traditions. The main reason for making a change was the fact that computers find it difficult to deal with two-dimensional constructions like

$$\frac{x_1 + 20}{x_2 - 20} + \sqrt{a^2 - \frac{2}{3}\sqrt{b}}.$$

One-dimensional sequences of tokens are much easier to input and to decode; hence programming languages generally put such formulas all on one line, by inserting parentheses, brackets, and asterisks as follows:

```
(x[1]+20)/(x[2]-20)+sqrt(a**2-(2/3)*sqrt(b)).
```

METAFONT will understand this formula, but it also accepts a notation that is shorter and closer to the standard conventions of mathematics:

```
(x1+20)/(x2-20)+sqrt(a**2-2/3sqrt b).
```

We observed in the previous chapter that METAFONT allows you to write '`x2`' instead of '`x[2]`'; similarly, you can write '`2x`' instead of '`2*x`' and '`2/3x`' instead of '`(2/3)*x`'. Such operations are extremely common in METAFONT programs, hence the language has been set up to facilitate them. On the other hand, META-FONT doesn't free you from all the inconveniences of computer languages; you must still write '`x*k`' for the product of x times k, and '`x[k]`' for the variable x subscripted by k, in order to avoid confusion with the suffixed variable '`x.k`'.

We learned in the previous chapter that there are eight types of variables: numeric, boolean, string, and so on. The same types apply to expressions; META-FONT deals not only with numeric expressions but also with boolean expressions, string expressions, and the others. For example, '$(0,0) \mathinner{.\,.} (x_1,y_1)$' is a path-valued expression, formed by applying the operator '..' to the subexpressions '$(0,0)$' and '(x_1,y_1)'; these subexpressions, in turn, have values of type "pair," and they have been built up from values of type "numeric." Each operation produces a result whose type can be determined from the types of the operands; furthermore, the simplest expressions (variables and constants) always have a definite type. Therefore the machine always knows what type of quantity it is dealing with, after it has evaluated an expression.

If an expression contains several operators, METAFONT has to decide which operation should be done first. For example, in the expression '$a - b + c$' it is important to compute '$a - b$' first, then to add c; if '$b + c$' were computed first, the result '$a - (b + c)$' would be quite different from the usual conventions of mathematics. On the other hand, mathematicians usually expect 'b/c' to be computed first in an expression like '$a - b/c$'; multiplications and divisions are usually performed before additions and subtractions, unless the contrary is specifically indicated by parentheses as in '$(a - b)/c$'. The general rule is to evaluate subexpressions in parentheses first, then to do operations in order of their "precedence"; if two operations have the same precedence, the left one is done first. For example, '$a - b/c$' is equivalent to '$a - (b/c)$' because division takes precedence over subtraction; but '$a - b + c$' is equivalent to '$(a - b) + c$' because left-to-right order is used on operators of equal precedence.

It's convenient to think of operators as if they are tiny magnets that attract their operands; the magnets for '$*$' and '$/$' are stronger than the magnets for '$+$' and '$-$', so they stick to their operands more tightly and we want to perform them first.

METAFONT distinguishes four (and only four) levels of precedence. The strongest magnets are those that join '2' to 'x' and 'sqrt' to 'b' in expressions like '$2x$' and 'sqrt b'. The next strongest are multiplicative operators like '$*$' and '$/$'; then come the additive operators like '$+$' and '$-$'. The weakest magnets are operators like '$..$' or '$<$'. For example, the expression

$$a + \text{sqrt } b/2x < c$$

is equivalent to the fully parenthesized formula

$$\big(a + ((\text{sqrt } b)/(2x))\big) < c.$$

▸**EXERCISE 8.1**
Insert parentheses into the formula '`z1+z2..z3/4*5..z6-7*8z9`', to show explicitly in what order METAFONT will do the operations.

 High-school algebra texts often avoid parentheses inside of parentheses by using braces and brackets. Therefore many people have been trained to write

$$\{a + [(\text{sqrt } b)/(2x)]\} < c$$

instead of the fully parenthesized formula above. However, professional mathematicians usually stick to only one kind of parentheses, because braces and brackets have other meanings that are more important. In this respect METAFONT is like the professionals: It reserves curly braces '`{}`' and square brackets '`[]`' for special purposes, so you should not try to substitute them for parentheses.

If you really want alternatives to parentheses, there is actually a way to get them. You can say, for example,

```
delimiters [[ ]];  delimiters {{  }}
```

after which double brackets and braces can be used in formulas like

$$\{\{a+[[(\text{sqrt } b)/(2x)]]\}\}<c.$$

The symbolic token '{{' has no relation to '{', and it has no primitive meaning, hence you are free to define it in any way you like; the **delimiters** command defines a new pair of delimiters. In formulas with mixed delimiters as defined here, METAFONT will check that '[[' matches only with ']]', '{{' only with '}}', and '(' only with ')'; thus you can more easily detect errors in large expressions. However, it's usually unnecessary to have any delimiters other than parentheses, because large expressions are rare, and because the rules of operator precedence make most parentheses superfluous.

If you're reading this chapter carefully, you may be thinking, "Hey wait! Isn't there a contradiction? A minute ago I was told that '2/3x' stands for '(2/3)*x', but now the rules of precedence appear to state that '2/3x' really stands for '2/(3x)'. What gives?" Indeed, you have an excellent point; but there is no contradiction, because of another rule that hasn't been mentioned yet. When two *numeric tokens* are divided, the magnetism of '/' is stronger than usual; in this case '/' has the same precedence as the implied multiplication operator in '3x'. Hence the operations in '2/3x' are carried out from left to right, as stated previously. (This is a good rule because it is almost always what a METAFONT programmer wants. However, one should bear in mind that 'a/3x' means 'a/(3x)' when a is *not* a numeric token.)

Because of the rule in the previous paragraph, the METAFONT programs in this book often say '$\frac{2}{3}x$' for what would be typed '2/3x' in a file. Such built-up fractions are never used except when the numerator and denominator are both numbers; a construction like 'a/3x' will always be rendered as '$a/3x$', not '$\frac{a}{3x}$'.

METAFONT knows how to do dozens of operations that haven't been mentioned yet in this book. Let's take a look at some of them, so that we will know they are available in case of need. It will be most instructive and most fun to learn about expressions by interacting with the computer; therefore you should prepare the following short file, called expr.mf:

```
string s[]; s1="abra";
path p[]; p1=(0,0)..(3,3); p2=(0,0)..(3,3)..cycle;
tracingonline:=1; scrollmode;
forever: message "gimme an expr: "; s0:=readstring;
show scantokens s0; endfor
```

 You don't need to understand what's in **expr.mf** when you read this chapter for the first time, because the file uses METAFONT in ways that will be explained carefully later. But here is a translation, in case you're curious: Line 1 declares all variables of the form s_k to be strings, and sets s_1 to the value **"abra"**. Line 2 declares all variables of the form p_k to be paths, and sets p_1 and p_2 to simple example paths.

Line 3 tells METAFONT to print diagnostic information online, i.e., on the terminal as well as in the log file; it also establishes '**scrollmode**', which means that the computer won't stop after error messages. Lines 4 and 5 set up an infinite loop in which METAFONT reads an expression from the terminal and shows the corresponding value.

If you start METAFONT and type '**expr**' when it asks for an input file name, it will read the file `expr.mf` and then it will say '**gimme an expr**'. Here's where the fun starts: You can type any expression, and METAFONT will compute and display its value. Try it; type '2+2' and ⟨return⟩, obtaining the value '>> 4'. Isn't that amazing? Here are some more things to try:

You type	*And the result is*
1.2-2.3	-1.1
1.3-2.4	-1.09999
1.3*1000	1300.00305
2.4*1000	2399.9939
3/8	0.375
.375*1000	375
1/3	0.33333
1/3*3	0.99998
0.99999	0.99998
1-epsilon	0.99998
1/(1/3)	3.00005
1/3.00005	0.33333
.1*10	1.00006
1+4epsilon	1.00006

These examples illustrate the small errors that occur because METAFONT does "fixed binary" arithmetic using integer multiples of $\frac{1}{65536}$. The result of $1.3-2.4$ is not quite the same as -1.1, because 1.3 is a little bit larger than $\frac{13}{10}$ and 2.4 is a little smaller than $\frac{24}{10}$. Small errors get magnified when they are multiplied by 1000, but even after magnification the discrepancies are negligible because they are just tiny fractions of a pixel. You may be surprised that 1/3 times 3 comes out to be .99998 instead of .99999; the truth is that both 0.99999 and 0.99998 represent the same value, namely $\frac{65535}{65536}$; METAFONT displays this value as 0.99998 because it is closer to .99998 than to .99999. Plain METAFONT defines *epsilon* to be $\frac{1}{65536}$, the smallest representable number that is greater than zero; therefore 1-epsilon is $\frac{65535}{65536}$, and 1+4epsilon is $\frac{65540}{65536}$.

You type	*And the result is*
4096	4095.99998 (with error message)
infinity	4095.99998
1000*1000	32767.99998 (with error message)

infinity+epsilon	4096
100*100	10000
.1(100*100)	1000.06104
(100*100)/3	3333.33333

METAFONT will complain that an 'Enormous number has been reduced' when you try to introduce constants that are 4096 or more. Plain METAFONT defines *infinity* to be 4096 − *epsilon*, which is the largest legal numeric token. On the other hand, it turns out that larger numbers can actually arise when an expression is being evaluated; METAFONT doesn't worry about this unless the resulting magnitude is at least 32768.

 ▶ **EXERCISE 8.2**
If you try '100*100/3' instead of '(100*100)/3', you get '3333.33282'. Why?

Sometimes METAFONT will compute things more accurately than you would expect from the examples above, because many of its internal calculations are done with multiples of 2^{-28} instead of 2^{-16}. For example, if $t = 3$ the result of '1/3t' will be exactly 1 (not 0.99998); the same thing happens if you write '1/3(3)'.

Now let's try some more complicated expressions, using undefined variables as well as constants. (Are you actually trying these examples, or are you just reading the book? It's far better to type them yourself and to watch what happens; in fact, you're also allowed to type things that *aren't* in the book!)

You type	*And the result is*
b+a	a+b
a+b	a+b
b+a-2b	a-b
2(a-b+.5)	2a-2b+1
.5(b-a)	-0.5a+0.5b
.5[a,b]	0.5a+0.5b
1/3[a,b]	0.66667a+0.33333b
0[a,b]	a
a[2,3]	a+2
t[a,a+1]	t+a
a*b	b (with error message)
1/b	b (with error message)

METAFONT has a preferred way to arrange variables in order when they are added together; therefore '$a + b$' and '$b + a$' give the same result. Notice that the mediation construction '.5[a, b]' specifies a number that's halfway between a and b, as explained in Chapter 2. METAFONT does not allow you to multiply two unknown numeric quantities together, nor can you divide by an unknown numeric; all of the unknown expressions that METAFONT works with must be "linear forms," i.e., they must be sums of variables with constant coefficients, plus an optional constant. (You might want to try typing 't[a,b]' now, in order to see what error message is given.)

You type	And the result is
sqrt 2	1.41422
sqrt 100	10
sqrt 100*100	1000
sqrt(100*100)	100
sqrt 100(100)	100
sqrt sqrt 100(100)	10
sqrt .01	0.09998
0.09998**2	0.01
2**1/2	1.41422
sqrt 2**2	2
sqrt -1	0 (with error message)
sqrt a	a (with error message)

Since sqrt has more "magnetism" than *, the formula sqrt 100*100 is evaluated as (sqrt 100)*100; but in 'sqrt 100(100)' the 100(100) is computed first. The reason is that '(sqrt 100)(100)' isn't a legal expression, so the operations in 'sqrt 100(100)' must be carried out from right to left. If you are unsure about the order of evaluation, you can always insert parentheses; but you'll find that METAFONT's rules of precedence are fairly natural as you gain experience.

▶ **EXERCISE 8.3**
Is 'sqrt 2**2' computed as '(sqrt 2)**2' or as 'sqrt(2**2)'?

Some METAFONT expressions have 'true' or 'false' values, instead of numbers; we will see later that they can be used to adapt METAFONT programs to special conditions.

You type	And the result is
0<1	true
0=1	false
a+1>a	true
a>=b	false (with error message)
"abc"<="b"	true
"B">"a!"	false
"b">"a?"	true
(1,2)<>(0,4)	true
(1,2)<(0,4)	false
(1,a)>(0,b)	true

`numeric a`	true
`known a`	false
`not pen a`	true
`known "a" and numeric 1`	true
`(0>1) or (a<a)`	false
`0>1 or a<a`	a (with error messages)

The tokens '`>=`', '`<=`', and '`<>`' stand respectively for the relations greater-than-or-equal-to, less-than-or-equal-to, and unequal-to. When strings are compared, METAFONT uses the order of words in a dictionary, except that it uses ASCII code to define ordering of individual characters; thus, all uppercase letters are considered to be less than all lowercase letters. (See Appendix C.) When pairs of numbers are compared, METAFONT considers only the x coordinates, unless the x coordinates are equal; in the latter case it compares the y coordinates. The type of an expression can be ascertained by an expression like '`pair a`', which is true if and only if a is a pair. The expression '`known a`' is true if and only if the value of a is fully known.

▶ **EXERCISE 8.4**
What causes the error messages in '`0>1 or a<a`'?

The rest of this chapter is entirely preceded by "dangerous bend" signs, so you can safely omit it on first reading (unless you're hooked and can't stop).

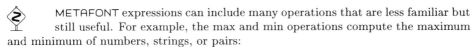

METAFONT expressions can include many operations that are less familiar but still useful. For example, the max and min operations compute the maximum and minimum of numbers, strings, or pairs:

You type	*And the result is*
`max(1,-2,4)`	4
`min(1,-2,4)`	-2
`max("a","b","ab")`	"b"
`min("a","b","ab")`	"a"
`max((1,5),(0,6),(1,4))`	(1,5)
`min((1,5),(0,6),(1,4))`	(0,6)
`max(.5a+1,.5a-1)`	0.5a+1

Numbers can be converted to integers in a variety of ways:

You type	*And the result is*
`floor 3.14159`	3
`floor -3.14159`	-4
`floor -epsilon`	-1
`floor infinity`	4095
`ceiling 3.14159`	4
`ceiling -3.14159`	-3

round 3.14159	3
round -3.14159	-3
round(1.1,2.8)	(1,3)
round(3.5,-3.5)	(4,-3)
round a	a+0.5 (with error message)
8 mod 3	2
-8 mod 3	1
.8 mod .3	0.2

The 'floor' operation computes the greatest integer that is less than or equal to its operand; this quantity is often denoted by $\lfloor x \rfloor$ in mathematics texts. Plain METAFONT also includes the analogous 'ceiling' operation $\lceil x \rceil$, which is the least integer greater than or equal to x. Furthermore, 'round x' is the integer nearest to x; plain METAFONT computes this by using the formula $\lfloor x + .5 \rfloor$, and applies it to both components of a pair if a pair is being rounded. The remainder of x with respect to y, written 'x mod y', is calculated by using the formula $x - y\lfloor x/y \rfloor$.

You type	*And the result is*
abs -7	7
abs(3,4)	5
length(3,4)	5
3++4	5
300++400	500
sqrt(300**2 + 400**2)	181.01933 (with error messages)
1++1	1.4142
0 ++ -7	7
5+-+4	3

The '++' operation is called *Pythagorean addition*; $a{+}{+}b$ is the same thing as $\sqrt{a^2 + b^2}$. Most of the square root operations in computer programs could probably be avoided if ++ were more widely available, because people seem to want square roots primarily when they are computing distances. Notice that $a{+}{+}b{+}{+}c = \sqrt{a^2 + b^2 + c^2}$; we have the identity $(a{+}{+}b){+}{+}c = a{+}{+}(b{+}{+}c)$ as well as $a{+}{+}b = b{+}{+}a$. It is better to use Pythagorean addition than to calculate $\sqrt{a^2 + b^2}$, because the computation of a^2 and b^2 might produce numbers that are too large even when $a{+}{+}b$ is rather small. There's also an inverse operation, Pythagorean subtraction, which is denoted by '+−+'; the quantity $a{+}{-}{+}b$ is equal to $\sqrt{a^2 - b^2}$.

▶ **EXERCISE 8.5**
When the author was preparing these examples he typed '0++-7' and was surprised to get the answer '0'. Why should this not have been a surprise?

▶ **EXERCISE 8.6**
(For mathematicians.) Although the Pythagorean addition operation is associative and commutative, METAFONT says that $5{+}{+}4{+}{+}2{+}{+}2 = 7 = 2{+}{+}2{+}{+}4{+}{+}5$ yet $2{+}{+}4{+}{+}5{+}{+}2 = 6.99998$. Why?

METAFONT uses the names 'sind' and 'cosd' for the trigonometric functions sine and cosine, because METAFONT's operations are designed to deal with angles expressed in degrees. But it turns out that programmers rarely need to refer to sines and cosines explicitly, because the 'dir' and 'angle' functions provide most of what a font designer needs.

You type	*And the result is*
sind 30	0.5
cosd 30	0.86603
sind -30	-0.5
cosd 360	1
sind 10 ++ cosd 10	1
dir 30	(0.86603,0.5)
dir -90	(0,-1)
angle(1,1)	45
angle(1,2)	63.43495
angle(1,-2)	-63.43495
sind 63.43495 / cosd 63.43495	1.99997
angle up	90
angle left	180
angle(-1000,-epsilon)	-180
angle dir 60	60.00008
angle(0,0)	0 (with error message)

Plain METAFONT defines 'dir x' to be the pair of values $(\cosd x, \sind x)$; this is a vector, which points x degrees above the rightward horizon. Conversely, the 'angle' operator determines the angle that corresponds to a given vector.

Logarithms and exponentials are computed with respect to an unusual base, designed to enhance the accuracy of calculations involving fixed-radix numbers in METAFONT's range. The values $\operatorname{mlog} x = 256 \ln x$ and $\operatorname{mexp} x = e^{x/256}$ produce reasonably good results when $x ** y$ is computed by the formula $\operatorname{mexp}(y * \operatorname{mlog} x)$.

You type	*And the result is*
mlog 2	177.44568
mexp mlog 2	2
mexp 8 mlog 2	256
mexp 256	2.71828
mlog 2.71828	255.99954
mlog 2.71829	256.00098
15 mlog 2	2661.68518
mexp 2661.68518	32767.99998
mexp 2661.68519	32767.99998 (with error message)
mexp-2661.68519	0.00003

METAFONT also generates two flavors of random numbers. It is very unlikely
that you will get the particular values shown in the following examples, when
you do the experiment yourself, because the results come out different each time the
computer is asked for a new random number (unless you have specified a "seed value"
as explained in Chapter 21).

You type	*And the result might be*
uniformdeviate 100	47.4241
uniformdeviate 100	97.28148
uniformdeviate -100	-36.16279
(normaldeviate,normaldeviate)	(0.46236,-1.87648)

The value of 'uniformdeviate 100' is a random number between 0 and 100; the value
of 'normaldeviate' is a normally distributed random number whose mean value is zero
and whose standard deviation is unity. Chapter 21 explains what this means and gives
several applications.

Besides all of these operations on numbers, METAFONT has a rich collection
of operations on pairs, some of which are indicated in the following examples:

You type	*And the result is*
right	(1,0)
(1,2)+(3,4)	(4,6)
1/3(3,10)	(1,3.33333)
z2-z1	(-x1+x2,-y1+y2)
.2[z1,z2]	(0.8x1+0.2x2,0.8y1+0.2y2)
3z	(3x,3y)
z scaled 3	(3x,3y)
z xscaled 2 yscaled 1/2	(2x,0.5y)
z shifted (2,3)	(x+2,y+3)
z shifted 3right	(x+3,y)
z slanted 1/6	(x+0.16667y,y)
z rotated 90	(-y,x)
z rotated 30	(-0.5y+0.86603x,0.86603y+0.5x)
xpart(z rotated 30)	-0.5y+0.86603x
ypart(z rotated 30)	0.86603y+0.5x
(1,2)*(3,4)	(3,4) (with error message)
(1,2)zscaled(3,4)	(-5,10)
(a,b)zscaled(3,4)	(3a-4b,4a+3b)
(a,b)zscaled dir 30	(0.86603a-0.5b,0.5a+0.86603b)
(1,2)dotprod(3,4)	11
(a,b)dotprod(3,4)	3a+4b
dir 21 dotprod dir 51	0.86603
(3,4)dotprod((30,40)rotated 90)	0

(Recall that plain METAFONT converts 'z$' into '(x$,y$)' when $ is any ⟨suffix⟩.) The operations exhibited here are almost all self-evident. When a point or vector is rotated, it is moved counterclockwise about $(0,0)$ through a given number of degrees. META-FONT computes the rotated coordinates by using sines and cosines in an appropriate way; you don't have to remember the formulas! Although you cannot use '*' to multiply a pair by a pair, you can use 'zscaled' to get the effect of complex number multiplication: Since $(1+2i)$ times $(3+4i)$ is $-5+10i$, we have $(1,2)$ zscaled $(3,4) = (-5,10)$. There's also a multiplication that converts pairs into numbers: (a,b) dotprod $(c,d) = ac + bd$. This is the "dot product," often written '$(a,b) \cdot (c,d)$' in mathematics texts; it turns out to be equal to $a++b$ times $c++d$ times the cosine of the angle between the vectors (a,b) and (c,d). Since cosd $90° = 0$, two vectors are perpendicular to each other if and only if their dot product is zero.

There are operations on strings, paths, and the other types too; we shall study such things carefully in later chapters. For now, it will suffice to give a few examples, keeping in mind that the file `expr.mf` defines s with any subscript to be a string, while p with any subscript is a path. Furthermore s_1 has been given the value `"abra"`, while p_1 is '$(0,0) \mathinner{\ldotp\ldotp} (3,3)$' and p_2 is '$(0,0) \mathinner{\ldotp\ldotp} (3,3) \mathinner{\ldotp\ldotp} cycle$'.

You type	*And the result is*
s2	unknown string s2
s1&"cad"&s1	"abracadabra"
length s1	4
length p1	1
length p2	2
cycle p1	false
cycle p2	true
substring (0,2) of s1	"ab"
substring (2,infinity) of s1	"ra"
point 0 of p1	(0,0)
point 1 of p1	(3,3)
point .5 of p1	(1.5,1.5)
point infinity of p1	(3,3)
point .5 of p2	(3,0)
point 1.5 of p2	(0,3)
point 2 of p2	(0,0)
point 2+epsilon of p2	(0.00009,-0.00009)
point -epsilon of p2	(-0.00009,0.00009)
point -1 of p1	(0,0)
direction 0 of p1	(1,1)
direction 0 of p2	(4,-4)
direction 1 of p2	(-4,4)

The length of a path is the number of '..' steps that it contains; the construction 'cycle ⟨path⟩' can be used to tell whether or not a particular path is cyclic. If you say just 'p1' you get to see path p_1 with its control points:

```
(0,0)..controls (1,1) and (2,2)
 ..(3,3)
```

Similarly, 'p2' is

```
(0,0)..controls (2,-2) and (5,1)
 ..(3,3)..controls (1,5) and (-2,2)
 ..cycle
```

and '**subpath (0,1) of p2**' is analogous to a substring:

```
(0,0)..controls (2,-2) and (5,1)
 ..(3,3)
```

The expression 'point t of p_2' gives the position of a point that moves along path p_2, starting with the initial point $(0,0)$ at $t = 0$, then reaching point $(3,3)$ at $t = 1$, etc.; the value at $t = 1/2$ is the third-order midpoint obtained by the construction of Chapter 3, using intermediate control points $(2,-2)$ and $(5,1)$. Since p_2 is a cyclic path of length 2, point $(t+2)$ of p_2 is the same as point t. Path p_1 is not cyclic, so its points turn out to be identical to point 0 when $t < 0$, and identical to point 1 when $t > 1$. The expression 'direction t of ⟨path⟩' is similar to 'point t of ⟨path⟩'; it yields a vector for the direction of travel at time t.

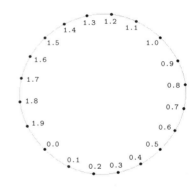

Paths are not necessarily traversed at constant speed. For example, the diagram at the right shows point t of p_2 at twenty equally spaced values of t. META-FONT moves faster in this case at time 1.0 than at time 1.2; but the points are spread out fairly well, so the concept of fractional time can be useful. The diagram shows, incidentally, that path p_2 is not an especially good approximation to a circle; there is no left-right symmetry, although the curve from point 1 to point 2 is a mirror image of the curve from point 0 to point 1. This lack of circularity is not surprising, since p_2 was defined by simply specifying two points, $(0,0)$ and $(3,3)$; at least four points are needed to get a path that is convincingly round.

The ampersand operation '**&**' can be used to splice paths together in much the same way as it concatenates strings. For example, if you type '**p2 & p1**', you get the path of length 3 that is obtained by breaking the cyclic connection at the end of path p_2 and attaching p_1:

```
(0,0)..controls (2,-2) and (5,1)
 ..(3,3)..controls (1,5) and (-2,2)
 ..(0,0)..controls (1,1) and (2,2)
 ..(3,3)
```

Concatenated paths must have identical endpoints at the junction.

You can even "slow down the clock" by concatenating subpaths that have non-integer time specifications. For example, here's what you get if you ask for 'subpath (0,.5) of p2 & subpath (.5,2) of p2 & cycle':

```
(0,0)..controls (1,-1) and (2.25,-0.75)
 ..(3,0)..controls (3.75,0.75) and (4,2)
 ..(3,3)..controls (1,5) and (-2,2)
 ..cycle
```

When t goes from 0 to 1 in subpath $(0, .5)$ of p_2, you get the same points as when t goes from 0 to .5 in p_2; when t goes from 0 to 1 in subpath $(.5, 2)$ of p_2, you get the same points as when t goes from .5 to 1 in p_2; but when t goes from 1 to 2 in subpath $(.5, 2)$ of p_2, it's the same as the segment from 1 to 2 in p_2.

Let's conclude this chapter by discussing the exact rules of precedence by which METAFONT decides what operations to do first. The informal notion of "magnetism" gives a good intuitive picture of what happens, but syntax rules express things unambiguously in borderline cases.

The four levels of precedence correspond to four kinds of formulas, which are called primaries, secondaries, tertiaries, and expressions. A *primary* is a variable or a constant or a tightly bound unit like '2x' or 'sqrt 2'; a *secondary* is a primary or a sequence of primaries connected by multiplicative operators like '*' or 'scaled'; a *tertiary* is a secondary or a sequence of secondaries connected by additive operators like '+' or '++'; an *expression* is a tertiary or a sequence of tertiaries connected by external operators like '<' or '..'. For example, the expression

```
a+b/2>3c*sqrt4d
```

is composed of the primaries 'a', 'b', '2', '3c', and 'sqrt4d'; the last of these is a primary containing '4d' as a primary within itself. The subformulas 'a', 'b/2', and '3c*sqrt4d' are secondaries; the subformulas 'a+b/2' and '3c*sqrt4d' are tertiaries.

If an expression is enclosed in parentheses, it becomes a primary that can be used to build up larger secondaries, tertiaries, etc.

The full syntax for expressions is quite long, but most of it falls into a simple pattern. If α, β, and γ are any "types"—numeric, boolean, string, etc.—then $\langle\alpha$ variable$\rangle$ refers to a variable of type α, $\langle\beta$ primary$\rangle$ refers to a primary of type β, and so on. Almost all of the syntax rules fit into the following general framework:

$\langle\alpha$ primary$\rangle \longrightarrow \langle\alpha$ variable$\rangle$ | $\langle\alpha$ constant$\rangle$ | ($\langle\alpha$ expression$\rangle$)
 | $\langle$operator that takes type β to type $\alpha\rangle\langle\beta$ primary$\rangle$
$\langle\alpha$ secondary$\rangle \longrightarrow \langle\alpha$ primary$\rangle$
 | $\langle\beta$ secondary$\rangle\langle$multiplicative op taking types β and γ to $\alpha\rangle\langle\gamma$ primary$\rangle$
$\langle\alpha$ tertiary$\rangle \longrightarrow \langle\alpha$ secondary$\rangle$
 | $\langle\beta$ tertiary$\rangle\langle$additive op taking types β and γ to $\alpha\rangle\langle\gamma$ secondary$\rangle$
$\langle\alpha$ expression$\rangle \longrightarrow \langle\alpha$ tertiary$\rangle$
 | $\langle\beta$ expression$\rangle\langle$external op taking types β and γ to $\alpha\rangle\langle\gamma$ tertiary$\rangle$

These schematic rules don't give the whole story, but they do give the general structure of the plot.

Chapter 25 spells out all of the syntax rules for all types of expressions. We shall consider only a portion of the numeric and pair cases here, in order to have a foretaste of the complete menu:

⟨numeric primary⟩ ⟶ ⟨numeric atom⟩
   | ⟨numeric atom⟩ [⟨numeric expression⟩ , ⟨numeric expression⟩]
   | **length** ⟨string primary⟩
   | **length** ⟨path primary⟩
   | **length** ⟨pair primary⟩
   | **angle** ⟨pair primary⟩
   | **xpart** ⟨pair primary⟩
   | **ypart** ⟨pair primary⟩
   | ⟨numeric operator⟩⟨numeric primary⟩
⟨numeric atom⟩ ⟶ ⟨numeric variable⟩
   | ⟨numeric token primary⟩
   | (⟨numeric expression⟩)
   | **normaldeviate**
⟨numeric token primary⟩ ⟶ ⟨numeric token⟩ / ⟨numeric token⟩
   | ⟨numeric token not followed by '/ ⟨numeric token⟩'⟩
⟨numeric operator⟩ ⟶ **sqrt** | **sind** | **cosd** | **mlog** | **mexp**
   | **floor** | **uniformdeviate** | ⟨scalar multiplication operator⟩
⟨scalar multiplication operator⟩ ⟶ ⟨plus or minus⟩
   | ⟨numeric token primary not followed by + or - or a numeric token⟩
⟨numeric secondary⟩ ⟶ ⟨numeric primary⟩
   | ⟨numeric secondary⟩⟨times or over⟩⟨numeric primary⟩
⟨times or over⟩ ⟶ ***** | **/**
⟨numeric tertiary⟩ ⟶ ⟨numeric secondary⟩
   | ⟨numeric tertiary⟩⟨plus or minus⟩⟨numeric secondary⟩
   | ⟨numeric tertiary⟩⟨Pythagorean plus or minus⟩⟨numeric secondary⟩
⟨plus or minus⟩ ⟶ **+** | **-**
⟨Pythagorean plus or minus⟩ ⟶ **++** | **+-+**
⟨numeric expression⟩ ⟶ ⟨numeric tertiary⟩

All of the finicky details about fractions and such things are made explicit by this syntax. For example, we can use the rules to deduce that 'sind-1/3x-2' is interpreted as '(sind(-(1/3x)))-2'; notice that the first minus sign in this formula is considered to be a "scalar multiplication operator," which comes in at the primary level, while the second one denotes subtraction and enters in the construction of ⟨numeric tertiary⟩. The mediation or "of-the-way" operation '$t[a, b]$' is handled at the primary level.

Several operations that haven't been discussed yet do not appear in the syntax above, but they fit into the same general pattern; for example, we will see later that 'ASCII⟨string primary⟩' and 'xxpart⟨transform primary⟩' are additional cases of the syntax for ⟨numeric primary⟩. On the other hand, several operations that we have discussed in this chapter do not appear in the syntax, because they are not primitives of METAFONT itself; they are defined in the plain METAFONT base (Appendix B). For example, 'ceiling' is analogous to 'floor', and '******' is analogous to '*****'. Chapter 20 explains how METAFONT allows extensions to its built-in syntax, so that additional operations can be added at will.

▶ **EXERCISE 8.7**
How does METAFONT interpret '2 2'? (There's a space between the 2's.)

 ▶ **EXERCISE 8.8**
According to `expr.mf`, the value of '1/2/3/4' is 0.66667; the value of 'a/2/3/4' is 0.375a. Explain why.

The rules of ⟨pair expression⟩ are similar to those for ⟨numeric expression⟩, so it's convenient to learn them both at the same time.

⟨pair primary⟩ ⟶ ⟨pair variable⟩
    | (⟨numeric expression⟩ , ⟨numeric expression⟩)
    | (⟨pair expression⟩)
    | ⟨numeric atom⟩ [⟨pair expression⟩ , ⟨pair expression⟩]
    | **point** ⟨numeric expression⟩ **of** ⟨path primary⟩
    | ⟨scalar multiplication operator⟩⟨pair primary⟩
⟨pair secondary⟩ ⟶ ⟨pair primary⟩
    | ⟨pair secondary⟩⟨times or over⟩⟨numeric primary⟩
    | ⟨numeric secondary⟩ * ⟨pair primary⟩
    | ⟨pair secondary⟩⟨transformer⟩
⟨transformer⟩ ⟶ **rotated** ⟨numeric primary⟩
    | **scaled** ⟨numeric primary⟩
    | **shifted** ⟨pair primary⟩
    | **slanted** ⟨numeric primary⟩
    | **transformed** ⟨transform primary⟩
    | **xscaled** ⟨numeric primary⟩
    | **yscaled** ⟨numeric primary⟩
    | **zscaled** ⟨pair primary⟩
⟨pair tertiary⟩ ⟶ ⟨pair secondary⟩
    | ⟨pair tertiary⟩⟨plus or minus⟩⟨pair secondary⟩
⟨pair expression⟩ ⟶ ⟨pair tertiary⟩

 ▶ **EXERCISE 8.9**
Try to guess the syntax rules for ⟨string primary⟩, ⟨string secondary⟩, ⟨string tertiary⟩, and ⟨string expression⟩, based solely on the examples that have appeared in this chapter. [*Hint:* The '**&**' operation has the same precedence as '..'.]

A maiden was sitting there who was lovely as any picture,
nay, so beautiful that no words can express it.
— JAKOB and WILHELM GRIMM, *Fairy Tales* (1815)

He looked astonished at the expression.
— EMILY BRONTË, *Wuthering Heights* (1847)

9
Equations

The variables in a METAFONT program receive their values by appearing in *equations*, which express relationships that the programmer wants to achieve. We've seen in the previous chapter that algebraic expressions provide a rich language for dealing with both numerical and graphical relationships. Thus it is possible to express a great variety of design objectives in precise form by stating that certain algebraic expressions should be equal to each other.

The most important things a METAFONT programmer needs to know about equations are (1) how to translate intuitive design concepts into formal equations, and (2) how to translate formal equations into intuitive design concepts. In other words, it's important to be able to *write* equations, and it's also important to be able to *read* equations that you or somebody else has written. This is not nearly as difficult as it might seem at first. The best way to learn (1) is to get a lot of practice with (2) and to generalize from specific examples. Therefore we shall begin this chapter by translating a lot of equations into "simple English."

Equation	*Translation*
$a = 3.14$	The value of a should be 3.14.
$3.14 = a$	The number 3.14 should be the value of a. (This means the same thing as '$a = 3.14$'; the left and right sides of an equation can be interchanged without affecting the meaning of that equation in any way.)
$mode = smoke$	The value of *mode* should be equal to the value of *smoke*. (Plain METAFONT assigns a special meaning to '*smoke*', so that if **mode_setup** is invoked when $mode = smoke$ the computer will prepare "smoke proofs" as explained in Chapter 5 and Appendix H.)
$y_3 = 0$	The y coordinate of point 3 should be zero; i.e., point 3 should be at the baseline. (Point 3 is also known as z_3, which is an abbreviation for the pair of coordinates (x_3, y_3), if you are using the conventions of plain METAFONT.)
$x_9 = 0$	The x coordinate of point 9 should be zero; i.e., point 9 should be at the left edge of the type box that encloses the current character.
$x_{1l} = curve\_sidebar$	The x coordinate of point $1l$ should be equal to the value of the variable called *curve_sidebar*. This puts z_{1l} a certain distance from the left edge of the type.

$$x_1 = x_2$$

Points 1 and 2 should have the same x coordinate; i.e., they should have the same horizontal position, so that one will lie directly above or below the other.

$$y_4 = y_5 + 1$$

Point 4 should be one pixel higher than point 5. (However, points 4 and 5 might be far apart; this equation says nothing about the relation between x_4 and x_5.)

$$y_6 = y_7 + 2mm$$

Point 6 should be two millimeters higher than point 7. (Plain METAFONT's **mode_setup** routine sets variable mm to the number of pixels in a millimeter, based on the resolution determined by *mode* and *mag*.)

$$x_4 = w - .01in$$

Point 3 should be one-hundredth of an inch inside the right edge of the type. (Plain METAFONT's **beginchar** routine sets variable w equal to the width of whatever character is currently being drawn, expressed in pixels.)

$$y_4 = .5h$$

Point 4 should be halfway between the baseline and the top of the type. (Plain METAFONT's **beginchar** sets h to the height of the current character, in pixels.)

$$y_6 = -d$$

Point 6 should be below the baseline, at the bottom edge of the type. (Each character has a "bounding box" that runs from $(0, h)$ at the upper left and (w, h) at the upper right to $(0, -d)$ and $(w, -d)$ at the lower left and lower right; variable d represents the depth of the type. The values of w, h, and d might change from character to character, since the individual pieces of type in a computer-produced font need not have the same size.)

$$y_8 = .5[h, -d]$$

Point 8 should be halfway between the top and bottom edges of the type.

$$w - x_5 = \tfrac{2}{3}x_6$$

The distance from point 5 to the right edge of the type should be two-thirds of the distance from point 6 to the left edge of the type. (Since w is at the right edge, $w - x_5$ is the distance from point 5 to the right edge.)

$z_0 = (0,0)$ Point 0 should be at the reference point of the current character, i.e., it should be on the baseline at the left edge of the type. This equation is an abbreviation for two equations, '$x_0 = 0$' and '$y_0 = 0$', because an equation between pairs of coordinates implies that the x and y coordinates must both agree. (Incidentally, plain META-FONT defines a variable called *origin* whose value is $(0,0)$; hence this equation could also have been written '$z_0 = origin$'.)

$z_9 = (w,h)$ Point 9 should be at the upper right corner of the current character's bounding box.

top $z_8 = (.5w, h)$ If the pen that has currently been "picked up" is placed at point 8, its top edge should be at the top edge of the type. Furthermore, x_8 should be $.5w$; i.e., point 8 should be centered between the left and right edges of the type. (Chapter 4 contains further examples of '*top*', as well as the corresponding operations '*bot*', '*lft*', and '*rt*'.)

$z_4 = \frac{3}{7}[z_5, z_6]$ Point 4 should be three-sevenths of the way from point 5 to point 6.

$z_{12} - z_{11} = z_{14} - z_{13}$ The vector that moves from point 11 to point 12 should be the same as the vector that moves from point 13 to point 14. In other words, point 12 should have the same direction and distance from point 11 as point 14 has from point 13.

$z_3 - z_2 =$ $(z_4 - z_2)$ rotated 15   Points 3 and 4 should be at the same distance from point 2, but the direction to point 3 should be 15 degrees counterclockwise from the direction to point 4.

▶ **EXERCISE 9.1**
Translate the following equations into "simple English":   (a) $x_7 - 9 = x_1$; (b) $z_7 = (x_4, .5[y_4, y_5])$;   (c) *lft* $z_{21} = rt\ z_{20} + 1$.

▶ **EXERCISE 9.2**
Now see if your knowledge of equation reading gives you the ability to write equations that correspond to the following objectives: (a) Point 13 should be just as far below the baseline as point 11 is above the baseline. (b) Point 10 should be one millimeter to the right of, and one pixel below, point 12. (c) Point 43 should be one-third of the way from the top left corner of the type to the bottom right corner of the type.

Let's return now to the six example points $(z_1, z_2, z_3, z_4, z_5, z_6)$ that were used so often in Chapters 2 and 3. Changing the notation slightly, we might say that the points are

$$(x_1, y_1) = (0, h); \qquad (x_2, y_2) = (.5w, h); \qquad (x_3, y_3) = (w, h);$$
$$(x_4, y_4) = (0, 0); \qquad (x_5, y_5) = (.5w, 0); \qquad (x_6, y_6) = (w, 0).$$

There are many ways to specify these points by writing a series of equations. For example, the six equations just given would do fine; or the short names z_1 through z_6 could be used instead of the long names (x_1, y_1) through (x_6, y_6). But there are several other ways to specify those points and at the same time to "explain" the relations they have to each other. One way is to define the x and y coordinates separately:

$$x_1 = x_4 = 0; \qquad x_2 = x_5 = .5w; \qquad x_3 = x_6 = w;$$
$$y_1 = y_2 = y_3 = h; \qquad y_4 = y_5 = y_6 = 0.$$

METAFONT allows you to state several equations at once, by using more than one equality sign; for example, '$y_1 = y_2 = y_3 = h$' stands for three equations, '$y_1 = y_2$', '$y_2 = y_3$', and '$y_3 = h$'.

In order to define the coordinates of six points, it's necessary to write twelve equations, because each equation contributes to the definition of one value, and because six points have twelve coordinates in all. However, an equation between pairs of coordinates counts as two equations between single numbers; that's why we were able to get by with only six '=' signs in the first set of equations, while twelve were used in the second.

Let's look at yet another way to specify those six points, by giving equations for their positions relative to each other:

$$z_1 - z_4 = z_2 - z_5 = z_3 - z_6$$
$$z_2 - z_1 = z_3 - z_2 = z_5 - z_4 = z_6 - z_5$$
$$z_4 = origin; \quad z_3 = (w, h).$$

First we say that the vectors from z_4 to z_1, from z_5 to z_2, and from z_6 to z_3, are equal to each other; then we say the same thing for the vectors from z_1 to z_2, z_2 to z_3, z_4 to z_5, and z_5 to z_6. Finally the corner points z_4 and z_3 are given explicitly. That's a total of seven equations between pairs of coordinates, so it should be more than enough to define the six points of interest.

However, it turns out that those seven equations are not enough! For example, the six points

$$z_1 = z_4 = (0, 0); \quad z_2 = z_5 = (.5w, .5h); \quad z_3 = z_6 = (w, h)$$

also satisfy the same equations. A closer look explains why: The two formulas

$$z_1 - z_4 = z_2 - z_5 \qquad \text{and} \qquad z_2 - z_1 = z_5 - z_4$$

actually say exactly the same thing. (Add $z_5 - z_1$ to both sides of the first equation and you get '$z_5 - z_4 = z_2 - z_1$'.) Similarly, $z_2 - z_5 = z_3 - z_6$ is the same as $z_3 - z_2 = z_6 - z_5$. Two of the seven equations give no new information, so we really have specified only five equations; that isn't enough. An additional relation such as '$z_1 = (0, h)$' is needed to make the solution unique.

▶ **EXERCISE 9.3**

(For mathematicians.)   Find a solution to the seven equations such that $z_1 = z_2$. Also find another solution in which $z_1 = z_6$.

At the beginning of a METAFONT program, variables have no values, except that plain METAFONT has assigned special values to variables like *smoke* and *origin*. Furthermore, when you begin a new character with **beginchar**, any previous values that may have been assigned to x or y variables are obliterated and forgotten. Values are gradually established as the computer reads equations and tries to solve them, together with any other equations that have already appeared in the program.

It takes ten equations to define the values of ten variables. If you have given only nine equations it may turn out that none of the ten variables has yet been determined; for example, the nine equations

$$g_0 = g_1 = g_2 = g_3 = g_4 = g_5 = g_6 = g_7 = g_8 = g_9$$

don't tell us any of the g values. However, the further equation

$$g_0 + g_1 = 1$$

will cause METAFONT to deduce that all ten of the g's are equal to $\frac{1}{2}$.

METAFONT always computes the values of as many variables as possible, based on the equations it has seen so far. For example, after the two equations

$$a + b + 2c = 3;$$
$$a - b - 2c = 1$$

the machine will know that $a = 2$ (because the sum of these two equations is '$2a = 4$'); but all it will know about b and c is that $b + 2c = 1$.

At any point in a program a variable is said to be either "known" or "unknown," depending on whether or not its value can be deduced uniquely from the equations that have been stated so far. The sample expressions in Chapter 8 indicate that METAFONT can compute a variety of things with unknown variables; but sometimes a quantity must be known before it can be used. For example, METAFONT can multiply an unknown numeric or pair variable by a known numeric value, but it cannot multiply two unknowns.

Equations can be given in any order, except that you might sometimes need to put certain equations first in order to make critical values known in the others. For example, METAFONT will find the solution $(a, b, c) = (2, 7, -3)$ to the equations '$a + b + 2c = 3; a - b - 2c = 1; b + c = 4$' if you give those equations in any other order, like '$b + c = 4; a - b - 2c = 1; a + b + 2c = 3$'. But if the equations had been '$a + b + 2c = 3; a - b - 2c = 1; a * (b + c) = 8$', you would not have been able to give the last one first, because METAFONT would have refused to multiply the unknown quantity a by another unknown quantity $b + c$. Here are the main things that METAFONT can do with unknown quantities:

$$-\langle\text{unknown}\rangle$$
$$\langle\text{unknown}\rangle + \langle\text{unknown}\rangle$$
$$\langle\text{unknown}\rangle - \langle\text{unknown}\rangle$$
$$\langle\text{unknown}\rangle * \langle\text{known}\rangle$$
$$\langle\text{known}\rangle * \langle\text{unknown}\rangle$$
$$\langle\text{unknown}\rangle/\langle\text{known}\rangle$$
$$\langle\text{known}\rangle[\langle\text{unknown}\rangle, \langle\text{unknown}\rangle]$$
$$\langle\text{unknown}\rangle[\langle\text{known}\rangle, \langle\text{known}\rangle]$$

Some of the operations of plain METAFONT, defined in Appendix B, also work with unknown quantities. For example, it's possible to say *top* $\langle\text{unknown}\rangle$, *bot* $\langle\text{unknown}\rangle$, *lft* $\langle\text{unknown}\rangle$, *rt* $\langle\text{unknown}\rangle$, and even

penpos$\langle\text{suffix}\rangle(\langle\text{unknown}\rangle, \langle\text{known}\rangle)$.

A METAFONT program can say '$\langle\text{unknown}\rangle[a,b]$' when $a - b$ is known, and variable a can be compared to variable b in boolean expressions like '$a < b$' when $a - b$ is known. The quantity $a - b$ might be known even when a and b aren't known by themselves.

You might wonder how METAFONT is able to keep its knowledge up-to-date, based on scraps of partial information that it receives from miscellaneous equations. The best way to understand this is to watch how it happens, by asking the computer to show certain calculations that it usually keeps to itself. Here's one way to do it: Run METAFONT and say

```
\tracingequations:=tracingonline:=1;
```

in response to the opening '******'. (Be sure to type the backslash '\', and to use ':=' instead of '='. We will see in Chapter 27 that METAFONT can be asked to "trace" many aspects of what it's doing.) Now type

```
a+b+2c=3;
```

the machine will reply by saying

```
## c=-0.5b-0.5a+1.5
```

since that is how it has digested your equation. (The '**##**' in this line identifies diagnostic information that comes from *tracingequations*.) Now type

```
a-b-2c=1;
```

METAFONT will read this as if you had said '**a-b-2(-0.5b-0.5a+1.5)=1**', since it has previously learned how to replace **c** by an expression that involves only **a** and **b**. This new equation can be simplified by multiplying out the left-hand side and collecting terms. The result is '**2a-3=1**', hence METAFONT will respond with

```
## a=2
```

and it will be your turn to type something again. Say

    showdependencies;

METAFONT's response will be

    c=-0.5b+0.5

indicating that there is only one variable whose value depends on others, and that its equation of dependency is now '$c = -0.5b + 0.5$'. (The previous dependency equation '$c = -0.5b - 0.5a + 1.5$' has been simplified to take account of the newly discovered value, $a = 2$.) Finally type

    b+c=4;

this spurs the computer on to say

    ## b=7
    #### c=-3

A line that begins with '`##`' states what METAFONT has deduced from the equation it has just read; a line that begins with '`####`' states an indirect consequence of that direct result, if some previously dependent variable has now become known.

 It's interesting to continue the computer experiment just begun by typing the following lines, one at a time, and watching what happens:

    a'+b'+.5c'=3;
    a'-b'-.5c'=1;
    g0=g1=g2=g3=g4;
    showdependencies;
    g0+g1=1;
    z1-z4=z2-z5=z3-z6;
    z2-z1=z3-z2=z5-z4=z6-z5;
    z4=origin;
    z3=(w,h);
    x1=0;
    y6=0;
    w=2h=100;
    end.

Notice that on the sixth line ('$z_1 - z_4 = \cdots$') METAFONT reports four equations, but on the next line ('$z_2 - z_1 = \cdots$') it reports only two. This happens because most of that line is redundant, as we have already observed.

 This computer session indicates that METAFONT deals with two kinds of unknown numeric variables: *dependent* variables and *independent* ones. Every variable is independent at the beginning of its life, but every equation causes one of the independent variables to become dependent or known. Each '`##`' line emitted by *tracingequations* shows a newly dependent-or-known variable, together with an equivalent expression that involves only independent variables. For example, the line '`## c=-0.5b-0.5a+1.5`' means that variable c has just become dependent and that it equals $-\frac{1}{2}b - \frac{1}{2}a + 1.5$, where variables b and a are independent. Similarly, '`## a=2`' means that a has just changed from independent to known. When an independent variable v changes to dependent or known, the equivalents of all dependent variables are updated so that they no longer depend on v; in this updating process some or all of them may change from dependent to known, whereupon a '`####`' line will be printed.

When METAFONT reads a numeric equation it replaces all known variables by their numeric values and all dependent variables by their equivalents. The resulting equation can be converted into the form

$$c_1 v_1 + \cdots + c_m v_m = \alpha$$

where the c's are nonzero constants and the v's are independent variables; α is a numeric constant that might be zero. If some c_k is so small that it probably would have been zero in a calculation free of rounding errors, it is replaced by zero and the corresponding v_k is removed from the equation. Now if $m = 0$, the equation is considered to be either *redundant* (if α is zero or extremely small) or *inconsistent* (otherwise). But if $m > 0$, METAFONT chooses an independent variable v_k for which c_k is maximum, and rewrites the equation in the form

$$\text{\#\#} \ v_k = (\alpha - c_1 v_1 - \cdots - c_{k-1} v_{k-1} - c_{k+1} v_{k+1} - \cdots - c_m v_m)/c_k.$$

Variable v_k becomes dependent (if $m > 1$) or known (if $m = 1$).

Inconsistent equations are equations that have no solutions. For example, if you say '$0 = 1$', METAFONT will issue an error message saying that the equation is "off by 1." A less blatant inconsistency arises if you say, e.g, '$a = b + 1$; $b = c + 1$; $c = a + 1$'; this last equation is off by three, for the former equations imply that $c = b - 1 = a - 2$. The computer will simply ignore an inconsistent equation when you resume processing after such an error.

Redundant equations are equations that say nothing new. For example, '$0 = 0$' is redundant, and so is '$a = b + c$' if you have previously said that $c = a - b$. METAFONT stops with an error message if you give it a redundant equation between two numeric expressions, because this usually indicates an oversight in the program. However, no error is reported when an equation between pairs leads to one or two redundant equations between numerics. For example, the equation '$z_3 = (0, h)$' will not trigger an error message when the program has previously established that $x_3 = 0$ or that $y_3 = h$ or both.

Sometimes you might have to work a little bit to put an equation into a form that METAFONT can handle. For example, you can't say

$$x/y = 2$$

when y is independent or dependent, because METAFONT allows division only by known quantities. The alternative

$$x = 2y$$

says the same thing and causes the computer no difficulties; furthermore it is a correct equation even when $y = 0$.

METAFONT's ability to remember previous equations is limited to "linear" dependencies as explained above. A mathematician might want to introduce the condition $x \geq 0$ by giving an equation such as '$x = \text{abs}\, x$'; but METAFONT is incapable of dealing with such a constraint. Similarly, METAFONT can't cope with an equation like '$x = \text{floor } x$', which states that x is an integer. Systems of equations that involve the absolute value and/or floor operation can be extremely difficult to solve, and METAFONT doesn't pretend to be a mathematical genius.

The rules given earlier explain how an independent variable can become dependent or known; conversely, it's possible for a dependent variable to become independent again, in unusual circumstances. For example, suppose that the equation $a + b + 2c = 3$ in our example above had been followed by the equation $d = b + c + a/4$. Then there would be two dependent variables,

```
## c=-0.5b-0.5a+1.5
## d=0.5b-0.25a+1.5
```

Now suppose that the next statement is '`numeric a`', meaning that the old value of variable a should be discarded. METAFONT can't simply delete an independent variable that has things depending on it, so it chooses a dependent variable to take a's place; the computer prints out

```
### 0.5a=-0.5b-c+1.5
```

meaning that $0.5a$ will be replaced by $-c - \frac{1}{2}b + \frac{3}{2}$ in all dependencies, before a is discarded. Variable c is now independent again; '**showdependencies**' will reveal that the only dependent variable is now d, which equals $0.75b + 0.5c + 0.75$. (This is correct, for if the variable a is eliminated from the two given equations we obtain $4d = 3b + 2c + 3$.) The variable chosen for independence is one that has the greatest coefficient of dependency with respect to the variable that will disappear.

A designer often wants to stipulate that a certain point lies on a certain line. This can be done easily by using a special feature of plain METAFONT called '*whatever*', which stands for an anonymous numeric variable that has a different unknown value each time you use it. For example,

$$z_1 = \textit{whatever}[z_2, z_3]$$

states that point 1 appears somewhere on the straight line that passes through points 2 and 3. (The expression $t[z_2, z_3]$ represents that entire straight line, as t runs through all values from $-\infty$ to $+\infty$. We want z_1 to be equal to $t[z_2, z_3]$ for some value of t, but we don't care what value it is.) The expression '*whatever*$[z_2, z_3]$' is legal whenever the difference $z_2 - z_3$ is known; it's usually used only when z_2 and z_3 are both known, i.e., when both points have been determined by prior equations.

Here are a few more examples of equations that involve '*whatever*', together with their translations into English. These equations are more fun than the "tame" ones we considered at the beginning of this chapter, because they show off more of the computer's amazing ability to deduce explicit values from implicit statements.

Equation	*Translation*
$z_5 - z_4 = \textit{whatever} * \text{dir } 30$	The angle between points 4 and 5 will be $30°$ above the horizon. (This equation can also be written '$z_4 = z_5 + \textit{whatever} * \text{dir } 30$', which states that point 4 is obtained by starting at

point 5 and moving by some unspecified multiple of dir 30.)

$z_7 - z_6 = whatever * (z_3 - z_2)$ — The line from point 6 to point 7 should be parallel to the line from point 2 to point 3.

$penpos_8(whatever, 60)$ — The simulated pen angle at point 8 should be 60 degrees; the breadth of the pen is unspecified, so it will be determined by other equations.

▶ **EXERCISE 9.4**
If z_1, z_2, z_3, and z_4 are known points, how can you tell METAFONT to compute the point z that lies on the intersection of the lines $z_1 .. z_2$ and $z_3 .. z_4$?

▶ **EXERCISE 9.5**
Given five points z_1, z_2, z_3, z_4, and z_5, explain how to compute z on the line $z_1 .. z_2$ such that the line $z .. z_3$ is parallel to the line $z_4 .. z_5$.

▶ **EXERCISE 9.6**
What METAFONT equation says that the line between points 11 and 12 is *perpendicular* to the line between points 13 and 14?

▶ **EXERCISE 9.7**
(For mathematicians.)   Given three points z_1, z_2, and z_3, explain how to compute the distance from z_1 to the straight line through z_2 and z_3.

▶ **EXERCISE 9.8**
(For mathematicians.)   Given three points z_1, z_2, z_3, and a length l, explain how to compute the two points on the line $z_2 .. z_3$ that are at distance l from z_1. (Assume that l is greater than the distance from z_1 to the line.)

▶ **EXERCISE 9.9**
The applications of *whatever* that we have seen so far have been in equations between *pairs* of numeric values, not in equations between simple numerics. Explain why an equation like '$a + 2b = whatever$' would be useless.

All of the equations so far in this chapter have been between numeric expressions or pair expressions. But METAFONT actually allows equations between any of the eight types of quantities. For example, you can write

```
s1="go"; s1&s1=s2
```

if s_1 and s_2 are string variables; this makes $s_1 =$ "go" and $s_2 =$ "gogo". Moreover, the subsequent equations

```
s3=s4; s5=s6; s3=s5; s4=s1&"sh"
```

will make it possible for the machine to deduce that $s_6 =$ "gosh".

But nonnumeric equations are not as versatile as numeric ones, because METAFONT does not perform operations on unknown quantities of other types. For example, the equation

```
"h"&s7="heck"
```

cannot be used to define $s_7 = $ "eck", because the concatenation operator **&** works only with strings that are already known.

After the declaration 'string s[]' and the equations 's1=s2=s3', the statement 'show s0' will produce the result 'unknown string s0'; but 'show s1' will produce 'unknown string s2'. Similarly, 'show s2' and 'show s3' will produce 'unknown string s3' and 'unknown string s1', respectively. In general, when several nonnumeric variables have been equated, they will point to each other in some cyclic order.

Let "X" equal my father's signature.
— FRED ALLEN, *Vogues* (1924)

ALL ANIMALS ARE EQUAL
BUT SOME ANIMALS ARE MORE EQUAL THAN OTHERS
— GEORGE ORWELL, *Animal Farm* (1945)

10

Assignments

Variables usually get values by appearing in equations, as described in the preceding chapter. But there's also another way, in which ':=' is used instead of '='. For example, the `io.mf` program in Chapter 5 said

```
stem# := trial_stem * pt#
```

when it wanted to define the value of `stem#`.

The colon-equal operator ':=' means "discard the previous value of the variable and assign a new one"; we call this an *assignment* operation. It was convenient for `io.mf` to define `stem#` with an assignment instead of an equation, because `stem#` was getting several different values within a single font. The alternative would have been to say

```
numeric stem#; stem# = trial_stem * pt#
```

(thereby specifically undefining the previous value of `stem#` before using it in an equation); this is more cumbersome.

The variable at the left of ':=' might appear also in the expression on the right. For example,

```
code := code + 1
```

means "increase the value of *code* by 1." This assignment would make no sense as an equation, since '*code* = *code* + 1' is inconsistent. The former value of *code* is still relevant on the right-hand side when '*code* + 1' is evaluated in this example, because old values are not discarded until the last minute; they are retained until just before a new assignment is made.

▶ **EXERCISE 10.1**
Is it possible to achieve the effect of '*code* := *code* + 1' by using equations and **numeric** declarations but not assignments?

Assignments are permitted only when the quantity at the left of the ':=' is a variable. For example, you can't say '`code+1:=code`'. More significantly, things like '`(x,y):=(0,0)`' are not permitted, although you can say '`w:=(0,0)`' if w has been declared to be a variable of type **pair**. This means that a statement like '`z1:=z2`' is illegal, because it's an abbreviation for the inadmissible construction '`(x1,y1):=(x2,y2)`'; we must remember that `z1` is not really a variable, it's a pair of variables.

The restriction in the previous paragraph is not terribly significant, because assignments play a relatively minor rôle in METAFONT programs. The best programming strategy is usually to specify equations instead of assignments, because equations indicate the relationships between variables in a declarative manner. A person who makes too many assignments is still locked into the habits of old-style "imperative" programming languages in which it is necessary to tell the computer exactly how to do everything; METAFONT's equation mechanism liberates us from that more complicated style of programming, because it lets the computer take over the job of solving equations.

The use of assignments often imposes a definite order on the statements of a program, because the value of a variable is different before and after an assignment takes place. Equations are simpler than assignments because they can usually be written down in any order that comes naturally to you.

Assignments do have their uses; otherwise METAFONT wouldn't bother with ':=' at all. But experienced METAFONT programmers introduce assignments sparingly—only when there's a good reason for doing so—because equations are generally easier to write and more enlightening to read.

METAFONT's internal quantities like *tracingequations* always have known numeric values, so there's no way to change them except by giving assignments. The computer experiment in Chapter 9 began with

    \tracingequations:=tracingonline:=1;

this illustrates the fact that multiple assignments are possible, just like multiple equations. Here is the complete syntax for equations and assignments:

⟨equation⟩ ⟶ ⟨expression⟩ = ⟨right-hand side⟩
⟨assignment⟩ ⟶ ⟨variable⟩ := ⟨right-hand side⟩
⟨right-hand side⟩ ⟶ ⟨expression⟩ | ⟨equation⟩ | ⟨assignment⟩

Notice that the syntax permits mixtures like '$a + b = c := d + e$'; this is the same as the assignment '$c := d + e$' and the equation '$a + b = c$'.

In a mixed equation/assignment like '$a + b = b := b + 1$', the old value of b is used to evaluate the expressions. For example, if b equals 3 before that statement, the result will be the same as '$a + 3 = b := 3 + 1$'; therefore b will be set to 4 and a will be set to 1.

▶ **EXERCISE 10.2**
Suppose that you want variable x_3 to become "like new," completely independent of any value that it formerly had; but you don't want to destroy the values of x_1 and x_2. You can't say '**numeric** $x[\,]$', because that would obliterate all the x_k's. What can you do instead?

▶ **EXERCISE 10.3**
Apply METAFONT to the short program

string $s[\,]$; $s_1 = s_2 = s_3 = s_4$; $s_5 = s_6$; $s_2 := s_5$; **showvariable** s;

and explain the results you get.

If other variables depend on v when v is assigned a new value, the other variables do not change to reflect the new assignment; they still act as if they depended on the previous (unknown) value of v. For example, if the equations '$2u = 3v = w$' are followed by the assignment '$w := 6$', the values of u and v won't become known, but METAFONT will still remember the fact that $v = .66667u$. (This is not a new rule; it's a consequence of the rules already stated. When an independent variable is discarded, a dependent variable may become independent in its place, as described in Chapter 9.)

▶ **EXERCISE 10.4**
Apply METAFONT to the program

$$tracingequations := tracingonline := 1;$$
$$a = 1; \quad a := a + b; \quad a := a + b; \quad a := a + b;$$
show $a, b;$

and explain the results you get.

At first his assignment had pleased,
but as hour after hour passed
with growing weariness,
he chafed more and more.

— C. E. MULFORD, *Hopalong Cassidy* (1910)

⟨*left part*⟩ ::= ⟨*variable*⟩ :=
⟨*left part list*⟩ ::= ⟨*left part*⟩ | ⟨*left part list*⟩⟨*left part*⟩
⟨*assignment statement*⟩ ::= ⟨*left part list*⟩⟨*arithmetic expression*⟩ |
⟨*left part list*⟩⟨*Boolean expression*⟩

— PETER NAUR et al., *Report on the Algorithmic language ALGOL 60* (1960)

11

Magnification and Resolution

A single METAFONT program can produce fonts of type for many different kinds of printing equipment, if the programmer has set things up so that the resolution can be varied. The "plain METAFONT" base file described in Appendix B establishes a set of conventions that make such variability quite simple; the purpose of the present chapter is to explain those conventions.

For concreteness let's assume that our computer has two output devices. One of them, called *cheapo*, has a resolution of 200 pixels per inch (approximately 8 per millimeter); the other, called *luxo*, has a resolution of 2000 pixels per inch. We would like to write METAFONT programs that are able to produce fonts for both devices. For example, if the file `newface.mf` contains a program for a new typeface, we'd like to generate a low-resolution font by invoking METAFONT with

> \mode=cheapo; input newface

and the same file should also produce a high-resolution font if we start with

> \mode=luxo; input newface

instead. Other people with different printing equipment should also be able to use `newface.mf` with their own favorite *mode* values.

The way to do this with plain METAFONT is to call **mode_setup** near the beginning of `newface.mf`; this routine establishes the values of variables like *pt* and *mm*, which represent the respective numbers of pixels in a point and a millimeter. For example, when *mode* = *cheapo*, the values will be $pt = 2.7674$ and $mm = 7.87402$; when *mode* = *luxo*, they will be $pt = 27.674$ and $mm = 78.74017$. The `newface.mf` program should be written in terms of such variables, so that the pixel patterns for characters will be about 10 times narrower and 10 times shorter in *cheapo* mode than they are in *luxo* mode. For example, a line that's drawn from $(0,0)$ to $(3mm, 0)$ will produce a line that's about 23.6 pixels long in *cheapo* mode, and about 236.2 pixels long in *luxo* mode; the former line will appear to be 3 mm long when printed by *cheapo*, while the latter will look 3 mm long when printed by *luxo*.

A further complication occurs when a typeface is being magnified; in such cases the font does not correspond to its normal size. For example, we might want to have a set of fonts for *cheapo* that are twice as big as usual, so that users can make transparencies for overhead projectors. (Such output could also be reduced to 50% of its size as printed, on suitable reproduction equipment, thereby increasing the effective resolution from 200 to 400.) TeX allows entire jobs to be magnified by a factor of 2 if the user says '\magnification=2000'; individual fonts can also be magnified in a TeX job by saying, e.g., '\font\f=newface scaled 2000'. The standard way to produce a font with two-fold magnification using the conventions of plain METAFONT is to say, e.g.,

> \mode=cheapo; mag=2; input newface;

this will make $pt = 5.5348$ and $mm = 15.74803$.

The **mode_setup** routine looks to see if *mag* has a known value; if not, it sets *mag* = 1. Similarly, if *mode* is unknown, **mode_setup** sets *mode* = *proof*.

Plain METAFONT also computes the values of several other dimension-oriented values in addition to *pt* and *mm*, corresponding to the dimensions that are understood by TEX. Here is the complete list:

pt	printer's point	($72.27\,\text{pt} = 1\,\text{in}$)
pc	pica	($1\,\text{pc} = 12\,\text{pt}$)
in	inch	($1\,\text{in} = 2.54\,\text{cm}$)
bp	big point	($72\,\text{bp} = 1\,\text{in}$)
cm	centimeter	($100\,\text{cm} = 1\,\text{meter}$)
mm	millimeter	($10\,\text{mm} = 1\,\text{cm}$)
dd	didot point	($1157\,\text{dd} = 1238\,\text{pt}$)
cc	cicero	($1\,\text{cc} = 12\,\text{dd}$)

In each case the values are rounded to the nearest $\frac{1}{65536}$th of a pixel.

Although such standard physical dimensions are available, they haven't been used very much in traditional typefaces; designers usually specify other units like '*em*' or '*x_height*' in order to define the sizes of letters, and such quantities generally have ad hoc values that vary from font to font. Plain META-FONT makes it easy to introduce ad hoc dimensions that will vary with the resolution and the magnification just as *pt* and *mm* do; all you have to do is define "sharped" dimensions that have the same name as your pixel-oriented dimensions, but with '#' tacked on as a suffix. For example, $em^{\#}$ and $x\_height^{\#}$ (typed '`em#`' and '`x_height#`') would be the sharped dimensions corresponding to *em* and *x_height*. Plain METAFONT has already defined the quantities $pt^{\#}$, $pc^{\#}$, $in^{\#}$, $bp^{\#}$, $cm^{\#}$, $mm^{\#}$, $dd^{\#}$, and $cc^{\#}$ for the standard units named above.

Sharped dimensions like $em^{\#}$ and $x\_height^{\#}$ should always be defined in terms of resolution-independent dimension variables like $pt^{\#}$, $in^{\#}$, etc., so that their values do not change in any way when *mode* and *mag* are varied. The '#' sign implies unchangeability. After **mode_setup** has been called, the pixel-oriented dimensions can be calculated by simply saying

define_pixels(*em*, *x_height*).

This statement is an abbreviation for

$$em := em^{\#} * hppp; \qquad x\_height := x\_height^{\#} * hppp$$

where *hppp* is an internal variable of METAFONT that represents the number of pixels per point in the horizontal dimension. Any number of ad hoc dimensions can be listed in a single **define_pixels** statement. Notice that '#' is not an operator that could convert *em* to $em^{\#}$; rounding errors would be mode-dependent.

Chapter 5's demonstration program `io.mf` contains several examples of ad hoc dimensions defined in this way, and it also contains the statement

define_blacker_pixels(*thin*, *thick*);

what's this? Well, Appendix B makes that statement an abbreviation for

$$thin := thin\# * hppp + blacker; \qquad thick := thick\# * hppp + blacker;$$

in other words, the sharped dimensions are being unsharped in this case by converting them to pixels and then adding '*blacker*'. The variable *blacker* is a special correction intended to help adapt a font to the idiosyncrasies of the current output device; **mode_setup** uses the value of *mode* to establish the value of *blacker*. For example, *cheapo* mode might want *blacker* = 0.65, while *luxo* mode might give best results when *blacker* = 0.1. The general convention is to add *blacker* to pixel-oriented variables that determine the breadth of pens and the thickness of stems, so that the letters will be slightly darker on machines that otherwise would make them appear too light. Different machines treat pixels quite differently, because they are often based on quite different physical principles. For example, the author once worked with an extremely high-resolution device that tended to shrink stem lines rather drastically when it used a certain type of photographic paper, and it was necessary to set *blacker* = 4 to get proper results on that machine; another high-resolution device seems to want *blacker* to be only 0.2. Experimentation is necessary to tune METAFONT's output to particular devices, but the author's experience suggests strongly that such a correction is worthwhile. When *mode* = *proof* or *smoke*, the value of *blacker* is taken to be zero, since the output in these modes is presumably undistorted.

▶ **EXERCISE 11.1**
Does '*mode* = *cheapo*; *mag* = 10' produce exactly the same font as '*mode* = *luxo*', under the assumptions of this chapter?

Line 7 of **io.mf** says '**define_corrected_pixels**(*o*)', and this is yet a third way of converting from true physical dimensions to pixel-oriented values. According to Appendix B, variable *o* is defined by the assignment

$$o := \text{round}(o\# * hppp * o\_correction) + eps$$

where *o_correction*, like *blacker*, is a magic number that depends on the output device for which fonts are being made. On a high-resolution device like *luxo*, the appropriate value for the *o_correction* factor is 1; but on a low-resolution device like *cheapo*, the author has obtained more satisfactory results with *o_correction* = 0.4. The reason is that '*o*' is used to specify the number of pixels by which certain features of characters "overshoot" the baseline or some other line to which they are visually related. High-resolution curves look better when they overshoot in this way, but low-resolution curves do not; therefore it is usually wise to curtail the amount of overshoot by applying the *o_correction* factor. In *proof* and *smoke* modes the factor is equal to 1.0, since these modes correspond to high resolution.

The properties of output devices are modeled also by a parameter that's called *fillin*, which represents the amount by which diagonal strokes tend to be darker than horizontal or vertical strokes. More precisely, let us say that a "corner" pixel is one whose color matches the color of five of its neighbors but not the other three, where the three exceptions include one horizontal neighbor, one vertical neighbor, and the diagonal neighbor between them. If a white corner pixel has apparent darkness f_1 and if a black corner pixel has apparent darkness $1 - f_2$, then the *fillin* is $f_1 - f_2$. (A "true" raster image would have $f_1 = f_2 = 0$, but physical properties often cause pixels to influence their neighbors.)

Each output device for which you will be generating fonts should be represented by a symbolic *mode* name in the implementation of METAFONT that you are using. Since these mode names vary from place to place, they are not standard aspects of the METAFONT language; for example, it is doubtful whether the hypothetical *cheapo* and *luxo* modes discussed in this chapter actually exist anywhere. The plain METAFONT base is intended to be extended to additional modes in a disciplined way, as described at the end of Appendix B.

It's easy to create a new symbolic mode, using plain METAFONT's '**mode_def**' convention. For example, the *luxo* mode we have been talking about could be defined by saying

> **mode_def** *luxo* =
> > *pixels_per_inch* := 2000;   % high res, almost 30 per point
> > *blacker* := .1;   % make pens a teeny bit blacker
> > *o_correction* := 1;   % keep the full overshoot
> > *fillin* := 0.1;   % compensate for darkened corners
> > *proofing* := 0;   % no, we're not making proofs
> > *fontmaking* := 1;   % yes, we are making a font
> > *tracingtitles* := 1; **enddef**; % yes, show titles online

The name of the mode should be a single symbolic token. The resolution should be specified by assigning a value to *pixels_per_inch*; all other dimension values (*pt*, *mm*, etc.) will be computed from this one by **mode_setup**. A mode definition should also assign values to the internal variables *blacker*, *o_correction*, and *fillin* (which describe the device characteristics), as well as *proofing*, *fontmaking*, and *tracingtitles* (which affect the amount of output that will be produced). In general, *proofing* and *fontmaking* are usually set to 0 and 1, respectively, in modes that are intended for font production rather than initial font design; *tracingtitles* is usually 0 for low-resolution fonts (which are generated quickly), but 1 for high-resolution fonts (which go more slowly), because detailed online progress reports are desirable when comparatively long jobs are running.

Besides the seven mandatory quantities '*pixels_per_inch*', ..., '*tracingtitles*' just discussed, a mode definition might assign a value to '*aspect_ratio*'. In the normal case when no *aspect_ratio* is specified, it means that the fonts to be output are are assumed to have square pixels. But if, for example, the **mode_def** sets *aspect_ratio* := 5/4, it means that the output pixels are assumed to be nonsquare in the ratio of 5 to 4; i.e., 5 vertical pixel units are equal to 4 horizontal pixel units. The pixel-oriented dimensions of plain METAFONT are given in terms of horizontal pixel units, so an aspect ratio of 5/4 together with 2000 pixels per inch would mean that there are 2500 vertical pixel units per inch; a square inch would consist of 2500 rows of pixels, with 2000 pixels in each row. (Stating this another way, each pixel would be $\frac{1}{2000}$ inches wide and $\frac{1}{2500}$ inches high.) In such a case, plain METAFONT will set the *currenttransform* variable so that all **draw** and **fill** commands stretch the curves by a factor of 5/4 in the vertical dimension; this compensates for the nonsquare pixels, so the typeface designer doesn't have to be aware of the fact that pixels aren't square.

Let's look now at a concrete example, so that it will be clear how the ideas of device-independent font design can be implemented in practice. We shall study a file `logo.mf` that generates the seven letters of METAFONT's logo. There also are "parameter" files `logo10.mf`, `logo9.mf`, etc., which use `logo.mf` to produce fonts in various sizes. For example, a font containing the 10-point characters 'METAFONT' could be generated for the hypothetical *luxo* printer by running METAFONT with the command line

```
\mode=luxo; input logo10
```

if *luxo* mode really existed.

The main purpose of `logo10.mf` is to establish the "sharped" values of several ad hoc dimensions; then it inputs `logo.mf`, which does the rest of the work. Here is the entire file `logo10.mf`:

```
% 10-point METAFONT logo
font_size 10pt#;       % the "design size" of this font
ht#:=6pt#;             % height of characters
xgap#:=0.6pt#;         % horizontal adjustment
u#:=4/9pt#;            % unit width
s#:=0;                 % extra space at the left and the right
o#:=1/9pt#;            % overshoot
px#:=2/3pt#;           % horizontal thickness of pen
input logo              % now generate the font
end                     % and stop.
```

Similar files `logo9.mf` and `logo8.mf` will produce 9-point 'METAFONT' and 8-point 'METAFONT'; the letters get a little wider in relation to their height, and the inter-character spacing gets significantly wider, as the size gets smaller:

```
% 9-point METAFONT logo        % 8-point METAFONT logo
font_size 9pt#;                font_size 8pt#;
ht#:=.9*6pt#;                  ht#:=.8*6pt#;
xgap#:=.9*0.6pt#;              xgap#:=.8*0.6pt#;
u#:=.91*4/9pt#;                u#:=.82*4/9pt#;
s#:=.08pt#;                    s#:=.2pt#;
o#:=1/10pt#;                   o#:=1/12pt#;
px#:=.9*2/3pt#;                px#:=.8*2/3pt#;
input logo                     input logo
end                            end
```

It is interesting to compare the font generated by `logo10.mf` to the font generated by `logo8.mf` with mag=10/8: Both fonts will have the same values of *ht*, *xgap*, and *px*, when the magnification has been taken into account. But the magnified 8-point font has a slightly larger value of *u* and a positive value of *s*; this changes 'METAFONT' to 'METAFONT'.

Every font has a "design size," which is a more-or-less arbitrary number that reflects the size of type it is intended to blend with. Users of TeX select magnified fonts in two ways, either by specifying an "at size" or by specifying a scale factor (times 1000). For example, the 8-point METAFONT logo can be used at 10/8 magnification by referring either to 'logo8 at 10pt' or to 'logo8 scaled 1250' in a TeX document. When an "at size" is specified, the amount of magnification is the stated size divided by the design size. A typeface designer can specify the design size by using plain METAFONT's '**font_size**' command as illustrated on the previous page. (If no design size is specified, METAFONT will set it to 128 pt, by default.)

The file `logo.mf` itself begins by defining three more ad hoc dimensions in terms of the parameters that were set by the parameter file; these dimensions will be used in several of the programs for individual letters. Then `logo.mf` makes the conversion to pixel units:

```
% Routines for the METAFONT logo
% (logo10.mf is a typical parameter file)
mode_setup;
ygap#:=(ht#/13.5u#)*xgap#;        % vertical adjustment
leftstemloc#:=2.5u#+s#;           % position of left stems
barheight#:=.45ht#;               % height of bar lines
define_pixels(s,u,xgap,ygap,leftstemloc,barheight);
py#:=.9px#; define_blacker_pixels(px,py); % pen dimensions
pickup pencircle xscaled px yscaled py; logo_pen:=savepen;
define_corrected_pixels(o);
```

There's nothing new here except the use of '*savepen*' in the second-last line; this, as we will see in Chapter 16, makes the currently-picked-up pen available for repeated use in the subsequent program.

After the initial definitions just shown, `logo.mf` continues with programs for each of the seven letters. For example, here is the program for 'E', which illustrates the use of $u^\#$, $s^\#$, $ht^\#$, *leftstemloc*, *barheight*, *xgap*, and *logo_pen*:

```
beginchar("E",14u#+2s#,ht#,0);
pickup logo_pen;
x1=x2=x3=leftstemloc;
x4=x6=w-x1+o; x5=x4-xgap;
y1=y6; y2=y5; y3=y4;
bot y1=0; top y3=h;
y2=barheight;
draw z6--z1--z3--z4; draw z2--z5;
labels(1,2,3,4,5,6);
endchar;
```

We have seen the essentials of the M and the T in Chapter 4; programs for the other letters will appear later.

▶**EXERCISE 11.2**
The ad hoc dimensions $ht\#$, $xgap\#$, $u\#$, $s\#$, $o\#$, and $px\#$ defined in the parameter files all affect the letter 'E' defined by this program. For each of these dimensions, tell what would happen to the 'E' if that dimension were increased slightly while all the others stayed the same.

 ▶**EXERCISE 11.3**
Guess the program for 'F' (which is almost the same as 'E').

 ▶**EXERCISE 11.4**
Write the complete programs for 'M' and 'T', based on the information in Chapter 4, but using the style of the program for 'E' above. The character widths should be $18u\# + 2s\#$ and $13u\# + 2s\#$, respectively.

 The file `logo.mf` also contains the following cryptic instructions, which cause the letter pairs 'TA' and 'FO' to be typeset closer together than their bounding boxes would imply:

```
ligtable "T": "A" kern -.5u#;
ligtable "F": "O" kern -u#;
```

Without these corrections 'METAFONT' would be 'METAFONT'. Uppercase letters are often subject to such spacing corrections, especially in logos; TeX will adjust the spacing if the typeface designer has supplied **ligtable** information like this.

 Finally, `logo.mf` closes with four more commands, which provide further information about how to typeset with this font:

```
font_quad    18u#+2s#;
font_normal_space   6u#+2s#;
font_normal_stretch   3u#;
font_normal_shrink   2u#;
```

A **font_quad** is the unit of measure that a TeX user calls one 'em' when this font is selected. The normal space, stretch, and shrink parameters define the interword spacing when text is being typeset in this font. Actually a font like `logo10` is rarely used to typeset anything except the one word, 'METAFONT'; but the spacing parameters have been included just in case somebody wants to typeset a sentence like 'AN EFFETE TOMATO OF MONTANA OFTEN ATE NONFAT TOFFEE'.

An optional '=' or ':=' sign may be typed after '**font_size**', '**font_quad**', etc., in case you think the file looks better that way.

Notice that "sharped" units must be given in the **ligtable** kerning commands and in the definition of device-independent parameters like **font_size** and **font_quad**. Appendix F discusses the complete rules of **ligtable** and other commands by which METAFONT programs can send important information to typesetting systems like TeX. Adding these extra bits of information to a METAFONT program after a font has been designed is something like adding an index to a book after that book has been written and proofread.

 ▶**EXERCISE 11.5**
What's the longest English word that can be typeset with the font `logo9`?

Let's summarize the general contents of `logo.mf`, now that we have seen it all, because it provides an example of a complete typeface description (even though there are only seven letters):

- The file begins by defining ad hoc dimensions and converting them to pixel units, using **mode_setup**, **define_pixels**, etc.

- Then come programs for individual letters. (These programs are often preceded by macro definitions for subroutines that occur several times. For example, we will see later that the 'A' and the 'O' of the logo are drawn with the help of a subroutine that makes half of a superellipse; the definition of this macro actually comes near the beginning of `logo.mf`, just before the programs for the letters.)

- Finally there are special commands like **ligtable** and **font_quad**, to define parameters of the font that are helpful when typesetting.

- The file is accompanied by parameter files that define ad hoc dimensions for different incarnations of the typeface.

We could make lots of different parameter files, which would produce lots of different (but related) variations on the METAFONT logo; thus, `logo.mf` defines a "meta-font" in the sense of Chapter 1.

▶ **EXERCISE 11.6**
What changes would be necessary to generalize the `logo` routines so that the bar-line height is not always 45 per cent of the character height?

Assignments (':=') have been used instead of equations ('=') in the parameter files `logo10.mf`, `logo9.mf`, and `logo8.mf`, as well as in the opening lines of `io.mf` in Chapter 5; this contradicts the advice in Chapter 10, where we are told to stick to equations unless assignments are absolutely necessary. The author has found it convenient to develop the habit of using assignments whenever ad hoc dimensions are being defined, because he often makes experimental files in which the ad hoc dimensions are changed several times. For example, it's a good idea to test a particular letter with respect to a variety of different parameter settings when that letter is first being designed; such experiments can be done easily by copying the ad hoc parameter definitions from parameter files into a test file, provided that the parameters have been defined with assignments instead of equations.

TEX users have found it convenient to have fonts in a series of magnifications that form a geometric series. A font is said to be scaled by 'magstep 1' if it has been magnified by 1.2; it is scaled by 'magstep 2' if it has been magnified by $1.2 \times 1.2 = 1.44$; it is scaled by 'magstep 3' if it has been magnified by $1.2 \times 1.2 \times 1.2 = 1.728$; and so on. Thus, if a job uses a font that is scaled by magstep 2, and if that entire job is magnified by magstep 1, the font actually used for printing will be scaled by magstep 3. The additive nature of magsteps makes it more likely that fonts will exist at the desired sizes when jobs are magnified. Plain METAFONT supports this convention by allowing constructions like

> `\mode=cheapo; mag=magstep 2; input logo9`

if you want to generate the 9-point METAFONT logo for the *cheapo* printer, magnified by 1.44 (i.e., by magstep 2). You can also write '`magstep 0.5`' for what TEX calls '`\magstephalf`'; this magnifies by $\sqrt{1.2}$.

The sharped forms of dimensions are actually represented by plain META-FONT in terms of printer's points, so that '$pt\#$' turns out to be equal to 1. However, it is best for programmers not to make use of this fact; a program ought to say, e.g., '$em\# := 10pt\#$', even though the '$pt\#$' in this construction is redundant, and even though the computer would run a few microseconds faster without it.

▶ **EXERCISE 11.7**
    Suppose you want to simulate a low-resolution printer on a high resolution device; for concreteness, let's say that *luxo* is supposed to produce the output of *cheapo*, with each black *cheapo* pixel replaced by a 10×10 square of black *luxo* pixels. Explain how to do this to the `logo10` font, by making appropriate changes to `logo.mf`. Your output file should be called `cheaplogo10.2000gf`.

A great Temptation must be withstood with great Resolution.
— WILLIAM BURKITT, *Expository Notes on the New Testament* (c. 1700)

What some invent, the rest enlarge.
— JONATHAN SWIFT, *Journal of a Modern Lady* (1729)

12

Boxes

Let's pause now to take a closer look at the "bounding boxes" that enclose individual characters. In olden days, metal type was cast on a rectangular body in which each piece of type had the same vertical extent, although the type widths would vary from character to character. Nowadays we are free of the mechanical constraints imposed by metal type, but the former metaphors are still useful: A typesetting system like TEX imagines that each character fits into a rectangular box, and words are typeset by putting such boxes snugly next to each other.

The main difference between the old conventions and the new ones is that type boxes are now allowed to vary in height as well as in width. For example, when TEX typesets 'A line of type.' it puts boxes together that essentially look like this: '☐ ▉▅▅ ▆▍ ▆▅▅▅'. (The 'A' appears in a box '☐' that sits on a given baseline, while the 'y' appears in a box '▯' that descends below the baseline.) TEX never looks inside a box to see what character actually appears there; TEX's job is to put boxes together in the right places on a page, based only on the box sizes. It is a typeface designer's job to decide how big the boxes should be and to create the characters inside the boxes.

Boxes are two-dimensional objects, but we ascribe three dimensions to them because the vertical component is divided into two quantities, the *height* (above the baseline) and the *depth* (below the baseline). The horizontal dimension is, of course, called the *width*. Here is a picture of a typical box, showing its so-called reference point and baseline:

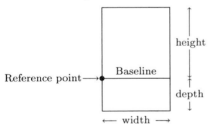

The example characters in previous chapters have all had zero depth, but we will soon be seeing examples in which both height and depth are relevant.

A character shape need not fit inside the boundaries of its box. Indeed, *italic* and *slanted* letters are put into ordinary boxes just as if they were not slanted, so they frequently stick out at the right. For example, the letter 'g' in the font you are now reading (cmr10) can be compared with the 'g' in the corresponding slanted font (cmsl10):

The slanted 'g' has been drawn as if its box were skewed right at the top and left at the bottom, keeping the baseline fixed; but TEX is told in both cases that the box is 5 pt wide, 4.3055 pt high, and 1.9444 pt deep. Slanted letters will be spaced properly in spite of the fact that their boxes have been straightened up, because the letters will match correctly at the baseline.

▷ Boxes also have a fourth dimension called the *italic correction*, which gives TEX additional information about whether or not a letter protrudes at the right. For example, the italic correction for an unslanted 'g' in `cmr10` is 0.1389 pt, while the corresponding slanted letter in `cmsl10` has an italic correction of 0.8565 pt. The italic correction is added to a box's width when math formulas like g^2 or g^2 are being typeset, and also in other cases as explained in *The TEXbook*.

Plain METAFONT's **beginchar** command establishes the width, height, and depth of a box. These dimensions should be given in terms of "sharped" quantities that do not vary with the resolution or magnification, because the size of a character's type box should not depend in any way on the device that will be used to output that character. It is important to be able to define documents that will not change even though the technology for printing those documents is continually evolving. METAFONT can be used to produce fonts for new devices by introducing new "modes," as we have seen in Chapter 11, but the new fonts should still give the same box dimensions to each character. Then the device-independent files output by TEX will not have to be changed in any way when they are printed or displayed with the help of new equipment.

The three dimensions in a **beginchar** command are given in reverse alphabetical order: First comes the width, then the height, then the depth. The **beginchar** routine converts these quantities into pixel units and assigns them to the three variables w, h, and d. In fact, **beginchar** rounds these dimensions to the nearest whole number of pixels; hence w, h, and d will always be integers.

METAFONT's pixels are like squares on graph paper, with pixel boundaries at points with integer coordinates. The left edge of the type box lies on the line $x = 0$, and the right edge lies on the line $x = w$; we have $y = h$ on the top edge and $y = -d$ on the bottom edge. There are w pixels in each row and $h + d$ in each column, so there are exactly $wh + wd$ pixels inside the type box.

Since w, h, and d are integers, they probably do not exactly match the box dimensions that are assumed by device-independent typesetting systems like TEX. Some characters will be a fraction of a pixel too wide; others will be a fraction of a pixel too narrow. However, it's still possible to obtain satisfactory results if the pixel boxes are stacked together based on their w values and if the accumulated error is removed in the spaces between words, provided that the box positions do not drift too far away from their true device-independent locations. A designer should strive to obtain letterforms that work well together when they are placed together in boxes that are an integer number of pixels wide.

▷▷ You might not like the value of w that **beginchar** computes by rounding the device-independent width to the nearest pixel boundary. For example, you might want to make the letter 'm' one pixel wider, at certain resolutions, so that its three stems are equally spaced or so that it will go better with your 'n'. In such a case you can assign a new value to w, at any time between **beginchar** and **endchar**. This new value will not affect the device-independent box width assumed by TeX, but it should be respected by the software that typesets `dvi` files using your font.

Here's an example of a character that has nonzero width, height, and depth; it's the left parenthesis in Computer Modern fonts like `cmr10`. Computer Modern typefaces are generated by METAFONT programs that involve lots of parameters, so this example also illustrates the principles of "meta-design": Many different varieties of left parentheses can be drawn by this one program. But let's focus our attention first on the comparatively simple way in which the box dimensions are established and used, before looking into the details of how a meta-parenthesis has actually been specified.

"Left parenthesis";
numeric $ht\#$, $dp\#$;
$ht\# = body\_height$; $.5[ht\#, -dp\#] = axis\#$;
beginchar($"("$, $7u\#$, $ht\#$, $dp\#$);
italcorr $ht\# * slant - .5u\#$;
pickup $fine.nib$;
$penpos_1(hair - fine, 0)$;
$penpos_2(.75[thin, thick] - fine, 0)$;
$penpos_3(hair - fine, 0)$;
$rt\ x_{1r} = rt\ x_{3r} = w - u$; $lft\ x_{2l} = x_1 - 4u$;
$top\ y_1 = h$; $y_2 = .5[y_1, y_3] = axis$;
filldraw $z_{1l}\{(z_{2l} - z_{1l})\ \text{xscaled}\ 3\} \ldots z_{2l}$
   $\ldots \{(z_{3l} - z_{2l})\ \text{xscaled}\ 3\} z_{3l}$
   $-- z_{3r}\{(z_{2r} - z_{3r})\ \text{xscaled}\ 3\} \ldots z_{2r}$
   $\ldots \{(z_{1r} - z_{2r})\ \text{xscaled}\ 3\} z_{1r} -- \text{cycle}$;
penlabels$(1, 2, 3)$; **endchar**;

The width of this left parenthesis is $7u\#$, where $u\#$ is an ad hoc parameter that figures in all the widths of the Computer Modern characters. The height and depth have been calculated in such a way that the top and bottom of the bounding box are equally distant from an imaginary line called the *axis*, which is important in mathematical typesetting. (For example, TeX puts the bar line at the axis in fractions like $\frac{1}{2}$; many symbols like '+' and '=', as well as parentheses, are centered on the axis line.) Our example program puts the axis midway between the top and bottom of the type by saying that '$.5[ht\#, -dp\#] = axis\#$'. We also place the top at position '$ht\# = body\_height\#$'; here $body\_height\#$ is the height of the tallest characters in the entire typeface. It turns out that $body\_height\#$ is exactly $7.5pt\#$ in `cmr10`, and $axis\# = 2.5pt\#$; hence $dp\# = 2.5pt\#$, and the parenthesis is exactly $10\,pt$ tall.

The program for '(' uses a **filldraw** command, which we haven't seen before in this book; it's basically a combination of **fill** and **draw**, where the filling is done with the currently-picked-up pen. Some of the Computer Modern fonts have characters with "soft" edges while others have "crisp" edges; the difference is due to the pen that is used to **filldraw** the shapes. This pen is a circle whose diameter is called *fine*; when *fine* is fairly large, **filldraw** will produce rounded corners, but when *fine* = 0 (as it is in cmr10) the corners will be sharp.

The statement '*penpos*$_1$(*hair* − *fine*, 0)' makes the breadth of a simulated broad-edge pen equal to *hair* − *fine* at position 1; i.e., the distance between z_{1l} and z_{1r} will be *hair* − *fine*. We will be filling a region between z_{1l} and z_{1r} with a circle-shaped pen nib whose diameter is *fine*; the center of that nib will pass through z_{1l} and z_{1r}, hence the pen will effectively add $\frac{1}{2}$*fine* to the breadth of the stroke at either side. The overall breadth at position 1 will therefore be $\frac{1}{2}$*fine* + (*hair* − *fine*) + $\frac{1}{2}$*fine* = *hair*. (Computer Modern's "hairline thickness" parameter, which governs the breadth of the thinnest strokes, is called *hair*.) Similarly, the statement '*penpos*$_2$(.75[*thin*, *thick*] − *fine*, 0)' makes the overall breadth of the pen at position 2 equal to .75[*thin*, *thick*], which is $\frac{3}{4}$ of the way between two other parameters that govern stroke breadths in Computer Modern routines. If *fine* is increased while *hair*, *thin*, and *thick* stay the same, the effect will simply be to produce more rounded corners at positions 1 and 3, with little or no effect on the rest of the shape, provided that *fine* doesn't get so large that it exceeds *hair*.

Here, for example, are five different left parentheses, drawn by our example program with various settings of the parameters:

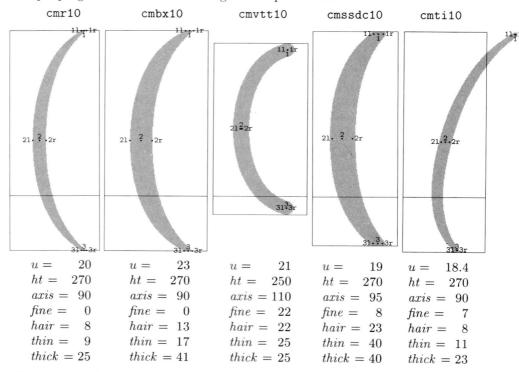

cmr10	cmbx10	cmvtt10	cmssdc10	cmti10
$u =$ 20	$u =$ 23	$u =$ 21	$u =$ 19	$u =$ 18.4
$ht =$ 270	$ht =$ 270	$ht =$ 250	$ht =$ 270	$ht =$ 270
$axis =$ 90	$axis =$ 90	$axis =$ 110	$axis =$ 95	$axis =$ 90
$fine =$ 0	$fine =$ 0	$fine =$ 22	$fine =$ 8	$fine =$ 7
$hair =$ 8	$hair =$ 13	$hair =$ 22	$hair =$ 23	$hair =$ 8
$thin =$ 9	$thin =$ 17	$thin =$ 25	$thin =$ 40	$thin =$ 11
$thick =$ 25	$thick =$ 41	$thick =$ 25	$thick =$ 40	$thick =$ 23

Parameter values are shown here in *proof* mode pixel units, 36 to the point.

(Thus, for example, the value of $u^\#$ in `cmr10` is $\frac{20}{36}pt^\#$.) Since `cmbx10` is a "bold extended" font, its unit width u is slightly larger than the unit width of `cmr10`, and its pen widths (especially *thick*) are significantly larger. The "variable-width typewriter" font `cmvtt10` has soft edges and strokes of almost uniform thickness, because *fine* and *hair* are almost as large as *thin* and *thick*. This font also has a raised axis and a smaller height. An intermediate situation occurs in `cmssdc10`, a "sans serif demibold condensed" font that is similar to the type used in the chapter titles of this book; *thick* = *thin* in this font, but hairlines are noticeably thinner, and *fine* provides slightly rounded corners. The "text italic" font `cmti10` has rounded ends, and the character shape has been slanted by .25; this means that each point (x, y) has been moved to position $(x + .25y, y)$, in the path that is filled by **filldraw**.

 The vertical line just of the right of the italic left parenthesis shows the italic correction of that character, i.e., the fourth box dimension mentioned earlier. This quantity was defined by the statement '**italcorr** $ht^\# * slant - .5u^\#$' in our program; here *slant* is a parameter of Computer Modern that is zero in all the unslanted fonts, but *slant* = .25 in the case of `cmti10`. The expression following **italcorr** should always be given in sharped units. If the value is negative, the italic correction will be zero; otherwise the italic correction will be the stated amount.

The author has obtained satisfactory results by making the italic correction roughly equal to .5u plus the maximum amount by which the character sticks out to the right of its box. For example, the top right end of the left parenthesis will be nearly at position $(w - u, ht)$ before slanting, so its x coordinate after slanting will be $w - u + ht * slant$; this will be the rightmost point of the character, if we assume that $slant \geq 0$. Adding .5u, subtracting w, and rewriting in terms of sharped units gives the stated formula. Notice that when $slant = 0$ the statement reduces to '**italcorr** $-.5u^\#$'; this means that unslanted left parentheses will have an italic correction of zero.

▶**EXERCISE 12.1**
Write a program for right parentheses, to go with these left parentheses.

The reader should bear in mind that the conventions of plain METAFONT and of Computer Modern are not hardwired into the METAFONT language; they are merely examples of how a person might use the system, and other typefaces may well be better served by quite different approaches. Our program for left parentheses makes use of **beginchar**, **endchar**, **italcorr**, **penlabels**, **pickup**, *penpos*, *lft*, *rt*, *top*, *z*, and **filldraw**, all of which are defined somewhat arbitrarily in Appendix B as part of the plain base; it also uses the quantities u, *body_height*, *axis*, *fine*, *hair*, *thin*, *thick*, and *slant*, all of which are arbitrary parameters that the author decided to introduce in his programs for Computer Modern. Once you understand how to use arbitrary conventions like these, you will be able to modify them to suit your own purposes.

▶**EXERCISE 12.2**
(For people who know TEX.) It's fairly clear that the width of a type box is important for typesetting, but what use does TEX make of the height and depth?

The primitive commands by which METAFONT actually learns the dimensions of each box are rarely used directly, since they are intended to be embedded in higher-level commands like **beginchar** and **italcorr**. But if you must know how things are done at the low level, here is the secret: There are four internal quantities called *charwd*, *charht*, *chardp*, and *charic*, whose values at the time of every **shipout** command are assumed to be the box dimensions for the character being shipped out, in units of printer's points. (See the definitions of **beginchar** and **italcorr** in Appendix B for examples of how these quantities can be manipulated.)

Besides *charwd* and its cousins, METAFONT also has four other internal variables whose values are recorded at the time of every **shipout**:

- *charcode* is rounded to the nearest integer and then converted to a number between 0 and 255, by adding or subtracting multiples of 256 if necessary; this "*c* code" is the location of the character within its font.

- *charext* is rounded to the nearest integer; the resulting number is a secondary code that can be used to distinguish between two or more characters with equal *c* codes. (TEX ignores *charext* and assumes that each font contains at most 256 characters; but extensions to TEX for oriental languages can use *charext* to handle much larger fonts.)

- *chardx* and *chardy* represent horizontal and vertical *escapement* in units of pixels. (Some typesetting systems use both of these device-dependent amounts to change their current position on a page, just after typesetting each character. Other systems, like the dvi software associated with TEX, assume that *chardy* = 0 but use *chardx* as the horizontal escapement whenever a horizontal movement by *chardx* does not cause the subsequent position to drift too far from the device-independent position defined by accumulated *charwd* values. Plain METAFONT's **endchar** routine keeps *chardy* = 0, but sets *chardx* := *w* just before shipping a character to the output. This explains why a change to *w* will affect the spacing between adjacent letters, as discussed earlier.)

Two characters with the same *c* code should have the same box dimensions and escapements; otherwise the second character will override the specifications of the first. The boolean expression '*charexists c*' can be used to determine whether or not a character with a particular *c* code has already been shipped out.

Let's conclude this chapter by contemplating a METAFONT program that generates the "dangerous bend" symbol, since that symbol appears so often in this book. It's a custom-made character intended to be used only at the very beginnings of paragraphs in which the baselines of the text are exactly 11 pt apart. Therefore it extends below its baseline by 11 pt; but it is put into a box of depth zero, because TEX would otherwise think that the first line of the paragraph contains an extremely deep character, and such depth would cause the second line to be moved down.

$$baselinedistance\# := 11pt\#; \quad \textbf{define\_pixels}(baselinedistance);$$
$$heavyline\# := 50/36pt\#; \quad \textbf{define\_blacker\_pixels}(heavyline);$$
$$\textbf{beginchar}(127, 25u\#, h\_height\# + border\#, 0); \quad \texttt{"Dangerous bend symbol"};$$
$$\textbf{pickup pencircle} \text{ scaled } rulethickness; \quad top\ y_1 = \tfrac{25}{27}h; \quad lft\ x_4 = 0;$$
$$x_1 + x_1 = x_{1a} + x_{1b} = x_{4b} + x_{2a} = x_4 + x_2 = x_{4a} + x_{2b} = x_{3b} + x_{3a} = x_3 + x_3 = w;$$
$$x_{4a} = x_{4b} = x_4 + u; \quad x_{3b} = x_{1a} = x_1 - 2u;$$
$$y_4 + y_4 = y_{4a} + y_{4b} = y_{3b} + y_{1a} = y_3 + y_1 = y_{3a} + y_{1b} = y_{2b} + y_{2a} = y_2 + y_2 = 0;$$
$$y_{1a} = y_{1b} = y_1 - \tfrac{2}{27}h; \quad y_{4b} = y_{2a} = y_4 + \tfrac{4}{27}h;$$

draw $z_{1a} .. z_1 .. z_{1b} \text{---} z_{2a} .. z_2 .. z_{2b} \text{---}$

$\qquad z_{3a} .. z_3 .. z_{3b} \text{---} z_{4a} .. z_4 .. z_{4b} \text{---}$ cycle;   % the signboard

$x_{10} = x_{11} = x_{12} = x_{13} = .5w - u; \quad x_{14} = x_{15} = x_{16} = x_{17} = w - x_{10};$

$y_{10} = y_{14} = \frac{28}{27}h; \quad bot \; y_{13} = -baselinedistance;$

$z_{11} = (z_{10} .. z_{13})$ intersectionpoint $(z_{1a}\{z_{1a} - z_{4b}\} .. z_1\{right\});$

$y_{15} = y_{11}; \quad y_{16} = y_{12} = -y_{11}; \quad y_{17} = y_{20} = y_{21} = y_{13};$

draw $z_{11} \text{--} z_{10} \text{--} z_{14} \text{--} z_{15};$ **draw** $z_{12} \text{--} z_{13};$ **draw** $z_{16} \text{--} z_{17};$ % the signpost

$x_{20} = w - x_{21}; \quad x_{21} - x_{20} = 16u;$ **draw** $z_{20} \text{--} z_{21};$ % ground level

$x_{36} = w - x_{31}; \quad x_{36} - x_{31} = 8u; \quad x_{32} = x_{33} = x_{36}; \quad x_{31} = x_{34} = x_{35};$

$y_{31} = -y_{36} = \frac{12}{27}h; \quad y_{32} = -y_{35} = \frac{9}{27}h; \quad y_{33} = -y_{34} = \frac{3}{27}h;$

pickup pencircle scaled *heavyline*;

draw $z_{32}\{z_{32} - z_{31}\} .. z_{33} \text{---} z_{34} .. z_{35}\{z_{36} - z_{35}\};$ % the dangerous bend

pickup penrazor xscaled *heavyline* rotated (angle$(z_{32} - z_{31}) + 90);$

draw $z_{31} \text{--} z_{32};$ **draw** $z_{35} \text{--} z_{36};$ % upper and lower bars

labels$(1a, 1b, 2a, 2b, 3a, 3b, 4a, 4b,$ **range** 1 **thru** $36);$

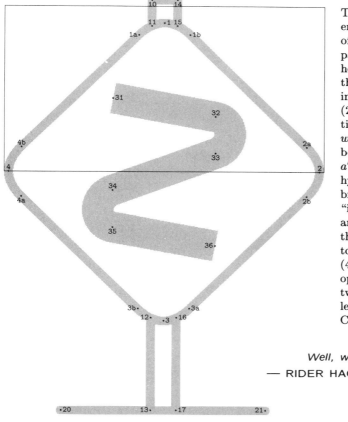

This program has several noteworthy points of interest: (1) The first parameter to **beginchar** here is 127, not a string; this puts the character into font location 127. (2) A sequence of equations like '$a = w - b; \; a' = w - b'$' can conveniently be shortened to '$a + b = a' + b' = w$'. (3) Three hyphens '---' is an abbreviation for a line with "infinite" tension, i.e., an almost straight line that connects smoothly to its curved neighbors. (4) An 'intersectionpoint' operation finds out where two paths cross; we'll learn more about this in Chapter 14.

Well, we are in the same box.
— RIDER HAGGARD, *Dawn* (1884)

A story, too,
may be boxed.
— DOROTHY COLBURN, *Newspaper Nomenclature* (1927)

13

Drawing, Filling, and Erasing

The pictures that METAFONT produces are made up of tiny pixels that are either
"on" or "off"; therefore you might imagine that the computer works behind the
scenes with some sort of graph paper, and that it darkens some of the squares
whenever you tell it to **draw** a line or to **fill** a region.

METAFONT's internal graph paper is actually more sophisticated than
this. Pixels aren't simply "on" or "off" when METAFONT is working on a picture;
they can be "doubly on" or "triply off." Each pixel contains a small *integer* value,
and when a character is finally shipped out to a font the black pixels are those
whose value is greater than zero. For example, the two commands

> **fill** $(0,3) \text{ -- } (9,3) \text{ -- } (9,6) \text{ -- } (0,6) \text{ -- cycle};$
> **fill** $(3,0) \text{ -- } (3,9) \text{ -- } (6,9) \text{ -- } (6,0) \text{ -- cycle}$

yield the following 9×9 pattern of pixel values:

```
0 0 0 1 1 1 0 0 0
0 0 0 1 1 1 0 0 0
0 0 0 1 1 1 0 0 0
1 1 1 2 2 2 1 1 1
1 1 1 2 2 2 1 1 1
1 1 1 2 2 2 1 1 1
0 0 0 1 1 1 0 0 0
0 0 0 1 1 1 0 0 0
0 0 0 1 1 1 0 0 0
```

Pixels that have been filled twice now have a value of 2.

When a simple region is "filled," its pixel values are all increased by 1;
when it is "unfilled," they are all decreased by 1. The command

> **unfill** $(1,4) \text{ -- } (8,4) \text{ -- } (8,5) \text{ -- } (1,5) \text{ -- cycle}$

will therefore change the pattern above to

```
0 0 0 1 1 1 0 0 0
0 0 0 1 1 1 0 0 0
0 0 0 1 1 1 0 0 0
1 1 1 2 2 2 1 1 1
1 0 0 1 1 1 0 0 1
1 1 1 2 2 2 1 1 1
0 0 0 1 1 1 0 0 0
0 0 0 1 1 1 0 0 0
0 0 0 1 1 1 0 0 0
```

The pixels in the center have not been erased (i.e., they will still be black if this
picture is output to a font), because they still have a positive value.

Incidentally, this example illustrates the fact that the edges between
METAFONT's pixels are lines that have integer coordinates, just as the squares
on graph paper do. For example, the lower left 'o' in the 9×9 array above
corresponds to the pixel whose boundary is '$(0,0) \text{ -- } (1,0) \text{ -- } (1,1) \text{ -- } (0,1) \text{ -- }$
cycle'. The (x, y) coordinates of the points inside this pixel lie between 0 and 1.

▶ **EXERCISE 13.1**
What are the (x, y) coordinates of the four corners of the *middle* pixel in the
9×9 array?

▶ **EXERCISE 13.2**
What picture would have been obtained if the **unfill** command had been given
before the two **fill** commands in the examples above?

▶ **EXERCISE 13.3**
Devise an **unfill** command that will produce the pixel values

```
0 0 0 1 1 1 0 0 0
0 0 0 1 0 1 0 0 0
0 0 0 1 0 1 0 0 0
1 1 1 2 1 2 1 1 1
1 0 0 1 0 1 0 0 1
1 1 1 2 1 2 1 1 1
0 0 0 1 0 1 0 0 0
0 0 0 1 0 1 0 0 0
0 0 0 1 1 1 0 0 0
```

when it is used just after the **fill** and **unfill** commands already given.

A "simple" region is one whose boundary does not intersect itself; more complicated effects occur when the boundary lines cross. For example,

> **fill** $(0, 1)$ -- $(9, 1)$ -- $(9, 4)$ -- $(4, 4)$ --
> $(4, 0)$ -- $(6, 0)$ -- $(6, 3)$ -- $(8, 3)$ -- $(8, 2)$ -- $(0, 2)$ -- cycle

produces the pixel pattern

```
0 0 0 0 1 1 1 1 1
0 0 0 0 1 1 0 0 1
1 1 1 1 2 2 1 1 1
0 0 0 0 1 1 0 0 0
```

Notice that some pixels receive the value 2, because they're "doubly filled." There's also a "hole" where the pixel values remain zero, even though they are surrounded by filled pixels; the pixels in that hole are not considered to be in the region, but the doubly filled pixels are considered to be in the region twice.

▶ **EXERCISE 13.4**
Show that the first 9×9 cross pattern on the previous page can be generated by a single **fill** command. (The nine pixel values in the center should be 2, as if two separate regions had been filled, even though you are doing only one **fill**.)

▶ **EXERCISE 13.5**
What do you think is the result of '**fill** $(0, 0)$ -- $(1, 0)$ -- $(1, 1)$ -- $(0, 1)$ -- $(0, 0)$ -- $(1, 0)$ -- $(1, 1)$ -- $(0, 1)$ -- cycle'?

A **fill** command can produce even stranger effects when its boundary lines cross in only one place. If you say, for example,

> **fill** $(0, 2)$ -- $(4, 2)$ -- $(4, 4)$ -- $(2, 4)$ -- $(2, 0)$ -- $(0, 0)$ -- cycle

METAFONT will produce the 4×4 pattern

```
0 0 1 1
0 0 1 1
- - 0 0
- - 0 0
```

where '-' stands for the value -1. Furthermore the machine will report that you have a "strange path" whose "turning number" is zero! What does this mean? Basically, it means that your path loops around on itself something like a figure 8; this causes a breakdown in METAFONT's usual rules for distinguishing the "inside" and "outside" of a curve.

Every cyclic path has a *turning number* that can be understood as follows. Imagine that you are driving a car along the path and that you have a digital compass that tells in what direction you're heading. For example, if the path is

$$(0,0) \text{ -- } (2,0) \text{ -- } (2,2) \text{ -- } (0,2) \text{ -- cycle}$$

you begin driving in direction $0°$, then you make four left turns. After the first turn, your compass heading is $90°$; after the second, it is $180°$; and after the third it is $270°$. (The compass direction increases when you turn left and decreases when you turn right; therefore it now reads $270°$, not $-90°$.) At the end of this cycle the compass will read $360°$, and if you go around again the reading will be $720°$. Similarly, if you had traversed the path

$$(0,0) \text{ -- } (0,2) \text{ -- } (2,2) \text{ -- } (2,0) \text{ -- cycle}$$

(which is essentially the same, but in the opposite direction), your compass heading would have started at $90°$ and ended at $-270°$; in this case each circuit would have *decreased* the reading by $360°$. It is clear that a drive around any cyclic path will change the compass heading by some multiple of $360°$, since you end in the same direction you started. The turning number of a path is defined to be t if the compass heading changes by exactly t times $360°$ when the path is traversed. Thus, the two example cycles we have just discussed have turning numbers of $+1$ and -1, respectively; and the "strange path" on the previous page that produced both positive and negative pixel values does indeed have a turning number of 0.

Here's how METAFONT actually implements a **fill** command, assuming that the cyclic path being filled has a *positive* turning number: The path is first "digitized," if necessary, so that it lies entirely on the edges of pixels; in other words, it is distorted slightly so that it is confined to the lines between pixels on graph paper. (Our examples so far in this chapter have not needed any such adjustments.) Then each individual pixel value is increased by j and decreased by k if an infinite horizontal line to the left of that pixel intersects the digitized path j times when the path is traveling downward and k times when it is traveling upward. For example, let's look more closely at the non-simple path on the previous page that enclosed a hole:

```
 a  a  a  a│b  b  b  b  b┐
 a  a  a  a│b  b│c  c│d┐
┌e  e  e  e│f  f│g  g  g┘
 a  a  a  a│b  b│h  h  h
```

Pixel d has $j = 2$ descending edges and $k = 1$ ascending edges to its left, so its net value increases by $j - k = 1$; pixels g are similar. Pixels c have $j = k = 1$, so they lie in a "hole" that is unfilled; pixels f have $j = 2$ and $k = 0$, so they are doubly filled. This rule works because, intuitively, the inside of a region lies at the *left* of a path whose turning number is positive.

▶ **EXERCISE 13.6**

True or false: When the turning number of a cyclic path is positive, a **fill** command increases each individual pixel value by $l - m$, if an infinite horizontal line to the *right* of that pixel intersects the digitized path l times when the path is traveling upward and m times when it is traveling downward. (For example, pixels e have $l = 2$ and $m = 1$; pixels c have $l = m = 1$.)

When the turning number is negative, a similar rule applies, except that the pixel values are *decreased* by j and *increased* by k; in this case the inside of the region lies at the *right* of the path.

But when the turning number is zero, the inside of the region lies sometimes at the left, sometimes at the right. METAFONT uses the rule for positive turning number and reports that the path is "strange." You can avoid this error message by setting '$turningcheck := 0$'; in this case the rule for positive turning number is always used for filling, even when the turning number is negative.

Plain METAFONT's **draw** command is different from **fill** in two important ways. First, it uses the currently-picked-up pen, thereby "thickening" the path. Second, it does not require that the path be cyclic. There is also a third difference, which needs to be mentioned although it is not quite as important: A **draw** command may increase the value of certain pixels by more than 1, even if the shape being drawn is fairly simple. For example, the pixel pattern

```
000000000000000000000000000000000000000000000000000000000000000000000000
000001111112222221111100000000000000000000000000001111111000000000000000
000011111111211111111110000000000000000000000000011111111110000000000000
000111111111110111111111110000000000000000000001111111111111110000000000
001111111111110001111111111100000000000000000011111111111111111000000000
001111111111110001111111111100000000000000000111111111111111111100000000
011111111111100001111111111110000000000000011111111111111111111110000000
011111111111100001111111111110000000000000111111111111111111111111000000
011111111111100001111111111110000000000001111111111111111111111111110000
011111111111100001111111111110000000000011111111111111111111111111110000
011111111111100001111111111110000000000111111111111111111111111111110000
011111111111100001111111111110000000001111111111111121111111111111110000
011111111111100001111111111110000000011111111111112211111111111111100000
011111111111100001111111111110000000011111111111122111111111111111000000
011111111111100001111111111110000000111111111112211221111111111111000000
011111111111100001111111111110000001111111111122110011111111111110000000
011111111111100001111111111110000001111111111122110000111111111110000000
011111111111100001111111111110000011111111111122110000112111111111110000
011111111111100001111111111110000011111111111112000001111111111111110000
011111111111100001111111111110000111111111111120000011111111111111100000
011111111111100001111111111110001111111111111100000011111111111110000000
011111111111100001111111111110001111111111111100000011111111111110000000
011111111111100001111111111110011111111111110000000001111111111100000000
011111111111100001111111111110011111111111100000000000111111110000000000
000000000000000001111111111110000000000001111110000000000011111000000000
```

was produced by two **draw** commands. The left-hand shape came from

> **pickup penrazor** scaled 10; % a pen of width 10 and height 0
> **draw** $(6, 1)\{up\} .. (13.5, 25) .. \{down\}(21, 1);$

it's not difficult to imagine why some of the top pixels get the value 2 here because an actual razor-thin pen would cover those pixels twice as it follows the given path. But the right-hand shape, which came from

> **pickup pencircle** scaled 16; **draw** $(41, 9) .. (51, 17) .. (61, 9)$

is harder to explain; there seems to be no rhyme or reason to the pattern of 2's in that case. METAFONT's method for drawing curves with thick pens is too complicated to explain here, so we shall just regard it as a curious process that occasionally shoots out extra spurts of ink in the interior of the shape that it's filling. Sometimes a pixel value even gets as high as 3 or more; but if we ignore such anomalies and simply consider the set of pixels that receive a positive value, we find that a reasonable shape has been drawn.

The left-parenthesis example in Chapter 12 illustrates the **filldraw** command, which is like **fill** in that it requires a cyclic path, and like **draw** in that it uses the current pen. Pixel values are increased inside the region that you would obtain by drawing the specified path with the current pen and then filling in the interior. Some of the pixel values in this region may increase by 2 or more. The turning number of the path should be nonzero.

Besides **fill**, **draw**, and **filldraw**, you can also say '**drawdot**', as illustrated at the beginning of Chapter 5. In this case you should specify only a single point; the currently-picked-up pen will be used to increase pixel values by 1 around that point. Chapter 24 explains that this gives slightly better results than if you were to draw a one-point path.

There's also an **undraw** command, analogous to **unfill**; it decreases pixel values by the same amount that **draw** would increase them. Furthermore— as you might expect—**unfilldraw** and **undrawdot** are the respective opposites of **filldraw** and **drawdot**.

If you try to use **unfill** and/or **undraw** in connection with **fill** and/or **draw**, you'll soon discover that something else is necessary. Plain METAFONT has a **cullit** command that replaces all negative pixel values by 0 and all positive pixel values by 1. This "culling" operation makes it possible to erase unwanted sections of a picture in spite of the vagaries of **draw** and **undraw**, and in spite of the fact that overlapping regions may be doubly filled.

The command '**erase fill** c' is an abbreviation for '**cullit**; **unfill** c; **cullit**'; this zeros out the pixel values inside the cyclic path c, and sets other pixel values to 1 if they were positive before erasing took place. (It works because the initial **cullit** makes all the values 0 or 1, then the **unfill** changes the values inside c to 0 or negative. The final **cullit** gets rid of the negative values, so that they won't detract from future filling and drawing.) You can also use '**draw**', '**filldraw**', or '**drawdot**' with '**erase**'; for example, '**erase draw** p' is an abbreviation for '**cullit**; **undraw** p; **cullit**', which uses the currently-picked-up pen as if it were an eraser applied to path p.

The cube at the right of this paragraph illustrates one of the effects that is easily obtained by erasing. First the eight points are defined, and the "back" square is drawn; then two lines of the "front" square are erased, using a somewhat thicker pen; finally the remaining lines are drawn with the ordinary pen:

$$s^{\#} := 5pt^{\#};\ \textbf{define\_pixels}(s);\ \%\ \text{side of the square}$$
$$z_1 = (0,0);\ z_2 = (s,0);\ z_3 = (0,s);\ z_4 = (s,s);$$
for $k = 1$ **upto** 4: $z_{k+4} = z_k + (\frac{2}{3}s, \frac{1}{3}s)$; **endfor**
pickup pencircle scaled .4pt; **draw** z_5 -- z_6 -- z_8 -- z_7 -- cycle;
pickup pencircle scaled 1.6pt; **erase draw** z_2 -- z_4 -- z_3;
pickup pencircle scaled .4pt; **draw** z_1 -- z_2 -- z_4 -- z_3 -- cycle;
for $k = 1$ **upto** 4: **draw** z_k -- z_{k+4}; **endfor**

At its true size the resulting cube looks like this: '▢'.

▶ **EXERCISE 13.7**
Modify the draw-and-erase construction in the preceding paragraph so that you get the *impossible cube* '▢' instead.

▶**EXERCISE 13.8**
Write a METAFONT program to produce the symbol ''. [*Hints:* The character is 10 pt wide, 7 pt high, and 2 pt deep. The starlike path can be defined by five points connected by "tense" lines as follows:

> **pair** *center*; *center* = $(.5w, 2pt)$;
> **numeric** *radius*; *radius* = $5pt$;
> **for** $k = 0$ **upto** 4: $z_k = center + (radius, 0)$ rotated$(90 + \frac{360}{5}k)$; **endfor**
> **def** :: = .. tension 5 .. **enddef**;
> **path** *star*; *star* = $z_0 :: z_2 :: z_4 :: z_1 :: z_3 ::$ cycle;

You probably want to work with subpaths of *star* instead of drawing the whole path at once, in order to give the illusion that the curves cross over and under each other.]

 ▶**EXERCISE 13.9**
What does the command '**fill** *star*' do, if *star* is the path defined above?

 ▶**EXERCISE 13.10**
Devise a macro called '**overdraw**' such that the command '**overdraw** *c*' will erase the inside of region *c* and will then draw the boundary of *c* with the currently-picked-up pen, assuming that *c* is a cyclic path that doesn't intersect itself. (Your macro could be used, for example, in the program

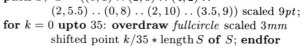

> **path** S; $S = ((0,1) .. (2,0) .. (4,2) ..$
> $(2, 5.5) .. (0, 8) .. (2, 10) .. (3.5, 9))$ scaled $9pt$;
> **for** $k = 0$ **upto** 35: **overdraw** *fullcircle* scaled $3mm$
> shifted point $k/35 *$ length S **of** S; **endfor**

to create the curious S shown here.)

 ▶**EXERCISE 13.11**
The Möbius Watchband Corporation has a logo that looks like this:

Explain how to produce it (or something very similar) with METAFONT.

 Chapter 7 points out that variables can be of type '**picture**', and Chapter 8 mentions that expressions can be of type '**picture**', but we still haven't seen any examples of picture variables or picture expressions. Plain METAFONT keeps the currently-worked-on picture in a picture variable called *currentpicture*, and you can copy it by equating it to a picture variable of your own. For example, if you say '**picture** $v[]$' at the beginning of your program, you can write equations like

> $v_1 = currentpicture$;

this makes v_1 equal to the picture that has been drawn so far; i.e., it gives v_1 the same array of pixel values that *currentpicture* now has.

Pictures can be added or subtracted; for example, $v_1 + v_2$ stands for the picture whose pixel values are the sums of the pixel values of v_1 and v_2. The "reverse-video dangerous bend" sign that heads this paragraph was made by substituting the following code for the '**endchar**' in the program at the end of Chapter 12:

> **picture** *dbend*; *dbend* = *currentpicture*;
> **endchar**; % end of the normal dangerous bend sign
> **beginchar**$(0, 25u^\#, h\_height^\# + border^\#, 0)$;
> **fill** $(0, -11pt) \text{ -- } (w, -11pt) \text{ -- } (w, h) \text{ -- } (0, h) \text{ -- cycle}$;
> *currentpicture* := *currentpicture* − *dbend*;
> **endchar**; % end of the reversed dangerous bend sign

The pixel values in *dbend* are all zero or more; thus the pixels with a positive value, after *dbend* has been subtracted from a filled rectangle, will be those that are inside the rectangle but zero in *dbend*.

We will see in Chapter 15 that pictures can also be shifted, reflected, and rotated by multiples of 90°. For example, the statement '*currentpicture* := *currentpicture* shifted $3right$' shifts the entire current picture three pixels to the right.

There's a "constant" picture called **nullpicture**, whose pixel values are all zero; plain METAFONT defines '**clearit**' to be an abbreviation for the assignment '*currentpicture*:=**nullpicture**'. The current picture is cleared automatically by every **beginchar** and **mode_setup** command, so you usually don't have to say '**clearit**' in your own programs.

Here's the formal syntax for picture expressions. Although METAFONT has comparatively few built-in operations that deal with entire pictures, the operations that do exist have the same syntax as the similar operations we have seen applied to numbers and pairs.

> ⟨picture primary⟩ ⟶ ⟨picture variable⟩
> | **nullpicture**
> | (⟨picture expression⟩)
> | ⟨plus or minus⟩⟨picture primary⟩
> ⟨picture secondary⟩ ⟶ ⟨picture primary⟩
> | ⟨picture secondary⟩⟨transformer⟩
> ⟨picture tertiary⟩ ⟶ ⟨picture secondary⟩
> | ⟨picture tertiary⟩⟨plus or minus⟩⟨picture secondary⟩
> ⟨picture expression⟩ ⟶ ⟨picture tertiary⟩

The "total weight" of a picture is the sum of all its pixel values, divided by 65536; you can compute this numeric quantity by saying

> **totalweight** ⟨picture primary⟩.

METAFONT divides by 65536 in order to avoid overflow in case of huge pictures. If the totalweight function returns a number whose absolute value is less than .5, as it almost always is, you can safely divide that number by *epsilon* to obtain the integer sum of all pixel values (since *epsilon* = 1/65536).

Let's turn to the computer again and try to evaluate some simple picture expressions interactively, using the general routine `expr.mf` of Chapter 8. When METAFONT says 'gimme', you can type

    hide(fill unitsquare) currentpicture

and the machine will respond as follows:

    >> Edge structure at line 5:
    row 0: 0+ 1- |

What does this mean? Well, '**hide**' is plain METAFONT's sneaky way to insert a command or sequence of commands into the middle of an expression; such commands are executed before the rest of the expression is looked at. In this case the command '**fill** *unitsquare*' sets one pixel value of the current picture to 1, because *unitsquare* is plain METAFONT's abbreviation for the path $(0,0)$ -- $(1,0)$ -- $(1,1)$ -- $(0,1)$ -- cycle. The value of *currentpicture* is displayed as '**row 0: 0+ 1-**', because this means "in row 0, the pixel value increases at $x = 0$ and decreases at $x = 1$."

METAFONT represents pictures internally by remembering only the vertical edges where pixel values change. For example, the picture just displayed has just two edges, both in row 0, i.e., both in the row between y coordinates 0 and 1. (Row k contains vertical edges whose x coordinates are integers and whose y coordinates run between k and $k+1$.) The fact that edges are represented, rather than entire arrays of pixels, makes it possible for METAFONT to operate efficiently at high resolutions, because the number of edges in a picture is essentially proportional to the resolution while the total number of pixels is proportional to the resolution *squared*. A ten-fold increase in resolution therefore calls for only a ten-fold (rather than a hundred-fold) increase in memory space and execution time.

 Continuing our computer experiments, let's declare a picture variable and fill a few more pixels:

    hide(picture V; fill unitsquare scaled 2; V=currentpicture) V

The resulting picture has pixel values $\frac{1}{2}\frac{1}{1}$, and its edges are shown thus:

    >> Edge structure at line 5:
    row 1: 0+ 2- |
    row 0: 0+ 2- 0+ 1- |

If we now type '-V', the result is similar but with the signs changed:

    >> Edge structure at line 5:
    row 1: 0- 2+ |
    row 0: 0- 2+ 0- 1+ |

(You should be doing the experiments as you read this.) A more interesting picture transformation occurs if we ask for 'V rotated-90'; the picture $\frac{2}{1}\frac{1}{1}$ appears below the baseline, hence the following edges are shown:

    >> Edge structure at line 5:
    row -1: | 0++ 1- 2-
    row -2: | 0+ 2-

Here '++' denotes an edge where the weight increases by 2. The edges appear *after* vertical lines '|' in this case, while they appeared *before* vertical lines in the previous examples; this means that METAFONT has sorted the edges by their x coordinates. Each **fill** or **draw** instruction contributes new edges to a picture, and unsorted edges accumulate until METAFONT needs to look at them in left-to-right order. (Type

```
V rotated-90 rotated 90
```

to see what V itself looks like when its edges have been sorted.) The expression

```
V +  V rotated 90 shifted 2right
```

produces an edge structure with both sorted and unsorted edges:

```
>> Edge structure at line 5:
row 1: 0+ 2- | 0+ 2-
row 0: 0+ 2- 0+ 1- | 0+ 1+ 2--
```

In general, addition of pictures is accomplished by simply combining the unsorted and sorted edges of each row separately.

▶ **EXERCISE 13.12**
Guess what will happen if you type 'hide(cullit) currentpicture' now; and verify your guess by actually doing the experiment.

▶ **EXERCISE 13.13**
Guess (and verify) what will happen when you type the expression

```
(V + V + V rotated 90 shifted 2right
   - V rotated-90 shifted 2up) rotated 90.
```

[You must type this monstrous formula all on one line, even though it's too long to fit on a single line in this book.]

If you ask for 'V rotated 45', METAFONT will complain that 45° rotation is too hard. (Try it.) After all, square pixels can't be rotated unless the angle of rotation is a multiple of 90°. On the other hand, 'V scaled-1' does work; you get

```
>> Edge structure at line 5:
row -1: 0- -2+ 0- -1+ |
row -2: 0- -2+ |
```

▶ **EXERCISE 13.14**
Why is 'V scaled-1' different from '-V'?

▶ **EXERCISE 13.15**
Experiment with 'V shifted (1.5,3.14159)' and explain what happens.

▶ **EXERCISE 13.16**
Guess and verify the result of 'V scaled 2'.

▶ **EXERCISE 13.17**
Why does the machine always speak of an edge structure 'at line 5'?

That completes our computer experiments. But before you log off, you might want to try typing 'totalweight V/epsilon', just to verify that the sum of all pixel values in V is 5.

The commands we have discussed so far in this chapter—**fill**, **draw**, **filldraw**, **unfill**, etc.—are not really primitives of METAFONT; they are macros of plain METAFONT, defined in Appendix B. Let's look now at the low-level operations on pictures that METAFONT actually performs behind the scenes. Here is the syntax:

⟨picture command⟩ ⟶ ⟨addto command⟩ | ⟨cull command⟩
⟨addto command⟩ ⟶ **addto** ⟨picture variable⟩ **also** ⟨picture expression⟩
  | **addto** ⟨picture variable⟩ **contour** ⟨path expression⟩⟨with list⟩
  | **addto** ⟨picture variable⟩ **doublepath** ⟨path expression⟩⟨with list⟩
⟨with list⟩ ⟶ ⟨empty⟩ | ⟨with list⟩⟨with clause⟩
⟨with clause⟩ ⟶ **withpen** ⟨pen expression⟩ | **withweight** ⟨numeric expression⟩
⟨cull command⟩ ⟶ **cull** ⟨picture variable⟩⟨keep or drop⟩⟨pair expression⟩
  | ⟨cull command⟩ **withweight** ⟨numeric expression⟩
⟨keep or drop⟩ ⟶ **keeping** | **dropping**

The ⟨picture variable⟩ in these commands should contain a known picture; the command modifies that picture, and assigns the resulting new value to the variable.

The first form of ⟨addto command⟩, '**addto** V **also** P', has essentially the same meaning as '$V := V + P$'. But the **addto** statement is more efficient, because it destroys the old value of V as it adds P; this saves both time and space. Earlier in this chapter we discussed the reverse-video dangerous bend, which was said to have been formed by the statement '$currentpicture := currentpicture - dbend$'. That was a little white lie; the actual command was '**addto** $currentpicture$ **also** $-dbend$'.

The details of the other forms of '**addto**' are slightly more complex, but (informally) they work like this, when $V = currentpicture$ and $q = currentpen$:

Plain METAFONT	Corresponding METAFONT primitives
fill c	**addto** V **contour** c
unfill c	**addto** V **contour** c **withweight** -1
draw p	**addto** V **doublepath** p **withpen** q
undraw p	**addto** V **doublepath** p **withpen** q **withweight** -1
filldraw c	**addto** V **contour** c **withpen** q
unfilldraw c	**addto** V **contour** c **withpen** q **withweight** -1

The second form of ⟨addto command⟩ is '**addto** V **contour** p', followed by optional clauses that say either '**withpen** q' or '**withweight** w'. In this case p must be a cyclic path; each pen q must be known; and each weight w must be either -3, -2, -1, $+1$, $+2$, or $+3$, when rounded to the nearest integer. If more than one pen or weight is given, the last specification overrides all previous ones. If no pen is given, the pen is assumed to be '**nullpen**'; if no weight is given, the weight is assumed to be $+1$. Thus, the second form of ⟨addto command⟩ basically identifies a picture variable V, a cyclic path p, a pen q, and a weight w; and it has the following meaning, assuming that $turningcheck$ is ≤ 0: If q is the null pen, path p is digitized and each pixel value is increased by $(j - k)w$, where j and k are the respective numbers of downward and upward path edges lying to the left of the pixel (as explained earlier in this chapter). If q is not the null pen, the action is basically the same except that p is converted to another path that "envelopes" p with respect to the shape of q; this modified path is digitized and filled as before. (The modified path may cross itself in unusual ways, producing strange squirts of ink as illustrated earlier. But it will be well behaved if path p defines a convex region, i.e., if a car that drives counterclockwise around p never turns toward the right at any time.)

If *turningcheck* > 0 when an '**addto**…**contour**' command is being performed, the action is the same as just described, provided that path p has a positive turning number. However, if p's turning number is negative, the action depends on whether or not pen q is simple or complex; a complex pen is one whose boundary contains at least two points. If the turning number is negative and the pen is simple, the weight w is changed to $-w$. If the turning number is negative and the pen is complex, you get an error message about a "backwards path." Finally, if the turning number is zero, you get an error message about a "strange path," unless the pen is simple and *turningcheck* ≤ 1. Plain METAFONT sets *turningcheck* $:= 2$; the **filldraw** macro in Appendix B avoids the "backwards path" error by explicitly reversing a path whose turning number is negative.

We mentioned that the command '**fill** $(0,2)$ -- $(4,2)$ -- $(4,4)$ -- $(2,4)$ -- $(2,0)$ -- $(0,0)$ -- cycle' causes METAFONT to complain about a strange path; let's take a closer look at the error message that you get:

```
> 0 ENE 1 NNE 2 (NNW WNW) WSW 3 SSW 4 WSW 5 (WNW NNW) NNE 0
! Strange path (turning number is zero).
```

What does this mean? The numbers represent "time" on the cyclic path, from the starting point at time 0, to the next key point at time 1, and so on, finally returning to the starting point. Code names like '`ENE`' stand for compass directions like "East by North East"; METAFONT decides in which of eight "octants" each part of a path travels, and `ENE` stands for all directions between the angles $0°$ and $45°$, inclusive. Thus, this particular strange path starts in octant `ENE` at time 0, then it turns to octant `NNE` after time 1. An octant name is parenthesized when the path turns through that octant without moving; thus, for example, octants `NNW` and `WNW` are bypassed on the way to octant `WSW`. It's possible to compute the turning number from the given sequence of octants; therefore, if you don't think your path is really strange, the abbreviated octant codes should reveal where METAFONT has decided to take an unexpected turn. (Chapter 27 explains more about strange paths.)

The third form of ⟨addto command⟩ is '**addto** V **doublepath** p', followed by optional clauses that define a pen q and a weight w as in the second case. If p is not a cyclic path, this case reduces to the second case, with p replaced by the doubled-up path 'p & reverse p & cycle' (unless p consists of only a single point, when the new path is simply 'p .. cycle'). On the other hand if p is a cyclic path, this case reduces to *two* addto commands of the second type, in one of which p is reversed; *turningcheck* is ignored during both of those commands.

An anomalous result may occur in the statement '**draw** p' or, more generally, in '**addto** V **doublepath** p **withpen** q' when p is a very small cyclic path and the current pen q is very large: Pixels that would be covered by the pen regardless of where it is placed on p might retain their original value. If this unusual circumstance hits you, the cure is simply to include the additional statement '**draw** z' or '**addto** V **doublepath** z **withpen** q', where z is any point of p, since this will cover all of the potentially uncovered pixels.

The **cull** command transforms a picture variable so that all of its pixel values are either 0 or a specified weight w, where w is determined as in an **addto** command. A pair of numbers (a, b) is given, where a must be less than or equal to b. To cull "**keeping** (a, b)" means that each new pixel value is w if and only if the corresponding old pixel value v was included in the range $a \leq v \leq b$; to cull "**dropping** (a, b)" means that each new pixel value is w if and only if the corresponding old pixel value v was *not* in that range. Thus, for example, '**cullit**' is an abbreviation for

> **cull** *currentpicture* **keeping** $(1, \textit{infinity})$

or for

> **cull** *currentpicture* **dropping** $(-\textit{infinity}, 0)$

(which both mean the same thing). A more complicated example is

> **cull** V_5 **dropping** $(-3, 2)$ **withweight** -2;

this changes the pixel values of V_5 to -2 if they were -4 or less, or if they were 3 or more; pixel values between -3 and $+2$, inclusive, are zeroed.

A cull command must not change pixel values from zero to nonzero. For example, METAFONT doesn't let you say '**cull** V_1 **keeping** $(0, 0)$', since that would give a value of 1 to infinitely many pixels.

▶ **EXERCISE 13.18**
What is the effect of the following sequence of commands?

> **picture** $V[\,]$;
> $V_1 = V_2 = \textit{currentpicture}$;
> **cull** V_1 **dropping** $(0, 0)$;
> **cull** V_2 **dropping** $(-1, 1)$;
> $\textit{currentpicture} := V_1 - V_2$;

▶ **EXERCISE 13.19**
Given two picture variables V_1 and V_2, all of whose pixel values are known to be either 0 or 1, explain how to replace V_1 by (a) $V_1 \cap V_2$; (b) $V_1 \cup V_2$; (c) $V_1 \oplus V_2$. [The *intersection* $V_1 \cap V_2$ has 1's where V_1 and V_2 both are 1; the *union* $V_1 \cup V_2$ has 0's where V_1 and V_2 both are 0; the *symmetric difference* or *selective complement* $V_1 \oplus V_2$ has 1's where V_1 and V_2 are unequal.]

▶ **EXERCISE 13.20**
Explain how to test whether or not two picture variables are equal.

▶ **EXERCISE 13.21**
Look at the definitions of **fill**, **draw**, etc., in Appendix B and determine the effect of the following statements:

a) **draw** p **withpen** q;
b) **draw** p **withweight** 3;
c) **undraw** p **withweight** w;
d) **fill** c **withweight** -2 **withpen** q;
e) **erase fill** c **withweight** 2 **withpen** *currentpen*;
f) **cullit withweight** 2.

▶ **EXERCISE 13.22**
Devise a **safefill** macro such that '**safefill** c' increases the pixel values of *currentpicture* by 1 in all pixels whose value would be changed by the command '**fill** c'. (Unlike **fill**, the **safefill** command never stops with a "strange path" error; furthermore, it never increases a pixel value by more than 1, nor does it decrease any pixel values, even when the cycle c is quite wild.)

▶ **EXERCISE 13.23**
Explain how to replace a character by its "outline": All black pixels whose four closest neighbors are also black should be changed to white, because they are in the interior. (Diagonally adjacent neighbors don't count.)

▶ **EXERCISE 13.24**
In John Conway's "Game of Life," pixels are said to be either alive or dead. Each pixel is in contact with eight neighbors. The live pixels in the $(n+1)$st generation are those who were dead and had exactly three live neighbors in the nth generation, or those who were alive and had exactly two or three live neighbors in the nth generation. Write a short METAFONT program that displays successive generations on your screen.

Blot out, correct, insert, refine,
Enlarge, diminish, interline;
Be mindful, when Invention fails,
To scratch your Head, and bite your Nails.
— JONATHAN SWIFT, *On Poetry: A Rapsody* (1733)

The understanding that can be gained from computer drawings
is more valuable than mere production.
— IVAN E. SUTHERLAND, *Sketchpad* (1963)

14

Paths

The boundaries of regions to be filled, and the trajectories of moving pens, are "paths" that can be specified by the general methods introduced in Chapter 3. METAFONT allows variables and expressions to be of type **path**, so that a designer can build new paths from old ones in many ways. Our purpose in this chapter will be to complete what Chapter 3 began; we shall look first at some special features of plain METAFONT that facilitate the creation of paths, then we shall go into the details of everything that METAFONT knows about pathmaking.

A few handy paths have been predefined in Appendix B as part of plain METAFONT, because they turn out to be useful in a variety of applications. For example, *quartercircle* is a path that represents one-fourth of a circle of diameter 1; it runs from point $(0.5, 0)$ to point $(0, 0.5)$. The METAFONT program

> **beginchar**$("a", 5pt^{\#}, 5pt^{\#}, 0)$;
> **pickup pencircle** scaled $(.4pt + blacker)$;
> **draw** *quartercircle* scaled $10pt$; **endchar**;

therefore produces the character '⌐' in position 'a' of a font.

▸ **EXERCISE 14.1**
Write a program that puts a *filled* quarter-circle '◣' into font position 'b'.

▸ **EXERCISE 14.2**
Why are the '⌐' and '◣' characters of these examples only 5 pt wide and 5 pt high, although they are made with the path '*quartercircle* scaled $10pt$'?

▸ **EXERCISE 14.3**
Use a *rotated* quarter-circle to produce '⌒' in font position 'c'.

▸ **EXERCISE 14.4**
Use *quartercircle* to produce '▽' in font position 'd'.

Plain METAFONT also provides a path called *halfcircle* that gives you '⌒'; this path is actually made from two quarter-circles, by defining

> *halfcircle* = *quartercircle* & *quartercircle* rotated 90.

And of course there's also *fullcircle*, a complete circle of unit diameter:

> *fullcircle* = *halfcircle* & *halfcircle* rotated 180 & cycle.

You can draw a circle of diameter D centered at (x, y) by saying

> **draw** *fullcircle* scaled D shifted (x, y);

similarly, '**draw** *fullcircle* xscaled A yscaled B' yields an ellipse with axes A and B.

Besides circles and parts of circles, there's also a standard square path called *unitsquare*; this is a cycle that runs from $(0, 0)$ to $(1, 0)$ to $(1, 1)$ to $(0, 1)$ and back to $(0, 0)$. For example, the command '**fill** *unitsquare*' adds 1 to a single pixel value, as discussed in the previous chapter.

▶ **EXERCISE 14.5**

Use *fullcircle* and *unitsquare* to produce the characters '◎' and '◈' in font positions 'e' and 'f', respectively. These characters should be 10 pt wide and 10 pt tall, and their centers should be 2.5 pt above the baseline.

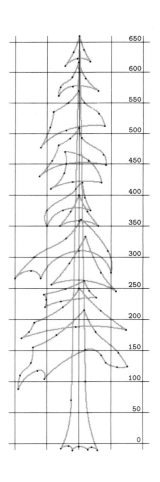

path $branch[\,]$, $trunk$;
$branch_1 = flex((0,660),(-9,633),(-22,610))$
    $\&\ flex((-22,610),(-3,622),(17,617))$
    $\&\ flex((17,617),(7,637),(0,660))\ \&\ cycle;$
$branch_2 = flex((30,570),(10,590),(-1,616))\ \&\ cycle;$
    $\&\ flex((-1,616),(-11,592),(-29,576),(-32,562))$
    $\&\ flex((-32,562),(-10,577),(30,570))\ \&\ cycle;$
$branch_3 = flex((-1,570),(-17,550),(-40,535))$
    $\&\ flex((-40,535),(-45,510),(-60,477))$
    $\&\ flex((-60,477),(-20,510),(40,512))$
    $\&\ flex((40,512),(31,532),(8,550),(-1,570))\ \&\ cycle;$
$branch_4 = flex((0,509),(-14,492),(-32,481))$
    $\&\ flex((-32,481),(-42,455),(-62,430))$
    $\&\ flex((-62,430),(-20,450),(42,448))$
    $\&\ flex((42,448),(38,465),(4,493),(0,509))\ \&\ cycle;$
$branch_5 = flex((-22,470),(-23,435),(-44,410))$
    $\&\ flex((-44,410),(-10,421),(35,420))$
    $\&\ flex((35,420),(15,455),(-22,470))\ \&\ cycle;$
$branch_6 = flex((18,375),(9,396),(5,420))$
    $\&\ flex((5,420),(-5,410),(-50,375),(-50,350))$
    $\&\ flex((-50,350),(-25,375),(18,375))\ \&\ cycle;$
$branch_7 = flex((0,400),(-13,373),(-30,350))$
    $\&\ flex((-30,350),(0,358),(30,350))$
    $\&\ flex((30,350),(13,373),(0,400))\ \&\ cycle;$
$branch_8 = flex((50,275),(45,310),(3,360))$
    $\&\ flex((3,360),(-20,330),(-70,300),(-100,266))$
    $\&\ flex((-100,266),(-75,278),(-60,266))$
    $\&\ flex((-60,266),(0,310),(50,275))\ \&\ cycle;$
$branch_9 = flex((10,333),(-15,290),(-43,256))$
    $\&\ flex((-43,256),(8,262),(58,245))$
    $\&\ flex((58,245),(34,275),(10,333))\ \&\ cycle;$
$branch_{10} = flex((8,262),(-21,249),(-55,240))$
    $\&\ flex((-55,240),(-51,232),(-53,220))$
    $\&\ flex((-53,220),(-28,229),(27,235))$
    $\&\ flex((27,235),(16,246),(8,262))\ \&\ cycle;$
$branch_{11} = flex((0,250),(-25,220),(-70,195))$
    $\&\ flex((-70,195),(-78,180),(-90,170))$
    $\&\ flex((-90,170),(-5,188),(74,183))$
    $\&\ flex((74,183),(34,214),(0,250))\ \&\ cycle;$
$branch_{12} = flex((8,215),(-35,175),(-72,155))$
    $\&\ flex((-72,155),(-75,130),(-92,110),(-95,88))$
    $\&\ flex((-95,88),(-65,117),(-54,104))$
    $\&\ flex((-54,104),(10,151),(35,142))$
    $..\ flex((42,130),(60,123),(76,124))$
    $\&\ flex((76,124),(62,146),(26,180),(8,215))\ \&\ cycle;$
$trunk = (0,660) \text{ --- } (-12,70)\ ..\ \{curl\,5\}(-28,-8)$
    $\&\ flex((-28,-8),(-16,-4),(-10,-11))$
    $\&\ flex((-10,-11),(0,-5),(14,-10))$
    $\&\ flex((14,-10),(20,-6),(29,-11))$
    $\&\ (29,-11)\{curl\,4\}\ ..\ (10,100)\text{ --- }cycle;$

Sometimes it's necessary to draw rather complicated curves, and plain METAFONT provides a '*flex*' operation that can simplify this task. The construction '*flex*(z_1, z_2, z_3)' stands for the path '$z_1 \mathbin{..} z_2\{z_3 - z_1\} \mathbin{..} z_3$', and similarly '*flex*$(z_1, z_2, z_3, z_4)$' stands for '$z_1 \mathbin{..} z_2\{z_4 - z_1\} \mathbin{..} z_3\{z_4 - z_1\} \mathbin{..} z_4$'; in general

$$flex(z_1, z_2, \ldots, z_{n-1}, z_n)$$

is an abbreviation for the path

$$z_1 \mathbin{..} z_2\{z_n - z_1\} \mathbin{..} \cdots \mathbin{..} z_{n-1}\{z_n - z_1\} \mathbin{..} z_n.$$

The idea is to specify two endpoints, z_1 and z_n, together with one or more intermediate points where the path is traveling in the same direction as the straight line from z_1 to z_n; these intermediate points are easy to see on a typical curve, so they are natural candidates for key points.

For example, the command

> **fill** $flex(z_1, z_2, z_3)$ & $flex(z_3, z_4, z_5)$
> & $flex(z_5, z_6, z_7)$ & $flex(z_7, z_8, z_9, z_1)$ & cycle

will fill the shape

after the points z_1, ..., z_9 have been suitably defined. This shape occurs as the fourth branch from the top of "El Palo Alto," a tree that is often used to symbolize Stanford University. The thirteen paths on the opposite page were defined by simply sketching the tree on a piece of graph paper, then reading off approximate values of key points "by eye" while typing the code into a computer. (A good radio or television program helps to stave off boredom when you're typing a bunch of data like this.) The entire figure involves a total of 47 flexes, most of which are pretty mundane; but $branch_{12}$ does contain an interesting subpath of the form

$$flex(z_1, z_2, z_3) \mathbin{..} flex(z_4, z_5, z_6),$$

which is an abbreviation for

$$z_1 \mathbin{..} z_2\{z_3 - z_1\} \mathbin{..} z_3 \mathbin{..} z_4 \mathbin{..} z_5\{z_6 - z_4\} \mathbin{..} z_6.$$

Since $z_3 \neq z_4$ in this example, a smooth curve runs through all six points, although two different flexes are involved.

Once the paths have been defined, it's easy to use them to make symbols like the white-on-black medallion shown here:

beginchar ("T", .5 $in^\#$, 1.25 $in^\#$, 0);
⟨Define the thirteen paths on the preceding pages⟩;
fill *superellipse* ((w, .5h), (.5w, h), (0, .5h), (.5w, 0), .8);
$branch_0 = trunk$;
for $n = 0$ **upto** 12:
   unfill *branch*[n] shifted (150, 50) scaled (w/300);
endfor endchar;

The oval shape that encloses this tree is a *superellipse*, which is another special kind of path provided by plain METAFONT. To get a general shape of this kind, you can write

$$superellipse\,(right\_point, top\_point, left\_point, bottom\_point, superness)$$

where '*superness*' controls the amount by which the curve differs from a true ellipse. For example, here are four superellipses, drawn with varying amounts of superness, using a **pencircle** xscaled 0.7*pt* yscaled 0.2*pt* rotated 30:

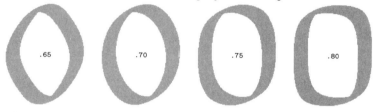

The *superness* should be between 0.5 (when you get a diamond) and 1.0 (when you get a square); values in the vicinity of 0.75 are usually preferred. The zero symbol '0' in this book's typewriter font was drawn as a superellipse of superness $2^{-.5} \approx .707$, which corresponds to a normal ellipse; the uppercase letter 'O' was drawn with superness $2^{-.25} \approx .841$, to help distinguish it from the zero. The ambiguous symbol 'O' (which is not in the font, but METAFONT can of course draw it) lies between these two extremes; its superness is 0.77.

A mathematical superellipse satisfies the equation $|x/a|^\beta + |y/b|^\beta = 1$, for some exponent β. It has extreme points $(\pm a, 0)$ and $(0, \pm b)$, as well as the "corner" points $(\pm\sigma a, \pm\sigma b)$, where $\sigma = 2^{-1/\beta}$ is the superness. The tangent to the curve at $(\sigma a, \sigma b)$ runs in the direction $(-a, b)$, hence it is parallel to a line from $(a, 0)$ to $(0, b)$. Gabriel Lamé invented the superellipse in 1818, and Piet Hein popularized the special case $\beta = 2.5$ [see Martin Gardner, *Mathematical Carnival* (New York: Knopf, 1975), 240–254]; this special case corresponds to a superness of $2^{-.4} \approx .7578582832552$. Plain METAFONT's *superellipse* routine does not produce a perfect superellipse, nor does *fullcircle* yield a true circle, but the results are close enough for practical purposes.

▶ **EXERCISE 14.6**
Try *superellipse* with superness values less than 0.5 or greater than 1.0; explain why you get weird shapes in such cases.

Let's look now at the symbols that are used between key points, when we specify a path. There are five such tokens in plain METAFONT:

..	free curve;
...	bounded curve;
--	straight line;
---	"tense" line;
&	splice.

In general, when you write '$z_0 .. z_1 .. \langle$etc.$\rangle .. z_{n-1} .. z_n$', METAFONT will compute the path of length n that represents its idea of the "most pleasing curve" through the given points z_0 through z_n. The symbol '...' is essentially the same as '..', except that it confines the path to a bounding triangle whenever possible, as explained in Chapter 3. A straight line segment '$z_{k-1} -- z_k$' usually causes the path to change course abruptly at z_{k-1} and z_k. By contrast, a segment specified by '$z_{k-1} --- z_k$' will be a straight line that blends smoothly with the neighboring curves; i.e., the path will enter z_{k-1} and leave z_k in the direction of $z_k - z_{k-1}$. (The *trunk* of El Palo Alto makes use of this option, and we have also used it to draw the signboard of the dangerous bend symbol at the end of Chapter 12.) Finally, the '&' operation joins two independent paths together at a common point, just as '&' concatenates two strings together.

Here, for example, is a somewhat silly path that illustrates all five basic types of joinery:

$z_0 = (0, 100)$; $z_1 = (50, 0)$; $z_2 = (180, 0)$;
for $n = 3$ **upto** 9: $z[n] = z[n-3] + (200, 0)$; **endfor**
draw $z_0 .. z_1 --- z_2 ... \{up\}z_3$
$\quad\quad$ & $z_3 .. z_4 -- z_5 ... \{up\}z_6$
$\quad\quad$ & $z_6 ... z_7 --- z_8 .. \{up\}z_9$.

The '...' operation is usually used only when one or both of the adjacent directions have been specified (like '$\{up\}$' in this example). Plain META-FONT's *flex* construction actually uses '...', not '..' as stated earlier, because this avoids inflection points in certain situations.

A path like '$z_0 --- z_1 --- z_2$' is almost indistinguishable from the broken line '$z_0 -- z_1 -- z_2$', except that if you enlarge the former path you will see that its lines aren't perfectly straight; they bend just a little, so that the curve is "smooth" at z_1 although there's a rather sharp turn there. (This means that the autorounding operations discussed in Chapter 24 will apply.) For example, the path

$(0,3)$ --- $(0,0)$ --- $(3,0)$ is equivalent to

$(0,3)$ .. controls $(-0.0002, 2.9998)$ and $(-0.0002, 0.0002)$
.. $(0,0)$ .. controls $(0.0002, -0.0002)$ and $(2.9998, -0.0002)$ .. $(3,0)$

while $(0,3)$ -- $(0,0)$ -- $(3,0)$ consists of two perfectly straight segments:

$(0,3)$ .. controls $(0,2)$ and $(0,1)$
.. $(0,0)$ .. controls $(1,0)$ and $(2,0)$ .. $(3,0)$.

▶ **EXERCISE 14.7**
Plain METAFONT's *unitsquare* path is defined to be '$(0,0)$ -- $(1,0)$ -- $(1,1)$ -- $(0,1)$ -- cycle'. Explain how the same path could have been defined using only '..' and '&', not '--' or explicit directions.

Sometimes it's desirable to take a path and change all its connecting links to '---', regardless of what they were originally; the key points are left unchanged. Plain METAFONT has a *tensepath* operation that does this. For example, *tensepath unitsquare* $= (0,0)$ --- $(1,0)$ --- $(1,1)$ --- $(0,1)$ --- cycle.

When METAFONT is deciding what curves should be drawn in place of '..' or '...', it has to give special consideration to the beginning and ending points, so that the path will start and finish as gracefully as possible. The solution that usually works out best is to make the first and last path segments very nearly the same as arcs of circles; an unadorned path of length 2 like 'z_0 .. z_1 .. z_2' will therefore turn out to be a good approximation to the unique circular arc that passes through (z_0, z_1, z_2), except in extreme cases. You can change this default behavior at the endpoints either by specifying an explicit direction or by specifying an amount of "curl." If you call for curliness less than 1, the path will decrease its curvature in the vicinity of the endpoint (i.e., it will begin to turn less sharply); if you specify curliness greater than 1, the curvature will increase. (See the definition of El Palo Alto's *trunk*, earlier in this chapter.)

Here, for example, are some pairs of parentheses that were drawn using various amounts of curl. In each case the shape was drawn by a statement of the form '**penstroke** $z_{0e}\{\text{curl}\,c\}$ .. z_{1e} .. $\{\text{curl}\,c\}z_{2e}$'; different values of c produce different-looking parentheses:

curl value	0	1	2	4	*infinity*
yields	()	()	()	()	()

(The parentheses of Computer Modern typefaces are defined by the somewhat more general scheme described in Chapter 12; explicit directions are specified at the endpoints, instead of curls, because this produces better results in unusual cases when the characters are extremely tall or extremely wide.)

The amount of curl should not be negative. When the curl is very large, METAFONT doesn't actually make an extremely sharp turn at the endpoint; instead, it changes the rest of the path so that there is comparatively little curvature at the neighboring point.

Chapter 3 points out that we can change METAFONT's default curves by specifying nonstandard "tension" between points, or even by specifying explicit control points to be used in the four-point method. Let us now study the full syntax of path expressions, so that we can come to a complete understanding of the paths that METAFONT is able to make. Here are the general rules:

⟨path primary⟩ ⟶ ⟨path variable⟩
   | (⟨path expression⟩)
   | **reverse** ⟨path primary⟩
   | **subpath** ⟨pair expression⟩ **of** ⟨path primary⟩
⟨path secondary⟩ ⟶ ⟨path primary⟩
   | ⟨path secondary⟩⟨transformer⟩
⟨path tertiary⟩ ⟶ ⟨path secondary⟩
⟨path expression⟩ ⟶ ⟨path subexpression⟩
   | ⟨path subexpression⟩⟨direction specifier⟩
   | ⟨path subexpression⟩⟨path join⟩ **cycle**
⟨path subexpression⟩ ⟶ ⟨path tertiary⟩ | ⟨pair tertiary⟩
   | ⟨path expression⟩⟨path join⟩⟨path tertiary⟩
⟨path join⟩ ⟶ ⟨direction specifier⟩⟨basic path join⟩⟨direction specifier⟩
⟨direction specifier⟩ ⟶ ⟨empty⟩
   | { **curl** ⟨numeric expression⟩ }
   | { ⟨pair expression⟩ }
   | { ⟨numeric expression⟩ , ⟨numeric expression⟩ }
⟨basic path join⟩ ⟶ **&** | .. | .. ⟨tension⟩ .. | .. ⟨controls⟩ ..
⟨tension⟩ ⟶ **tension** ⟨tension amount⟩
   | **tension** ⟨tension amount⟩ **and** ⟨tension amount⟩
⟨tension amount⟩ ⟶ ⟨numeric primary⟩
   | **atleast** ⟨numeric primary⟩
⟨controls⟩ ⟶ **controls** ⟨pair primary⟩
   | **controls** ⟨pair primary⟩ **and** ⟨pair primary⟩

The operations '...' and '--' and '---' are conspicuously absent from this syntax; that is because Appendix B defines them as macros:

   ...   is an abbreviation for '.. tension atleast 1 ..';
   --   is an abbreviation for '{curl 1} .. {curl 1}';
   ---   is an abbreviation for '.. tension *infinity* ..'.

These syntax rules specify a wide variety of possibilities, even though they don't mention '--' and such things explicitly, so we shall now spend a little while looking carefully at their implications. A path expression essentially has the form

$$p_0 \quad j_1 \quad p_1 \quad j_2 \quad \cdots \quad j_n \quad p_n$$

where each p_k is a tertiary expression of type pair or path, and where each j_k is a "path join." A path join begins and ends with a "direction specifier," and has a "basic path join" in the middle. A direction specifier can be empty, or it can be '{curl c}' for some $c \geq 0$, or it can be a direction vector enclosed in braces. For example, '{*up*}' specifies an upward direction, because plain METAFONT defines *up* to be the pair $(0, 1)$. This same direction could be specified by '{$(0, 1)$}' or '{$(0, 10)$}', or without parentheses as '{$0, 1$}'. If a specified direction vector turns out to be $(0, 0)$, METAFONT behaves as if no direction had been specified; i.e., '$\{0,0\}$' is equivalent to '$\langle\text{empty}\rangle$'. An empty direction specifier is implicitly filled in by rules that we shall discuss later.

A basic path join has three essential forms: (1) '&' simply concatenates two paths, which must share a common endpoint.   (2) '.. tension α and β ..' means that a curve should be defined, having respective "tensions" α and β. Both α and β must be equal to 3/4 or more; we shall discuss tension later in this chapter. (3) '.. controls u and v ..' defines a curve with intermediate control points u and v.

Special abbreviations are also allowed, so that the long forms of basic path joins can usually be avoided: '..' by itself stands for '.. tension 1 and 1 ..', while '.. tension α ..' stands for '.. tension α and α ..', and '.. controls u ..' stands for '.. controls u and u ..'.

Our examples so far have always constructed paths from points; but the syntax shows that it's also possible to write, e.g., 'p_0 .. p_1 .. p_2' when the p's themselves are paths. What does this mean? Well, every such path will already have been changed into a sequence of curves with explicit control points; METAFONT expands such paths into the corresponding sequence of points and basic path joins of type (3). For example, '$((0,0)$ .. $(3,0))$ .. $(3,3)$' is essentially the same as '$(0,0)$ .. controls $(1,0)$ and $(2,0)$ .. $(3,0)$ .. $(3,3)$', because '$(0,0)$ .. $(3,0)$' is the path '$(0,0)$ .. controls $(1,0)$ and $(2,0)$ .. $(3,0)$'. If a cycle is expanded into a subpath in this way, its cyclic nature will be lost; its last point will simply be a copy of its first point.

Now let's consider the rules by which empty direction specifiers can inherit specifications from their environment. An empty direction specifier at the beginning or end of a path, or just next to the '&' operator, is effectively replaced by '$\{\text{curl}\,1\}$'. This rule should be interpreted properly with respect to cyclic paths, which have no beginning or end; for example, 'z_0 .. z_1 & z_1 .. z_2 .. cycle' is equivalent to 'z_0 .. $z_1\{\text{curl}\,1\}$&$\{\text{curl}\,1\}z_1$ .. z_2 .. cycle'.

If there's a nonempty direction specifier after a point but not before it, the nonempty one is copied into both places. Thus, for example, '.. $z\{w\}$' is treated as if it were '.. $\{w\}z\{w\}$'. If there's a nonempty direction specifier before a point but not after it, the nonempty one is, similarly, copied into both places, except if it follows a basic path join that gives explicit control points. The direction specifier that immediately follows '.. controls u and v ..' is always ignored.

An empty direction specifier next to an explicit control point inherits the direction of the adjacent path segment. More precisely, '.. z .. controls u and v ..' is treated as if it were '.. $\{u - z\}z$ .. controls u and v ..' if $u \neq z$, or as if it were '.. $\{\text{curl}\,1\}z$ .. controls u and v ..' if $u = z$. Similarly, '.. controls u and v .. z ..' is treated as if z were followed by $\{z - v\}$ if $z \neq v$, by $\{\text{curl}\,1\}$ otherwise.

After the previous three rules have been applied, we might still be left with cases in which there are points surrounded on both sides by empty direction specifiers. METAFONT must choose appropriate directions at such points, and it does so by applying the following algorithm due to John Hobby [*Discrete and Computational Geometry* **1** (1986), to appear]: Given a sequence

$$z_0\{d_0\} \text{ .. tension } \alpha_0 \text{ and } \beta_1 \text{ .. } z_1 \text{ .. tension } \alpha_1 \text{ and } \beta_2 \text{ .. } z_2$$
$$\langle\text{etc.}\rangle\ z_{n-1} \text{ .. tension } \alpha_{n-1} \text{ and } \beta_n \text{ .. } \{d_n\}z_n$$

for which interior directions need to be determined, we will regard the z's as if they were complex numbers. Let $l_k = |z_k - z_{k-1}|$ be the distance from z_{k-1} to z_k, and let $\psi_k = \arg((z_{k+1} - z_k)/(z_k - z_{k-1}))$ be the turning angle at z_k. We wish to find direction vectors $w_0, w_1, \ldots, w_n$ so that the given sequence can effectively be replaced by

$$z_0\{w_0\} \,.. \text{ tension } \alpha_0 \text{ and } \beta_1 \,.. \{w_1\}z_1\{w_1\} \,.. \text{ tension } \alpha_1 \text{ and } \beta_2 \,.. \{w_2\}z_2$$
$$\langle\text{etc.}\rangle \ z_{n-1}\{w_{n-1}\} \,.. \text{ tension } \alpha_{n-1} \text{ and } \beta_n \,.. \{w_n\}z_n.$$

Since only the directions of the w's are significant, not the magnitudes, it suffices to determine the angles $\theta_k = \arg(w_k/(z_{k+1} - z_k))$. For convenience, we also let $\phi_k = \arg((z_k - z_{k-1})/w_k)$, so that

$$\theta_k + \phi_k + \psi_k = 0. \tag{$*$}$$

Hobby's paper introduces the notion of "mock curvature" according to which the following equations should hold at interior points:

$$\beta_k^2 l_k^{-1}(\alpha_{k-1}^{-1}(\theta_{k-1} + \phi_k) - 3\phi_k) = \alpha_k^2 l_{k+1}^{-1}(\beta_{k+1}^{-1}(\theta_k + \phi_{k+1}) - 3\theta_k). \tag{$**$}$$

We also need to consider boundary conditions. If d_0 is an explicit direction vector w_0, we know θ_0; otherwise d_0 is 'curl γ_0' and we set up the equation

$$\alpha_0^2(\beta_1^{-1}(\theta_0 + \phi_1) - 3\theta_0) = \gamma_0\beta_1^2(\alpha_0^{-1}(\theta_0 + \phi_1) - 3\phi_1). \tag{$***$}$$

If d_n is an explicit vector w_n, we know ϕ_n; otherwise d_n is 'curl γ_n' and we set

$$\beta_n^2(\alpha_{n-1}^{-1}(\theta_{n-1} + \phi_n) - 3\phi_n) = \gamma_n\alpha_{n-1}^2(\beta_n^{-1}(\theta_{n-1} + \phi_n) - 3\theta_{n-1}). \tag{$***'$}$$

It can be shown that the conditions $\alpha_k \geq 3/4$, $\beta_k \geq 3/4$, $\gamma_k \geq 0$ imply that there is a unique solution to the system of equations consisting of $(*)$ and $(**)$ for $0 < k < n$ plus the two boundary equations; hence the desired quantities $\theta_0, \ldots, \theta_{n-1}$ and $\phi_1, \ldots, \phi_n$ are uniquely determined. (The only exception is the degenerate case $n = \gamma_0\gamma_1 = 1$.)

 A similar scheme works for cycles, when there is no '$\{d_0\}$' or '$\{d_n\}$'. In this case equations $(*)$ and $(**)$ hold for all k.

▶ **EXERCISE 14.8**
Write out the equations that determine the directions chosen for the general cycle '$z_0 \,..$ tension α_0 and $\beta_1 \,.. z_1 \,..$ tension α_1 and $\beta_2 \,.. z_2 \,..$ tension α_2 and $\beta_3 \,..$ cycle' of length 3. (You needn't try to solve the equations.)

Whew — these rules have determined the directions at all points. To complete the job of path specification, we need merely explain how to change a segment like '$z_0\{w_0\} \,..$ tension α and $\beta \,.. \{w_1\}z_1$' into a segment of the form '$z_0 \,..$ controls u and $v \,.. z_1$'; i.e., we finally want to know METAFONT's magic recipe for choosing the control points u and v. If $\theta = \arg(w_0/(z_1 - z_0))$ and $\phi = \arg((z_1 - z_0)/w_1)$, the control points are

$$u = z_0 + e^{i\theta}(z_1 - z_0)f(\theta, \phi)/\alpha, \qquad v = z_1 - e^{-i\phi}(z_1 - z_0)f(\phi, \theta)/\beta,$$

where $f(\theta, \phi)$ is another formula due to John Hobby:

$$f(\theta, \phi) = \frac{2 + \sqrt{2}\,(\sin\theta - \frac{1}{16}\sin\phi)(\sin\phi - \frac{1}{16}\sin\theta)(\cos\theta - \cos\phi)}{3\,(1 + \frac{1}{2}(\sqrt{5} - 1)\cos\theta + \frac{1}{2}(3 - \sqrt{5})\cos\phi)}.$$

There's yet one more complication. If the tensions α and/or β have been preceded by the keyword 'atleast', the values of α and/or β are increased, if necessary, to the minimum values such that u and v do not lie outside the "bounding triangle," which is discussed near the end of Chapter 3.

What do these complex rules imply, for METAFONT users who aren't "into" mathematics? The most important fact is that the rules for paths are invariant under shifting, scaling, and rotation. In other words, if the key points z_k of a path are all shifted, scaled, and/or rotated in the same way, the resulting path will be the same as you would get by shifting, scaling, and/or rotating the path defined by the unmodified z_k's (except of course for possible rounding errors). However, this invariance property does not hold if the points or paths are xscaled and yscaled by separate amounts.

Another consequence of the rules is that tension specifications have a fairly straightforward interpretation in terms of control points, when the adjacent directions have been given: The formulas for u and v simply involve division by α and β. This means, for example, that a tension of 2 brings the control points halfway in towards the neighboring key points, and a tension of *infinity* makes the points very close indeed; contrariwise, tensions less than 1 move the control points out.

Tension and curl specifications also influence METAFONT's choices of directions at the key points. That is why, for example, the construction '$z_{k-1} \text{ --- } z_k$' (which means 'z_{k-1} .. tension *infinity* .. z_k') affects the direction of a larger path as it enters z_{k-1} and leaves z_k.

The rules imply that a change in the position of point z_n causes a change in the curve near point z_0, when METAFONT has to choose directions at all points between z_0 and z_n. However, this effect is generally negligible except in the vicinity of the changed point. You can verify this by looking, for example, at the control points that METAFONT chooses for the path '$(0,0) .. (1,0) .. (2,0) .. (3,0) .. (4,0) \ldots \{up\}(5,y)$', as y varies.

▶**EXERCISE 14.9**
Run METAFONT on the 'expr' file of Chapter 8, and ask to see the path expression '*unitsquare* shifted $(0,1)$ .. *unitsquare* shifted $(1,0)$'. Account for the results that you get.

▶**EXERCISE 14.10**
We've said that '--' is plain METAFONT's abbreviation for '$\{\text{curl} 1\} .. \{\text{curl} 1\}$'. Would there be any essential difference if '--' were defined to mean '$\{\text{curl} 2\} .. \{\text{curl} 2\}$'?

▶**EXERCISE 14.11**
Look closely at the syntax of ⟨path expression⟩ and explain what METAFONT does with the specification '$(0,0) .. (3,3) .. \text{cycle}\{\text{curl} 1\}$'.

Now let's come back to simpler topics relating to paths. Once a path has been specified, there are lots of things you can do with it, besides drawing and filling and suchlike. For example, if p is a path, you can reverse its direction by saying 'reverse p'; the reverse of 'z_0 .. controls u and v .. z_1' is 'z_1 .. controls v and u .. z_0'.

▶**EXERCISE 14.12**
True or false: length reverse p = length p, for all paths p.

It's convenient to associate "time" with paths, by imagining that we move along a path of length n as time passes from 0 to n. (Chapter 8 has already illustrated this notion, with respect to an almost-but-not-quite-circular path called p2; it's a good idea to review the discussion of paths and subpaths in Chapter 8 now before you read further.) Given a path

$$p = z_0 \mathinner{\ldotp\ldotp} \text{controls } u_0 \text{ and } v_1 \mathinner{\ldotp\ldotp} z_1 \langle \text{etc.} \rangle z_{n-1} \mathinner{\ldotp\ldotp} \text{controls } u_{n-1} \text{ and } v_n \mathinner{\ldotp\ldotp} z_n$$

and a number t, METAFONT determines 'point t of p' as follows: If $t \le 0$, the result is z_0; if $t \ge n$, the result is z_n; otherwise if $k \le t < k+1$, it is $(t-k)[z_k, u_k, v_{k+1}, z_{k+1}]$, where we generalize the '$t[\alpha, \beta]$' notation so that $t[\alpha, \beta, \gamma]$ means $t[t[\alpha, \beta], t[\beta, \gamma]]$ and $t[\alpha, \beta, \gamma, \delta]$ means $t[t[\alpha, \beta, \gamma], t[\beta, \gamma, \delta]]$. (This is a Bernshteĭn polynomial in t, cf. Chapter 3.) Given a cyclic path

$$c = z_0 \mathinner{\ldotp\ldotp} \text{controls } u_0 \text{ and } v_1 \mathinner{\ldotp\ldotp} z_1 \langle \text{etc.} \rangle z_{n-1} \mathinner{\ldotp\ldotp} \text{controls } u_{n-1} \text{ and } v_n \mathinner{\ldotp\ldotp} \text{cycle}$$

and a number t, METAFONT determines 'point t of c' in essentially the same way, except that t is first reduced modulo n so as to lie in the range $0 \le t < n$.

▶ **EXERCISE 14.13**
True or false: point t of $(z_0 \mathbin{--} z_1) = t[z_0, z_1]$.

Given a path p and two time values $t_1 \le t_2$, 'subpath (t_1, t_2) of p' contains all the values 'point t of p' as t varies from t_1 to t_2. There's no problem understanding how to define this subpath when t_1 and t_2 are integers; for example,

$$\text{subpath } (2, 4) \text{ of } p = z_2 \mathinner{\ldotp\ldotp} \text{controls } u_2 \text{ and } v_3 \mathinner{\ldotp\ldotp} z_3 \mathinner{\ldotp\ldotp} \text{controls } u_3 \text{ and } v_4 \mathinner{\ldotp\ldotp} z_4$$

in the notation above, if we assume that $n \ge 4$. The fractional case is handled by "stretching time" in one segment of the curve; for example, if $0 < t < 1$ we have

$$\text{subpath } (0, t) \text{ of } p = z_0 \mathinner{\ldotp\ldotp} \text{controls } t[z_0, u_0] \text{ and } t[z_0, u_0, v_1] \mathinner{\ldotp\ldotp} t[z_0, u_0, v_1, z_1];$$
$$\text{subpath } (t, 1) \text{ of } p = t[z_0, u_0, v_1, z_1] \mathinner{\ldotp\ldotp} \text{controls } t[u_0, v_1, z_1] \text{ and } t[v_1, z_1] \mathinner{\ldotp\ldotp} z_1.$$

These two subpaths together account for all points of '$z_0 \mathinner{\ldotp\ldotp} \text{controls } u_0 \text{ and } v_1 \mathinner{\ldotp\ldotp} z_1$'. To get subpath (t_1, t_2) of p when $0 < t_1 < t_2 < 1$, METAFONT applies this construction twice, by computing subpath $(t_1/t_2, 1)$ of subpath $(0, t_2)$ of p.

The operation 'subpath (t_1, t_2) of p' is defined for all combinations of times (t_1, t_2) and paths p by the following rules: Let $n = \text{length}\,p$. (1) If $t_1 > t_2$, subpath (t_1, t_2) of p = reverse subpath (t_2, t_1) of p. Henceforth we shall assume that $t_1 \le t_2$. (2) If $t_1 = t_2$, subpath (t_1, t_2) of p = point t_1 of p, a path of length zero. Henceforth we shall assume that $t_1 < t_2$. (3) If $t_1 < 0$ and p is a cycle, subpath (t_1, t_2) of p = subpath $(t_1 + n, t_2 + n)$ of p. If $t_1 < 0$ and p is not a cycle, subpath (t_1, t_2) of p = subpath $(0, \max(0, t_2))$ of p. Henceforth we shall assume that $t_1 \ge 0$. (4) If $t_1 \ge n$ and p is a cycle, subpath (t_1, t_2) of p = subpath $(t_1 - n, t_2 - n)$ of p. If $t_1 < n < t_2$ and p is a cycle, subpath (t_1, t_2) of p = subpath (t_1, t_2) of $(p \,\&\, p \,\&\, \text{cycle})$. If $t_2 > n$ and p is not a cycle, subpath (t_1, t_2) of p = subpath $(\min(t_1, n), n)$ of p. Henceforth we shall assume that $0 \le t_1 < t_2 \le n$. (5) If $t_1 \ge 1$, subpath (t_1, t_2) of p = subpath $(t_1 - 1, t_2 - 1)$ of subpath $(1, n)$ of p, where subpath $(1, n)$ of p is obtained by removing the first segment of p. Henceforth we shall assume that $0 \le t_1 < 1$. (6) If $t_2 > 1$, subpath (t_1, t_2) of p = subpath $(t_1, 1)$ of $p \,\&\,$ subpath $(1, t_2)$ of p. Henceforth we shall assume that $0 \le t_1 < t_2 \le 1$. (7) The remaining cases were defined in the preceding paragraph.

▸ **EXERCISE 14.14**
What is the length of 'subpath $(2.718, 3.142)$ of p'?

Besides 'point t of p', METAFONT allows you to speak of 'postcontrol t of p' and 'precontrol t of p'; this gives access to the control points of a path. Let

$$p = z_0 \ .. \ \text{controls} \ u_0 \ \text{and} \ v_1 \ .. \ z_1 \ \langle \text{etc.} \rangle \ z_{n-1} \ .. \ \text{controls} \ u_{n-1} \ \text{and} \ v_n \ .. \ z_n.$$

If $t < n$, postcontrol t of p is the first control point in subpath (t, n) of p; if $t \geq n$, postcontrol t of p is z_n. If $t > 0$, precontrol t of p is the last control point in subpath $(0, t)$ of p; if $t \leq 0$, precontrol t of p is z_n. In particular, if t is an integer, postcontrol t of p is u_t for $0 \leq t < n$, and precontrol t of p is v_t for $0 < t \leq n$.

The ability to extract key points and control points makes it possible to define interesting operations such as plain METAFONT's *interpath* function, which allows you to interpolate between paths. For example, '*interpath*$(1/3, p, q)$' will produce a path of length n whose points are $1/3$[point t of p, point t of q] for $0 \leq t \leq n$, given any paths p and q of length n. It can be defined by a fairly simple program:

> **vardef** *interpath*(**expr** a, p, q) =
> **for** $t = 0$ **upto** length $p - 1$: a[point t of p, point t of q]
>   .. controls a[postcontrol t of p, postcontrol t of q]
>   and a[precontrol $t + 1$ of p, precontrol $t + 1$ of q] .. **endfor**
> **if** cycle p: cycle   % assume that p, q are both cycles or both noncycles
> **else**: a[point *infinity* of p, point *infinity* of q] **fi enddef**;

On February 14, 1979, the author bought a box of chocolates and placed the box on a piece of graph paper (after suitably disposing of the contents). The experimental data gathered in this way led to a "definitive" heart shape:

$$heart = (100, 162) \ .. \ (140, 178)\{right\} \ .. \ (195, 125)\{down\}$$
$$.. \ (100, 0)\{\text{curl } 0\} \ .. \ \{up\}(5, 125) \ .. \ \{right\}(60, 178) \ .. \ (100, 162);$$

It is interesting to interpolate between *heart* and other paths, by using a program like

> **for** $n = 0$ **upto** 10: **draw** *interpath*$(n/10, p, heart)$; **endfor**.

For example, the left illustration below was obtained by taking

$$p = (100, 0) \ \text{--} \ (300, 0) \ \text{--} \ (200, 0) \ \text{--} \ (100, 0) \ \text{--} \ (0, 0) \ \text{--} \ (-100, 0) \ \text{--} \ (100, 0);$$

notice that *interpath* doesn't necessarily preserve smoothness at the key points. The right illustration was obtained by duplicating point $(100, 0)$ in *heart* (thereby making it a path of length 7) and taking

$$p = (100, 200) \ \text{--} \ (200, 200) \ \text{--} \ (200, 100)$$
$$\text{--} \ (200, 0) \ \text{--} \ (0, 0) \ \text{--} \ (0, 100) \ \text{--} \ (0, 200) \ \text{--} \ (100, 200).$$

Plain METAFONT allows you to say 'direction t of p' in order to determine the direction in which path p is moving at time t. This is simply an abbreviation for '(postcontrol t of p) − (precontrol t of p)'. Sometimes a path veers abruptly and has no unique direction; in this case the direction function gives a result somewhere between the two possible extremes. For example, the *heart* path above turns a corner at time 3; 'direction 3 of *heart*' turns out to be $(-93.29172, 0)$, but 'direction $3 -$ *epsilon* of *heart*' is $(-46.64589, -31.63852)$ and 'direction $3 +$ *epsilon* of *heart*' is $(-46.64589, 31.63852)$.

Conversely, METAFONT can tell you when a path heads in a given direction. You just ask for 'directiontime w of p', where w is a direction vector and p is a path. This operation is best understood by looking at examples, so let's resume our dialog with the computer by applying METAFONT to the 'expr' file as in Chapter 8. When METAFONT first says '**gimme**', our opening strategy this time will be to type

```
hide(p3 = (0,0){right}..{up}(1,1)) p3
```

so that we have a new path to play with. Now the fun begins:

You type	*And the result is*
directiontime right of p3	0
directiontime up of p3	1
directiontime down of p3	-1
directiontime (1,1) of p3	0.5
directiontime left of reverse p3	1
direction directiontime (1,2) of p3 of p3	(0.23126,0.46251)
directiontime right of subpath(epsilon,1) of p3	0
directiontime right of subpath(2epsilon,1)of p3	-1
directiontime (1,1) of subpath(epsilon,1) of p3	0.49998
direction epsilon of p3	(0.55226,0)
direction 2epsilon of p3	(0.55229,0.00003)
directiontime dir 30 of p3	0.32925
angle direction 0.32925 of p3	29.99849
angle direction 0.32925+epsilon of p3	30.00081
directionpoint up of p3	(1,1)

Note that directiontime yields -1 if the specified direction doesn't occur. At time *epsilon*, path p_3 is still traveling right, but at time 2*epsilon* it has begun to turn upward. The 'directionpoint' operation is analogous to directiontime, but it gives the point on the path rather than the time of arrival.

You type	*And the result is*
directiontime up of fullcircle	0
directiontime left of fullcircle	2
directiontime right of fullcircle	6
directiontime (-1,1) of fullcircle	1
directiontime (epsilon,infinity) of fullcircle	8

directiontime right of unitsquare	0
directiontime up of unitsquare	1
directiontime (1,1) of unitsquare	1
directiontime (-1,1) of unitsquare	2

If a path travels in a given direction more than once, directiontime reports only the first time. The *unitsquare* path has sharp turns at the corners; directiontime considers that all directions between the incoming and outgoing ones are instantaneously present.

It's possible to construct pathological paths in which unusual things happen. For example, the path $p = (0,0)$ .. controls $(1,1)$ and $(0,1)$ .. $(1,0)$ has a "cusp" at time 0.5, when it comes to a dead stop and turns around. (If you ask for 'direction 0.5 of p', the answer is zero, while direction $0.5 - \epsilon$ of p is $(0, 2\epsilon)$ and direction $0.5 + \epsilon$ of p is $(0, -2\epsilon)$.) The directiontime operation assumes that all possible directions actually occur when a path comes to a standstill, hence 'directiontime *right* of p' will be 0.5 in this case even though it might be argued that p never turns to the right. Paths with cusps are numerically unstable, and they might become "strange" after transformations are applied, because rounding errors might change their turning numbers. The path p in this example has control points that correspond to tensions of only 0.28 with respect to the initial and final directions; since METAFONT insists that tensions be at least 0.75, this anomalous path could never have arisen if the control points hadn't been given explicitly.

▶ **EXERCISE 14.15**
Write macros called *posttension* and *pretension* that determine the effective tensions of a path's control points at integer times t. For example, '*pretension* 1 of $(z_0$ .. tension α and β .. $z_1)$' should be β (approximately). Test your macro by computing *posttension* 0 of $((0,0)\{right\} \ldots \{up\}(1,10))$.

We have now discussed almost all of the things that METAFONT can do with paths; but there's one more important operation to consider, namely intersection. Given two paths p and q, you can write

p intersectiontimes q

and the result will be a pair of times (t, u) such that point t of $p \approx$ point u of q. For example, using the **expr** routine,

You type	*And the result is*
unitsquare intersectiontimes fullcircle	(0.50002,0)
unitsquare intersectiontimes fullcircle rotated 90	(0.50002,6)
reverse unitsquare intersectiontimes fullcircle	(0.50002,2)
fullcircle intersectiontimes unitsquare	(0,0.50002)
halfcircle rotated 45 intersectiontimes unitsquare	(1,3.5)
halfcircle rotated 89 intersectiontimes unitsquare	(0.02196,3.5)
halfcircle rotated 90 intersectiontimes unitsquare	(0,3.50002)
halfcircle rotated 91 intersectiontimes unitsquare	(-1,-1)
halfcircle rotated 45 intersectiontimes fullcircle	(0,1)
fullcircle intersectiontimes (-0.5,0)	(4,0)

```
unitsquare intersectionpoint fullcircle              (0.5,0)
reverse unitsquare intersectionpoint fullcircle      (0,0.5)
```

Notice that the result is $(-1, -1)$ if the paths don't intersect. The last two examples illustrate the 'intersectionpoint' operator, which yields the common point of intersection. Both intersectiontimes and intersectionpoint apply at the tertiary level of precedence, hence parentheses were not needed in these examples.

▶ **EXERCISE 14.16**
J. H. Quick (a student) wanted to construct a path r that started on some previously defined path p and proceeded up to the point where it touched another path q, after which r was supposed to continue on path q. So he wrote

path r; **numeric** t, u; $(t, u) = p$ intersectiontimes q;
$r =$ subpath $(0, t)$ of p & subpath $(u, \mathit{infinity})$ of q;

but it didn't work. Why not?

If the paths intersect more than once, METAFONT has a somewhat peculiar way of deciding what times (t, u) should be reported by 'p intersectiontimes q'. Suppose p has length m and q has length n. (Paths of length 0 are first changed into motionless paths of length 1.) METAFONT proceeds to examine subpath $(k, k+1)$ of p versus subpath $(l, l+1)$ of q, for $k = 0, \ldots, m-1$ and $l = 0, \ldots, n-1$, with l varying most rapidly. This reduces the general problem to the special case of paths of length 1, and the times (t, u) for the first such intersection found are added to (k, l). But within paths of length 1 the search for intersection times is somewhat different: Instead of reporting the "lexicographically smallest" pair (t, u) that corresponds to an intersection, METAFONT finds the (t, u) whose "shuffled binary" representation $(.t_1 u_1 t_2 u_2 \ldots)_2$ is minimum, where $(.t_1 t_2 \ldots)_2$ and $(.u_1 u_2 \ldots)_2$ are the radix-2 representations of t and u.

▶ **EXERCISE 14.17**
(A mathematical puzzle.) The path $p = (0,0)$ .. controls $(2,2)$ and $(0,1)$ .. $(1,0)$ loops on itself, so there are times $t < u$ such that point t of $p \approx$ point u of p. Devise a simple way to compute (t, u) in a METAFONT program, without using the subpath operation.

Let's conclude this chapter by applying what we've learned about paths to a real-life example. The *Journal of Algorithms* has been published since 1980 by Academic Press, and its cover page carries the following logo, which was designed by J. C. Knuth to blend with the style of type used elsewhere on that page:

A METAFONT program to produce this logo will make it possible for the editors of the journal to use it on letterheads in their correspondence. Here is one way to do the job, without needing to erase anything:

1 **beginchar**(`"A"`, $29mm^\#$, $25mm^\#$, 0); $\;thick^\# := 2mm^\#$; $\;thin^\# := 5/4mm^\#$;
2 **define_whole_blacker_pixels**($thick$, $thin$);
3 **forsuffixes** $\$ = a, b, c$: **transform** $\$$;
4   **forsuffixes** $e = l, r$: **path** $\$e, \$'e$; **numeric** $t\$[\,]e$; **endfor endfor**
5 $penpos_1(thick, 0)$; $penpos_2(thick, 90)$; $penpos_3(thick, 180)$; $penpos_4(thick, 270)$;
6 $penpos_5(thick, 0)$; $penpos_6(thick, 90)$; $penpos_7(thick, 180)$; $penpos_8(thick, 270)$;
7 $x_2 = x_4 = x_6 = x_8 = .5[x_5, x_7] = .5w$; $\;x_{1r} = w$; $\;x_{3r} = 0$; $\;x_5 - x_7 = y_6 - y_8$;
8 $y_1 = y_3 = y_5 = y_7 = .5[y_6, y_8] = .5h$; $\;y_{2r} = h$; $\;y_{4r} = 0$; $\;y_{6r} = .75h$;
9 **forsuffixes** $e = l, r$: $a.e = b'e = c'e = superellipse(z_{1e}, z_{2e}, z_{3e}, z_{4e}, .75)$;
10     $a'e = b.e = c.e = superellipse(z_{5e}, z_{6e}, z_{7e}, z_{8e}, .72)$; **endfor**
11 $penpos_{a1}(thin, 0)$; $\;penpos_{a5}(whatever, -90)$; $\;penpos_{a9}(thin, 180)$;
12 $x_{a1l} - x_{a9l} = 1/3(x_{5l} - x_{7l})$; $\;x_{a5} = .5w$; $\;y_{a1} = y_{a9}$; $\;y_{a5r} = 4/7h$;
13 $x_{a3l} = x_{a1l}$; $\;x_{a3r} = x_{a1r}$; $\;x_{a4r} = 1/6[x_{a3r}, x_{1l}]$; $\;x_0 = .5w$; $\;y_0 = .52h$;
14 $x_{a6l} + x_{a4l} = x_{a6r} + x_{a4r} = x_{a7l} + x_{a3l} = x_{a7r} + x_{a3r} = x_{a9} + x_{a1} = w$;
15 $y_{a3r} = y_{a4r} = y_{a6r} = y_{a7r} = .2[y_{2l}, y_0]$; $\;y_{a3l} = y_{a4l} = y_{a6l} = y_{a7l} = y_{a3r} - thin$;
16 $z_{a4l} = z_{a4r} + (thin, 0)\,\mathrm{rotated}(\mathrm{angle}(z_{a4r} - z_{a5r}) + 90)$
17       $+ whatever * (z_{a4r} - z_{a5r})$; $\;z_{a4l} - z_{a5l} = whatever * (z_{a4r} - z_{a5r})$;
18 $z = a.r$ intersectionpoint $(z_0\,\text{-- } (w, 0))$; $\;y_{a1} - y_{a5} = \mathrm{length}(z - z_0)$;
19 $b = identity$ shifted $(0, y_0 - y_{a1})$ rotatedaround$(z_0, 90 - \mathrm{angle}(z_0 - (w, 0)))$;
20 $c = b$ reflectedabout (z_2, z_4);
21 **for** $n = 1, 3, 4, 5, 6, 7, 9$: **forsuffixes** $e = l, , r$: **forsuffixes** $\$ = b, c$:
22     $z_{\$[n]e} = z_{a[n]e}$ transformed $\$$; **endfor endfor endfor**
23 **forsuffixes** $e = l, r$: **forsuffixes** $\$ = a, b, c$:
24     $z_{\$2e} = \$r$ intersectionpoint $(z_{\$1e}\,\text{-- } z_{\$3e})$;
25     $z_{\$8e} = \$r$ intersectionpoint $(z_{\$9e}\,\text{-- } z_{\$7e})$;
26     $t_{\$1e} = \mathrm{xpart}(\$e$ intersectiontimes $(z_{\$1l}\,\text{-- } z_{\$3l}))$;
27     $t_{\$9e} = \mathrm{xpart}(\$e$ intersectiontimes $(z_{\$9l}\,\text{-- } z_{\$7l}))$;
28     $t_{\$4e} = \mathrm{xpart}(\$'e$ intersectiontimes $(z_{\$5r}\,\text{-- } z_{\$4l}))$;
29     $t_{\$6e} = \mathrm{xpart}(\$'e$ intersectiontimes $(z_{\$5r}\,\text{-- } z_{\$6l}))$; **endfor endfor**
30 **penstroke** subpath(t_{a9e}, t_{b6e}) of $a.e$;
31 **penstroke** subpath(t_{b4e}, t_{c4e}) of $b'e$;
32 **penstroke** subpath$(t_{c6e}, t_{a1e} + 8)$ of $c'e$;
33 **penstroke** subpath(t_{a6e}, t_{b9e}) of $a'e$;
34 **penstroke** subpath(t_{b1e}, t_{c1e}) of $b.e$;
35 **penstroke** subpath$(t_{c9e}, t_{a4e} + 8)$ of $c.e$;
36 **forsuffixes** $\$ = a, b, c$: **penlabels**($\$1, \$2, \$3, \$4, \$5, \$6, \$7, \$8, \$9$);
37   **penstroke** $z_{\$2e}\,\text{-- } z_{\$3e}\,\text{-- } z_{\$4e}\,\text{-- } z_{\$5e}\,\text{-- } z_{\$6e}\,\text{-- } z_{\$7e}\,\text{-- } z_{\$8e}$; **endfor**
38 **penlabels**(**range** 0 **thru** 8); **endchar**;

Lines 5–10 of this program define the main superellipses of the figure. The outer superellipse is eventually drawn as three separate strokes in lines 30–32, and the inner one is drawn as three strokes in lines 33–35. The rest of the figure consists of three arrows, whose point labels are prefaced by the respective labels a, b, c. Lines 11–18 define the 'a' arrow; then lines 19–22 transform these points into the 'b' and 'c' arrows, anticipating some of the things we shall discuss in Chapter 15. Thirty-six intersections between arrows and superellipses are computed in lines 23–29, and the arrows are finally drawn by the penstrokes specified in lines 36–37.

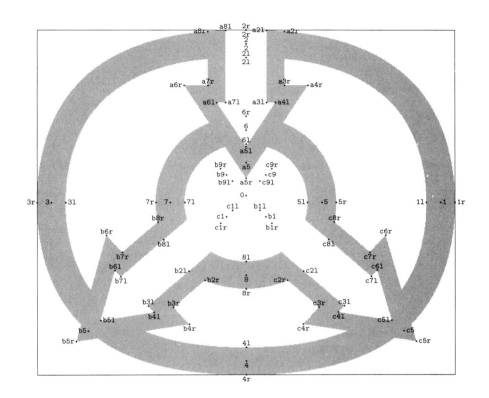

The route is indicated by dots,
the days' journeys are expressed by numbers,
and letters are used to locate notable places and sites.
. . . We arrived at the Arroyo de San Francisco,
beside which stream is the redwood tree I spoke of yesterday;
I measured its height with the Graphometer
and reckoned it to be fifty yards high, more or less.
— FRAY PEDRO FONT, *Diary* (1776)

The practical teaching of the masters of Art was summed by the O of Giotto.
— JOHN RUSKIN, *The Cestus of Aglaia* (1865)

15
Transformations

Points, paths, pens, and pictures can be shifted, scaled, rotated, and revamped in a variety of ways. Our aim in this chapter will be to learn all about the built-in metamorphoses of METAFONT, because they can make programs simpler and more versatile.

The basic transformations have already appeared in many examples, but let's start by reviewing them here:

$$
\begin{aligned}
(x, y) \text{ shifted } (a, b) &= (x + a, y + b); \\
(x, y) \text{ scaled } s &= (sx, sy); \\
(x, y) \text{ xscaled } s &= (sx, y); \\
(x, y) \text{ yscaled } s &= (x, sy); \\
(x, y) \text{ slanted } s &= (x + sy, y); \\
(x, y) \text{ rotated } \theta &= (x \cos \theta - y \sin \theta, x \sin \theta + y \cos \theta); \\
(x, y) \text{ zscaled } (u, v) &= (xu - yv, xv + yu).
\end{aligned}
$$

One of the nice things about METAFONT is that you don't have to remember the sine-and-cosine formulas of trigonometry; you just have to know that '(x, y) rotated θ' means 'the vector (x, y) rotated θ degrees counterclockwise around $(0, 0)$', and the computer does all the necessary calculations by itself. The operation of zscaling may look a bit strange, but it is simply a combination of rotating by angle (u, v) and scaling by length (u, v).

Plain METAFONT provides two more transformations that are commonly needed: You can say '(x, y) rotatedaround (z_0, θ)' if you want to rotate around point z_0 instead of point $(0, 0)$. And you can say '(x, y) reflectedabout (z_1, z_2)' if you want to find the point directly opposite (x, y) on the other side of the straight line that runs through z_1 and z_2.

All of these operations are special manifestations of a single glorious maneuver that can be written in the general form

$$(x, y) \text{ transformed } t.$$

Here t is a variable (or primary expression) of type **transform**; it stands for any desired sequence of shiftings, scalings, slantings, etc., all in one fell swoop.

You can give equations between transforms, just as you can give equations between other types of things in METAFONT programs. Thus, for example, you might say

transform $t[\ ]$; $t_2 = t_1$ shifted $(2, 2)$ rotated 30;

then an expression like '(x, y) transformed t_1 shifted $(2, 2)$ rotated 30' can be abbreviated to '(x, y) transformed t_2', which is simpler and faster.

There's a special transform variable called *identity* with the amazing property that

$$(x, y) \text{ transformed } identity = (x, y)$$

for all x and y. You might think that *identity* is useless, since it does nothing, but in fact it's a natural starting point for building other transforms. For example, line 19 of the program at the end of the previous chapter says

$$b = identity \text{ shifted } (0, y_0 - y_{a1}) \text{ rotatedaround}(z_0, theta);$$

this defines the transform variable b to be a compound transformation that is used on lines 21 and 22 to construct the lower left arrow as a shifted and rotated copy of the upper arrow, in the character being drawn.

 A **transform** variable t represents six numbers $(t_x, t_y, t_{xx}, t_{xy}, t_{yx}, t_{yy})$, in much the same way as a **pair** variable represents two numbers (x, y). The general transformation '(x, y) transformed t' is simply an abbreviation for

$$(t_x + x\,t_{xx} + y\,t_{xy},\ t_y + x\,t_{yx} + y\,t_{yy});$$

thus, for example, 't_{xy}' appears in the xpart of the transform as the coefficient of y. If you say '**show** t' when t is a completely unknown transform, the computer will type

>> (xpart t,ypart t,xxpart t,xypart t,yxpart t,yypart t)

just as it would type '>> (xpart u,ypart u)' for a completely unknown variable u of type **pair**. You can access individual components of a transform by referring to '$xpart\ t$', '$ypart\ t$', '$xxpart\ t$', etc.

 Once again, we can learn best by computer experiments with the **expr** file (cf. Chapter 8); this time the idea is to play with transforms:

You type	And the result is
identity	(0,0,1,0,0,1)
identity shifted (a,b)	(a,b,1,0,0,1)
identity scaled s	(0,0,s,0,0,s)
identity xscaled s	(0,0,s,0,0,1)
identity yscaled s	(0,0,1,0,0,s)
identity slanted s	(0,0,1,s,0,1)
identity rotated 90	(0,0,0,-1,1,0)
identity rotated 30	(0,0,0.86603,-0.5,0.5,0.86603)
identity rotatedaround ((2,3),90)	(5,1,0,-1,1,0)
(x,y) rotatedaround ((2,3),90)	(-y+5,x+1)
(x,y) reflectedabout ((0,0),(0,1))	(-x,y)
(x,y) reflectedabout ((0,0),(1,1))	(y,x)
(x,y) reflectedabout ((5,0),(0,10))	(-0.8y-0.6x+8,0.6y-0.8x+4)

 ▶ **EXERCISE 15.1**
Guess the result of '(x,y) reflectedabout ((0,0),(1,0))'.

 ▶ **EXERCISE 15.2**
What transform takes (x, y) into $(-x, -y)$?

▶ **EXERCISE 15.3**
True or false: $(-(x, y))$ transformed $t = -((x, y)$ transformed $t)$.

In order to have some transform variables to work with, it's necessary to 'hide' some declarations and commands before giving the next exprs:

You type	And the result is
`hide(transform t[]) t1`	`(xpart t1,ypart t1,xxpart...)`
`hide(t1=identity zscaled(1,2)) t1`	`(0,0,1,-2,2,1)`
`hide(t2=t1 shifted (1,2)) t2`	`(1,2,1,-2,2,1)`
`t2 xscaled s`	`(s,2,s,-2s,2,1)`
`unknown t2`	`false`
`transform t2`	`true`
`t1=t2`	`false`
`t1<t2`	`true`
`inverse t2`	`(-1,0,0.2,0.4,-0.4,0.2)`
`inverse t2 transformed t2`	`(0,0,0.99998,0,0,0.99998)`
`hide(t3 transformed t2=identity) t3`	`(-1,0,0.2,0.4,-0.4,0.2)`

The *inverse* function finds the transform that undoes the work of another; the equation that defines t_3 above shows how to calculate an inverse indirectly, without using *inverse*.

Like numeric expressions and pair expressions, transform expressions can be either "known" or "unknown" at any given point in a program. (If any component of a transform is unknown, the whole transform is regarded as unknown.) You are always allowed to use the constructions

⟨known⟩ transformed ⟨known⟩
⟨unknown⟩ transformed ⟨known⟩
⟨known⟩ transformed ⟨unknown⟩

but METAFONT will balk at '⟨unknown⟩ transformed ⟨unknown⟩'. This is not the most lenient rule that could have been implemented, but it does have the virtue of being easily remembered.

▶ **EXERCISE 15.4**

If z_1 and z_2 are unknown pairs, you can't say 'z_1 shifted z_2', because 'shifted z_2' is an unknown transform. What can you legally say instead?

▶ **EXERCISE 15.5**

Suppose *dbend* is a picture variable that contains a normal dangerous bend sign, as in the "reverse-video" example of Chapter 13. Explain how to transform it into the left-handed dangerous bend that heads this paragraph.

The next three lines illustrate the fact that you can specify a transform completely by specifying the images of three points:

You type	And the result is
`hide((0,0)transformed t4=(1,2)) t4`	`(1,2,xxpart t4,xypart t4,...)`
`hide((1,0)transformed t4=(4,5)) t4`	`(1,2,3,xypart t4,3,yypart t4)`
`hide((1,4)transformed t4=(0,0)) t4`	`(1,2,3,-1,3,-1.25)`

The points at which the transform is given shouldn't all lie on a straight line.

Now let's use transformation to make a little ornament, based on a '$\cup$' shape replicated four times:

The following program merits careful study:

```
 1   beginchar("4", 11pt#, 11pt#, 0);
 2   pickup pencircle scaled 3/4pt yscaled 1/3 rotated 30;
 3   transform t;
 4   t = identity rotatedaround((.5w, .5h), −90);
 5   x₂ = .35w;  x₃ = .6w;
 6   y₂ = .1h;  topy₃ = .4h;
 7   path p;  p = z₂{right} ... {up}z₃;
 8   top z₁ = point .5 of p transformed t;
 9   draw z₁ ... p;
10   addto currentpicture also currentpicture transformed t;
11   addto currentpicture also currentpicture transformed (t transformed t);
12   labels(1, 2, 3);  endchar;
```

Lines 3 and 4 compute the transform that moves each '$\cup$' to its clockwise neighbor. Lines 5–7 compute the right half of the '$\cup$'. Line 8 is the most interesting: It puts point z_1 on the rotated path. Line 9 draws the '$\cup$', line 10 changes it into two, and line 11 changes two into four. The parentheses on line 11 could have been omitted, but it is much faster to transform a transform than to transform a picture.

 METAFONT will transform a picture expression only when t_{xx}, t_{xy}, t_{yx}, and t_{yy} are integers and either $t_{xy} = t_{yx} = 0$ or $t_{xx} = t_{yy} = 0$; furthermore, the values of t_x and t_y are rounded to the nearest integers. Otherwise the transformation would not take pixel boundaries into pixel boundaries.

▶ **EXERCISE 15.6**
Explain how to rotate the ornament by 45°.

Plain METAFONT maintains a special variable called *currenttransform*, behind the scenes. Every **fill** and **draw** command is affected by this variable; for example, the statement '**fill** *p*' actually fills the interior of the path

> *p* transformed *currenttransform*

instead of *p* itself. We haven't mentioned this before, because *currenttransform* is usually equal to *identity*; but nonstandard settings of *currenttransform* can be used for special effects that are occasionally desired. For example, it's possible to change 'METAFONT' to '*METAFONT*' by simply saying

> *currenttransform* := *identity* slanted 1/4

and executing the programs of `logo.mf` that are described in Chapter 11; no other changes to those programs are necessary.

It's worth noting that the pen nib used to draw '*METAFONT*' was not slanted when *currenttransform* was changed; only the "tracks" of the pen, the paths in **draw** commands, were modified. Thus the slanted image was not simply obtained by slanting the unslanted image.

When fonts are being made for devices with nonsquare pixels, plain META-FONT will set *currenttransform* to '*identity* yscaled *aspect_ratio*', and **pickup** will similarly yscale the pen nibs that are used for drawing. In this case the slanted '*METAFONT*' letters should be drawn with

> *currenttransform* := *identity* slanted 1/4 yscaled *aspect_ratio*.

▶ **EXERCISE 15.7**
Our program for '⟨⟩' doesn't work when pixels aren't square. Fix it so that it handles a general *aspect_ratio*.

Change begets change. Nothing propagates so fast.
— CHARLES DICKENS, *Martin Chuzzlewit* (1843)

There are some that never know how to change.
— MARK TWAIN, *Joan of Arc* (1896)

16

Calligraphic Effects

Pens were introduced in Chapter 4, and we ought to make a systematic study of what METAFONT can do with them before we spill any more ink. The purpose of this chapter will be to explore the uses of "fixed" pen nibs—i.e., variables and expressions of type **pen**—rather than to consider the creation of shapes by means of outlines or penstrokes.

When you say '**pickup** ⟨pen expression⟩', the macros of plain META-FONT do several things for you: They create a representation of the specified pen nib, and assign it to a pen variable called *currentpen*; then they store away information about the top, bottom, left, and right extents of that pen, for use in *top*, *bot*, *lft*, and *rt* operations. A **draw** or **drawdot** or **filldraw** command will make use of *currentpen* to modify the current picture.

You can also say '**pickup** ⟨numeric expression⟩'; in this case the numeric expression designates the code number of a previously picked-up pen that was saved by '**savepen**'. For example, the `logo.mf` file in Chapter 11 begins by picking up the pen that's used to draw 'METAFONT', then it says '*logo_pen* := **savepen**'. Every character program later in that file begins with the command '**pickup** *logo_pen*', which is a fast operation because it doesn't require the generation of a new pen representation inside the computer.

Caution: Every time you use **savepen**, it produces a new integer value and stashes away another pen for later use. If you keep doing this, METAFONT's memory will become cluttered with the representations of pens that you may never need again. The command '**clear_pen_memory**' discards all previously saved pens and lets METAFONT start afresh.

But what is a ⟨pen expression⟩? Good question. So far in this book, almost everything that we've picked up was a pencircle followed by some sequence of transformations; for example, the *logo_pen* of Chapter 11 was '**pencircle** xscaled *px* yscaled *py*'. Chapter 13 also made brief mention of another kind of pen, when it said

   pickup penrazor scaled 10;

this command picks up an infinitely thin pen that runs from point $(-5, 0)$ to point $(5, 0)$ with respect to its center. Later in this chapter we shall make use of pens like

   pensquare xscaled 30 yscaled 3 rotated 30;

this pen has a rectangular boundary measuring 30 pixels × 3 pixels, inclined at an angle of 30° to the baseline.

You can define pens of any convex polygonal shape by saying '**makepen** *p*', where *p* is a cyclic path. It turns out that METAFONT looks only at the key points of *p*, not the control points, so we may as well assume that *p* has the form z_0 -- z_1 -- ⟨etc.⟩ -- cycle. This path must have the property that it turns left at every key point (i.e., z_{k+1} must lie to the left of the line from z_{k-1} to z_k, for all k), unless the cycle contains fewer than three key points; furthermore the path must have a turning number of 1 (i.e., it must not make more than one counterclockwise loop). Plain META-FONT's **penrazor** stands for '**makepen** $((-.5, 0)$ -- $(.5, 0)$ -- *cycle*)', and **pensquare** is an abbreviation for '**makepen** (*unitsquare* shifted $-(.5, .5)$))'. But **pencircle** is not defined via **makepen**; it is a primitive operation of METAFONT. It represents a true circle of diameter 1, passing through the points $(\pm.5, 0)$ and $(0, \pm.5)$.

 The complete syntax for pen expressions is rather short, because you can't really do all that much with pens. But it also contains a surprise:

⟨pen primary⟩ ⟶ ⟨pen variable⟩
   | (⟨pen expression⟩)
   | **nullpen**
⟨future pen primary⟩ ⟶ **pencircle**
   | **makepen** ⟨path primary⟩
⟨pen secondary⟩ ⟶ ⟨pen primary⟩
⟨future pen secondary⟩ ⟶ ⟨future pen primary⟩
   | ⟨future pen secondary⟩⟨transformer⟩
   | ⟨pen secondary⟩⟨transformer⟩
⟨pen tertiary⟩ ⟶ ⟨pen secondary⟩
   | ⟨future pen secondary⟩
⟨pen expression⟩ ⟶ ⟨pen tertiary⟩

The constant '**nullpen**' is just the single point $(0, 0)$, which is invisible—unless you use it in **filldraw**, which then reduces to **fill**. (A **beginchar** command initializes *currentpen* to **nullpen**, in order to reduce potentially dangerous dependencies between the programs for different characters.) The surprise in these rules is the notion of a "future pen," which stands for a path or an ellipse that has not yet been converted into METAFONT's internal representation of a true pen. The conversion process is rather complicated, so METAFONT procrastinates until being sure that no more transformations are going to be made. A true pen is formed at the tertiary level, when future pens are no longer permitted in the syntax.

 The distinction between pens and future pens would make no difference to a user, except for another surprising fact: All of METAFONT's pens are convex polygons, even the pens that are made from **pencircle** and its variants! Thus, for example, the pen you get from an untransformed pencircle is identical to the pen you get by specifying the diamond-shaped nib

    makepen $((.5, 0) \mathbin{\text{--}} (0, .5) \mathbin{\text{--}} (-.5, 0) \mathbin{\text{--}} (0, -.5) \mathbin{\text{--}} \text{cycle})$.

And the pens you get from '**pencircle** scaled 20' and '**pencircle** xscaled 30 yscaled 20' are polygons with 24 and 32 sides, respectively:

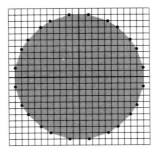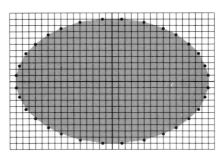

The vertices of the polygons, shown as heavy dots in this illustration, all have "half-integer" coordinates; i.e., each coordinate is either an integer or an integer plus 1/2. Every polygon that comes from a **pencircle** is symmetric under 180° rotation; furthermore, there will be reflective left/right and top/bottom symmetry if the future pen is a circle, or if it's an ellipse that has not been rotated.

This conversion to polygons explains why future pens must, in general, be distinguished from ordinary ones. For example, the extra parentheses in '(**pencircle** xscaled 30) yscaled 20' will yield a result quite different from the elliptical polygon just illustrated. The parentheses force conversion of '**pencircle** xscaled 30' from future pen to pen, and this polygon turns out to be

$$(12.5, -0.5) \text{ -- } (15, 0) \text{ -- } (12.5, 0.5)$$
$$\text{ -- } (-12.5, 0.5) \text{ -- } (-15, 0) \text{ -- } (-12.5, -0.5) \text{ -- cycle},$$

an approximation to a 30 × 1 ellipse. Then yscaling by 20 yields

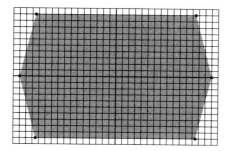

Why does METAFONT work with polygonal approximations to circles, instead of true circles? That's another good question. The main reason is that suitably chosen polygons give better results than the real thing, when digitization is taken into account. For example, suppose we want to draw a straight line of slope 1/2 that's exactly one pixel thick, from $(0, y)$ to $(200, y + 100)$. The image of a perfectly circular pen of diameter 1 that travels along this line has outlines that run from $(0, y \pm \alpha)$ to $(200, y + 100 \pm \alpha)$, where $\alpha = 1/\sqrt{5} \approx 0.559$. If we digitize these outlines and fill the region between them, we find that for some values of y (e.g., $y = 0.1$) the result is a repeating pixel pattern like '$\ldots$ ⁂'; but for other values of y (e.g., $y = 0.3$) the repeating pattern of pixels is 50 percent darker: '$\ldots$ ⁂'. Similarly, some diagonal lines of slope 1 digitize to be twice as dark as others, when a truly circular pen is considered. But the diamond-shaped nib that METAFONT uses for a pencircle of diameter 1 does not have this defect; all straight lines of the same slope will digitize to lines of uniform darkness. Moreover, curved lines drawn with the diamond nib always yield one pixel per column when they move more-or-less horizontally (with slopes between $+1$ and -1), and they always yield one pixel per row when they move vertically. By contrast, the outlines of curves drawn with circular pens produce occasional "blots." Circles and ellipses of all diameters can profitably be replaced by polygons whose sub-pixel corrections to the ideal shape will produce better digitizations; METAFONT does this in accordance with the interesting theory developed by John D. Hobby in his Ph.D. dissertation (Stanford University, 1985).

It's much easier to compute the outlines of a polygonal pen that follows a given curve than to figure out the corresponding outlines of a truly circular pen; thus polygons win over circles with respect to both quality and speed. When a curve is traveling in a direction between the edge vectors $z_{k+1} - z_k$ and $z_k - z_{k-1}$ of a polygonal pen, the curve's outline will be offset from its center by z_k. If you want fine control over this curve-drawing process, METAFONT provides the primitive operation 'penoffset w of p', where w is a vector and p is a pen. If $w = (0, 0)$, the result is $(0, 0)$; if the direction of w lies strictly between $z_{k+1} - z_k$ and $z_k - z_{k-1}$, the result is z_k; and if w has the same direction as $z_{k+1} - z_k$ for some k, the result is either z_k or z_{k+1}, whichever METAFONT finds most convenient to compute.

▶ **EXERCISE 16.1**
Explain how to use penoffset to find the point or points at the "top" of a pen (i.e., the point or points with largest y coordinate).

The primitive operation '**makepath** p', where p is a (polygonal) pen whose vertices are $z_0, z_1, \ldots, z_{n-1}$, produces the path '$z_0$ .. controls z_0 and z_1 .. z_1 .. ⟨etc.⟩ .. z_{n-1} .. controls z_{n-1} and z_0 .. cycle', which is one of the paths that might have generated p. This gives access to all the offsets of a pen.

When a **pencircle** is transformed by any of the operations in Chapter 15, it changes into an ellipse of some sort, since all of METAFONT's transformations preserve ellipse-hood. The diameter of the ellipse in each direction θ is decreased by $2\min(|\sin\theta|, |\cos\theta|)$ times the current value of *fillin*, before converting to a polygon; this helps to compensate for the variation in thickness of diagonal strokes with respect to horizontal or vertical strokes, on certain output devices. (METAFONT uses *fillin* only when creating polygons from ellipses, but users can of course refer to *fillin* within their own routines for drawing strokes.) The final polygon will never be perfectly flat like **penrazor**, even if you say 'xscaled 0' and/or 'yscaled 0'; its center will always be surrounded at least by the basic diamond nib that corresponds to a circle of diameter 1.

▶ **EXERCISE 16.2**
Run METAFONT on the **expr** file of Chapter 8 and look at what is typed when you ask for '`pencircle`' and '`pencircle scaled 1.1`'. (The first will exhibit the diamond nib, while the second will show a polygon that's equivalent to **pensquare**.) Continue experimenting until you find the "threshold" diameter where METAFONT decides to switch between these two polygons.

METAFONT's polygonal pens work well for drawing lines and curves, but this pleasant fact has an unpleasant corollary: They do not always digitize well at the endpoints, where curves start and stop. The reason for this is explored further in Chapter 24; polygon vertices that give nice uniform stroke widths might also be "ambiguous" points that cause difficulties when we consider rounding to the raster. Therefore a special **drawdot** routine is provided for drawing one-point paths. It is sometimes advantageous to apply **drawdot** to the first and last points of a path p, after having said '**draw** p'; this can fatten up the endpoints slightly, making them look more consistent with each other.

Plain METAFONT also provides two routines that can be used to clean up endpoints in a different way: The command '**cutoff** (z, θ)' removes half of the *currentpen* image at point z, namely all points of the pen that lie in directions between

$(\theta - 90)°$ and $(\theta + 90)°$ from the center point. And the command '**cutdraw** p' is an abbreviation for the following three commands:

> **draw** p;　**cutoff** (point 0 of p, 180 + angle direction 0 of p);
> **cutoff** (point *infinity* of p, angle direction *infinity* of p).

The effect is to draw a curve whose ends are clipped perpendicular to the starting and ending directions. For example, the command

> **cutdraw** z_4 .. controls z_1 and z_2 .. z_6

produces the following curve, which invites comparison with the corresponding uncut version at the end of Chapter 3:

 Here's another example of **cutoff**, in which the endpoints of METAFONT's 'T' have been cropped at $10°$ angles to the perpendicular of the stroke direction:

```
pickup logo_pen;
top lft z1=(0,h); top rt z2=(w,h);
top z3=(.5w,h); z4=(.5w,0);
draw z1--z2;
cutoff(z1,170); cutoff(z2,-10);
draw z3--z4; cutoff(z4,-80).
```

The **cutoff** macro of Appendix B deals with several things that we've been studying recently, so it will be instructive to look at it now (slightly simplified):

> **def cutoff** (**expr** $z, theta$) =
> cut_pic := **nullpicture**;
>   **addto** cut_pic **doublepath** z **withpen** *currentpen*;
>   **addto** cut_pic **contour** $((0,-1)$ -- $(1,-1)$ -- $(1,1)$ -- $(0,1)$ -- cycle)
>   scaled $1.42(1 + \max(pen\_lft, pen\_rt, pen\_top, pen\_bot))$
>   rotated *theta* shifted z;
>   **cull** cut_pic **keeping** $(2,2)$ **withweight** -1;
>   **addto** *currentpicture* **also** cut_pic **enddef**.

The main work is done in a separate picture variable called cut_pic, so that neighboring strokes won't be affected. First cut_pic is set to the full digitized pen image (by making a **doublepath** from a single point). Then a rectangle that includes the cutoff region is added in; pen_lft, pen_rt, pen_top, and pen_bot are the quantities used to compute the functions *lft*, *rt*, *top*, and *bot*, so they bound the size of the pen. The culling operation produces the intersection of pen and rectangle, which is finally subtracted from *currentpicture*.

 We shall conclude this chapter by studying two examples of how METAFONT's pen-and-curve-drawing facilities can combine in interesting ways. First, let's examine two "tilde" characters

which were both created by a single command of the form

draw z_1 .. controls z_2 and z_3 .. z_4.

The left example was done with a **pencircle** xscaled $.8pt$ yscaled $.2pt$ rotated 50, and the right example was exactly the same but with **pensquare**. The control points z_2 and z_3 that made this work were defined by

$$y_2 - y_1 = y_4 - y_3 = 3(y_4 - y_1);$$
$$z_2 - z_1 = z_4 - z_3 = whatever * \text{dir } 50.$$

The second pair of equations is an old calligrapher's trick, namely to start and finish a stroke in the direction of the pen you're holding. The first pair of equations is a mathematician's trick, based on the fact that the Bernshteın polynomial $t[0, 3, -2, 1]$ goes from 0 to 1 to 0 to 1 as t goes from 0 to .25 to .75 to 1.

 Next, let's try to draw a fancy serif with the same two pens, holding them at a 20° angle instead of a 50° angle. Here are two examples

that can be created by '**filldraw**' commands:

filldraw z_1 .. controls z_2 .. z_3
     $-- (flex(z_3, .5[z_3, z_4] + dishing, z_4))$ shifted $(0, -epsilon)$
     $-- z_4$ .. controls z_5 .. z_6 -- cycle.

The *dishing* parameter causes a slight rise between z_3 and z_4; the *flex* has been lowered by *epsilon* in order to avoid the danger of "strange paths," which might otherwise be caused by tiny loops at z_3 or z_4. But the most interesting thing about this example is the use of double control points, z_2 and z_5, in two of the path segments. (Recall that 'controls z_2' means the same thing as 'controls z_2 and z_2'.) These points were determined by the equations

$$x_2 = x_1; \quad z_2 = z_3 + whatever * \text{dir } 20;$$
$$x_5 = x_6; \quad z_5 = z_4 + whatever * \text{dir } -20;$$

thus, they make the strokes vertical at z_1 and z_6, parallel to the pen angle at z_3, and parallel to the complementary angle at z_4.

The pen, probably more than any other tool,
has had the strongest influence upon lettering
in respect of serif design . . .
It is probable that the letters [of the Trajan column]
were painted before they were incised,
and though their main structure is attributed to the pen
and their ultimate design to the technique of the chisel,
they undoubtedly owe much of their freedom
to the influence of the brush.

— L. C. EVETTS, *Roman Lettering* (1938)

Remember that it takes time, patience, critical practice
and knowledge to learn any art or craft.
No "art experience" is going to result from any busy work
for a few hours experimenting with the edged pen.
. . . Take as much time as you require,
and do not become impatient.
If it takes a month to get it,
then be happy that it takes only a month.

— LLOYD REYNOLDS, *Italic Calligraphy & Handwriting* (1969)

17
Grouping

We have now covered all the visual, graphic aspects of METAFONT—its points, paths, pens, and pictures; but we still don't know everything about METAFONT's organizational, administrative aspects—its programs. The next few chapters of this book therefore concentrate on how to put programs together effectively.

A METAFONT program is a sequence of statements separated by semi-colons and followed by '**end**'. More precisely, the syntax rules

⟨program⟩ ⟶ ⟨statement list⟩ **end**
⟨statement list⟩ ⟶ ⟨empty⟩ | ⟨statement⟩ ; ⟨statement list⟩

define a ⟨program⟩ in terms of a ⟨statement⟩.

But what are statements? Well, they are of various kinds. An "equation" states that two expressions are supposed to be equal. An "assignment" assigns the value of an expression to a variable. A "declaration" states that certain variables will have a certain type. A "definition" defines a macro. A "title" gives a descriptive name to the character that is to follow. A "command" orders METAFONT to do some specific operation, immediately. The "empty statement" tells METAFONT to do absolutely nothing. And a "compound statement" is a list of other statements treated as a group.

⟨statement⟩ ⟶ ⟨equation⟩ | ⟨assignment⟩ | ⟨declaration⟩
        | ⟨definition⟩ | ⟨title⟩ | ⟨command⟩ | ⟨empty⟩
        | **begingroup** ⟨statement list⟩ ⟨statement⟩ **endgroup**

We've given the syntax for ⟨equation⟩ and ⟨assignment⟩ in Chapter 10; the syntax for ⟨declaration⟩ appeared in Chapter 7; ⟨definition⟩ and ⟨title⟩ and ⟨command⟩ will appear in later chapters. Our main concern just now is with the final type of ⟨statement⟩, where **begingroup** and **endgroup** bind other statements into a unit, just as parentheses add structure to the elements of an algebraic expression.

The main purpose of grouping is to protect the values of variables in one part of the program from being clobbered in another. A symbolic token can be given a new meaning inside a group, without changing the meaning it had outside that group. (Recall that METAFONT deals with three basic kinds of tokens, as discussed in Chapter 6; it is impossible to change the meaning of a numeric token or a string token, but symbolic tokens can change meanings freely.)

There are two ways to protect the values of variables in a group. One is called a ⟨save command⟩, and the other is called an ⟨interim command⟩:

⟨save command⟩ ⟶ **save** ⟨symbolic token list⟩
⟨symbolic token list⟩ ⟶ ⟨symbolic token⟩
        | ⟨symbolic token list⟩ , ⟨symbolic token⟩
⟨interim command⟩ ⟶ **interim** ⟨internal quantity⟩ := ⟨right-hand side⟩

The symbolic tokens in a **save** command all lose their current meanings, but those old meanings are put into a safe place and restored at the end of the current group. Each token becomes undefined, as if it had never appeared before. For

example, the command

> **save** x, y

effectively causes all previously known variables like x_1 and y_{5r} to become inaccessible; the variable x_1 could now appear in a new equation, where it would have no connection with its out-of-group value. You could also give the silly command

> **save save**;

this would make the token '**save**' itself into a ⟨tag⟩ instead of a ⟨spark⟩, so you couldn't use it to save anything else until the group ended.

 An **interim** command is more restrictive than a **save**, since it applies only to an ⟨internal quantity⟩. (Recall that internal quantities are special variables like *tracingequations* that take numeric values only; a complete list of all the standard internal quantities can be found in Chapter 25, but that list isn't exhaustive because you can define new ones for your own use.) METAFONT treats an interim command just like an ordinary assignment, except that it undoes the assignment when the group ends.

 If you save something two or more times in the same group, the first saved value takes precedence. For example, in the construction

> **begingroup**
> . . .
> **interim** *autorounding* := 0;   **save** x;
> . . .
> **interim** *autorounding* := 1;   **save** x;
> . . .
> **endgroup**

the values of *autorounding* and x after the end of the group will be their previous values just before the statement '**interim** *autorounding* := 0'. (Incidentally, these might not be the values they had upon entry to the group).

 Tokens and internal quantities regain their old meanings and values at the end of a group only if they were explicitly saved in a **save** or **interim** command. All other changes in meaning and/or value will survive outside the group.

 The **beginchar** operation of plain METAFONT includes a **begingroup**, and **endchar** includes **endgroup**. Thus, for example, interim assignments can be made in a program for one character without any effect on other characters.

 A ⟨save command⟩ that's not in a group simply clears the meanings of the symbolic tokens specified; their old meanings are not actually saved, because they never will have to be restored. An ⟨interim command⟩ outside a group acts just like a normal assignment.

 If you set the internal quantity *tracingrestores* to a positive value, METAFONT will make a note in your transcript file whenever it is restoring the former value of a symbolic token or internal quantity. This can be useful when you're debugging a program that doesn't seem to make sense.

Groups can also be used within algebraic expressions. This is the other important reason for grouping; it allows METAFONT to do arbitrarily complicated things while in the middle of other calculations, thereby greatly increasing the power of macro definitions (which we shall study in the next chapter). A *group expression* has the general form

> begingroup ⟨statement list⟩ ⟨expression⟩ endgroup

and it fits into the syntax of expressions at the primary level. The meaning of a group expression is: "Perform the list of statements, then evaluate the expression, then restore anything that was saved in this group."

Group expressions belong in the syntax rules for each type of expression, but they were not mentioned in previous chapters because it would have been unnecessarily distracting. Thus, for example, the syntax for ⟨numeric primary⟩ actually includes the additional alternative

> begingroup ⟨statement list⟩⟨numeric expression⟩ endgroup.

The same goes for ⟨pair primary⟩, ⟨picture primary⟩, etc.; Chapter 25 has the complete rules of syntax for all types of expressions.

▶**EXERCISE 17.1**
What is the value of the expression

> begingroup x:=x+1; x endgroup + begingroup x:=2x; x endgroup

if x initially has the value a? What would the value have been if the two group expressions had appeared in the opposite order? Verify your answers using the **expr** routine of Chapter 8.

▶**EXERCISE 17.2**
Appendix B defines *whatever* to be an abbreviation for the group expression '**begingroup save ?; ? endgroup**'. Why does this work?

▶**EXERCISE 17.3**
What is the value of '**begingroup save ?; (?, ?) endgroup**'?

▶**EXERCISE 17.4**
According to exercise 10.2, the assignment '$x_3 := whatever$' will make the numeric variable x_3 behave like new, without affecting other variables like x_2. Devise a similar stratagem that works for arrays of **picture** variables.

It is often difficult
to account for some beginners grouping right away
and others proving almost hopeless.
— A. G. FULTON, *Notes on Rifle Shooting* (1913)

Rock bands prefer San Francisco groupies to New York groupies.
— ELLEN WILLIS, *But Now I'm Gonna Move* (1971)

18

Definitions
(also called Macros)

You can often save time writing METAFONT programs by letting single tokens stand for sequences of other tokens that are used repeatedly. For example, Appendix B defines '`---`' to be an abbreviation for '`.. tension` *infinity* `..`', and this definition is preloaded as part of the plain METAFONT base. Programs that use such definitions are not only easier to write, they're also easier to read. But Appendix B doesn't contain every definition that every programmer might want; the present chapter therefore explains how you can make definitions of your own.

In the simplest case, you just say

def ⟨symbolic token⟩ = ⟨replacement text⟩ **enddef**

and the symbolic token will henceforth expand into the tokens of the replacement text. For example, Appendix B says

```
def --- = ..tension infinity.. enddef.
```

The replacement text can be any sequence of tokens not including '**enddef**'; or it can include entire subdefinitions like '**def** ... **enddef**', according to certain rules that we shall explain later.

Definitions get more interesting when they include *parameters*, which are replaced by *arguments* when the definition is expanded. For example, Appendix B also says

```
def rotatedaround(expr z,theta) =
  shifted -z rotated theta shifted z enddef;
```

this means that an expression like 'z_1 rotatedaround $(z_2, 30)$' will expand into 'z_1 shifted $-z_2$ rotated 30 shifted z_2'.

The parameters '`z`' and '`theta`' in this definition could have been any symbolic tokens whatever; there's no connection between them and appearances of '`z`' and '`theta`' outside the definition. (For example, '`z`' would ordinarily stand for '`(x,y)`', but it's just a simple token here.) The definition could even have been written with "primitive" tokens as parameters, like

```
def rotatedaround(expr;,+) =
  shifted-; rotated+shifted; enddef;
```

the effect would be exactly the same. (Of course, there's no point in doing such a thing unless you are purposely trying to make your definition inscrutable.)

When '`rotatedaround`' is used, the arguments that are substituted for `z` and `theta` are first evaluated and put into "capsules," so that they will behave like primary expressions. Thus, for example, 'z_1 rotatedaround $(z_2 + z_3, 30)$' will not expand into 'z_1 shifted $-z_2 + z_3$ rotated 30 shifted $z_2 + z_3$'—which means something entirely different—but rather into 'z_1 shifted $-\alpha$ rotated 30 shifted α', where α is a nameless internal variable that contains the value of $z_2 + z_3$.

 A capsule value cannot be changed, so an **expr** parameter should not appear at the left of the assignment operator '`:=`'.

Macros are great when they work, but complicated macros sometimes surprise their creators. METAFONT provides "tracing" facilities so that you can see what the computer thinks it's doing, when you're trying to diagnose the reasons for unexpected behavior. If you say '*tracingmacros* := 1', the transcript file of your run will record every macro that is subsequently expanded, followed by the values of its arguments as soon as they have been computed. For example, 'rotatedaround $(up, 30)$' might produce the following lines of diagnostic information:

```
rotatedaround(EXPR0)(EXPR1)->shifted-(EXPR0)rotated(EXPR1)sh
ifted(EXPR0)
(EXPR0)<-(0,1)
(EXPR1)<-30
```

Here's another example from Appendix B. It illustrates the usefulness of group expressions in macro definitions:

def reflectedabout (**expr** p, q) =
  transformed **begingroup**
    save T; **transform** T;
    p transformed $T = p$;
    q transformed $T = q$;
    xxpart $T = -$yypart T;
    xypart $T = $ yxpart T;
    T **endgroup enddef**;

thus a new transform, T, is computed in the midst of another expression, and the macro 'reflectedabout(p, q)' essentially expands into 'transformed T'.

Some macros, like 'rotatedaround', are meant for general-purpose use. But it's also convenient to write special-purpose macros that simplify the development of particular typefaces. For example, let's consider the METAFONT logo from this standpoint. The program for 'E' in Chapter 11 starts with

```
beginchar("E",14u#+2s#,ht#,0); pickup logo_pen;
```

and the programs for 'M', 'T', etc., all have almost the same beginning. Therefore we might as well put the following definition near the top of the file `logo.mf`:

```
def beginlogochar(expr code, unit_width) =
 beginchar(code,unit_width*u#+2s#,ht#,0);
 pickup logo_pen enddef;
```

Then we can start the 'E' by saying simply

```
beginlogochar("E",14);
```

similar simplifications apply to all seven letters. Notice from this example that macros can be used inside macros (since '**beginchar**' and '**pickup**' are themselves macros, defined in Appendix B); once you have defined a macro, you have essentially extended the METAFONT language. Notice also that **expr** parameters can be expressions of any type; for example, "E" is a string, and the first parameter of 'rotatedaround' is a pair.

Chapter 11 didn't give the programs for 'A' or 'O'. It turns out that those programs can be simplified if we write them in terms of an auxiliary subroutine called 'super_half'. For example, here is how the 'O' is made:

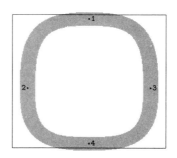

```
beginlogochar("O",15);
x1=x4=.5w; top y1=h+o; bot y4=-o;
x2=w-x3=1.5u+s; y2=y3=barheight;
super_half(2,1,3);
super_half(2,4,3);
labels(1,2,3,4); endchar;
```

The super_half routine is supposed to draw half of a superellipse, through three points whose subscripts are specified.

We could define super_half as a macro with three **expr** parameters, referring to the first point as '$z[i]$', say; but there's a better way. Parameters to macros can be classified as suffixes, by saying **suffix** instead of **expr**. In this case the actual arguments may be any ⟨suffix⟩, i.e., any sequence of subscripts and tags that complete the name of a variable as explained in Chapter 7. Here's what super_half looks like, using this idea:

```
def super_half(suffix i,j,k) =
 draw z.i{0,y.j-y.i}
  ... (.8[x.j,x.i],.8[y.i,y.j]){z.j-z.i}
  ... z.j{x.k-x.i,0}
  ... (.8[x.j,x.k],.8[y.k,y.j]){z.k-z.j}
  ... z.k{0,y.k-y.j} enddef;
```

▶ **EXERCISE 18.1**
Would the program for 'O' still work if the two calls of super_half had been 'super_half(3,1,2)' and 'super_half(3,4,2)'?

▶ **EXERCISE 18.2**
Guess the program for METAFONT's 'A', which has the same width as 'O'.

Besides parameters of type **expr** and **suffix**, METAFONT also allows a third type called **text**. In this case the actual argument is any sequence of tokens, and this sequence is not evaluated beforehand; a text argument is simply copied in place of the corresponding parameter. This makes it possible to write macros that deal with lists of things. For example, Appendix B's '**define_pixels**' macro is defined thus:

```
def define_pixels(text t) =
 forsuffixes a=t: a := a# * hppp; endfor enddef;
```

This means that 'define_pixels(em,cap)' will expand into

```
forsuffixes a=em,cap: a := a# * hppp; endfor
```

which, in turn, expands into the tokens 'em := em# * hppp; cap := cap# * hppp;' as we will see in Chapter 19.

Let's look now at a subroutine for drawing serifs, since this typifies the sort of special-purpose macro one expects to see in the design of a meta-typeface. Serifs can take many forms, so we must choose from myriads of possibilities. We shall consider two rather different approaches, one based on outline-filling and the other based on the use of a fixed pen nib. In both cases it will be necessary to omit some of the refinements that would be desirable in a complete typeface design, to keep the examples from getting too complicated.

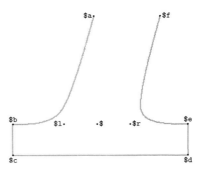

Our first example is a serif routine that constructs six points $z_{\$a}$, $z_{\$b}$, ..., $z_{\$f}$ around a given triple of "penpos" points $z_{\$l}$, $z_{\$}$, $z_{\$r}$; here $ is a suffix that's a parameter to the *serif* macro. Other parameters are: *breadth*, the distance between the parallel lines that run from $z_{\$l}$ to $z_{\$a}$ and from $z_{\$r}$ to $z_{\$f}$; *theta*, the direction angle of those two lines; *left_jut*, the distance from $z_{\$l}$ to $z_{\$b}$; and *right_jut*, the distance from $z_{\$r}$ to $z_{\$e}$. (The serif "juts out" by the amounts of the jut parameters.)   There's also a *serif_edge* macro, which constructs the path shown. The routines refer to three variables that are assumed to apply to all serifs: *slab*, the vertical distance from $z_{\$b}$ and $z_{\$e}$ to $z_{\$c}$ and $z_{\$d}$; *bracket*, the vertical distance from $z_{\$a}$ and $z_{\$f}$ to $z_{\$l}$ and $z_{\$r}$; and *serif_darkness*, a fraction that controls how much of the triangular regions ($z_{\$a}, z_{\$l}, z_{\$b}$) and ($z_{\$f}, z_{\$r}, z_{\$e}$) will be filled in.

> **def** *serif* (**suffix** $)(**expr** *breadth*, *theta*, *left_jut*, *right_jut*) =
> $penpos_{\$}(breadth/\text{abs sind } theta, 0)$;
> $z_{\$a} - z_{\$l} = z_{\$f} - z_{\$r} = (bracket/\text{abs sind } theta) * \text{dir } theta$;
> $y_{\$c} = y_{\$d}$; $y_{\$b} = y_{\$e} = y_{\$}$; $y_{\$b} - y_{\$c} =$ **if** $theta < 0 : -$ **fi** *slab*;
> $x_{\$b} = x_{\$c} = x_{\$l} - left\_jut$; $x_{\$d} = x_{\$e} = x_{\$r} + right\_jut$;
> **labels**($a, $b, $c, $d, $e, $f) **enddef**;

> **def** *serif_edge* **suffix** $ =
> (*serif_bracket*($a, $l, $b) -- $z_{\$c}$
> ‑‑ $z_{\$d}$ -- **reverse** *serif_bracket*($f, $r, $e)) **enddef**;

> **def** *serif_bracket*(**suffix** i, j, k) =
> $(z.i\{z.j - z.i\} \ldots serif\_darkness[z.j, .5[z.i, z.k]]\{z.k - z.i\}$
> $\ldots z.k\{z.k - z.j\})$ **enddef**;

 ▶ **EXERCISE 18.3**
Under what circumstances will the *serif_edge* go through points $z_{\$l}$ and $z_{\$r}$?

 ▶ **EXERCISE 18.4**
Should this *serif* macro be used before points $z_{\$l}$, $z_{\$}$, and $z_{\$r}$ have been defined, or should those points be defined first?

Here are two sample letters that show how these serif routines might be used. The programs assume that the font has several additional ad hoc parameters: u, a unit of character width; ht, the character height; *thin* and *thick*, the two stroke weights; and *jut*, the amount by which serifs protrude on a "normal" letter like 'H'.

$$\mathbf{beginchar}(\texttt{"A"}, 13u^\#, ht^\#, 0);$$

$z_1 = (.5w, 1.05h);$ % top point

$x_{4l} = w - x_{5r} = u; \quad y_{4l} = y_{5r} = slab;$ % bottom points

numeric $theta[\,];$

$theta_4 = \text{angle}(z_1 - z_{4l});$ % left stroke angle

$theta_5 = \text{angle}(z_1 - z_{5r});$ % right stroke angle

$serif\,(4, thin, theta_4, .6jut, jut);$ % left serifs

$serif\,(5, thick, theta_5, jut, .6jut);$ % right serifs

$z_0 = z_{4r} + whatever * \text{dir } theta_4$

     $= z_{5l} + whatever * \text{dir } theta_5;$ % inside top point

fill $z_1 \;\text{-{}-}\; serif\_edge_4 \;\text{-{}-}\; z_0$ % the left stroke

     $\&\; z_0 \;\text{-{}-}\; serif\_edge_5 \;\text{-{}-}\; z_1 \;\&\; \text{cycle};$ % the right stroke

$penpos_2(whatever, theta_4);$

$penpos_3(whatever, theta_5);$

$y_{2r} = y_{3r} = .5[y_4, y_0];$ % crossbar height

$y_{2l} = y_{3l} = y_{2r} - thin;$ % crossbar thickness

$z_2 = whatever[z_1, z_{4r}];$

$z_3 = whatever[z_1, z_{5l}];$

penstroke $z_{2e} \;\text{-{}-}\; z_{3e};$ % the crossbar

penlabels$(0, 1, 2, 3, 4, 5);$ **endchar**;

$$\mathbf{beginchar}(\texttt{"I"}, 6u^\#, ht^\#, 0);$$

$x_1 = x_2 = .5w;$

$y_1 = h - y_2; \quad y_2 = slab;$

$serif\,(1, thick, -90, 1.1jut, 1.1jut);$ % upper serifs

$serif\,(2, thick, 90, 1.1jut, 1.1jut);$ % lower serifs

fill $serif\_edge_2 \;\text{-{}-}\; \text{reverse } serif\_edge_1 \;\text{-{}-}\; \text{cycle};$ % the stroke

penlabels$(1, 2);$ **endchar**;

The illustration was prepared with $thin = .5pt$, $thick = 1.1pt$, $u = .6pt$, $ht = 7pt$, $slab = .25pt$, $jut = .9pt$, $bracket = pt$, and $serif\_darkness = 1/3$.

▶ **EXERCISE 18.5**

Could the equations defining y_1 and y_2 in the program for "I" have been replaced by '$y_{1c} = h$' and '$y_{2c} = 0$'?

▶ **EXERCISE 18.6**

Write the program for an "H" to go with these letters.

A second approach to serifs can be based on the example at the end of Chapter 16. In this case we assume that *broad_pen* is a '**pensquare** xscaled *px* yscaled *py* rotated *phi*' for some $px > py$ and some small angle *phi*. Thicker strokes will be made by using this pen to fill a larger region; the serif routine is given the distance *xx* between $z_{\$l}$ and $z_{\$r}$. There's a pair variable called *dishing* that controls the curvature between $z_{\$c}$ and $z_{\$d}$. Top and bottom serifs are similar, but they are sufficiently different that it's easier to write separate macros for each case.

def *bot_serif* (**suffix** $)(**expr** *xx*, *theta*, *left_jut*, *right_jut*) =
  $penpos_{\$}(xx, 0)$; $z_{\$a} - z_{\$l} = z_{\$f} - z_{\$r} = (bracket/\text{abs sind } theta) * \text{dir } theta$;
  $y_{\$c} = topy_{\$l}$; $y_{\$d} = y_{\$r}$; $x_{\$c} = x_{\$l} - left\_jut$; $x_{\$d} = x_{\$r} + right\_jut$;
  $z_{\$b} = z_{\$l} + whatever * \text{dir } theta = z_{\$c} + whatever * \text{dir } phi$;
  $z_{\$e} = z_{\$r} + whatever * \text{dir } theta = z_{\$d} + whatever * \text{dir } -phi$;
  labels($a, $b, $c, $d, $e, $f) **enddef**;
def *bot_serif_edge* **suffix** $ =
  $(z_{\$a}$ .. controls $z_{\$b}$ .. $z_{\$c}$
    -- $(flex(z_{\$c}, .5[z_{\$c}, z_{\$d}] + dishing, z_{\$d}))$ shifted $(0, -epsilon)$
    -- $z_{\$d}$ .. controls $z_{\$e}$ .. $z_{\$f})$ **enddef**;

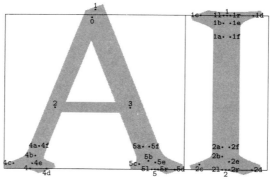

beginchar("A", 13$u^{\#}$, $ht^{\#}$, 0); **pickup** *broad_pen*;
$z_1 = (.5w, top\ h)$; *lft* $x_{4l} = w - rt\ x_{5r} = 1.2u$; $y_{4l} = y_{5r} = 0$;
numeric *theta*[]; $theta_4 = \text{angle}(z_1 - z_{4l})$; $theta_5 = \text{angle}(z_1 - z_{5r})$;
numeric *xxx*; $px * \text{sind}(theta_5 - phi) + xxx * \text{sind } theta_5 = px * \text{cosd } phi + xx$;
$bot\_serif(4, 0, theta_4, .8jut, .8jut)$; $bot\_serif(5, xxx, theta_5, .6jut, .8jut)$;
$z_0 = z_{4r} + whatever * \text{dir } theta_4 = z_{5l} + whatever * \text{dir } theta_5$;
filldraw z_1 -- $bot\_serif\_edge_4$ -- z_0 & z_0 -- $bot\_serif\_edge_5$ -- z_1 & cycle;
top $y_2 = top\ y_3 = .45bot\ y_0$; $z_2 = whatever[z_1, z_{4r}]$; $z_3 = whatever[z_1, z_{5l}]$;
draw z_2 -- z_3; **penlabels**(0, 1, 2, 3, 4, 5); **endchar**;

beginchar("I", 6$u^{\#}$, $ht^{\#}$, 0); **pickup** *broad_pen*;
$x_1 = x_2 = .5w$; $y_1 = h$; $y_2 = 0$;
$top\_serif(1, xx, -90, 1.1jut, 1.1jut)$; $bot\_serif(2, xx, 90, 1.1jut, 1.1jut)$;
filldraw $bot\_serif\_edge_2$ -- reverse $top\_serif\_edge_1$ -- cycle;
penlabels(1, 2); **endchar**;

In the illustration, $px = .8pt$, $py = .2pt$, $phi = 20$, $xx = .3pt$, $u = .6pt$, $ht = 7pt$, $jut = .9pt$, $bracket = pt$, and $dishing = (.25pt, 0)$ rotated 20.

▶ **EXERCISE 18.7**
Write the missing code for *top_serif* and *top_serif_edge*.

▶ **EXERCISE 18.8**
(For mathematicians.) Explain the equation for *xxx* in the program for "**A**".

▶ **EXERCISE 18.9**
Write the program for an "**H**" to go with these letters.

A close look at the *serif_edge* routines in these examples will reveal that some parentheses are curiously lacking: We said '**def** *serif_edge* **suffix** $' instead of '**def** *serif_edge*(**suffix** $)', and we used the macro by saying '*serif_edge*₅' instead of '*serif_edge*(5)'. The reason is that METAFONT allows the final parameter of a macro to be without delimiters; this is something that could not have been guessed from a study of previous examples. It is time now to stop looking at specific cases and to start examining the complete set of rules for macro definitions. Here is the syntax:

⟨definition⟩ ⟶ ⟨definition heading⟩⟨is⟩⟨replacement text⟩ **enddef**

⟨is⟩ ⟶ **=** | **:=**

⟨definition heading⟩ ⟶ **def** ⟨symbolic token⟩⟨parameter heading⟩
    | ⟨vardef heading⟩
    | ⟨leveldef heading⟩

⟨parameter heading⟩ ⟶ ⟨delimited parameters⟩⟨undelimited parameters⟩

⟨delimited parameters⟩ ⟶ ⟨empty⟩
    | ⟨delimited parameters⟩ **(** ⟨parameter type⟩⟨parameter tokens⟩ **)**

⟨parameter type⟩ ⟶ **expr**
    | **suffix**
    | **text**

⟨parameter tokens⟩ ⟶ ⟨symbolic token⟩
    | ⟨parameter tokens⟩ **,** ⟨symbolic token⟩

⟨undelimited parameters⟩ ⟶ ⟨empty⟩
    | **primary** ⟨symbolic token⟩
    | **secondary** ⟨symbolic token⟩
    | **tertiary** ⟨symbolic token⟩
    | **expr** ⟨symbolic token⟩
    | **expr** ⟨symbolic token⟩ **of** ⟨symbolic token⟩
    | **suffix** ⟨symbolic token⟩
    | **text** ⟨symbolic token⟩

(We'll discuss ⟨vardef heading⟩ and ⟨leveldef heading⟩ in Chapter 20.) The basic idea is that we name the macro to be defined, then we name zero or more delimited parameters (i.e., parameters in parentheses), then we name zero or more undelimited parameters. Then comes an '=' sign, followed by the replacement text, and **enddef**. The '=' sign might also be ':='; both mean the same thing.

Delimited parameters are of type **expr**, **suffix**, or **text**; two or more parameters of the same type may be listed together, separated by commas. For example, '(**expr** a, b)' means exactly the same thing as '(**expr** a)(**expr** b)'. Undelimited parameters have eight possible forms, as shown in the syntax.

The ⟨replacement text⟩ is simply filed away for future use, not interpreted, when METAFONT reads a definition. But a few tokens are treated specially:

- **def**, **vardef**, **primarydef**, **secondarydef**, and **tertiarydef** are considered to introduce definitions inside definitions.

- **enddef** ends the replacement text, unless it matches a previous **def**-like token (as listed in the preceding rule).

- Each ⟨symbolic token⟩ that stands for a parameter, by virtue of its appearance in the ⟨parameter heading⟩ or ⟨leveldef heading⟩, is changed to a special internal "parameter token" wherever it occurs in the replacement text. Whenever this special token is subsequently encountered, METAFONT will substitute the appropriate argument.

- **quote** disables any special interpretation of the immediately following token. A '**quote**' doesn't survive in the replacement text (unless, of course, it has been quoted).

▶**EXERCISE 18.10**
Check your understanding of these rules by figuring out what the replacement text is, in the following weird definition:

```
def foo(text t) expr e of p :=
  def t = e enddef; quote def quote t = p enddef
```

METAFONT does not expand macros when it reads a ⟨definition⟩; but at almost all other times it will replace a defined token by the corresponding replacement text, after finding all the arguments. The replacement text will then be read as if it had been present in the program all along.

How does METAFONT determine the arguments to a macro? Well, it knows what kinds of arguments to expect, based on the parameter heading. Let's consider delimited arguments first:

- A delimited **expr** argument should be of the form '(⟨expression⟩)'; the expression is evaluated and put into a special "capsule" token that will be substituted for the parameter wherever it appears in the replacement text.

- A delimited **suffix** argument should be of the form '(⟨suffix⟩)'; subscripts that occur in the suffix are evaluated and replaced by numeric tokens. The result is a list of zero or more tokens that will be substituted for the parameter wherever it appears in the replacement text.

- A delimited **text** argument should be of the form '(⟨text⟩)', where ⟨text⟩ is any sequence of tokens that is balanced with respect to the delimiters surrounding it. This sequence of tokens will be substituted for the parameter wherever it appears in the replacement text.

- When there are two or more delimited parameters, you can separate the arguments by commas instead of putting parentheses around each one. For example, three delimited arguments could be written either as '$(a)(b)(c)$' or '$(a, b)(c)$' or '$(a)(b, c)$' or '(a, b, c)'. However, this abbreviation doesn't work after text arguments, which must be followed by ')' because text arguments can include commas.

Chapter 8 points out that you can use other delimiters besides parentheses. In general, a comma following a delimited **expr** or **suffix** argument is equivalent to two tokens ')' ('', corresponding to whatever delimiters enclose that comma.

▶ **EXERCISE 18.11**
After 'def f(expr a)(text b,c)=...enddef' and 'delimiters {{ }}', what are the arguments in 'f{{x,(,}}((}}))'?

The rules for undelimited arguments are similar. An undelimited **primary**, **secondary**, **tertiary**, or **expr** is the longest syntactically correct ⟨primary⟩, ⟨secondary⟩, ⟨tertiary⟩, or ⟨expression⟩ that immediately follows the delimited arguments. An undelimited '**expr** x of y' specifies two arguments, found by taking the longest syntactically correct ⟨expression⟩ of ⟨primary⟩. In each of these cases, the expression might also be preceded by an optional '=' or ':='. An undelimited **suffix** is the longest ⟨suffix⟩ that immediately follows the delimited arguments; METAFONT also allows '(⟨suffix⟩)' in this case, but not '=⟨suffix⟩' or ':=⟨suffix⟩'. An undelimited **text** essentially runs to the end of the current statement; more precisely, it runs to the first ';' or '**endgroup**' or '**end**' that is not part of a group within the argument.

Appendix B contains lots of macros that illustrate these rules. For example,

def fill expr c = addto *currentpicture* contour c enddef;
def erase text t = cullit; t withweight -1; cullit enddef;

these are slight simplifications of the real definitions, but they retain the basic ideas. The command '**erase fill** p' causes '**fill** p' to be the **text** argument to **erase**, after which 'p' becomes the **expr** argument to **fill**.

▶ **EXERCISE 18.12**
The '**pickup**' macro in Appendix B starts with '**def pickup secondary** q'; why is the argument a secondary instead of an expression?

▶ **EXERCISE 18.13**
Explain why the following '*hide*' macro allows you to hide any sequence of statements in the midst of an expression:

def *hide*(text t) = *gobble* begingroup t; endgroup enddef;
def *gobble* primary g = enddef;

DEFINI'TION, s. [definitio, *Latin*.]
1. A short description of a thing by its properties.
— SAMUEL JOHNSON, *A Dictionary of the English Language* (1755)

DEFINI"TION, n. [L. definitio. *See* Define.]
1. A brief description of a thing by its properties;
as a definition of wit or of a circle.
— NOAH WEBSTER, *An American Dictionary of the English Language* (1828)

19

Conditions
and Loops

If decisions never had to be made, life would be much easier, and so would programming. But sometimes it is necessary to choose between alternatives, and METAFONT allows programs to take different paths depending on the circumstances. You just say something like

> **if** not *decisions*: *life* := *programming* := *easier*(*much*)
> **elseif** *choice* = *a*: *program_a*
> **else**: *program_b* **fi**

which reduces, for example, to '*program_b*' if and only if *decisions* = **true** and *choice* ≠ *a*. The normal left-to-right order of program interpretation can also be modified by specifying "loops," which tell the computer to read certain tokens repeatedly, with minor variations, until some condition becomes true. We have seen many examples of these mechanisms already; the purpose of the present chapter is to discuss the entire range of possibilities.

METAFONT's conditions and loops are different from those in most other programming languages, because the conditional or iterated code does not have to fit into the syntactic structure. For example, you can write strange things like

> `p = (if b: 0,0)..(1,5 else: u,v fi)`

where the conditional text '0, 0) .. (1, 5' makes no sense by itself, although it becomes meaningful when read in context. In this respect conditions and loops behave like macros. They specify rules of token transformation that can be said to take place in METAFONT's "mouth" before the tokens are actually digested in the computer's "stomach."

The first conditional example above has three alternatives, in the form

> **if** ⟨boolean$_1$⟩: ⟨text$_1$⟩ **elseif** ⟨boolean$_2$⟩: ⟨text$_2$⟩ **else**: ⟨text$_3$⟩ **fi**

and the second example has just two; there can be any number of '**elseif**' clauses before '**else**:'. Only one of the conditional texts will survive, namely the first one whose condition is true; '**else**:' is always true. You can also omit '**else**:' entirely, in which case '**else**: ⟨empty⟩' is implied just before the closing '**fi**'. For example, plain METAFONT's **mode_setup** routine includes the conditional command

> **if** unknown *mag*: *mag* := 1; **fi**

whose effect is to set *mag* equal to 1 if it hasn't already received a value; in this case there's only one alternative.

▶ **EXERCISE 19.1**
Would it be wrong to put the ';' after the '**fi**' in the example just given?

 The informal rules just stated can, of course, be expressed more formally as rules of syntax:

⟨condition⟩ ⟶ `if` ⟨boolean expression⟩ : ⟨conditional text⟩⟨alternatives⟩ `fi`
⟨alternatives⟩ ⟶ ⟨empty⟩
    | `else` : ⟨conditional text⟩
    | `elseif` ⟨boolean expression⟩ : ⟨conditional text⟩⟨alternatives⟩

Every conditional construction begins with 'if' and ends with 'fi'. The conditional texts are any sequences of tokens that are balanced with respect to 'if' and 'fi'; furthermore, 'elseif' and 'else' can occur in a conditional text only when enclosed by 'if' and 'fi'.

Each 'if' and 'elseif' must be followed by a ⟨boolean expression⟩, i.e., by an expression whose value is either '**true**' or '**false**'. Boolean expressions are named after George Boole, the founder of algebraic approaches to logic. Chapter 7 points out that variables can be of type **boolean**, and numerous examples of boolean expressions appear in Chapter 8. It's time now to be more systematic, so that we will know the facts about boolean expressions just as we have become well-versed in numeric expressions, pair expressions, picture expressions, path expressions, transform expressions, and pen expressions. Here are the relevant syntax rules:

⟨boolean primary⟩ ⟶ ⟨boolean variable⟩
    | `true` | `false`
    | (⟨boolean expression⟩)
    | `begingroup` ⟨statement list⟩⟨boolean expression⟩ `endgroup`
    | `known` ⟨primary⟩ | `unknown` ⟨primary⟩
    | ⟨type⟩⟨primary⟩ | `cycle` ⟨primary⟩
    | `odd` ⟨numeric primary⟩
    | `not` ⟨boolean primary⟩
⟨boolean secondary⟩ ⟶ ⟨boolean primary⟩
    | ⟨boolean secondary⟩ `and` ⟨boolean primary⟩
⟨boolean tertiary⟩ ⟶ ⟨boolean secondary⟩
    | ⟨boolean tertiary⟩ `or` ⟨boolean secondary⟩
⟨boolean expression⟩ ⟶ ⟨boolean tertiary⟩
    | ⟨numeric expression⟩⟨relation⟩⟨numeric tertiary⟩
    | ⟨pair expression⟩⟨relation⟩⟨pair tertiary⟩
    | ⟨transform expression⟩⟨relation⟩⟨transform tertiary⟩
    | ⟨boolean expression⟩⟨relation⟩⟨boolean tertiary⟩
    | ⟨string expression⟩⟨relation⟩⟨string tertiary⟩
⟨relation⟩ ⟶ `<` | `<=` | `>` | `>=` | `=` | `<>`

Most of these operations were already explained in Chapter 8, so it's only necessary to mention the more subtle points now. A ⟨primary⟩ of any type can be tested to see whether it has a specific type, and whether it has a known or unknown value based on the equations so far. In these tests, a ⟨future pen primary⟩ is considered to be of type **pen**. The test 'cycle p' is true if and only if p is a cyclic path. The 'odd' function first rounds its argument to an integer, then tests to see if the integer is odd. The 'not' function changes true to false and vice versa. The 'and' function yields true only if both arguments are true; the 'or' function yields true unless both arguments are false. Relations on pairs, transforms, or strings are decided by the first unequal component from left to right. (A transform is considered to be a 6-tuple as in Chapter 15.)

▶**EXERCISE 19.2**
What do you think: Is **false** > **true**?

▶**EXERCISE 19.3**
Could '(odd n) and not (odd $-n$)' possibly be true?

▶ **EXERCISE 19.4**
Could '(cycle p) and not (known p)' possibly be true?

▶ **EXERCISE 19.5**
Define an 'even' macro such that 'even n' is true if and only if round(n) is an even integer. [*Hint:* There's a slick answer.]

Boolean expressions beginning with a ⟨type⟩ should not come at the very beginning of a statement, because METAFONT will think that a ⟨declaration⟩ is coming up instead of an ⟨expression⟩. Thus, for example, if b is a boolean variable, the equation '**path** $p = b$' should be rewritten either as '$b = $ **path** p' or as '(**path** p) $= b$'.

A boolean expression like '$x = y$' that involves the equality relation looks very much like an equation. METAFONT will consider '$=$' to be a ⟨relation⟩ unless the expression to its left occurs at the very beginning of a ⟨statement⟩ or the very beginning of a ⟨right-hand side⟩. If you want to change an equation into a relation, just insert parentheses, as in '($x = y$) $= b$' or '$b = (x = y)$'.

After a ⟨path join⟩, the token 'cycle' is not considered to be the beginning of a ⟨boolean primary⟩. (Cf. Chapter 14.)

The boolean expression '**path** $((0,0))$' is false, even though '$((0,0))$' meets Chapter 14's syntax rules for ⟨path primary⟩, via (⟨path expression⟩) and (⟨path subexpression⟩) and (⟨pair tertiary⟩). A pair expression is not considered to be of type **path** unless the path interpretation is mandatory.

▶ **EXERCISE 19.6**
Evaluate 'length $((3,4))$' and 'length $((3,4)\{0,0\})$' and 'length reverse $(3,4)$'.

OK, that covers all there is to be said about conditions. What about loops? It's easiest to explain loops by giving the syntax first:

⟨loop⟩ ⟶ ⟨loop header⟩:⟨loop text⟩ `endfor`
⟨loop header⟩ ⟶ `for` ⟨symbolic token⟩⟨is⟩⟨for list⟩
  | `for` ⟨symbolic token⟩⟨is⟩⟨progression⟩
  | `forsuffixes` ⟨symbolic token⟩⟨is⟩⟨suffix list⟩
  | `forever`
⟨is⟩ ⟶ `=` | `:=`
⟨for list⟩ ⟶ ⟨expression⟩ | ⟨empty⟩
  | ⟨for list⟩ , ⟨expression⟩ | ⟨for list⟩ , ⟨empty⟩
⟨suffix list⟩ ⟶ ⟨suffix⟩
  | ⟨suffix list⟩ , ⟨suffix⟩
⟨progression⟩ ⟶ ⟨initial value⟩ `step` ⟨step size⟩ `until` ⟨limit value⟩
⟨initial value⟩ ⟶ ⟨numeric expression⟩
⟨step size⟩ ⟶ ⟨numeric expression⟩
⟨limit value⟩ ⟶ ⟨numeric expression⟩
⟨exit clause⟩ ⟶ `exitif` ⟨boolean expression⟩ `;`

As in macro definitions, '$=$' and '$:=$' are interchangeable here.

This syntax shows that loops can be of four kinds, which we might indicate schematically as follows:

> **for** $x = \epsilon_1, \epsilon_2, \epsilon_3$: text($x$) **endfor**
> **for** $x = \nu_1$ **step** ν_2 **until** ν_3: text(x) **endfor**
> **forsuffixes** $s = \sigma_1, \sigma_2, \sigma_3$: text($s$) **endfor**
> **forever**: text **endfor**

The first case expands to 'text(ϵ_1) text(ϵ_2) text(ϵ_3)'; the ϵ's here are expressions of any type, not necessarily "known," and they are evaluated and put into capsules before being substituted for x. The ϵ's might also be empty, in which case text(ϵ) is omitted. The second case is more complicated, and it will be explained carefully below; simple cases like '1 **step** 2 **until** 7' are equivalent to short lists like '1, 3, 5, 7'. The third case expands to 'text(σ_1) text(σ_2) text(σ_3)'; the σ's here are arbitrary suffixes (possibly empty), in which subscripts will have been evaluated and changed to numeric tokens before being substituted for x. The final case expands into the sequence 'text text text ...', ad infinitum; there's an escape from this (and from the other three kinds of loop) if an ⟨exit clause⟩ appears in the text, as explained below.

Notice that if the loop text is a single statement that's supposed to be repeated several times, you should put a ';' just before the **endfor**, not just after it; METAFONT's loops do not insert semicolons automatically, because they are intended to be used in the midst of expressions as well as with statements that are being iterated.

Plain METAFONT defines '**upto**' as an abbreviation for '**step** 1 **until**', and '**downto**' as an abbreviation for '**step** −1 **until**'. Therefore you can say, e.g., '**for** $x = 1$ **upto** 9: ' instead of '**for** $x = 1, 2, 3, 4, 5, 6, 7, 8, 9$: '.

When you say '**for** $x = \nu_1$ **step** ν_2 **until** ν_3', METAFONT evaluates the three numeric expressions, which must have known values. Then it reads the loop text. If $\nu_2 > 0$ and $\nu_1 > \nu_3$, or if $\nu_2 < 0$ and $\nu_1 < \nu_3$, the loop is not performed at all. Otherwise text(ν_1) is performed, ν_1 is replaced by $\nu_1 + \nu_2$, and the same process is repeated with the new value of ν_1.

▶ **EXERCISE 19.7**
Read the rules in the previous paragraph carefully, then explain for what values of x the loop is performed if you say (a) '**for** $x = 1$ **step** 2 **until** 0'. (b) '**for** $x = 1$ **step** −2 **until** 0'. (c) '**for** $x = 1$ **step** 0 **until** 0'. (d) '**for** $x = 0$ **step** .1 **until** 1'.

A ⟨loop text⟩ is rather like the ⟨replacement text⟩ of a macro. It is any sequence of tokens that is balanced with respect to unquoted appearances of **for/forsuffixes/forever** and **endfor** delimiters. METAFONT reads the entire loop text quickly and stores it away before trying to perform it or to expand macros within it. All occurrences of the controlled ⟨symbolic token⟩ in the loop text are changed to special internal parameter tokens that mean "insert an argument here," where the argument is of type **expr** in the case of **for**, of type **suffix** in the case of **forsuffixes**. This rule implies, in particular, that the symbolic token has no connection with similarly named variables elsewhere in the program.

▶**EXERCISE 19.8**
What values are shown by the following program?

```
n=0; for n=1: m=n; endfor show m,n; end.
```

The *flex* routine described in Chapter 14 provides an interesting example of how loops can be used inside of macros inside of expressions:

pair $z_-[\,]$, dz_-; **numeric** n_-;   % private variables
def *flex*(**text** t) =   % t is a list of pairs
  hide($n_- := 0$;
    for $z = t$: $z_-[\text{incr } n_-] := z$; **endfor**
    $dz_- := z_-[n_-] - z_-[1]$)
  $z_-[1]$ **for** $k = 2$ **upto** $n_- - 1$: $\ldots z_-[k]\{dz_-\}$ **endfor**
  $\ldots z_-[n_-]$ **enddef**;

The first loop stores the given pairs temporarily in an array, and it also counts how many there are; this calculation is "hidden." Then the actual flex-path is contributed to the program with the help of a second loop. (Appendix B uses the convention that symbolic tokens ending in '$-$' should not appear in a user's program; this often makes it unnecessary to '**save**' tokens.)

When METAFONT encounters the construction '**exitif** ⟨boolean expression⟩;', it evaluates the boolean expression. If the expression is true, the (innermost) loop being iterated is terminated abruptly. Otherwise, nothing special happens.

▶**EXERCISE 19.9**
Define an '**exitunless**' macro such that '**exitunless** ⟨boolean expression⟩;' will exit the current loop if the boolean expression is false.

▶**EXERCISE 19.10**
Write a METAFONT program that sets $p[k]$ to the kth prime number, for $1 \le k \le 30$. Thus, $p[1]$ should be 2, $p[2] = 3$, etc.

▶**EXERCISE 19.11**
When you run METAFONT on the file '**expr.mf**' of Chapter 8, you get into a '**forever**' loop that can be stopped if you type, e.g., '**0 end**'. But what can you type to get out of the loop without ending the run? (The goal is to make METAFONT type '**∗**', without incurring any error messages.)

If? thou Protector of this damned Strumpet,
Talk'st thou to me of Ifs: thou art a Traytor,
Off with his Head.

— WILLIAM SHAKESPEARE, *Richard the Third* (1593)

Use not vain repetitions.

— *Matthew 6:7* (c. 70 A.D.)

20

More About Macros

Chapter 18 gave the basic facts about macro definitions, but it didn't tell the whole story. It's time now for the Ultimate Truth to be revealed.

 But this whole chapter consists of "dangerous bend" paragraphs, since the subject matter will be appreciated best by people who have worked with METAFONT for a little while. We shall discuss the following topics:

- Definitions that begin with '**vardef**'; these embed macros into the variables of a program and extend the unary operators of METAFONT expressions.
- Definitions that begin with '**primarydef**', '**secondarydef**', or '**tertiarydef**'; these extend the binary operators of METAFONT expressions.
- Other primitives of METAFONT that expand into sequences of tokens in a macro-like way, including '**input**' and '**scantokens**'.
- Rules that explain when tokens are subject to expansion and when they aren't.

First let's consider the ⟨vardef heading⟩ that was left undefined in Chapter 18. The ordinary macros discussed in that chapter begin with

def ⟨symbolic token⟩⟨parameter heading⟩

and then comes '=', etc. You can also begin a definition by saying

vardef ⟨declared variable⟩⟨parameter heading⟩

instead; in this case the ⟨declared variable⟩ might consist of several tokens, and you are essentially defining a variable whose "value" is of type "macro." For example, suppose you decide to say

pair $a.p$; **pen** $a.q$; **path** $a.r$; **vardef** $a.s = \ldots$ **enddef**;

then $a.p$, $a.q$, and $a.r$ will be variables of types **pair**, **pen**, and **path**, but $a.s$ will expand into a sequence of tokens. (The language SIMULA68 demonstrated that it is advantageous to include procedures as parts of variable data structures; METAFONT does an analogous thing with macros.)

After a definition like '**def** $t = \ldots$', the token t becomes a "spark"; i.e., you can't use it in a suffix. But after '**vardef** $t = \ldots$', the token t remains a "tag," because macro expansion will take place only when t is the first token in a variable name. Some of the definitions in Appendix B are vardefs instead of defs for just that reason; for example,

vardef dir **primary** $d = \textit{right}$ rotated d **enddef**

allows a user to have variable names like '`p5dir`'.

A variable is syntactically a primary expression, and METAFONT would get unnecessarily confused if the replacement texts of vardef macros were very different from primary expressions. Therefore, the tokens '**begingroup**' and '**endgroup**' are automatically inserted at the beginning and end of every vardef replacement text. If you say '**showvariable** a' just after making the declarations and definition above, the machine will reply as follows:

```
a.p=pair
a.q=unknown pen
a.r=unknown path
a.s=macro:->begingroup...endgroup
```

The 'incr' macro of Appendix B increases its argument by 1 and produces the increased value as its result. The inserted '**begingroup**' and '**endgroup**' come in handy here:

> **vardef** incr **suffix** $ = $:= $ + 1;　$ **enddef**.

Notice that the argument is a **suffix**, not an **expr**, because every variable name is a special case of a ⟨suffix⟩, and because an **expr** parameter should never appear to the left of ':='. Incidentally, according to the rules for undelimited suffix parameters in Chapter 18, you're allowed to say either 'incr v' or 'incr(v)' when applying incr to v.

There's another kind of vardef, in which the variable name being defined can have any additional suffix when it is used; this suffix is treated as an argument to the macro. In this case you write

> **vardef** ⟨declared variable⟩@# ⟨parameter heading⟩

and you can use @# in the replacement text (where it behaves like any other **suffix** parameter). For example, Appendix B says

> **vardef** z@# = (x@#, y@#) **enddef**;

this is the magic definition that makes 'z_{3r}' equivalent to '(x_{3r}, y_{3r})', etc. In fact, we now know that '$z3r$' actually expands into eleven tokens:

> ```
> begingroup (x3r, y3r) endgroup
> ```

▶ **EXERCISE 20.1**
True or false: After '**vardef** a@# **suffix** b = ... **enddef**', the suffix argument b will always be empty.

Plain METAFONT includes a *solve* macro that uses binary search to find numerical solutions to nonlinear equations, which are too difficult to resolve in the ordinary way. To use *solve*, you first define a macro f such that $f(x)$ is either **true** or **false**; then you say

> *solve* $f(true\_x, false\_x)$

where *true_x* and *false_x* are values such that $f(true_x) = $ **true** and $f(false_x) = $ **false**. The resulting value x will be at the cutting edge between truth and falsity, in the sense that x will be within a given *tolerance* of values for which f yields both outcomes.

> **vardef** *solve*@#(**expr** *true_x, false_x*) =
> tx_- := *true_x*;　fx_- := *false_x*;
> **forever**: x_- := $.5[tx_-, fx_-]$;　**exitif** abs($tx_- - fx_-$) ≤ *tolerance*;
> **if** @#(x_-) :　tx_- **else** :　fx_- **fi**:=x_-;　**endfor**;
> x_- **enddef**;

For example, the *solve* routine makes it possible to solve the following interesting problem posed by Richard Southall: Given points z_1, z_2, z_3, z_4 such that $x_1 < x_2 < x_3 < x_4$ and $y_1 < y_2 = y_3 > y_4$, find the point z between z_2 and z_3 such that METAFONT will choose to travel *right* at z in the path

> $z_1 \{z_2 - z_1\} .. z .. \{z_4 - z_3\} z_4.$

If we try $z = z_2$, METAFONT will choose a direction at z that has a positive (upward) y-component; but at $z = z_3$, METAFONT's chosen direction will have a negative (downward) y-component. Somewhere in between is a "nice" value of z for which the curve will not rise above the line $y = y_2$. What is this z?

Chapter 14 gives equations from which z could be computed, in principle, but those equations involve trigonometry in a complicated fashion. It's nice to know that we can find z rather easily in spite of those complexities:

> **vardef** *upward*(**expr** x) =
> ypart direction 1 of $(z_1\{z_2 - z_1\} \mathbin{..} (x, y_2) \mathbin{..} \{z_4 - z_3\}z_4) > 0$ **enddef**;
> $z = (solve\ upward(x_2, x_3), y_2)$.

▶ **EXERCISE 20.2**
It might happen in unusual cases that *upward*(x) is **false** for all $x_2 \leq x \leq x_3$, hence *solve* is being invoked under invalid assumptions. What result does it give then?

▶ **EXERCISE 20.3**
Use *solve* to find $\sqrt[3]{10}$, and compare the answer to the cube root obtained in the normal way.

The syntax for ⟨declared variable⟩ in Chapter 7 allows for collective subscripts as well as tags in the name of the variable being declared. Thus, you can say

> **vardef** $a[\,]b[\,] = \ldots$ **enddef**;

what does this mean? Well, it means that all variables like **a1b2** are macros with a common replacement text. Every vardef has two implicit suffix parameters, '**#@**' and '**@**', which can be used in the replacement text to discover what subscripts have actually been used. Parameter '**@**' is the final token of the variable name ('2' in this example); parameter '**#@**' is everything preceding the final token (in this case '**a1b**'). These notations are supposed to be memorable because '**@**' is where you're "at," while '**#@**' is everything before and '**@#**' is everything after.

▶ **EXERCISE 20.4**
After '**vardef p[]dir=(#@dx,#@dy) enddef**', what's the expansion of '**p5dir**'?

▶ **EXERCISE 20.5**
Explain how it's possible to retrieve the first subscript in the replacement text of **vardef a[]b[]** (thereby obtaining, for example, '1' instead of '**a1b**').

▶ **EXERCISE 20.6**
Say '**showvariable incr,z**' to METAFONT and explain the machine's reply.

A vardef wipes out all type declarations and macro definitions for variables whose name begins with the newly defined macro variable name. For example, '**vardef a**' causes variables like **a.p** and **a1b2** to disappear silently; '**vardef a.s**' wipes

out a.s.p, etc. Moreover, after 'vardef a' is in effect, you are not allowed to say
'pair a.p' or 'vardef a[]', since such variables would be inaccessible.

 The syntax for ⟨definition⟩ in Chapter 18 was incomplete, because ⟨vardef
heading⟩ and ⟨leveldef heading⟩ were omitted. Here are the missing rules:

⟨vardef heading⟩ ⟶ **vardef** ⟨declared variable⟩⟨parameter heading⟩
| **vardef** ⟨declared variable⟩ **@#** ⟨parameter heading⟩
⟨leveldef heading⟩ ⟶ ⟨leveldef⟩⟨parameter⟩⟨symbolic token⟩⟨parameter⟩
⟨leveldef⟩ ⟶ **primarydef** | **secondarydef** | **tertiarydef**
⟨parameter⟩ ⟶ ⟨symbolic token⟩

The new things here are **primarydef**, **secondarydef**, and **tertiarydef**, which permit
you to extend METAFONT's repertoire of binary operators. For example, the 'dotprod'
operator is defined as follows in Appendix B:

primarydef w dotprod $z =$
    (xpart w * xpart z + ypart w * ypart z) **enddef**.

METAFONT's syntax for expressions has effectively gained a new rule

⟨numeric secondary⟩ ⟶ ⟨pair secondary⟩ dotprod ⟨pair primary⟩

in addition to the other forms of ⟨numeric secondary⟩, because of this primarydef.

The names '**primarydef**', '**secondarydef**', and '**tertiarydef**' may seem off
by one, because they define operators at one level higher up: A primarydef
defines a binary operator that forms a secondary expression from a secondary and a primary; such operators are at the same level as '*' and 'rotated'. A secondarydef defines
a binary operator that forms a tertiary expression from a tertiary and a secondary;
such operators are at the same level as '+' and 'or'. A tertiarydef defines a binary
operator that forms an expression from an expression and a tertiary; such operators
are at the same level as '<' and '&'.

Plain METAFONT's 'intersectionpoint' macro is defined by a **secondarydef**
because it is analogous to 'intersectiontimes', which occurs at the same level
(namely the secondary → tertiary level).

secondarydef p intersectionpoint $q =$
    begingroup save x_-, y_-; $(x_-, y_-) = p$ intersectiontimes q;
    if $x_- < 0$: **errmessage**("The paths don't intersect"); $(0,0)$
    else: .5[point x_- of p, point y_- of q] **fi endgroup enddef**;

Notice that **begingroup** and **endgroup** are necessary here; they aren't inserted automatically as they would have been in a **vardef**.

▶ **EXERCISE 20.7**
Define a 'transum' macro operation that yields the sum of two transforms.
(If $t_3 = t_1$ transum t_2, then z transformed $t_3 = z$ transformed $t_1 + z$ tranformed t_2,
for all pairs z.)

Now we've covered all the types of ⟨definition⟩, and it's time to take stock and think about the total picture. METAFONT's mastication process converts an input file into a long sequence of tokens, as explained in Chapter 6, and its digestive processes work strictly on those tokens. When a symbolic token is about to be digested, METAFONT looks up the token's current meaning, and in certain cases METAFONT will expand that token into a sequence of other tokens before continuing; this "expansion process" applies to macros and to **if** and **for**, as well as to certain other special primitives that we shall consider momentarily. Expansion continues until an unexpandable token is found; then the digestion process can continue. Sometimes, however, the expansion is not carried out; for example, after METAFONT has digested a **def** token, it stops all expansion until just after it reaches the corresponding **enddef**. A complete list of all occasions when tokens are not expanded appears later in this chapter.

Let's consider all the tokens that cause expansion to occur, whenever expansion hasn't been inhibited:

- Macros. When a macro is expanded, METAFONT first reads and evaluates the arguments (if any), as already explained. (Expansion continues while **expr** and **suffix** arguments are being evaluated, but it is suppressed within **text** arguments.) Then METAFONT replaces the macro and its arguments by the replacement text.

- Conditions. When 'if' is expanded, METAFONT reads and evaluates the boolean expression, then skips ahead, if necessary, until coming to either 'fi' or a condition that's true; then it will continue to read the next token. When 'elseif' or 'else' or 'fi' is expanded, a conditional text has just ended, so METAFONT skips to the closing 'fi' and the expansion is empty.

- Loops. When 'for' or 'forsuffixes' or 'forever' is expanded, METAFONT reads the specifications up to the colon, then reads the loop text (without expansion) up to the **endfor**. Finally it rereads the loop text repeatedly, with expansion. When 'exitif' is expanded, METAFONT evaluates the following boolean expression and throws away the semicolon; if the expression proves to be true, the current loop is terminated.

- **scantokens** ⟨string primary⟩. When 'scantokens' is expanded, METAFONT evaluates the following primary expression, which should be of type **string**. This string is converted to tokens by the rules of Chapter 6, as if it had been input from a file containing just one line of text.

- **input** ⟨filename⟩. When 'input' is expanded, the expansion is null, but METAFONT prepares to read from the specified file before looking at any more tokens from its current source. A ⟨filename⟩ is subject to special restrictions explained on the next page.

- **endinput**. When 'endinput' is expanded, the expansion is null. But the next time METAFONT gets to the end of an **input** line, it will stop reading from the file containing that line.

- **expandafter**. When 'expandafter' is expanded, METAFONT first reads one more token, without expanding it; let's call this token t. Then METAFONT reads the token that comes after t (and possibly more tokens, if that token takes an argument), replacing it by its expansion. Finally, METAFONT puts t back in front of that expansion.

- \. When '\' is expanded, the expansion is null, i.e., empty.

The syntax for ⟨filename⟩ is not standard in METAFONT, because different operating systems have different conventions. You should ask your local system wizards for details on just how they have decided to implement file names. The situation is complicated by the fact that METAFONT's process of converting to tokens is irreversible; for example, 'x01' and 'x1.0' both yield identical sequences of tokens. Therefore METAFONT doesn't even try to convert a file name to tokens; an **input** operation must appear only in a text file, not in a list of tokens like the replacement text of a macro! (You can get around this restriction by saying

> **scantokens** "input foo"

or, more generally,

> **scantokens** ("input " & *fname*)

if *fname* is a string variable containing the ⟨filename⟩ you want to input.) Although file names have nonstandard syntax, a sequence of six or fewer ordinary letters and/or digits followed by a space should be a file name that works in essentially the same way on all installations of METAFONT. Uppercase letters are considered to be distinct from their lowercase counterparts, on many systems.

Here now is the promised list of all cases when expandable tokens are not expanded. Some of the situations involve primitives that haven't been discussed yet, but we'll get to them eventually. Expansion is suppressed at the following times:

- When tokens are being deleted during error recovery (see Chapter 5).
- When tokens are being skipped because conditional text is being ignored.
- When METAFONT is reading the definition of a macro.
- When METAFONT is reading a loop text, or the symbolic token that immediately follows **for** or **forsuffixes**.
- When METAFONT is reading the **text** argument of a macro.
- When METAFONT is reading the initial symbolic token of a ⟨declared variable⟩ in a type declaration.
- When METAFONT is reading the symbolic tokens to be defined by **delimiters**, **inner**, **let**, **newinternal**, or **outer**.
- When METAFONT is reading the symbolic tokens to be shown by **showtoken** or **showvariable**.
- When METAFONT is reading the token after **expandafter**, **everyjob**, or the '=' following **let**.

The expansion process is not suppressed while reading the suffix that follows the initial token of a ⟨declared variable⟩, not even in a ⟨vardef heading⟩.

The two lieutenants,
Fonteius Capito in Germany,
and Claudius Macro in Africa,
who opposed his advancement,
were put down.

— SUETONIUS, *Sergius Sulpicius Galba* (c. 125 A.D.)

By introducing macro instructions in the source language,
the designer can bring about the same ease of programming
as could be achieved by giving the computer
a more powerful operation list than it really has.
But naturally, one does not get the same advantages
in terms of economy of memory space and computer time
as would be obtained if the more powerful instructions
were really built into the machine.

— O. DOPPING, *Computers & Data Processing* (1970)

21
Random Numbers

It's fun to play games with METAFONT by writing programs that incorporate an element of chance. You can generate unpredictable shapes, and you can add patternless perturbations to break up the rigid symmetry that is usually associated with mathematical constructions. Musicians who use computers to synthesize their compositions have found that music has more "life" if its rhythms are slightly irregular and offbeat; perfect 1–2–3–4 pulses sound pretty dull by contrast. The same phenomenon might prove to be true in typography.

METAFONT allows you to introduce controlled indeterminacy in two ways: (1) 'uniformdeviate t' gives a number u that's randomly distributed between 0 and t; (2) 'normaldeviate' gives a random number x that has the so-called normal distribution with mean zero and variance one.

More precisely, if $t > 0$ and $u = $ uniformdeviate t, we will have $0 \leq u < t$, and for each fraction $0 \leq p \leq 1$ we will have $0 \leq u < pt$ with approximate probability p. If $t < 0$, the results are similar but negated, with $0 \geq u > t$. Finally if $t = 0$, we always have $u = 0$; this is the only case where $u = t$ is possible.

A normaldeviate, x, will be positive about half the time and negative about half the time. Its distribution is "bell-shaped" in the sense that a particular value x occurs with probability roughly proportional to $e^{-x^2/2}$; the graph of this function looks something like a bell. The probability is about 68% that $|x| < 1$, about 95% that $|x| < 2$, and about 99.7% that $|x| < 3$. It's a pretty safe bet that $|x| < 4$.

Instead of relying on mathematical formulas to explain this random behavior, we can actually see the results graphically by letting METAFONT draw some "scatter plots." Consider the following program, which draws a $10\,\mathrm{pt} \times 10\,\mathrm{pt}$ square and puts 100 little dots inside it:

> **beginchar** (**incr** *code*, $10pt^{\#}, 10pt^{\#}, 0$);
> **pickup pencircle** scaled $.3pt$; **draw** *unitsquare* scaled w;
> **pickup pencircle** scaled $1pt$;
> **for** $k = 1$ **upto** 100:
>   **drawdot**(uniformdeviate w, uniformdeviate w); **endfor endchar**.

The resulting "characters," if we repeat the experiment ten times, look like this:

And if we replace 'uniformdeviate w' by '$.5w + w/6 * $ normaldeviate', we get

Finally, if we say '**drawdot**(uniformdeviate w, $.5w + w/6 * $ normaldeviate)' the results are a mixture of the other two cases:

▶ **EXERCISE 21.1**
Consider the program fragment '**if** uniformdeviate $1 < 1/3$: *case_a* **else**: *case_b* **fi**'. True or false: *case_b* will occur about three times as often as *case_a*.

▶**EXERCISE 21.2**

METAFONT's uniformdeviate operator usually doesn't give you an integer. Explain how to generate random integers between 1 and n, in such a way that each value will be about equally likely.

▶**EXERCISE 21.3**

What does the formula '(uniformdeviate 1)$[z_1, z_2]$' represent?

▶**EXERCISE 21.4**

Guess what the following program will produce:

```
beginchar(incr code,100pt#,10pt#,0);
for n:=0 upto 99:
  fill unitsquare xscaled 1pt yscaled uniformdeviate h
    shifted (n*pt,0); endfor endchar.
```

▶**EXERCISE 21.5**

And what does this puzzle program draw?

```
beginchar(incr code,24pt#,10pt#,0);
numeric count[];
pickup pencircle scaled 1pt;
for n:=1 upto 100:
 x:=.5w+w/6*normaldeviate;
 y:=floor(x/pt);
 if unknown count[y]: count[y]:=-1; fi
 drawdot(x,pt*incr count[y]); endfor endchar.
```

Let's try now to put more "life" in the METAFONT logo, by asking Lady Luck to add small perturbations to each of the key points. First we define *noise*,

vardef *noise* = normaldeviate * *craziness* **enddef**;

the *craziness* parameter will control the degree of haphazard variation. Then we can write the following program for the logo's 'N':

beginlogochar(**"N"**, 15);
$x_1 = leftstemloc + noise$;
$x_2 = leftstemloc + noise$;
$w - x_4 = leftstemloc + noise$;
$w - x_5 = leftstemloc + noise$;
$bot\ y_1 = noise - o$;
$top\ y_2 = h + o + noise$;
$y_3 = y_4 + ygap + noise$;
$bot\ y_4 = noise - o$;
$top\ y_5 = h + o + noise$;
$z_3 = whatever[z_4, z_5]$;
draw z_1 -- z_2 -- z_3; **draw** z_4 -- z_5; **labels**$(1, 2, 3, 4, 5)$; **endchar**.

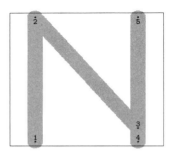

The illustration here was drawn with *craziness* = 0, so there was no noise.

Three trials of the 9 pt 'N' with *craziness* = .1*pt* gave the following results:

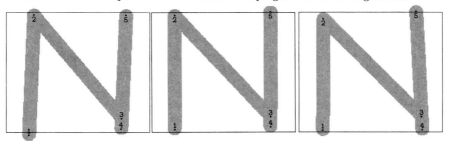

And here's what happens if you do similar things to all the letters of METAFONT, with *craziness* decreasing from .45*pt* to zero in steps of .05*pt*:

METAFONT
METAFONT
METAFONT
METAFONT
METAFONT
METAFONT
METAFONT
METAFONT
METAFONT
METAFONT

 Every time you run a program that refers to random numbers, you'll get different results, because METAFONT uses the date and time of day to change its generator. This unpredictable behavior is normally what you want, but it can be troublesome if your program draws a lovely shape that you'd like to see again. Or perhaps one of your runs will uncover a program bug; you won't be able to diagnose the problem, because it probably won't recur! The solution is to say

randomseed := ⟨numeric expression⟩

and to remember the value of that numeric expression. (The value will automatically be recorded in the transcript file of your run.) You will get the same sequence of uniform and normal deviates on any two runs that begin with the same **randomseed**, because METAFONT's numbers are only "pseudo-random."

> *A musician whom I knew amused himself*
> *by tuning his piano arbitrarily, without any rhyme or reason.*
> *Afterwards he played Beethoven's* Sonate Pathétique *by heart.*
> *It was an unbelievable delight to hear an old piece come back to life.*
> *I had heard this sonata for twenty years,*
> *never dreaming that it was capable of being developed further.*
> — AUGUST STRINDBERG, *Chance in Artistic Creation* (1894)

> *[Education] must lead us from chance and arbitrariness*
> *to rational clarity and intellectual order.*
> — L. MIES VAN DER ROHE, *Inaugural Address* (1938)

22

Strings

METAFONT is not a word processor, but a METAFONT programmer can process words and other short strings of symbols in rudimentary ways. Strings can help explain what a program is doing; for example, the `io.mf` file of Chapter 5 mentions `"The letter O"` as a title that should appear on proofsheets, and it also says `"O"` in order to identify the position of a character in the output font.

Chapter 6 points out that a ⟨string token⟩ is any sequence of characters enclosed in double-quote (`"`) marks, except that you're not allowed to use the double-quote character itself in this way. If you need that character, plain META-FONT provides it in a string of length 1 called *ditto*. Thus

> `"A string expression can contain a '" & ditto & "' mark"`

even though a ⟨string token⟩ cannot.

A string expression can be used all by itself as a statement, just as if it were an equation or declaration or command. Such a statement is called a ⟨title⟩, provided that it is immediately followed by a ';'. If *tracingtitles* > 0 when a title is encountered, METAFONT will type the title on the user's terminal. If *proofing* > 0 when a title is encountered, METAFONT will copy the title into the output file, so that it can be put onto proofsheets by postprocessors such as the `GFtoDVI` program described in Appendix H.

 Appendix H explains how to specify the strings that are used as labels for the key points on proofsheets.

 Here's the full syntax for string expressions. All of the activity except for concatenation ('&') takes place at the primary level:

⟨string primary⟩ ⟶ ⟨string token⟩
    | ⟨string variable⟩
    | (⟨string expression⟩)
    | **begingroup** ⟨statement list⟩⟨string expression⟩ **endgroup**
    | **jobname**
    | **readstring**
    | **str** ⟨suffix⟩
    | **char** ⟨numeric primary⟩
    | **decimal** ⟨numeric primary⟩
    | **substring** ⟨pair primary⟩ **of** ⟨string primary⟩
⟨string secondary⟩ ⟶ ⟨string primary⟩
⟨string tertiary⟩ ⟶ ⟨string secondary⟩
⟨string expression⟩ ⟶ ⟨string tertiary⟩
    | ⟨string expression⟩ **&** ⟨string tertiary⟩

The new features here are `jobname`, `readstring`, `str`, `char`, `decimal`, and `substring`; we shall consider each of them in turn.

 The name of your job (**jobname**) is the name of the first file you input, provided that the first line of instructions to METAFONT (the '`**`' line or command line) causes input of some file. Otherwise the job name is `mfput`, as in Experiment 1 of Chapter 5.

When you say '**readstring**', METAFONT stops and waits for the user to type a line at the terminal. The value of **readstring** is the contents of this line, with trailing spaces eliminated. (You probably should use the **message** command first, to give the user a clue about what to type; for example, see the **expr.mf** file of Chapter 8, which gets its input expressions via **readstring**. The **stop** macro of Appendix B makes use of the fact that **readstring** halts the computer; it doesn't actually look at the string.)

An arbitrary ⟨suffix⟩ is converted to a string by **str**, using the method by which METAFONT displays suffix arguments in diagnostic typeouts. Negative subscripts are enclosed in square brackets; spaces or dots are inserted between tokens whose characters belong to the same class (according to the table in Chapter 6). For example, if $n = 1$ then '**str** $x[n]a$' is "x1a"; '**str** $x\,n\,a$' is "x.n.a".

The result of '**char** n' is a string of length 1, representing the character whose ASCII code is n. (Appendix C explains this code.) The value of n is first rounded to the nearest integer, then multiples of 256 are added or subtracted if necessary until $0 \le n < 256$; this defines **char** n in all cases.

The decimal representation of a known numeric value x is available in string form as '**decimal** x'. If x is negative, the first character of this string will be '-'. If x is not an integer, a decimal point will be included, followed by as many digits as are necessary to characterize the value. (These conventions are the same as those illustrated in the example outputs of Chapter 8.)

The rules for substring are like the rules for subpath in Chapter 14. META-FONT thinks of a string as if its characters were written in the squares of a piece of graph paper, between coordinates $x = 0$ and $x = n$, where n is the length of the string. In simple cases, substring (a, b) then refers to the characters between $x = a$ and $x = b$. The rules for the general case are slightly more involved: If $b < a$, the result will be the reverse of substring (b, a). Otherwise a and b are replaced respectively by $\max(0, \min(n, \text{round } a))$ and $\max(0, \min(n, \text{round } b))$; this leads to the simple case $0 \le a \le b \le n$ described above, when the resulting string has length $b - a$.

Strings can be converted into numbers, although Chapter 8 didn't mention this fact in its syntax for ⟨numeric primary⟩. The primitive operations are

> **ASCII** ⟨string primary⟩ | **oct** ⟨string primary⟩ | **hex** ⟨string primary⟩

where 'ASCII' returns the ASCII code of the first character of the string, 'oct' computes an integer from a string representing octal notation (radix 8), and 'hex' computes an integer from a string representing hexadecimal notation (radix 16). For example,

> ASCII "100" $= 49$;   oct "100" $= 64$;   hex "100" $= 256$.

Several exceptional conditions need to be mentioned: (1) ASCII "" $= -1$; otherwise ASCII yields an integer between 0 and 255. (2) The characters in the string argument to 'oct' must all be digits in the range 0–7. (3) The characters in the string argument to 'hex' must all be digits in the range 0–9, A–F, or a–f. (4) The number that results from 'oct' or 'hex' must be less than 4096. Thus, 'oct "7777"' and 'hex "FFF"' are the maximum legal values.

▶ **EXERCISE 22.1**
Under what circumstances is (a) ASCII **char** $n = n$? (b) **char** ASCII $s = s$?

▶ **EXERCISE 22.2**
Why are there primitive operations to convert from strings to numbers assuming octal notation and hexadecimal notation, but not assuming decimal notation?

▶ **EXERCISE 22.3**
Write an *octal* macro that converts a nonnegative integer to an octal string.

A ⟨message command⟩ allows you to communicate directly or indirectly with the user. It has the general syntax

⟨message command⟩ ⟶ ⟨message op⟩⟨string expression⟩
⟨message op⟩ ⟶ **message** | **errmessage** | **errhelp**

If you say '**message** s', the characters of s will be typed on the terminal, at the beginning of a new line; '**errmessage** s' is similar, but the string will be preceded by "! " and followed by ".", followed by lines of context as in METAFONT's normal error messages. If the user asks for help after an **errmessage** error, the most recent **errhelp** string will be typed (unless it was empty).

METAFONT doesn't allow you to have an array of different macros $m[i]$; but you can have an array of strings that have macro-like behavior, via **scantokens**. The **mode_def** construction of Appendix B exploits this idea.

Many other useful Practises
mecanicks perform by this Theo.
as the finding the length of strings.
— WILLIAM ALINGHAM, *Geometry Epitomized* (1695)

Forgive me, if my trembling Pen displays
What never yet was sung in mortal Lays.
But how shall I attempt such arduous String?
— JAMES THOMSON, *The Castle of Indolence* (1748)

23

Online
Displays

How do you get pictures to appear on your screen? Plain METAFONT provides the '**showit**' command, which displays the *currentpicture*. Furthermore you can ask for '**screenchars**'; this automatically does a **showit** at the time of each **endchar**. And you can see all the action by asking for '**screenstrokes**'; this automatically does a **showit** after every **draw** or **fill**.

The above-described features of plain METAFONT are implemented from low-level primitive commands, by macros that appear in Appendix B. At the lowest level, METAFONT obeys commands such as '**display** *currentpicture* **inwindow** 1'; there's also an '**openwindow**' command that defines a correspondence between META-FONT coordinates and screen coordinates. The syntax is

⟨display command⟩ ⟶ **display** ⟨picture variable⟩ **inwindow** ⟨window⟩
⟨window⟩ ⟶ ⟨numeric expression⟩
⟨openwindow command⟩ ⟶ **openwindow** ⟨window⟩⟨window spec⟩
⟨window spec⟩ ⟶ ⟨screen place⟩ **at** ⟨pair expression⟩
⟨screen place⟩ ⟶ **from** ⟨screen coordinates⟩ **to** ⟨screen coordinates⟩
⟨screen coordinates⟩ ⟶ ⟨pair expression⟩

A ⟨window⟩ is an integer between 0 and 15, inclusive; it represents one of sixteen "windows" or "portholes" that METAFONT provides between its pictures and the outside world. The ⟨window⟩ mentioned in a **display** command must previously have been "opened" by an **openwindow** command.

METAFONT's windows should not be confused with the so-called windows provided by many modern operating systems. If you have such a system, you'll probably find that all of METAFONT's pictorial output appears in one operating-system window, and all of its terminal I/O appears in another, and you might be running other jobs (like the system editor) in another. METAFONT's windows are not so fancy as this; they are just internal subwindows of one big picture window.

The command '**openwindow** k **from** (r_0, c_0) **to** (r_1, c_1) **at** (x, y)' associates a rectangular area of the user's screen (or of the user's big picture window) with pixels in METAFONT's coordinate system. All of the numbers in this command (namely k, r_0, c_0, r_1, c_1, x, and y) are rounded to the nearest integer if they aren't integers already. Furthermore r_0 is replaced by $\max(0, \min(maxr, r_0))$ and r_1 is replaced by $\max(r_0, \min(maxr, r_1))$, where $maxr$ is the maximum number of rows on the screen; similar adjustments are made to c_0 and c_1. The two (r, c) values are row and column numbers on the screen; the topmost row is conventionally taken to be row zero, and the leftmost column is taken to be column zero. (These conventions for screen coordinates are quite different from the normal Cartesian coordinate system used everywhere else in METAFONT, but somehow they seem appropriate when applied to screens.) Point (x, y) of METAFONT's raster will be equated to the upper left corner of the rectangle, i.e., to the upper left corner of the pixel in screen column c_0 of screen row r_0. The window itself occupies $r_1 - r_0$ rows and $c_1 - c_0$ columns. It follows that the pixel in column c_1 of row r_1 is not in the window itself, but it is the screen pixel diagonally just below and to the right of the lower right corner of the window.

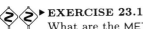 **EXERCISE 23.1**
What are the METAFONT coordinates of the boundary of such a window?

If you run METAFONT on a system that doesn't support general bitmap displays, the **display** and **openwindow** commands will do nothing. You'll have to look at hardcopy output, offline. (But your METAFONT might run a bit faster.)

The syntax for **display** insists that you display a ⟨picture variable⟩, not a ⟨picture expression⟩; thus, you can't '**display nullpicture**'. Plain METAFONT defines a special variable *blankpicture* that's entirely blank, just so that you can easily display nothing whenever you like.

A window may be opened any number of times, hence moved to different locations on the screen. Opening a window blanks the corresponding screen rectangle as if you had displayed *blankpicture*.

The effect of overlapping windows is undefined, because METAFONT does not always repaint pixels that have remained unchanged between displays.

Changes to a picture do not change the displays that were generated from it, until you give another display command explicitly. Thus, the images emblazoned on your screen might not exist any longer in METAFONT's picture memory.

Plain METAFONT has an '**openit**' macro that opens *currentwindow*; this variable *currentwindow* is always zero unless you change it yourself. The **showit** macro displays *currentpicture* in *currentwindow*; and it's also designed to call **openit**— but only the very first time **showit** is invoked. This means that the screen normally won't be touched until the moment you first try to display something.

Appendix E explains how to manage a more elaborate scheme in which six windows can be used to show how meta-characters vary under six different font-parameter settings. The author used such a six-window system when developing the Computer Modern typefaces; here is a typical example of what appeared on his terminal when the letter 'a' was being refined:

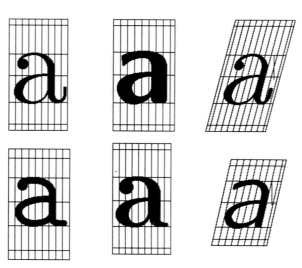

▶ **EXERCISE 23.2**

The **openit** macro in Appendix B specifies $(-50, 300)$ as the upper left corner point of the window used for showing all the pictures. This might clip off the bottom of a large character, if your screen is limited to, say, 360 rows. How could you change **openit** so that the character images will be raised 20 rows higher than they would be in the standard setting?

▶ **EXERCISE 23.3**

Design a '**new_window**' routine that allocates windows 1, 2, ..., 15. If the user says '**new_window $(u,v)**', where **$** is any suffix and **u,v** are pairs of coordinates for two opposite corners of a rectangle, your macro should map that rectangle to the next available screen rectangle and open it as window number **window$**. The allocation should be left to right, top to bottom; assume that the screen is an infinite rectangle, *screen_cols* wide.

Editing will be done on-line with a display scope and keyboard.
— RICHARD L. VENEZKY, in *American Documentation* (1968)

In future I might be obliged to turn for material to the tube.
— IGOR STRAVINSKY, in *Harper's* (1970)

24

Discreteness
and Discretion

Pixel patterns are indistinguishable from continuous curves, when the pixels are small enough. After all, the human eye is composed of discrete receptors, and visible light has a finite wavelength. Our hypothetical *luxo* printer of Chapter 11, with its resolution of 2000 pixels per inch, would surely be able to produce printed pages of high quality, if it existed; the physical properties of ink would smooth out all the tiny bumps, obliterating all the evidence that the letterforms had been digitized. However, it will always be less expensive to work with devices of lower resolution, and we want the output of METAFONT to look as good as possible on the machines that we can afford to buy. The purpose of this chapter is to discuss the principles of "discreet rounding," i.e., to consider the tasteful application of mathematical techniques by which METAFONT can be made to produce satisfactory shapes even when the resolution is rather coarse.

The technical material in this chapter is entirely marked with danger signs, since careful rounding tends to make METAFONT programs more complex; a novice user will not wish to worry about such details. On the other hand, an expert METAFONTer will take pains to round things properly even when preparing high-resolution fonts, since the subtle refinements we are about to discuss will often lead to significantly better letterforms.

We should realize before we begin that it would be a mistake to set our hopes too high. Mechanically generated letters that are untouched by human hands and unseen by human eyes can never be expected to compete with alphabets that are carefully crafted to look best on a particular device. There's no substitute for actually looking at the letters and changing their pixels until the result looks right. Therefore our goal should not be to make hand-tuning obsolete; it should rather be to make hand-tuning tolerable. Let us try to create meta-designs so that we would never want to change more than a few pixels per character, say half a dozen, regardless of the resolution. At low resolutions, six pixels will of course be a significant percentage of the whole, and at higher resolutions six well-considered pixel changes can still lead to worthwhile improvements. The point is that if our design comes close enough, a person with a good bitmap-editing program will be able to optimize an entire font in less than an hour. This is an attainable goal, if rounding is done judiciously.

METAFONT tries to adjust curves automatically, so that they are well adapted to the raster, if the internal quantities *autorounding* and/or *smoothing* have positive values. (Plain METAFONT sets *autorounding* := 2 and *smoothing* := 1, so you generally get these features unless you turn them off yourself.) But all the examples in this chapter will be generated with *autorounding* := *smoothing* := 0 unless otherwise mentioned, because this will keep METAFONT's automatic mechanisms from interfering with our experiments. We shall discuss the pros and cons of automatic rounding after we have explored the general problem in more detail.

The first thing we need to understand about rounding is METAFONT's procedure for digitizing a path. A path of length n can be regarded as a trajectory $z(t)$ that is traced out as t varies from 0 to n. In these terms, the corresponding digitized path is most easily described by the formula 'round $z(t)$' for $0 \leq t \leq n$; each

$z(t)$ is rounded to the nearest point with integer coordinates. For example, if a path goes through point $(3.1, 5.7)$, its digitization will go through point $(3, 6)$. The digitized trajectory makes discrete jumps at certain values of t, when round $z(t)$ hops from one point to another; the two points will be one pixel apart, and we can imagine that the digitized path traverses the horizontal or vertical edge between them when it jumps.

When an ordinary region is being filled, this rule for digitizing paths boils down to a simple criterion that's easy to visualize: *A pixel belongs to the digitized region if and only if its center point lies inside the original undigitized path.* For example, two versions of Chapter 5's Ionian 'O' are shown here at a resolution of 200 pixels per inch, using the characteristics of *lowres* mode in Appendix B:

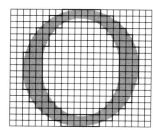 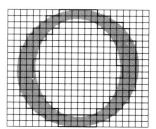

The heavy broken lines are digitized paths, and the pixels inside these ragged boundaries are those whose centers lie in the shaded regions.

The 'O' on the left has digitized well; but the one on the right has problems, because it was based on curves that were generated without taking the raster into account. The difference between these two letters is entirely due to line 8 of the program in Chapter 5, which says

$$curve\_sidebar = \text{round } 1/18em;$$

this equation determines the position of the leftmost and rightmost edges of the 'O' before digitization, and it leads to the nice digitized form in the left-hand example. Without the word 'round', we get the inferior right-hand example, which was obtained by exactly the same METAFONT program except that *curve_sidebar* was set to $1/18em$ exactly. One little token—which changed an exact calculation to an approximate, rounded calculation—made all the difference!

Curves that are placed in arbitrary positions on a raster can lead to digital disasters, even though the curves themselves aren't bad. For example, suppose we take the right-hand example above and shift it just 0.05 and 0.10 pixels to the right:

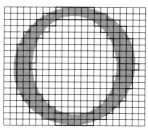 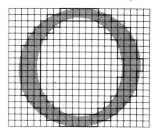

The first shift of 0.05 pixels causes a tiny pimple to appear at the right edge; after another small shift the pimple has grown into a mole, and the left edge has become too flat.

A designer who is asked to make a digital 'O' that is 22 pixels wide will certainly have pixels in mind when making the design. Therefore it's not surprising that our program to generate a digital 'O' should pay attention to actual pixel positions by rounding *curve_sidebar* as in this example. We have distorted the infinite-resolution curve slightly so that it will digitize well, before digitizing it.

A path $z(t)$ will digitize well if the digitization process doesn't change it too much; thus, we want $z(t)$ to be essentially the same as round $z(t)$, at all the important places. But what places are "important"? Experience shows that the most critical points are those where the path travels horizontally or vertically, i.e., where it runs parallel to the raster lines. It's best to arrange things so that a curve becomes parallel to the raster lines just when it touches or nearly touches those lines; then it will appear to have the right curvature after digitization. The worst case occurs when a curve becomes parallel to the raster just when it's halfway between raster lines; then it gets a pimple or a flat spot.

Diagonal slopes, where a curve has a $\pm 45°$ tangent angle, are also potential sources of unwanted pimples and flats. Similarly, at higher resolutions it is sometimes possible to detect small glitches when a curve travels with slopes of $\pm 1/2$ or $\pm 2/1$. Rational slopes m/n where m and n are small integers turn out to be somewhat dangerous. But diagonals are of secondary importance; horizontal and vertical slopes lead to more severe problems.

These considerations suggest a simple general principle for adapting the outlines of shapes to be digitized: *If you know that the outline will have a vertical tangent at some point, round the x coordinate to an integer and leave the y coordinate unchanged. If you know that the outline will have a horizontal tangent at some point, round the y coordinate to an integer and leave the x coordinate unchanged.*

Incidentally, the horizontal tangent points in our 'O' examples were taken care of by the fact that '**define_corrected_pixels**' makes the overshoot parameter o nearly an integer, together with the fact that **beginchar** makes h an integer. If the y coordinates had not been rounded at the horizontal tangent points, our bad examples would have looked even worse.

Before we go further into the study of rounding, we had better face up to a technicality that's sometimes important: We said that the pixels of a digitized region are those whose centers lie inside the undigitized region; but this rule is vague about what happens when the centers happen to fall precisely on the undigitized boundary. Similarly, when we said that round $z(t)$ jumps from one point to an adjacent point, we ignored the fact that a curve such as $z(t) = (t, t)$ actually jumps from $(0, 0)$ to $(1, 1)$ when it is rounded as t passes $1/2$; those points are not adjacent. METAFONT skirts both of these problems in an interesting way: It shifts all of its paths to the right by an infinitesimal amount δ, and it also shifts them upward by an even smaller infinitesimal amount $\delta\epsilon$, so that no path actually touches a pixel center. Here δ and ϵ are positive numbers that are chosen to be so small that their actual values don't matter. For example, the path $z(t) = (t, t)$ becomes $(t + \delta, t + \delta\epsilon)$, which jumps from $(0, 0)$ to $(1, 0)$ to $(1, 1)$ because it momentarily rounds to $(1, 0)$ when $t = 1/2 - 2\delta\epsilon$.

Points of the form $(m + 1/2, n + 1/2)$, where m and n are integers, lie in the centers of their pixels. They are called "ambiguous" points because we can't round them to the nearest integer neighbor without deciding which of four adjacent points is to be considered the nearest. If we imagine taking a curved outline and shifting it slowly to the right, the digitized image makes abrupt transitions when the outline passes over an ambiguous point. When a path comes near an ambiguous point, the path is farthest away from its digitization. Thus the ambiguous points are points of instability, and digitizing works best when paths don't get too close to them.

Let's consider now what happens when we **draw** with a pen, instead of filling an outline. It may seem that the simplest possible **draw** command would be something like this:

pickup pencircle; **draw** $(0, 0) \ldots (10, 0)$;

what could be easier? But a closer look shows that this is actually about the worst case that could be imagined! A circular pen of diameter 1 that goes from $(0,0)$ to $(10,0)$ has upper and lower boundaries that go from $(0, \pm 1/2)$ to $(10, \pm 1/2)$, and both of these boundaries run smack through lots of ambiguous points. METAFONT has to decide whether to fill the row of pixels with $0 \leq y \leq 1$ or the lower row with $-1 \leq y \leq 0$, neither of which is centered on the given line. According to the rule stated earlier, METAFONT shifts the path very slightly to the right and very, very slightly up; thus the pixels actually filled are bounded by $(0,0)$ -- $(10,0)$ -- $(10,1)$ -- $(0,1)$ -- cycle.

▶ **EXERCISE 24.1**
Continuing this example, what pixels would have been filled if the path had been '$(0,0) \ldots (10, -epsilon)$'?

In general when we **draw** with a fixed pen, good digitizations depend on where the edges of the pen happen to fall, not on the path followed by the pen's center. Thus, for example, if the path we're drawing has a vertical tangent at point z_1, we don't necessarily want x_1 to be an integer; we want *lft* x_1 and *rt* x_1 to be integers. If there's a horizontal tangent at z_2, we want *top* y_2 and *bot* y_2 to be integers. The pens created by **pencircle** always have the property that $(lft\ x) - (rt\ x)$ and $(top\ y) - (bot\ y)$ are integers; hence both edges will be in good or bad positions simultaneously.

Suppose that we want x_1 to be approximately equal to α, and we also want it to be at a good place for vertical tangents with respect to the pen that has currently been picked up. One way to define x_1 is to say

lft $x_1 = \text{round}(lft\ \alpha)$;

this does the right thing, because it makes *lft* x_1 an integer and it also makes $x_1 \approx \alpha$. Similarly, to make $y_2 \approx \beta$ good for horizontal tangents, we can say

top $x_2 = \text{round}(top\ \beta)$.

Such operators occur frequently in practice, so plain METAFONT provides convenient abbreviations: We can say simply

$x_1 = good.x\ \alpha$; $y_2 = good.y\ \beta$

instead of using indirect equations for *lft* x_1 and *top* y_2.

Let's look one last time at the letters of the METAFONT logo, in order to make them round properly. Chapter 11 describes a file `logo.mf` that draws the seven characters, but we can improve the results by making pixel-oriented refinements. In the first place, we can replace the command

$$\textbf{define\_pixels}(s, u, xgap, ygap, leftstemloc, barheight)$$

by something better: Looking at the uses of these ad hoc dimensions, we see that $xgap$ and $ygap$ ought to be integers; $leftstemloc$ should be a $good.x$ value for $logo\_pen$; and $barheight$ should be a $good.y$ value. Therefore we say

> **define_pixels**(s, u);
> **define_whole_pixels**$(xgap, ygap)$;
> **define_good_x_pixels**$(leftstemloc)$;
> **define_good_y_pixels**$(barheight)$;

these commands, provided by plain METAFONT, will do the right thing. (The $logo\_pen$ should be picked up before the last two commands are given.) These few changes, and a change to the 'O', suffice to fix all the letters except 'T'.

▶ **EXERCISE 24.2**
The program for METAFONT's 'O' appears in Chapter 18. What changes would you suggest to make it digitize well?

The 'T' presents a new problem, because we want it to be symmetric between left and right. If the pen breadth is odd, we want the character width w to be odd, so that there will be as many pixels to the left of the stem as there are to the right. If the pen breadth is even, we want w to be even. Therefore we have a 50-50 chance of being unhappy with the value of w that is computed by **beginchar**.

▶ **EXERCISE 24.3**
Prove that the value of w is satisfactory for 'T' with respect to the $logo\_pen$ if and only if $.5w$ is a good x value for vertical strokes.

If w is not a good value, we want to replace it by either $w+1$ or $w-1$, whichever is closer to the device-independent width from which w was rounded. For example, if w was rounded to 22 from the ideal width 21.7, we want to change it to 21 rather than 23. Plain METAFONT's **change_width** routine does this. Hence we have the following program for 'T', in place of the simpler version found in exercise 11.4:

> **beginlogochar**$(\texttt{"T"}, 13)$;
> **if** $.5w <> good.x\ .5w$: **change_width**; **fi**
> $lft\ x_1 = -eps$;
> $x_2 = w - x_1$;
> $x_3 = x_4 = .5w$;
> $y_1 = y_2 = y_3$; $top\ y_1 = h$; $bot\ y_4 = -o$;
> **draw** $z_1\ \texttt{--}\ z_2$; **draw** $z_3\ \texttt{--}\ z_4$;
> **labels**$(1, 2, 3, 4)$; **endchar**.

Chapter 4 said that 'T' was the simplest of the seven logo letters, but it has turned out to be the trickiest.

This program has one unexplained feature. Why was *lft* x_1 set to $-eps$ instead of zero? The answer requires an understanding of the pen polygons discussed in Chapter 16. The edges of those polygons are highly likely to pass through ambiguous points when the center of the pen has integer or half-integer coordinates. METAFONT shifts paths slightly to the right and up, in order to resolve ambiguities; therefore if ambiguous points occur at the left and right edges of the 'T', some pixels will be lost at the left but gained at the right. The constant *eps* is 0.00049, which is small but positive enough that METAFONT will surely notice it. Subtracting *eps* from x_1 and adding *eps* to x_2 avoids ambiguous edge points and keeps the result symmetric.

Since the overshoot '*o*' is always *eps* more than an integer, it is unnecessary to do anything similar at point z_4; the equation '*bot* $y_4 = -o$' is sufficient.

Point z_3 in the middle of the 'M' is in a satisfactory position because *bot* $y_3 = ygap - o$. If *bot* y_3 were exactly an integer, the M would often turn out to be unsymmetric, because of ambiguous points on the boundary at z_3.

▶ **EXERCISE 24.4**
True or false: If *currentpen* is **pencircle** xscaled *px* yscaled *py*, the command '**draw** $(-epsilon, 0)$ .. $(+epsilon, 0)$' will produce an image that has both left-right and top-bottom symmetry. (Assume that *autorounding*=*smoothing*=0.)

▶ **EXERCISE 24.5**
The polygon for '**pencircle** scaled 3' is an octagon whose vertices are at the points $(\pm 0.5, \pm 1.5)$ and $(\pm 1.5, \pm 0.5)$. Prove that if you '**draw** (x, y)' with this pen, the result never has both top-bottom and left-right symmetry.

Rounding can also help to position points at which we don't have horizontal or vertical tangents. For example, consider the "sharp sign" or "hash mark" character that's drawn by the following program:

$u^{\#} := \frac{10}{18} pt^{\#}$;   **define_pixels**$(u)$;
beginchar $(0, 15u^{\#}, \frac{250}{36} pt^{\#}, \frac{70}{36} pt^{\#})$;
pickup pencircle
       scaled $(.4pt + blacker)$;
lft $x_1 = $ round $u - eps$;
$x_3 = x_1$;
$x_2 = x_4 = w - x_1$;
$y_1 = y_2 = good.y(.5[-d, h] + pt)$;
$y_3 = y_4 = h - d - y_1$;
draw z_1 -- z_2;   **draw** z_3 -- z_4;
lft $x_6 = $ round $3u$;
$x_7 = w - x_6$;
$x_8 = good.x .5w$;
$x_5 - x_6 = x_7 - x_8$;
top $y_5 = $ *top* $y_7 = h + eps$;
bot $y_6 = $ *bot* $y_8 = -d - eps$;
draw z_5 -- z_6;   **draw** z_7 -- z_8;
labels(**range** 1 **thru** 8);
endchar.

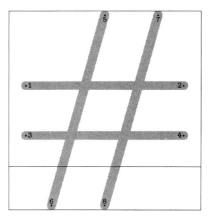

If we digitize this character according to *lowres* mode at 200 pixels per inch, we get the following results:

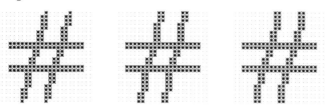

The left-hand example was obtained by omitting the 'round' and '*good.x*' instructions in the equations for x_6 and x_8. This meant that points z_6 and z_8 fell into different, possibly unlucky, raster positions, so the two diagonal strokes digitized differently even though they came from essentially identical undigitized lines. The middle example was produced by the given program without changes. And the right-hand example was produced by drawing the diagonals in a more complicated way: The commands '**draw** z_5 -- z_6; **draw** z_7 -- z_8;' were replaced by

$$y_{15} = y_1; \quad z_{15} = whatever[z_5, z_6]; \quad y_{36} = y_3; \quad z_{36} = whatever[z_5, z_6];$$
$$y_{27} = y_2; \quad z_{27} = whatever[z_7, z_8]; \quad y_{48} = y_4; \quad z_{48} = whatever[z_7, z_8];$$

$$\textbf{draw } z_5 \text{ -- } (good.x(x_{15} + .5), y_1) \text{ -- } (good.x(x_{15} - .5), y_1)$$
$$\text{ -- } (good.x(x_{36} + .5), y_3) \text{ -- } (good.x(x_{36} - .5), y_3) \text{ -- } z_6;$$
$$\textbf{draw } z_7 \text{ -- } (good.x(x_{27} + .5), y_2) \text{ -- } (good.x(x_{27} - .5), y_2)$$
$$\text{ -- } (good.x(x_{48} + .5), y_4) \text{ -- } (good.x(x_{48} - .5), y_4) \text{ -- } z_8;$$

The idea here was to control the goodness of the points where the diagonals intersect the horizontal bar lines, and to hide one of the "jaggies" inside each bar line. If we do the same three experiments but triple the resolution, we get similar results but the differences are not quite so obvious:

When letters are drawn by filling outlines, the left and right outlines are digitized independently; therefore corresponding outlines should usually be offset from each other by an integer amount whenever possible. For example, suppose that the letter 'n' is being drawn with commands like

$$penpos_2(stem, 0); \quad penpos_4(stem, 0)$$

to specify the stroke widths at the base of the two stems. We will therefore have $x_{2r} - x_{2l} = x_{4r} - x_{4l} = stem$. If *stem* is not an integer, say $stem = 2.7$, we might have $x_{2l} = 2.1$, $x_{2r} = 4.8$, $x_{4l} = 9.6$, $x_{4r} = 12.3$; then $x_{2r} - x_{2l}$ will digitize to $5 - 2 = 3$, so the left stem will be three pixels wide, but the right stem will be only $12 - 10 = 2$ pixels wide. We could get around this problem by insisting that either x_{2l} or x_{2r} be an integer, and that either x_{4l} or x_{4r} be an integer; then both stems would be three pixels wide. But other quantities calculated from *stem* (e.g., the breadth of diagonal strokes) would then be based on a value of 2.7 instead of the stem width 3 that an observer of the font actually perceives. Therefore it is best to make *stem* an integer. The proper way to do this is generally to say

define_whole_blacker_pixels(*stem*);

this command computes *stem* from *stem*# by the formula

$$stem := max(1, \text{round}(stem\# * hppp + blacker)).$$

(Notice that this rounding operation is not allowed to reduce *stem* to zero at low resolutions.)

Even when the *stem* width is an integer in the 'n' example, we probably want to arrange things so that x_{2l}, x_{2r}, x_{4l}, and x_{4r} are integers, because this will give the least distortion under digitization. Suppose, however, that it's most convenient to define the pen position at the center of the stroke instead of at the edge; i.e., the program would say just '$x_2 = \alpha$' if rounding were not taken into account. How should x_2 be defined, when we want x_{2l} to be an integer? We could say

$$x_2 = \alpha; \quad x_{2l} := \text{round } x_{2l}; \quad x_{2r} := \text{round } x_{2r}; \quad x_2 := .5[x_{2l}, x_{2r}]$$

but that's too complicated; moreover, it will fail if any other variables depend on x_2, x_{2l}, or x_{2r}, because such dependencies are forgotten when new values are assigned. In the case of fixed pens we solved this problem by saying '$x_2 = good.x\ \alpha$'; but the *good.x* function doesn't know about *stem*. One solution is to say

$$x_{2l} = \text{round}(\alpha - .5stem),$$

or equivalently, '$x_{2r} = \text{round}(\alpha + .5stem)$'. This does the job all right, but it isn't completely satisfying. It requires knowledge of the breadth that was specified in the $penpos_2$ command, and it works only when the penpos angle is 0. If the penpos command is changed, the corresponding equation for rounding must be changed too. There's another solution that's more general and more attractive once you get used to it:

$$x_{2l} = \text{round}(x_{2l} - (x_2 - \alpha)).$$

Why does this work? The argument to 'round' must be a known value, but both x_{2l} and x_2 are unknown. Fortunately, their difference $x_{2l} - x_2$ is known, because of the $penpos_2$ command. The rounding operation makes $x_2 \approx \alpha$ because it makes x_{2l} approximately equal to the value of x_{2l} minus the difference between x_2 and α.

▶ **EXERCISE 24.6**
The generality of this technique can be appreciated by considering the following more difficult problem that the author faced while designing a 'w': Suppose you want $x_1 - x_2$ to be an integer and $x_3 \approx x_4$, and suppose that x_2, $x_3 - x_1$, and $x_4 + x_1$ are known; but x_1 is unknown, hence x_3 and x_4 are also unknown. According to our general idea, we want to specify an equation of the form '$x_1 - x_2 = \text{round}(x_1 - x_2 + f)$', where $x_1 - x_2 + f$ is known and f is a formula that should be approximately zero. In this case $x_3 - x_4$ is approximately zero, and $(x_3 - x_1) - (x_4 + x_1)$ is known; what value of f should we choose?

In many fonts, such as the one you are now reading, curved lines swell out so that the thick parts of 'o' are actually a bit broader than the stems of 'n'. Therefore the Computer Modern font routines discussed in Appendix E have two parameters, *stem*# and *curve*#, to govern the stroke thickness. For example, the font **cmr9** used in the present paragraph has *stem*# = $2/3pt$# and *curve*# = $7/9pt$#. Both of these should be integers, hence the **font_setup** macro in Appendix E dutifully says

  define_whole_blacker_pixels(*stem*, *curve*).

Although this looks good on paper, it can cause problems at certain low resolutions, because the rounding operation might make *stem* and *curve* rather different from each other even though *stem*# and *curve*# are fairly close. For example, the resolution might be just at the value where **cmr9**'s *stem* turns out to be only 2 but *curve* is 3. Curves shouldn't be that much darker than stems; they would look too splotchy. Therefore plain METAFONT has a '**lowres_fix**' subroutine, and Appendix E says

  lowres_fix(*stem*, *curve*) 1.2

after *stem* and *curve* have been defined as above. In this particular case **lowres_fix** will reset *curve* := *stem* if it turns out that the ratio *curve*/*stem* is greater than 1.2 times the ratio *curve*#/*stem*#. Since *curve*#/*stem*# = 7/6 in the case of **cmr9**, this means that the ratio *curve*/*stem* after rounding is allowed to be at most 1.4; if *curve* = 3 and *stem* = 2, the *curve* parameter will be lowered to 2. In general the command

  lowres_fix($d_1, d_2, \ldots, d_n$) r

will set $d_n := \cdots d_2 := d_1$ if $\max(d_1, d_2, \ldots, d_n)/\min(d_1, d_2, \ldots, d_n)$ is greater than $r \cdot \max(d_1\#, d_2\#, \ldots, d_n\#)/\min(d_1\#, d_2\#, \ldots, d_n\#)$.

▶ **EXERCISE 24.7**
 Good digitization can also require attention to the shapes of the digitized angles where straight lines meet. The purpose of the present exercise is to illustrate the relevant ideas by studying the '▶' symbol, for which a program appears in Chapter 4. If that program is used without change to produce low-resolution triangles, the results might turn out to be unsatisfactory because, for example, the point of the triangle at the right might digitize into a snubnosed or asymmetric shape. If y_3 is an integer, the triangle will be top-bottom symmetric, but the right-hand

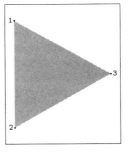

tip will be two pixels tall and this will look too blunt. Therefore we should choose y_3 to be an integer plus 1/2. Given this value of y_3, what will be the shape of the rightmost four columns of the digitized tip, as x_3 varies?

▶ **EXERCISE 24.8**
 Continuing the previous exercise, assume that x_1 is an integer. What value of y_1 will make the upper tip of the triangle look like '' after digitization?

▶ **EXERCISE 24.9**
 Concluding the previous exercise, modify the program of Chapter 4 so that the upper tip and the upper part of the right tip both digitize to the shape ''.

So far in this chapter we've assumed that pixels are square. But sometimes we need to prepare output for devices with general rectangular pixels, and this adds an extra dimension of complexity to rounding. Plain METAFONT sets things up so that *currenttransform* multiplies all y coordinates by *aspect_ratio*, when paths are filled or drawn, or when pens are picked up. Furthermore the *top* and *bot* functions divide the amount of offset by *aspect_ratio*. This means that METAFONT programs can still be written as if pixels were square; the normal 'angle' and 'direction' functions, etc., can be used. But the good places for rounding horizontal tangents are not at integer values of y in general, they are actually at values that will become integers after multiplication by the aspect ratio.

The *vround* function rounds its argument to the nearest y coordinate that corresponds to a pixel boundary in the general case. Thus if *aspect_ratio* = 1, *vround* simply rounds to the nearest integer, just like 'round'; but if, say, *aspect_ratio* = 4/3, then *vround* will round to the nearest multiple of 3/4. Plain METAFONT uses *vround* instead of 'round' when it computes an overshoot correction, and also when **beginchar** computes the values of h and d. The *good.y* function produces a good y value that takes *aspect_ratio* properly into account.

▶ **EXERCISE 24.10**
Without looking at Appendix B, try to guess how the *vround* and *good.y* macros are defined.

▶ **EXERCISE 24.11**
What are the "ambiguous points" when pixels are not square?

The METAFONT logo as we have described it so far will round properly with respect to arbitrary aspect ratios if we make only a few more refinements. The value of *ygap* should be vrounded instead of rounded, so we initialize it by saying

> **define_whole_vertical_pixels**(*ygap*).

Furthermore we should say

> $ho^\# := o^\#$; **define_horizontal_corrected_pixels**(*ho*);

and *ho* should replace *o* in the equations for x_4 in the programs for 'E' and 'F'. Everything else should work satisfactorily as it stands.

Appendix B includes macros *good.top*, *good.bot*, *good.lft*, and *good.rt* that take pairs as arguments. If you say, for example, '$z_3 = good.top(\alpha, \beta)$' it means that z_3 will be near (α, β) and that when z_3 is modified by *currenttransform* the top point of *currentpen* placed at the transformed point will be in a good raster position.

METAFONT's '*autorounding*' feature tries to adjust curves to the raster for you, but it is a mixed blessing. Here's how it works: If the internal quantity *autorounding* is positive, the x coordinates of all paths that are filled or drawn are rounded to good raster positions wherever there's a vertical tangent; and the y coordinates are rounded to good raster positions wherever there's a horizontal tangent. The rest of the curve is distorted appropriately, as if the raster were stretching or shrinking slightly. If *autorounding* > 1, you get even more changes: paths are perturbed slightly at ±45° tangent directions, so that second-order pimples and flat spots don't appear there.

For example, if we return to the Ionian 'O' with which we began this chapter, let's suppose that *curve_sidebar* was left unrounded. We saw that the result was bad when *autorounding* was 0; when *autorounding* = 1 and 2 we get this:

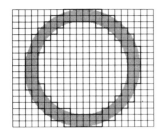 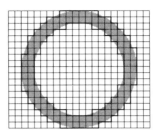

The stroke has gotten a lot thinner at the sides, by comparison with the original design (which, incidentally, can be seen in the illustrations below). Although autorounding has produced a fairly recognizable O shape, the character of the original has been lost, especially in the case *autorounding* = 2; indeed, the inner outline has been brought towards the center, in the upper left and lower right sectors, and this has made the digitized inner boundary perfectly symmetric!

There's an internal quantity called *granularity*, normally equal to 1, which affects autorounding by effectively scaling up the raster size. If, for example, *granularity* = 4, the autorounded x coordinates and y coordinates will become multiples of 4 instead of simply integers. The illustrations above were produced by setting *granularity* = 10 and *mag* = 10; this made the effects of autorounding visible. The granularity should always be an integer.

Besides *autorounding*, there's a 'smoothing' feature that becomes active when *smoothing* > 0. The basic idea is to try to make the edges of a curve follow a regular progression instead of wobbling. A complete discussion of the smoothing algorithm is beyond the scope of this manual, but an example should make the general idea clear: Let's use the letters R and D to stand for single-pixel steps to the right and down, respectively. If a digitized path goes '*RDDRDRDDD*', say, the number of downward steps per rightward step is first decreasing, then increasing; the *smoothing* process changes this to '*RDDRDDRDD*'. If smoothing is applied to the Ionian 'O' shapes above, nothing happens; but if we go back to the original obtained with *autorounding* = 0, we get a few changes:

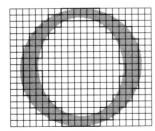 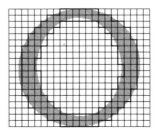

Three pixels have been added by *smoothing* in the right-hand illustration; e.g., a pattern *RDRDDDDRDD* has become *RDDRDDDDRDD*.

If you do your own rounding, it turns out that autorounding and smoothing usually change very few pixels, if any; thus your safest strategy is probably to turn them off in such cases. If you define your strokes by outlines, autorounding and smoothing apply independently to the left and right edges, so they may hurt as often as they help; again, they should probably be turned off. But if you are drawing with fixed pens, autorounding generally works well and saves a lot of fuss. If the pens are circles or nearly circles, smoothing is also helpful; but if the pens are more "calligraphic," they are supposed to produce nonsmooth edges occasionally, so you had better set *smoothing* := 0.

If you "slant" a font by modifying *currenttransform* as described in Chapter 15, positions of horizontal tangency will remain the same. But positions of vertical tangency will change drastically, and they will probably not fall in known parts of your design. This means, for example, that autorounding will be helpful in a slanted pen-generated font like the '*METAFONT*' logo. However, the author found that the outline-generated letters of Computer Modern *italic* came out better with *autorounding* = 0, because autorounding tended to make some characters too dark and others too light.

The effect of autorounding can be studied numerically if you set *tracingspecs* to a positive value; this displays METAFONT's internal calculations as it finds horizontal, vertical, and diagonal tangent points. (METAFONT prepares to digitize paths by first subdividing each Bézier segment into pieces that travel in only one "octant" direction.) For example, if *autorounding* = 0 and *tracingspecs* = 1, and if *curve_sidebar* is left unrounded, the file io.log will contain the following information about the outer curve of the 'O':

```
Path at line 15, before subdivision into octants:
(1.53745,9.05344)..controls (1.53745,4.0051) and (5.75407,-0.0005)
 ..(10.85146,-0.0005)..controls (16.2217,-0.0005) and (20.46255,4.51297)
 ..(20.46255,9.94656)..controls (20.46255,14.99715) and (16.23842,19.0005)
 ..(11.13652,19.0005)..controls (5.77066,19.0005) and (1.53745,14.48491)
 ..cycle

Cycle spec at line 15, after subdivision:
(1.53745,9.05344) % beginning in octant 'SSE'
   ..controls (1.53745,6.58784) and (2.54324,4.37099)
 ..(4.16621,2.74802) % segment 0
% entering octant 'ESE'
   ..controls (5.8663,1.04793) and (8.24362,-0.0005)
 ..(10.85146,-0.0005) % segment 0
% entering octant 'ENE'
```

... and so on; there are lots more numbers! What does this all mean? Well, the first segment of the curve, from $(1.53745, 9.05344)$ to $(10.85146, -0.0005)$, has been subdivided into two parts at the place where the slope is -1. The first of these parts travels basically 'South by South East' and the second travels 'East by South East'. The other three segments are subdivided in a similar way (not shown here). If you try the same experiment but with *autorounding* = 1, some rather different numbers emerge:

```
Cycle spec at line 15, after subdivision and autorounding:
(2,9.05347) % beginning in octant 'SSE'
   ..controls (2,6.50525) and (3.02194,4.2227)
 ..(4.65768,2.58696) % segment 0
% entering octant 'ESE'
   ..controls (6.26239,0.98225) and (8.45784,0)
 ..(10.85872,0) % segment 0
% entering octant 'ENE'
```

Point $(1.53745, 9.05344)$, where there was a vertical tangent, has been rounded to $(2, 9.05347)$; point $(10.85146, -.00005)$, where there was a horizontal tangent, has been rounded to $(10.85872, 0)$; the intermediate control points have been adjusted accordingly. (Rounding of x coordinates has been done separately from y coordinates.) Finally, with *autorounding* $= 2$, additional adjustments are made so that the $45°$ transition point will occur at what METAFONT thinks is a good spot:

```
Cycle spec at line 15, after subdivision and double autorounding:
(2,9.05347) % beginning in octant 'SSE'
   ..controls (2,6.67609) and (3.07103,4.42897)
 ..(4.78535,2.71465) % segment 0
% entering octant 'ESE'
   ..controls (6.46927,1.03073) and (8.62747,0)
 ..(10.85872,0) % segment 0
% entering octant 'ENE'
```

(Notice that $4.78535 + 2.71465 = 7.50000$; when the slope is -1 at a transition point (x, y), the curve stays as far away as possible from ambiguous points near the transition if $x + y + .5$ is an integer.)

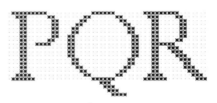

— PIERRE LE BÉ, *Béle Prérie* (1601)

— MATTHEW CARTER, *Bell Centennial* (1978)

25
Summary of Expressions

We've seen that METAFONT can handle a wide variety of algebraic expressions; now it's time to consolidate what we have learned. The purpose of this chapter and the one that follows is to present a precise and concise summary of everything that METAFONT knows how to do.

We shall be concerned here solely with METAFONT's *primitive* operations, rather than with the higher-level features of the plain METAFONT base that comprise the bulk of typical programs. Therefore novice users should put off reading Chapters 25 and 26 until they feel a need to know what goes on at the more mundane levels inside the computer. Appendix B contains a summary of the features of plain METAFONT, together with a ready-reference guide to the things that most people want to know about METAFONT usage.

The remainder of this chapter is set in small type, like that of the present paragraph, since it is analogous to material that is marked "doubly dangerous" in other chapters. Instead of using dangerous bend signs repeatedly, let us simply agree that Chapters 25 and 26 are dangerous by definition.

Chapter 8 introduced the general idea of expressions and the four-fold "primary, secondary, tertiary, expression" hierarchy on which their syntax is based. META-FONT's variables can have any of eight types: **boolean, numeric, pair, path, pen, picture, string,** and **transform**. Its expressions can actually have nine different types, although the ninth one—"vacuous"—is not particularly interesting since it has only one possible value. Here is the overall syntax:

⟨primary⟩ ⟶ ⟨boolean primary⟩ | ⟨numeric primary⟩
    | ⟨pair primary⟩ | ⟨path primary⟩
    | ⟨pen primary⟩ | ⟨future pen primary⟩
    | ⟨picture primary⟩ | ⟨string primary⟩
    | ⟨transform primary⟩ | ⟨vacuous primary⟩

⟨secondary⟩ ⟶ ⟨boolean secondary⟩ | ⟨numeric secondary⟩
    | ⟨pair secondary⟩ | ⟨path secondary⟩
    | ⟨pen secondary⟩ | ⟨future pen secondary⟩
    | ⟨picture secondary⟩ | ⟨string secondary⟩
    | ⟨transform secondary⟩ | ⟨vacuous secondary⟩

⟨tertiary⟩ ⟶ ⟨boolean tertiary⟩ | ⟨numeric tertiary⟩
    | ⟨pair tertiary⟩ | ⟨path tertiary⟩
    | ⟨pen tertiary⟩ | ⟨picture tertiary⟩
    | ⟨string tertiary⟩ | ⟨transform tertiary⟩
    | ⟨vacuous tertiary⟩

⟨expression⟩ ⟶ ⟨boolean expression⟩ | ⟨numeric expression⟩
    | ⟨pair expression⟩ | ⟨path expression⟩
    | ⟨pen expression⟩ | ⟨picture expression⟩
    | ⟨string expression⟩ | ⟨transform expression⟩
    | ⟨vacuous expression⟩

We shall discuss the different types of expressions in alphabetic order; thus, if you are dying to know what a "vacuous" expression is, you should skip to the end of the chapter.

■ Boolean expressions were discussed in Chapter 19. The full syntax has one more operation, 'charexists', that was not mentioned there:

⟨boolean primary⟩ ⟶ ⟨boolean variable⟩ | ⟨boolean argument⟩
    | **true** | **false**
    | (⟨boolean expression⟩)
    | **begingroup** ⟨statement list⟩⟨boolean expression⟩ **endgroup**
    | **known** ⟨primary⟩ | **unknown** ⟨primary⟩
    | ⟨type⟩⟨primary⟩ | **cycle** ⟨primary⟩
    | **odd** ⟨numeric primary⟩
    | **charexists** ⟨numeric primary⟩
    | **not** ⟨boolean primary⟩
⟨boolean secondary⟩ ⟶ ⟨boolean primary⟩
    | ⟨boolean secondary⟩ **and** ⟨boolean primary⟩
⟨boolean tertiary⟩ ⟶ ⟨boolean secondary⟩
    | ⟨boolean tertiary⟩ **or** ⟨boolean secondary⟩
⟨boolean expression⟩ ⟶ ⟨boolean tertiary⟩
    | ⟨numeric expression⟩⟨relation⟩⟨numeric tertiary⟩
    | ⟨pair expression⟩⟨relation⟩⟨pair tertiary⟩
    | ⟨transform expression⟩⟨relation⟩⟨transform tertiary⟩
    | ⟨boolean expression⟩⟨relation⟩⟨boolean tertiary⟩
    | ⟨string expression⟩⟨relation⟩⟨string tertiary⟩
⟨relation⟩ ⟶ < | <= | > | >= | = | <>

The expression 'charexists x' is true if and only if a **shipout** command has previously been done with *charcode* $= x$. (The value of x is first rounded to an integer, and reduced to the range $0 \le x < 256$ by adding or subtracting multiples of 256.)

In these rules, tokens like '**true**' that appear in typewriter type stand for any tokens whose current meaning is the same as the meaning of '**true**' when METAFONT starts from scratch; the particular token '**true**'—whose meaning may indeed change as a program runs—is not really involved.

The special tokens '(' and ')' in these rules do not refer to parentheses; they refer to any matching pair of delimiters defined by a **delimiters** command.

A ⟨boolean variable⟩ denotes a ⟨variable⟩ whose type is **boolean**; a ⟨numeric variable⟩ is a ⟨variable⟩ whose type is **numeric**; and so on. The syntax for ⟨variable⟩ was discussed in Chapter 7. A ⟨boolean argument⟩ is an **expr** argument to a macro, where the value of the expression is of type **boolean**; **expr** arguments are put into special "capsule" tokens as explained in Chapter 18.

■ Numeric expressions have the richest syntax of all, because they form the nucleus of the entire METAFONT language:

⟨numeric atom⟩ ⟶ ⟨numeric variable⟩ | ⟨numeric argument⟩
    | ⟨numeric token atom⟩
    | ⟨internal quantity⟩
    | **normaldeviate**
    | (⟨numeric expression⟩)
    | **begingroup** ⟨statement list⟩⟨numeric expression⟩ **endgroup**
⟨numeric token atom⟩ ⟶ ⟨numeric token⟩ / ⟨numeric token⟩
    | ⟨numeric token not followed by '/⟨numeric token⟩'⟩

⟨numeric primary⟩ ⟶ ⟨numeric atom⟩
    | ⟨numeric atom⟩ [⟨numeric expression⟩ , ⟨numeric expression⟩]
    | **length** ⟨numeric primary⟩ | **length** ⟨pair primary⟩
    | **length** ⟨path primary⟩ | **length** ⟨string primary⟩
    | **ASCII** ⟨string primary⟩ | **oct** ⟨string primary⟩ | **hex** ⟨string primary⟩
    | ⟨pair part⟩⟨pair primary⟩ | ⟨transform part⟩⟨transform primary⟩
    | **angle** ⟨pair primary⟩
    | **turningnumber** ⟨path primary⟩ | **totalweight** ⟨picture primary⟩
    | ⟨numeric operator⟩⟨numeric primary⟩
    | **directiontime** ⟨pair expression⟩ **of** ⟨path primary⟩
⟨pair part⟩ ⟶ **xpart** | **ypart**
⟨transform part⟩ ⟶ ⟨pair part⟩ | **xxpart** | **xypart** | **yxpart** | **yypart**
⟨numeric operator⟩ ⟶ **sqrt** | **sind** | **cosd** | **mlog** | **mexp**
    | **floor** | **uniformdeviate** | ⟨scalar multiplication operator⟩
⟨scalar multiplication operator⟩ ⟶ ⟨plus or minus⟩
    | ⟨numeric token atom not followed by + or − or a numeric token⟩
⟨numeric secondary⟩ ⟶ ⟨numeric primary⟩
    | ⟨numeric secondary⟩⟨times or over⟩⟨numeric primary⟩
⟨times or over⟩ ⟶ ***** | **/**
⟨numeric tertiary⟩ ⟶ ⟨numeric secondary⟩
    | ⟨numeric tertiary⟩⟨plus or minus⟩⟨numeric secondary⟩
    | ⟨numeric tertiary⟩⟨Pythagorean plus or minus⟩⟨numeric secondary⟩
⟨plus or minus⟩ ⟶ **+** | **−**
⟨Pythagorean plus or minus⟩ ⟶ **++** | **+−+**
⟨numeric expression⟩ ⟶ ⟨numeric tertiary⟩

Each of the operations mentioned in this syntax has already been explained somewhere in this book; Appendix I tells where.

This is a good time to list all of the internal quantities that are initially present in METAFONT:

tracingtitles	show titles online when they appear
tracingequations	show each variable when it becomes known
tracingcapsules	show capsules as well as variables
tracingchoices	show the control points chosen for paths
tracingspecs	show subdivision of paths into octants before digitizing
tracingpens	show vertices of pens as they are made from future pens
tracingcommands	show commands and operations before they're performed
tracingrestores	show when a symbol or internal quantity is restored
tracingmacros	show macros before they are expanded
tracingedges	show digitized edges as they are computed
tracingoutput	show digitized edges as they are output
tracingonline	show long diagnostics on the terminal and in the log
tracingstats	log the memory usage at end of job
pausing	show lines on the terminal before they are read
showstopping	stop after each **show** command
fontmaking	produce font metric output
proofing	produce proof mode output

turningcheck	reorient clockwise paths, flag strange ones
warningcheck	advise when a variable value gets large
smoothing	remove certain glitches from digitized curves
autorounding	move paths to "good" tangent points
granularity	the pixel size for *autorounding*
fillin	the extra darkness of diagonals (to be counteracted)
year	the current year (e.g., 1986)
month	the current month (e.g, 3 ≡ March)
day	the current day of the month
time	the number of minutes past midnight when job started
charcode	the number of the next character to be output
charext	the extension code of the next character to be output
charwd	the width of the next character to be output, in points
charht	the height of the next character to be output, in points
chardp	the depth of the next character to be output, in points
charic	the italic correction of the next character, in points
chardx	the device's x movement for the next character, in pixels
chardy	the device's y movement for the next character, in pixels
designsize	the approximate size of the current typeface, in points
hppp	the number of horizontal pixels per point
vppp	the number of vertical pixels per point
xoffset	the horizontal displacement of shipped-out characters
yoffset	the vertical displacement of shipped-out characters
boundarychar	the right boundary character for ligatures and kerns

All of these quantities are numeric. They are initially zero at the start of a job, except for *year*, *month*, *day*, and *time*, which are initialized to the time the run began; furthermore, *boundarychar* is initially −1. A *granularity* of zero is equivalent to *granularity* = 1. A preloaded base file like plain METAFONT will usually give nonzero values to several other internal quantities on this list.

■ Now we come to expressions of type **pair**, which are the second most important elements of METAFONT programs:

⟨pair primary⟩ ⟶ ⟨pair variable⟩ | ⟨pair argument⟩
        | (⟨numeric expression⟩ , ⟨numeric expression⟩)
        | (⟨pair expression⟩)
        | **begingroup** ⟨statement list⟩⟨pair expression⟩ **endgroup**
        | ⟨numeric atom⟩ [⟨pair expression⟩ , ⟨pair expression⟩]
        | ⟨scalar multiplication operator⟩⟨pair primary⟩
        | **point** ⟨numeric expression⟩ **of** ⟨path primary⟩
        | **precontrol** ⟨numeric expression⟩ **of** ⟨path primary⟩
        | **postcontrol** ⟨numeric expression⟩ **of** ⟨path primary⟩
        | **penoffset** ⟨pair expression⟩ **of** ⟨pen primary⟩
        | **penoffset** ⟨pair expression⟩ **of** ⟨future pen primary⟩
⟨pair secondary⟩ ⟶ ⟨pair primary⟩
        | ⟨pair secondary⟩⟨times or over⟩⟨numeric primary⟩
        | ⟨numeric secondary⟩ ∗ ⟨pair primary⟩
        | ⟨pair secondary⟩⟨transformer⟩

⟨transformer⟩ ⟶ **rotated** ⟨numeric primary⟩
    | **scaled** ⟨numeric primary⟩
    | **shifted** ⟨pair primary⟩
    | **slanted** ⟨numeric primary⟩
    | **transformed** ⟨transform primary⟩
    | **xscaled** ⟨numeric primary⟩
    | **yscaled** ⟨numeric primary⟩
    | **zscaled** ⟨pair primary⟩
⟨pair tertiary⟩ ⟶ ⟨pair secondary⟩
    | ⟨pair tertiary⟩⟨plus or minus⟩⟨pair secondary⟩
    | ⟨path tertiary⟩ **intersectiontimes** ⟨path secondary⟩
⟨pair expression⟩ ⟶ ⟨pair tertiary⟩

A pair is a special case of a path (namely, it's a path of length zero); Chapter 19 explains that METAFONT doesn't change the type from pair to path unless there is no other way to meet the syntax rules.

■ Speaking of paths, they come next in our survey:

⟨path primary⟩ ⟶ ⟨path variable⟩ | ⟨path argument⟩
    | (⟨path expression⟩)
    | **begingroup** ⟨statement list⟩⟨path expression⟩ **endgroup**
    | **makepath** ⟨pen primary⟩
    | **makepath** ⟨future pen primary⟩
    | **reverse** ⟨path primary⟩
    | **subpath** ⟨pair expression⟩ **of** ⟨path primary⟩
⟨path secondary⟩ ⟶ ⟨path primary⟩ | ⟨path secondary⟩⟨transformer⟩
⟨path tertiary⟩ ⟶ ⟨path secondary⟩
⟨path subexpression⟩ ⟶ ⟨path tertiary⟩ | ⟨pair tertiary⟩
    | ⟨path expression⟩⟨path join⟩⟨path tertiary⟩
⟨path join⟩ ⟶ ⟨direction specifier⟩⟨basic path join⟩⟨direction specifier⟩
⟨direction specifier⟩ ⟶ ⟨empty⟩
    | { **curl** ⟨numeric expression⟩ }
    | { ⟨pair expression⟩ }
    | { ⟨numeric expression⟩ , ⟨numeric expression⟩ }
⟨basic path join⟩ ⟶ **&**
    | ..
    | .. ⟨tension⟩ ..
    | .. ⟨controls⟩ ..
⟨tension⟩ ⟶ **tension** ⟨tension amount⟩
    | **tension** ⟨tension amount⟩ **and** ⟨tension amount⟩
⟨tension amount⟩ ⟶ ⟨numeric primary⟩
    | **atleast** ⟨numeric primary⟩
⟨controls⟩ ⟶ **controls** ⟨pair primary⟩
    | **controls** ⟨pair primary⟩ **and** ⟨pair primary⟩
⟨path expression⟩ ⟶ ⟨path subexpression⟩
    | ⟨path subexpression⟩⟨direction specifier⟩
    | ⟨path subexpression⟩⟨path join⟩ **cycle**

Chapter 14 tells all about path creation.

- Pens and future pens coexist as follows:

⟨pen primary⟩ ⟶ ⟨pen variable⟩ | ⟨pen argument⟩
    | `nullpen`
    | (⟨pen expression⟩)
    | `begingroup` ⟨statement list⟩⟨pen expression⟩ `endgroup`
⟨future pen primary⟩ ⟶ `pencircle`
    | `makepen` ⟨path primary⟩
⟨pen secondary⟩ ⟶ ⟨pen primary⟩
⟨future pen secondary⟩ ⟶ ⟨future pen primary⟩
    | ⟨future pen secondary⟩⟨transformer⟩
    | ⟨pen secondary⟩⟨transformer⟩
⟨pen tertiary⟩ ⟶ ⟨pen secondary⟩
    | ⟨future pen secondary⟩
⟨pen expression⟩ ⟶ ⟨pen tertiary⟩

See Chapter 16 for a thorough discussion of pen usage.

- Pictures can be null, added, or subtracted:

⟨picture primary⟩ ⟶ ⟨picture variable⟩ | ⟨picture argument⟩
    | `nullpicture`
    | (⟨picture expression⟩)
    | `begingroup` ⟨statement list⟩⟨picture expression⟩ `endgroup`
    | ⟨plus or minus⟩⟨picture primary⟩
⟨picture secondary⟩ ⟶ ⟨picture primary⟩
    | ⟨picture secondary⟩⟨transformer⟩
⟨picture tertiary⟩ ⟶ ⟨picture secondary⟩
    | ⟨picture tertiary⟩⟨plus or minus⟩⟨picture secondary⟩
⟨picture expression⟩ ⟶ ⟨picture tertiary⟩

Chapter 13 is the definitive reference for picture operations.

- Strings are still fresh in our minds from Chapter 22, but we should repeat the syntax again for completeness here.

⟨string primary⟩ ⟶ ⟨string variable⟩ | ⟨string argument⟩
    | ⟨string token⟩
    | `jobname`
    | `readstring`
    | (⟨string expression⟩)
    | `begingroup` ⟨statement list⟩⟨string expression⟩ `endgroup`
    | `str` ⟨suffix⟩
    | `char` ⟨numeric primary⟩
    | `decimal` ⟨numeric primary⟩
    | `substring` ⟨pair primary⟩ `of` ⟨string primary⟩
⟨string secondary⟩ ⟶ ⟨string primary⟩
⟨string tertiary⟩ ⟶ ⟨string secondary⟩
⟨string expression⟩ ⟶ ⟨string tertiary⟩
    | ⟨string expression⟩ `&` ⟨string tertiary⟩

There's nothing more to say about strings.

■ Chapter 15 explains transforms, but gives no formal syntax. The rules are:

⟨transform primary⟩ ⟶ ⟨transform variable⟩ | ⟨transform argument⟩
    | (⟨transform expression⟩)
    | **begingroup** ⟨statement list⟩⟨transform expression⟩ **endgroup**
⟨transform secondary⟩ ⟶ ⟨transform primary⟩
    | ⟨transform secondary⟩⟨transformer⟩
⟨transform tertiary⟩ ⟶ ⟨transform secondary⟩
⟨transform expression⟩ ⟶ ⟨transform tertiary⟩

Note that *identity* doesn't appear here; it is a variable defined in Appendix B, not a primitive of the language.

■ Finally, we come to the new kind of expression, which wasn't mentioned in previous chapters because it is so trivial.

⟨vacuous primary⟩ ⟶ ⟨vacuous argument⟩
    | ⟨compound⟩
    | (⟨vacuous expression⟩)
    | **begingroup** ⟨statement list⟩⟨vacuous expression⟩ **endgroup**
⟨vacuous secondary⟩ ⟶ ⟨vacuous primary⟩
⟨vacuous tertiary⟩ ⟶ ⟨vacuous secondary⟩
⟨vacuous expression⟩ ⟶ ⟨vacuous tertiary⟩

A ⟨compound⟩ is defined in Chapter 26.

▶ **EXERCISE 25.1**
Construct minimal examples of each of the nine types of expression (boolean, numeric, ..., vacuous). You should use only "sparks" in your constructions, not ⟨tag⟩ tokens or capsules; in particular, variables are not permitted (otherwise this exercise would be too easy). Your expressions should be as short as possible in the sense of *fewest tokens*; the number of keystrokes needed to type them is irrelevant.

This is of you very well remembred,
and well and sommaryly rehersed.
— THOMAS MORE, *A Dialogue Concernynge Heresyes* (1529)

Below the tomato blobs was a band of white with vertical black stripes,
to which he could assign no meaning whatever,
till some one else came by, murmuring:
"What expression he gets with his foreground!"
... Ah, they were all Expressionists now, he had heard, on the Continent.
So it was coming here too, was it?
— JOHN GALSWORTHY, *To Let* (1921)

26

Summary of
the Language

The grand tour of METAFONT's syntax that was begun in the previous chapter is concluded in this one, so that a complete reference guide is available for people who need to know the details. (Another summary appears in Appendix B.)

METAFONT actually has a few features that didn't seem to be worth mentioning in earlier chapters, so they will be introduced here as part of our exhaustive survey. If there is any disagreement between something that was said previously and something that will be said below, the facts in the present chapter should be regarded as better approximations to the truth.

We shall study METAFONT's digestive processes, i.e., what METAFONT does in response to the tokens that arrive in its "stomach." Chapter 6 describes the process by which input files are converted to lists of tokens in METAFONT's "mouth," and Chapters 18–20 explain how expandable tokens are converted to unexpandable ones in METAFONT's "gullet" by a process similar to regurgitation. In particular, conditions and loops are handled by the expansion mechanism, and we need not discuss them further. When unexpandable tokens finally reach METAFONT's gastro-intestinal tract, the real activities begin; expressions are evaluated, equations are solved, variables are declared, and commands are executed. In this chapter we shall discuss the primitive operations that actually draw pictures and produce output.

Let's start by looking at the full syntax for ⟨program⟩ and for ⟨statement⟩:

⟨program⟩ ⟶ ⟨statement list⟩ **end** | ⟨statement list⟩ **dump**
⟨statement list⟩ ⟶ ⟨empty⟩ | ⟨statement⟩ ; ⟨statement list⟩
⟨statement⟩ ⟶ ⟨empty⟩ | ⟨title⟩
     | ⟨equation⟩ | ⟨assignment⟩
     | ⟨declaration⟩ | ⟨definition⟩
     | ⟨compound⟩ | ⟨command⟩
⟨title⟩ ⟶ ⟨string expression⟩
⟨compound⟩ ⟶ **begingroup** ⟨statement list⟩⟨non-title statement⟩ **endgroup**
⟨command⟩ ⟶ ⟨save command⟩
     | ⟨interim command⟩
     | ⟨newinternal command⟩
     | ⟨randomseed command⟩
     | ⟨let command⟩
     | ⟨delimiters command⟩
     | ⟨protection command⟩
     | ⟨everyjob command⟩
     | ⟨show command⟩
     | ⟨message command⟩
     | ⟨mode command⟩
     | ⟨picture command⟩
     | ⟨display command⟩
     | ⟨openwindow command⟩
     | ⟨shipout command⟩
     | ⟨special command⟩
     | ⟨font metric command⟩

The ⟨empty⟩ statement does nothing, but it is very handy because you can always feel safe when you put extra semicolons between statements. A ⟨title⟩ does almost nothing, but it provides useful documentation as explained in Chapter 22. The syntax of ⟨equation⟩ and ⟨assignment⟩ can be found in Chapter 10; ⟨declaration⟩ is in Chapter 7; ⟨definition⟩ is in Chapters 18 and 20. We shall concentrate in this chapter on the various types of *commands*, especially on those that haven't been mentioned before.

> ⟨save command⟩ ⟶ **save** ⟨symbolic token list⟩
> ⟨symbolic token list⟩ ⟶ ⟨symbolic token⟩
> | ⟨symbolic token list⟩ **,** ⟨symbolic token⟩
> ⟨interim command⟩ ⟶ **interim** ⟨internal quantity⟩ **:=** ⟨right-hand side⟩

The **save** and **interim** commands cause values to be restored at the end of the current group, as discussed in Chapter 17.

> ⟨newinternal command⟩ ⟶ **newinternal** ⟨symbolic token list⟩

Each of the symbolic tokens specified in a **newinternal** command will henceforth behave exactly as an ⟨internal quantity⟩, initially zero. Thus, they can be used in **interim** commands; they are tags but not external tags (see Chapter 7). Since META-FONT can access internal quantities quickly, you can use them to gain efficiency.

> ⟨randomseed command⟩ ⟶ **randomseed** **:=** ⟨numeric expression⟩

The **randomseed** command specifies a "seed" value that defines the pseudo-random numbers to be delivered by 'uniformdeviate' and 'normaldeviate' (cf. Chapter 21). The default value, if you don't specify your own seed, is *day + time * epsilon*.

> ⟨let command⟩ ⟶ **let** ⟨symbolic token⟩⟨is⟩⟨symbolic token⟩
> ⟨is⟩ ⟶ **=** | **:=**

The **let** command changes the current meaning of the left-hand token to the current meaning of the right-hand token. For example, after '**let** *diamonds* = **forever**', the token *diamonds* will introduce loops. If the left-hand token was the first token of any variable names, those variables all disappear. If the right-hand token was the first token in any variable names, those variables remain unchanged, and the left-hand token becomes an unknown, independent variable. (The purpose of **let** is to redefine primitive meanings or macro meanings, not to equate variables in any way.) If the right-hand symbol is one of a pair of matching delimiters, the subsequent behavior of the left-hand symbol is undefined. For example, it's a bad idea to say '**let** [[= (; **let**]] =)'.

> ⟨delimiters command⟩ ⟶ **delimiters** ⟨symbolic token⟩⟨symbolic token⟩

The **delimiters** command gives new meanings to the two symbolic tokens; henceforth they will match each other (and only each other). For example, Appendix B says '**delimiters** ()'; without this command, parentheses would be ordinary symbolic tokens. Any distinct symbolic tokens can be defined to act as delimiters, and many different pairs of delimiters can be in use simultaneously.

> ⟨protection command⟩ ⟶ **outer** ⟨symbolic token list⟩
> | **inner** ⟨symbolic token list⟩

A "forbidden" stamp is added to or removed from symbolic tokens by an **outer** or **inner** command, without changing the essential meanings of those tokens. A token that has been called **outer** should not appear when METAFONT is skipping over tokens at high speed; the program will stop and insert an appropriate delimiter, if an **outer** token is sensed in the wrong place, since such tokens are supposed to occur only at "quiet" times. (Unquiet times occur when METAFONT is skipping tokens because of a false condition, or because it is reading the replacement text of a macro or the loop text of a loop, or because it is scanning the text argument to a macro, or because it is flushing erroneous tokens that were found at the end of a statement.) Without such protection, a missing right delimiter could cause METAFONT to eat up your whole program before any error was detected; **outer** tokens keep such errors localized. An **inner** command undoes the effect of **outer**; so does 'let', and so does any other command or definition that changes the meaning of a symbolic token. All tokens are initially **inner**.

⟨everyjob command⟩ ⟶ everyjob ⟨symbolic token⟩

The command '**everyjob** S' tells METAFONT that token S should be inserted first, just before the input file is read, when a job starts. (This is meaningful only in a base file that will be loaded or preloaded at the beginning of a run; it is analogous to TEX's \everyjob command.)

⟨show command⟩ ⟶ show ⟨expression list⟩
　　| showvariable ⟨symbolic token list⟩
　　| showtoken ⟨symbolic token list⟩
　　| showdependencies
　　| showstats

A simple **show** command displays the value of each expression, in turn. Paths, pens, and pictures are shown only in the transcript file, unless *tracingonline* is positive. The **showvariable** command gives the structure of all variables that begin with a given external tag, together with their values in an abbreviated form; this allows you to see which of its subscripts and attributes have occurred. For example, if you're using plain METAFONT conventions, '**showvariable** x, y' will show all coordinates that have been defined since the last **beginchar**. The **showtoken** command gives the current meaning of a token, so that you can tell whether it is primitive or not, **outer** or not. (If **showvariable** is applied to a spark instead of a tag, it gives the same information as **showtoken**.) Every unknown numeric variable that's currently dependent is shown by **showdependencies** (except that unknown capsules are shown only when *tracingcapsules* is positive). And finally, **showstats** gives information about METAFONT's current memory usage. Each of these commands will stop and say '! OK.', if the internal quantity *showstopping* has a positive value; this gives you a chance to enter more **show** commands interactively, while you're trying to debug a program.

⟨message command⟩ ⟶ ⟨message op⟩⟨string expression⟩
⟨message op⟩ ⟶ message | errmessage | errhelp

Communication with the user is possible via **message**, **errmessage**, and **errhelp**, as discussed in Chapter 22.

⟨mode command⟩ ⟶ batchmode | nonstopmode
　　| scrollmode | errorstopmode

The four "mode commands" control the amount of interaction during error recovery, just as in TEX. A job starts in **errorstopmode**, and you can also resurrect this mode by interrupting METAFONT; **scrollmode**, **nonstopmode**, and **batchmode** are the modes you get into by hitting 'S', 'R', or 'Q', respectively, in response to error messages (cf. Chapter 5).

⟨picture command⟩ ⟶ ⟨addto command⟩ | ⟨cull command⟩
⟨addto command⟩ ⟶ **addto** ⟨picture variable⟩ **also** ⟨picture expression⟩
    | **addto** ⟨picture variable⟩ **contour** ⟨path expression⟩⟨with list⟩
    | **addto** ⟨picture variable⟩ **doublepath** ⟨path expression⟩⟨with list⟩
⟨with list⟩ ⟶ ⟨empty⟩ | ⟨with list⟩⟨with clause⟩
⟨with clause⟩ ⟶ **withpen** ⟨pen expression⟩ | **withweight** ⟨numeric expression⟩
⟨cull command⟩ ⟶ **cull** ⟨picture variable⟩⟨keep or drop⟩⟨pair expression⟩
    | ⟨cull command⟩ **withweight** ⟨numeric expression⟩
⟨keep or drop⟩ ⟶ **keeping** | **dropping**

The **addto** and **cull** commands are the principal means of making changes to pictures; they are discussed fully in Chapter 13.

⟨display command⟩ ⟶ **display** ⟨picture variable⟩ **inwindow** ⟨window⟩
⟨window⟩ ⟶ ⟨numeric expression⟩
⟨openwindow command⟩ ⟶ **openwindow** ⟨window⟩⟨window spec⟩
⟨window spec⟩ ⟶ ⟨screen place⟩ **at** ⟨pair expression⟩
⟨screen place⟩ ⟶ **from** ⟨screen coordinates⟩ **to** ⟨screen coordinates⟩
⟨screen coordinates⟩ ⟶ ⟨pair expression⟩

Chapter 23 explains how to display stuff on your screen via **display** and **openwindow**.

⟨shipout command⟩ ⟶ **shipout** ⟨picture expression⟩

You may have wondered how METAFONT actually gets pictorial information into a font. Here at last is the answer: '**shipout** v' puts the pixels of positive weight, as defined by the picture expression v, into a generic font output file, where they will be the bitmap image associated with character number $charcode \bmod 256 + charext * 256$. The pixels of v are shifted by $(xoffset, yoffset)$ as they are shipped out. (However, no output is done if $proofing < 0$. The values of $xoffset$, $yoffset$, $charcode$, and $charext$ are first rounded to integers, if necessary.) This command also saves the values of $charwd$, $charht$, $chardp$, $charic$, $chardx$, and $chardy$; they will be associated with the current $charcode$ when font metric information is produced. (See Appendices F and G for the basic principles of font metric information and generic font files.)

⟨special command⟩ ⟶ **special** ⟨string expression⟩
    | **numspecial** ⟨numeric expression⟩

The **special** and **numspecial** commands send alphabetic and numeric information to the generic font output file, if *proofing* is nonnegative. For example, the labels on proofsheets are specified in this way by macros of plain METAFONT. Appendices G and H provide further details.

We have now discussed every kind of command but one; and the remaining one is even more special than the ⟨special command⟩, so we had better defer its discussion to an appendix. Appendix F will complete the syntax by defining ⟨font metric command⟩. For now, we merely need to know that font metric commands specify fussy font facts; examples are the kerning and '**font_normal_space**' statements in the METAFONT logo program of Chapter 11.

And there's one more loose end to tie up, going back to the very first syntax rule in this chapter: The token '**dump**' can be substituted for '**end**', if a special version of METAFONT called 'INIMF' is being used. This writes a file containing the macros defined so far, together with the current values of variables and the current meanings of symbolic tokens, so that they can be loaded as a base file. (It is analogous to TEX's \dump command.) Base files are discussed at the end of Appendix B.

 ▶ **EXERCISE 26.1**
Run METAFONT with the input

```
\newinternal a;
let b=a; outer a,b,c;
let c=b; delimiters a::;
showtoken a,b,c; end
```

and explain the computer's responses.

Our life is frittered away by detail.
An honest man has hardly need
to count more than his ten fingers,
or in extreme cases he may add his ten toes,
and lump the rest. Simplicity, simplicity, simplicity!
I say, let your affairs be as two or three,
and not a hundred or a thousand . . .
Simplify, simplify.

— HENRY DAVID THOREAU, *Walden* (1854)

The awesome memory of thy ever attentive computer
accepts all words as truth.
Think, therefore, in analytical, modular steps,
for the truth or untruth spoken through thy fingertips
will be acted upon unerringly.

— HERMANN ZAPF, *The Ten Commandments of Photo-Typesetting* (1982)

27

Recovery
from
Errors

OK, everything you need to know about METAFONT has been explained—unless you happen to be fallible. If you don't plan to make any errors, don't bother to read this chapter. Otherwise you might find it helpful to make use of some of the ways that METAFONT tries to pinpoint bugs in your programs.

In the trial runs you did when reading Chapter 5, you learned the general form of error messages, and you also learned the various ways in which you can respond to METAFONT's complaints. With practice, you will be able to correct most errors "online," as soon as METAFONT has detected them, by inserting and deleting a few things. On the other hand, some errors are more devastating than others; one error might cause some other perfectly valid construction to be loused up. Furthermore, METAFONT doesn't always diagnose your errors correctly, since the number of ways to misunderstand the rules is vast; METAFONT is a rather simple-minded computer program that doesn't readily comprehend the human point of view. In fact, there will be times when you and METAFONT disagree about something that you feel makes perfectly good sense. This chapter tries to help avoid a breakdown in communication by explaining how to learn METAFONT's reasons for its actions.

Ideally you'll be in a mellow mood when you approach METAFONT, and you will regard any error messages as amusing puzzles—"Why did the machine do that?"—rather than as personal insults. METAFONT knows how to issue more than a hundred different sorts of error messages, and you probably never will encounter all of them, because some types of mistakes are very hard to make.

Let's go back to the 'badio.mf' example file of Chapter 5, since it has more to teach us. If you have a better memory than the author, you'll recall that the first error message was

```
>> mode.setup
! Isolated expression.
<to be read again>
                     ;
1.1 mode setup;
                   % an intentional error!
?
```

In Chapter 5 we just charged ahead at this point, but it would be more normal for a mature METAFONTer to think "Shucks, I meant to type 'mode_setup', but I forgot the underscore. Luckily this didn't cause any harm; METAFONT just found an isolated expression, '*mode.setup*', which it will ignore. So let me now insert the correct command, '**mode_setup**'."

Good thinking; so you type 'I mode_setup', right? Wrong . . . sorry. Lots of error messages occur before METAFONT has read a semicolon in preparation for another statement; the important clue in this case comes from the two lines

```
<to be read again>
                     ;
```

which tell us that the semicolon is still pending. So the correct response would have been to type 'I; mode_setup' instead. Without the semicolon, you get what appears at first to be a horrible mess:

```
! Extra tokens will be flushed.
<to be read again>
                        warningcheck
mode_setup->warningcheck
                        :=0;if.unknown.mode:mode=proof;fi...
<insert>  mode_setup

<to be read again>
                        ;
1.1 mode setup;
                % an intentional error!
?
```

But relax, there's a simple way out. The help message says 'Please insert a semicolon now in front of anything that you don't want me to delete'; all you have to do is type 'I;' and the net effect will be the same as if you had correctly inserted a semicolon before mode_setup in the first place.

The moral of this story is: *When you insert a new statement during error recovery, you frequently need to put a semicolon just ahead of it.* But if you forget, METAFONT gives you another chance.

After proceeding through badio with the interactions suggested in Chapter 5, we will come again to the error

```
>> 0.08682thinn+144
! Undefined x coordinate has been replaced by 0.
```

(This is where the erroneous 'thinn' was detected.) The help message for this error has some curious advice:

```
(Chapter 27 of The METAFONTbook explains that
you might want to type 'I ???' now.)
```

Chapter 27? That's us! What happens if we do type 'I ???' now? We get

```
x4l=0.08682thinn+144
y4=-0.4924thinn+259.0005
x4r=-0.08682thinn+144
y4r=-0.9848thinn+259.0005
! OK.
```

It is now abundantly clear that 'thin' was misspelled. Plain METAFONT defines '???' to be a macro that shows all of the current dependencies between numeric variables and stops with 'OK'; this is useful because a badly typed variable name might have become a dependent variable instead of an independent variable, in which case it would be revealed by '???' but not by the error message.

One more example of online error correction should suffice to make the general strategy clear. Suppose you accidentally type square brackets instead of parentheses; the computer will scream:

```
! A primary expression can't begin with '['.
<inserted text>
                      0
<to be read again>
                      [
<*> show round[
              1 + sqrt43];
?
```

(By coincidence, the help message for this particular error also refers to Chapter 27.) When METAFONT needs to see an expression, because of the tokens it has already digested, it will try to insert '0' in order to keep going. In this case we can see that zero isn't what we intended; so we type '7' to delete the next seven tokens, and the computer comes back with

```
<*> show round[1 + sqrt43]
                          ;
?
```

Now 'I (1 + sqrt43)' will insert the correct formula, and the program will be able to continue happily as if there were no mistake.

▶ **EXERCISE 27.1**
Why was '7' the right number of tokens to delete?

▶ **EXERCISE 27.2**
If the user hadn't deleted or inserted anything, but had just plunged ahead, METAFONT would have come up with another error:

```
>> 0
! Extra tokens will be flushed.
<to be read again>
                      [
<to be read again>
                      (7.55743)
<to be read again>
                      ]
<*> show round[1 + sqrt43]
                          ;
?
```

Explain what happened. What should be done next?

It's wise to remember that the first error in your program may well spawn spurious "errors" later on, because anomalous commands can inflict serious injury on METAFONT's ability to cope with the subsequent material. But most of the time you will find that a single run through the machine will locate all of the places in which your input conflicts with METAFONT's rules.

 Sometimes an error is so bad that METAFONT is forced to quit prematurely. For example, if you are running in **batchmode** or **nonstopmode**, METAFONT makes an "emergency stop" if it needs input from the terminal; this happens when a necessary file can't be opened, or when no **end** was found in the input. Here are some of the messages you might get just before METAFONT gives up the ghost:

> `Fatal base file error; I'm stymied.`

This means that the preloaded base you have specified cannot be used, because it was prepared for a different version of METAFONT.

> `That makes 100 errors; please try again.`

METAFONT has scrolled past 100 errors since the last statement ended, so it's probably in an endless loop.

> `I can't go on meeting you like this.`

A previous error has gotten METAFONT out of whack. Fix it and try again.

> `This can't happen.`

Something is wrong with the METAFONT you are using. Complain fiercely.

 There's also a dreadful message that METAFONT issues only with great reluctance. But it can happen:

> `METAFONT capacity exceeded, sorry.`

This, alas, means that you have tried to stretch METAFONT too far. The message will tell you what part of METAFONT's memory has become overloaded; one of the following eighteen things will be mentioned:

> `number of strings` (strings and names of symbolic tokens and files)
> `pool size` (the characters in such strings)
> `main memory size` (pairs, paths, pens, pictures, token lists, transforms, etc.)
> `hash size` (symbolic token names)
> `input stack size` (simultaneous input sources)
> `number of internals` (internal quantities)
> `rounding table size` (transitions between octants in cycles)
> `parameter stack size` (macro parameters)
> `buffer size` (characters in lines being read from files)
> `text input levels` (**input** files and error insertions)
> `path size` (key points per path)
> `move table size` (rows of picture being simultaneously accessed)
> `pen polygon size` (pen offsets per octant)
> `ligtable size` (accumulated **ligtable** instructions)
> `kern` (distinct kern amounts)
> `extensible` (built-up characters)
> `headerbyte` (largest **headerbyte** address)
> `fontdimen` (largest **fontdimen** address)

The current amount of memory available will also be shown.

If you have a job that doesn't overflow METAFONT's capacity, yet you want to see just how closely you have approached the limits, just set *tracingstats* to a positive value before the end of your job. The log file will then conclude with a report on your actual usage of the first nine things named above (i.e., the number of strings, ..., the buffer size), in that order. Furthermore, the **showstats** command can be used to discover the current string memory and main memory usage at any time during a run. The main memory statistics are broken into two parts; '490&5950' means, for example, that 490 words are being used for "large" things like pens, capsules, and transforms, while 5950 words are being used for "small" things like tokens and edges.

What can be done if METAFONT's capacity is exceeded? All of the above-listed components of the capacity can be increased, except the memory for kerns and extensible characters, provided that your computer is large enough; in fact, the space necessary to increase one component can usually be obtained by decreasing some other component, without increasing the total size of METAFONT. If you have an especially important application, you may be able to convince your local system people to provide you with a special METAFONT whose capacities have been hand-tailored to your needs. But before taking such a drastic step, be sure that you are using METAFONT properly. If you have specified a gigantic picture that has lots of transitions between black and white pixels, you should change your approach, because METAFONT has to remember every change between adjacent pixel values in every currently accessible picture. If you keep saving different pens, you might be wasting memory as discussed in Chapter 16. If you have built up an enormous macro library, you should realize that METAFONT has to remember all of the replacement texts that you define; therefore if memory space is in short supply, you should load only the macros that you need.

Some erroneous METAFONT programs will overflow any finite memory capacity. For example, after 'def recurse=(recurse)enddef', the use of recurse will immediately bomb out:

```
! METAFONT capacity exceeded, sorry [input stack size=30].
recurse->(recurse
                  )
recurse->(recurse
                  )
recurse->(recurse
                  )
...
```

The same sort of error will obviously occur no matter how much you increase META-FONT's input stack size.

Most implementations of METAFONT allow you to interrupt the program in some way. This makes it possible to diagnose the causes of infinite loops, if the machine doesn't stop because of memory limitations. METAFONT switches to **errorstopmode** when interrupted; hence you have a chance to insert commands into the input: You can abort the run, or you can **show** or change the current contents of variables, etc. In such cases you will probably want to "hide" your diagnostic commands, for example by typing

```
I hide(showstopping:=1; alpha:=2; show x)
```

so that you don't mess up the expression METAFONT is currently evaluating. Interruption can also give you a feeling for where METAFONT is spending most of its time, if you happen to be using an inefficient macro, since random interrupts will tend to occur in whatever place METAFONT visits most often.

METAFONT's second most frustrating error messages are its occasional claims that you have "strange" paths. Sometimes a glance at your output will make it clear that you did indeed specify a path that crossed over itself, something like a figure-8; but sometimes a path that looks fine to you will be rejected by the computer. In such cases you need to decipher METAFONT's octant codes, which look scary at first although they turn out to be helpful when you get used to them. For example, let's reconsider **branch4** of El Palo Alto, from the program in Chapter 14:

```
branch4=
flex((0,509),(-14,492),(-32,481))
&flex((-32,481),(-42,455),(-62,430))
&flex((-62,430),(-20,450),(42,448))
&flex((42,448),(38,465),(4,493),(0,509))
&cycle;
```

If the number 450 in the third flex had been 452 instead, METAFONT would have stopped and told you this:

```
> 0 SSW WSW 1 2 SSW 3 WSW 4 (WNW NNW) NNE ENE 5 ESE 6 (ENE)
  NNE NNW 7 WNW NNW 8 NNE 0 (NNW WNW WSW)
! Strange path (turning number is zero).
<to be read again>
                       ;
<for(4)> ...]shifted(150,50)scaled(w/300);
                                              ENDFOR
p.4,1.94 endfor
                   endchar;
?
```

The 'for(4)' in the fifth-last line implies that **branch4** is at fault, because it says that the **for** loop index is 4; but the octant codes like 'SSW' are your only clues about why **branch4** is considered strange. (A simpler example appeared in Chapter 13, which you might want to review now.) You probably also have a proofmode diagram:

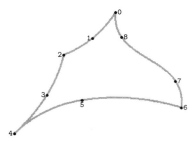

Starting at time 0, and at the point $(0, 509)$, the path goes South by Southwest, then West by Southwest until time 2 (the end of the first flex). Then it goes SSW again, and **WSW** again (that's the second flex). But at time 4, the path makes a sharp turn through the directions **WNW** and **NNW**, *without moving* (because these octant codes are in parentheses). Aha! That's where the path was supposed to turn counterclockwise, through **SSW** and **SSE** and **ESE**; METAFONT turned clockwise because it was the shortest way to go. The path actually makes a little loop at time 4, between the end of the second flex and the beginning of the third. Therefore its turning number is indeed zero, and the path is strange by definition.

 ▶ **EXERCISE 27.3**
At what point do the second and third flexes cross, in this example?

  There are three main ways to avoid problems with strange paths. One is to stay away from paths that turn so abruptly. Or you can displace the paths by *epsilon*, as in the serif example at the end of Chapter 16. (Displacing by *eps* would be even safer.) Or you can discipline yourself to fill all cycles counterclockwise, so that you can set *turningcheck* := 0; this means that METAFONT won't check for strange paths, but that's OK because tiny little loops won't hurt anything if you are filling cycles in the correct direction.

  Sometimes the octant codes of a strange path are shown backwards, because the system may have tried to reverse the path to get rid of its strangeness.

Sooner or later—hopefully sooner—you'll get METAFONT to process your whole file without stopping once to complain. But maybe the output still won't be right; the mere fact that METAFONT didn't stop doesn't mean that you can avoid looking at proofsheets. At this stage it's usually easy to see how to fix typographic errors by correcting the input; hardcopy proofs such as those discussed in Appendix H usually clear up obvious mistakes, especially if you have remembered to label the key points in your constructions.

But your output may contain seemingly inexplicable errors. If you can't find out what went wrong, try the old trick of simplifying your program: Remove all the things that do work, until you obtain the shortest possible input file that fails in the same way as the original. The shorter the file, the easier it will be for you or somebody else to pinpoint the problem.

  One of the important tricks for shortening a buggy program is to assign a positive value to *tracingspecs*, because this will put all the key points and control points of a problematic path into your log file. (See the example at the end of Chapter 24, "before subdivision.") If something is wrong with the treatment of some path, you can copy the path's description from the log file and use it directly in METAFONT input, thereby avoiding all the complexity of equations that might have been involved in that path's original creation.

  We've just talked about *tracingstats* and *tracingspecs*; METAFONT is able to produce lots of other kinds of tracing. For example, Chapter 22 discusses *tracingtitles*, Chapter 18 discusses *tracingmacros*, Chapter 17 discusses *tracingrestores*, and Chapter 9 discusses *tracingequations*. You can also invoke *tracingchoices*, which shows all paths before and after their control points are chosen according to the rules in Chapter 14; or *tracingpens*, which shows the pen polygons that arise when a future pen becomes a full-fledged **pen**; or *tracingoutput*, which shows every picture that's shipped out, using edge-transitions to represent the pixel values as illustrated in Chapter 13. Each of these types of tracing is enabled by assigning a positive value to the corresponding internal quantity; for example, you can simply set *tracingpens* := 1 (or **interim** *tracingpens* := 1) if you want the data about pens.

If *tracingcommands* = 1, METAFONT shows every command just before it is carried out. If *tracingcommands* = 2, METAFONT also shows every expandable token just before it is expanded (except that macros are separate, they're traced only when *tracingmacros* > 0). And if *tracingcommands* = 3, METAFONT also shows every algebraic operation just before it is evaluated. Thus you can get "stream of consciousness" information about everything METAFONT is doing.

Digitized output can be monitored by setting *tracingedges* = 1. For example, if we ask METAFONT to draw the Ionian 'O' of Chapter 5 at a resolution of 100 pixels per inch (*lowres* mode with *mag* = .5), *tracingedges* will report as follows:

```
Tracing edges at line 15: (weight 1)
(1,5)(1,2)(2,2)(2,1)(3,1)(3,0)(8,0)(8,1)(9,1)(9,2)(10,2)(10,8)(9,8)
(9,9)(8,9)(8,10)(3,10)(3,9)(2,9)(2,8)(1,8)(1,5).

Tracing edges at line 15: (weight -1)
(3,5)(3,2)(4,2)(4,1)(7,1)(7,2)(8,2)(8,8)(7,8)(7,9)(4,9)(4,8)(3,8)(3,5).
```

By following these edges (and negating their weights on the inner boundary) we find that the character at this low resolution is symmetric:

Further information about digitization comes out when *tracingedges* > 1, if fixed pens are used to **draw** or **filldraw** a shape. In this case detailed information is presented about the activity in each octant direction; straight line "transition" edges are also reported whenever METAFONT changes from one penoffset to another.

The *tracing*... commands put all of their output into your log file, unless the *tracingonline* parameter is positive; in the latter case, all diagnostic information goes to the terminal as well as to the log file. Plain METAFONT has a **tracingall** macro that turns on the maximum amount of tracing of all kinds. It not only sets up *tracingcommands*, *tracingedges*, *tracingspecs*, and so on, it also sets *tracingonline* := 1, and it sets *showstopping* := 1 so that you can do interactive debugging via **show** commands. This is the works. There's also **loggingall**, which is like **tracingall** except that it doesn't touch *tracingonline* or *showstopping*. You can say **interact** if you want just *tracingonline* := *showstopping* := 1. Finally, there's **tracingnone**, which shuts off every form of tracing after you've had enough.

Some production versions of METAFONT have been streamlined for speed. These implementations don't look at the value of *tracingstats*, nor do you get extra information when *tracingedges* > 1, because METAFONT runs faster when it doesn't have to maintain statistics or keep tabs on whether tracing is required. If you want all of METAFONT's diagnostic tools, you should be sure to use the right version.

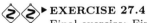 If you set *pausing* := 1, METAFONT will give you a chance to edit each line of input as it is read from the file. In this way you can make temporary patches (e.g., you can insert **show**... commands) while troubleshooting, without changing the actual contents of the file, and you can keep METAFONT running at human speed.

Final hint: When working on a large font, it's best to prepare only a few characters at a time. Set up a "test" file and a "master" file, and do your work in the test file. (Appendix E suggests a convenient way to prepare control files that supply parameters to individual test characters as well as to the whole font.) After the characters come out looking right, you can append them to the master file; and you can run the master file through METAFONT occasionally, in order to see how the font is shaping up. Characters can always be moved back to the test file if you have to fix some unexpected problems.

▸ **EXERCISE 27.4**
Final exercise: Find all of the lies in this manual, and all of the jokes.

Final exhortation: GO FORTH now and create *masterpieces of digital typography!*

*With respect to the directions of the route
I may have made some errors.*
— FRAY PEDRO FONT, *Diary* (1776)

*The road to wisdom? Well, it's plain
and simple to express:*
Err
and err
and err again
but less
and less
and less.
— PIET HEIN, *Grooks* (1966)

A
Answers to All the Exercises

The preface to this manual points out the wisdom of trying to figure out each exercise before you look up the answer here. But these answers are intended to be read, since they occasionally provide additional information that you are best equipped to understand when you have just worked on a problem.

2.1. Point $5 = (100, 0)$ is closer than any of the others. (See the diagram below.)

2.2. False. But they all do have the same y coordinate.

2.3. 5 units to the *left* of the reference point, and 15 units up.

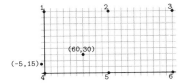

2.4. $(200, -60)$.

2.5. *top lft* $z_1 = (0, b)$; *top* $z_2 = (a, b)$; *top rt* $z_3 = (2a - 1, b)$; *bot lft* $z_4 = (0, 0)$; *bot* $z_5 = (a, 0)$; *bot rt* $z_6 = (2a - 1, 0)$. Adjacent characters will be separated by exactly one column of white pixels, if character is $2a$ pixels wide, because the right edge of black pixels is specified here to have the x coordinate $2a - 1$.

2.6. *right* $= (1, 0)$; *left* $= (-1, 0)$; *down* $= (0, -1)$; *up* $= (0, 1)$.

2.7. True; this is $(2, 3) - (5, -2)$.

2.8. $0[z_1, z_2] = z_1$, because we move none of the way towards z_2; similarly $1[z_1, z_2]$ simplifies to z_2, because we move all of the way. If we keep going in the same direction until we've gone twice as far as the distance from z_1 to z_2, we get to $2[z_1, z_2]$. But if we start at point z_1 and face z_2, then back up exactly half the distance between them, we wind up at $(-.5)[z_1, z_2]$.

2.9. (a) True; both are equal to $z_1 + \frac{1}{2}(z_2 - z_1)$. (b) False, but close; the right-hand side should be $\frac{2}{3}z_1 + \frac{1}{3}z_2$. (c) True; both are equal to $(1 - t)z_1 + tz_2$.

2.10. There are several reasons. (1) The equations in a METAFONT program should represent the programmer's intentions as directly as possible; it's hard to understand those intentions if you are shown only their ultimate consequences, since it's not easy to reconstruct algebraic manipulations that have gone on behind the scenes. (2) It's easier and safer to let the computer do algebraic calculations, rather than to do them by hand. (3) If the specifications for z_1 and z_5 change, the formula $(\frac{1}{2}[x_1, x_5], b)$ still gives a reasonable value for z_3. It's almost always good to anticipate the need for subsequent modifications.

However, the stated formula for z_3 isn't the only reasonable way to proceed. We could, for example, give two equations

$$x_3 - x_1 = x_5 - x_3; \qquad y_3 = b;$$

the first of these states that the horizontal distance from 1 to 3 is the same as the horizontal distance from 3 to 5. We'll see later that METAFONT is able to solve a wide variety of equations.

2.11. The following four equations suffice to define the four unknown quantities x_2, y_2, x_4, and y_4: $z_4 - z_2 = whatever * \text{dir } 20$; $\frac{1}{2}[y_2, y_4] = \frac{2}{3}[y_3, y_1]$; $z_2 = whatever[z_1, z_3]$; $z_4 = whatever[z_3, z_5]$.

3.1. The direction at z_2 is parallel to the line $z_4 \mathinner{\ldotp\ldotp} z_3$, but the vector $z_4 - z_3$ specifies a direction towards z_4, which is 180° different from the direction $z_3 - z_4$ that was discussed in the text. Thus, we have a difficult specification to meet, and META-FONT draws a pretzel-shaped curve that loops around in a way that's too ugly to show here. The first part of the path, from z_4 to z_2, is mirror symmetric about the line $z1 \mathinner{\ldotp\ldotp} z5$ that bisects $z_4 \mathinner{\ldotp\ldotp} z_2$, so it starts out in a south-by-southwesterly direction; the second part is mirror symmetric about the vertical line that bisects $z_2 \mathinner{\ldotp\ldotp} z_3$, so when the curve ends at z_3 it's traveling roughly northwest. The moral is: Don't specify a direction that runs opposite to (i.e., is the negative of) the one you really want.

3.2. **draw** $z_5 \mathinner{\ldotp\ldotp} z_4\{z_4 - z_2\} \mathinner{\ldotp\ldotp} z_1 \mathinner{\ldotp\ldotp} z_3 \mathinner{\ldotp\ldotp} z_6\{z_2 - z_6\} \mathinner{\ldotp\ldotp}$ cycle.

4.1. (a) An ellipse 0.8 pt tall and 0.2 pt wide ('❙'); (b) a circle of diameter 0.8 pt (rotation doesn't change a circle!); (c) same as (a).

4.2. Six individual points will be drawn, instead of lines or curves. These points will be drawn with the current pen. However, for technical reasons explained in Chapter 24, the **draw** command does its best work when it is moving the pen; the pixels you get at the endpoints of curves are not always what you would expect, especially at low resolutions. It is usually best to say '**drawdot**' instead of '**draw**' when you are drawing only one point.

4.3. True, for all of the pens discussed so far. But false in general, since we will see later that pens might extend further upward than downward; i.e., t might be unequal to b in the equations for *top* and *bot*.

4.4. $x_2 = x_1$; $x_3 = \frac{1}{2}[x_2, x_4]$; $x_4 = x_5$; *bot* $y_1 = -o$; *top* $y_2 = h + o$; $y_4 = y_2$; $y_5 = y_1$; **draw** $z_1 \mathinner{\ldotp\ldotp} z_2$; **draw** $z_2 \mathinner{\ldotp\ldotp} z_3$; **draw** $z_3 \mathinner{\ldotp\ldotp} z_4$; **draw** $z_4 \mathinner{\ldotp\ldotp} z_5$. We will learn later that the four **draw** commands can be replaced by

> **draw** $z_1 \mathbin{-\!\!-} z_2 \mathbin{-\!\!-} z_3 \mathbin{-\!\!-} z_4 \mathbin{-\!\!-} z_5$;

in fact, this will make METAFONT run slightly faster.

4.5. Either say '**fill** $z_5 \mathinner{\ldotp\ldotp} z_4 \mathinner{\ldotp\ldotp} z_1 \mathinner{\ldotp\ldotp} z_3 \mathinner{\ldotp\ldotp} z_6 \mathinner{\ldotp\ldotp} z_5 \mathinner{\ldotp\ldotp}$ cycle', which doubles point z_5 and abandons smoothness there, or '**fill** $z_5\{\text{curl}\,1\} \mathinner{\ldotp\ldotp} z_4 \mathinner{\ldotp\ldotp} z_1 \mathinner{\ldotp\ldotp} z_3 \mathinner{\ldotp\ldotp} z_6 \mathinner{\ldotp\ldotp} \{\text{curl}\,1\}$cycle'. In the latter case you can omit either one of the curl specifications, but not both.

4.6. After the six original points have been defined, say

> **fill** $z_5 \mathinner{\ldotp\ldotp} z_4 \mathinner{\ldotp\ldotp} z_1 \mathinner{\ldotp\ldotp} z_3 \mathinner{\ldotp\ldotp} z_6 \mathinner{\ldotp\ldotp}$ cycle;
> $z_0 = (.8[x_1, x_2], .5[y_1, y_4])$;
> **for** $k = 1$ **upto** 6: $z'_k = .2[z_k, z_0]$; **endfor**
> **unfill** $z'_5 \mathinner{\ldotp\ldotp} z'_4 \mathinner{\ldotp\ldotp} z'_1 \mathinner{\ldotp\ldotp} z'_3 \mathinner{\ldotp\ldotp} z'_6 \mathinner{\ldotp\ldotp}$ cycle.

4.7. $\frac{1}{2}[North, \frac{1}{2}[North, West]] = \frac{1}{2}[90, \frac{1}{2}[90, 180]] = \frac{1}{2}[90, 135] = 112.5$.

4.8. 30°, 60°, 210°, and 240°. Since it's possible to add or subtract 360° without changing the meaning, the answers −330°, −300°, −150°, and −120° are also correct.

4.9. $z_{1l} = (25, 30)$, $z_{1r} = (25, 20)$.

4.10. He said '**penstroke** $z_{1e}\{up\} \mathinner{\ldotp\ldotp} z_{2e}\{left\} \mathinner{\ldotp\ldotp} z_{3e}\{down\} \mathinner{\ldotp\ldotp} z_{4e}\{right\} \mathinner{\ldotp\ldotp}$ cycle'.

4.11. We use angles perpendicular to (w, h) and $(w, -h)$ at the diagonal endpoints:

$x_{1l} = x_{4l} = 0$;
$x_2 = x_5 = .5w$;
$x_{3r} = x_{6r} = w$;
$y_{1r} = y_2 = y_{3l} = h$;
$y_{4r} = y_5 = y_{6l} = 0$;
$z_{1'} = .25[z_1, z_6]$; $z_{6'} = .75[z_1, z_6]$;
$theta_1 := \text{angle}(w, -h) + 90$;
$penpos_1(b, theta_1)$; $penpos_6(b, theta_1)$;
$z_7 = .5[z_1, z_6]$; $penpos_7(.6b, theta_1)$;
$penpos_{1'}(b, theta_1)$; $penpos_{6'}(b, theta_1)$;
penstroke $z_{1e} .. z_{1'e}\{z_{6'} - z_{1'}\} .. z_{7e} .. \{z_{6'} - z_{1'}\}z_{6'e} .. z_{6e}$;
$z_{3'} = .25[z_3, z_4]$; $z_{4'} = .75[z_3, z_4]$;
$theta_3 := \text{angle}(-w, -h) + 90$;
$penpos_3(b, theta_3)$; $penpos_4(b, theta_3)$;
$z_8 = .5[z_1, z_6]$; $penpos_8(.6b, theta_3)$;
$penpos_{3'}(b, theta_3)$; $penpos_{4'}(b, theta_3)$;
penstroke $z_{3e} .. z_{3'e}\{z_{4'} - z_{3'}\} .. z_{8e} .. \{z_{4'} - z_{3'}\}z_{4'e} .. z_{4e}$;
$penpos_2(b, 0)$; $penpos_5(b, 0)$; **penstroke** $z_{2e} .. z_{5e}$.

5.1. The width is `0.8em#`, and an `em#` is 10 true points, so the box will be exactly 8 pt wide in device-independent units. The height will be 7 pt. (And the depth below the baseline will be 0 pt.)

5.2. $8 \times 3.6 = 28.8$ rounds to the value $w = 29$; similarly, $h = 25$. (And $d = 0$.)

5.3. Here's one way, using a variable *slab* to control the pen breadth at the ends of the stroke:

```
slab#:=.8pt#; define_blacker_pixels(slab);
beginchar("S",5/9em#,cap#,0); "The letter S";
penpos1(slab,70); penpos2(.5slab,80);
penpos3(.5[slab,thick],200); penpos5(.5[slab,thick],210);
penpos6(.7slab,80);
penpos7(.25[slab,thick],72);
x1=x5; y1r=.94h+o;
x2=x4=x6=.5w; y2r=h+o; y4=.54h; y6l=-o;
x3r=.04em; y3=.5[y4,y2];
x5l=w-.03em; y5=.5[y4,y6];
.5[x7l,x7]=.04em; y7l=.12h-o;
path trial; trial=z3{down}..z4..{down}z5;
pair dz; dz=direction 1 of trial;
penpos4(thick,angle dz-90);
penstroke z1e..z2e{left}..z3e{down}
    ..z4e{dz}..z5e{down}..z6e{left}..z7e;
penlabels(1,2,3,4,5,6,7); endchar;
```

Notice that the pen angle at point 4 has been found by letting METAFONT construct a trial path through the center points, then using the perpendicular direction. The letters work reasonably well at their true size: 'SO IO IS ISIS.'

5.4. After an "isolated expression," METAFONT thinks it is at the end of a state-ment or command, so it expects to see a semicolon next. You should type, e.g., 'I; mode_setup' to keep METAFONT happy.

5.5. Yes.

6.1. (a) No, the second token represents $\frac{1}{65536}$. (A token has the same meaning as '0' if and only if its decimal value is strictly less than $2^{-17} = .00000\,76293\,94531\,25$.) (b) Yes; both tokens represent $\frac{1}{65536}$, because 1 is the nearest integer to both $.00001 \times 65536 = .65536$ and $0.00002 \times 65536 = 1.31072$. (c) No, 0.00003 represents $\frac{2}{65536}$. (d) Yes, they both mean "enormous number that needs to be reduced"; METAFONT complains in both cases and substitutes the largest legal numeric token. (Rounding 4095.999999 to the nearest multiple of $\frac{1}{65536}$ yields 4096, which is too big.)

6.2. $\boxed{\text{xx}}$, $\boxed{\text{3.1}}$ (a numeric token), $\boxed{\text{.6}}$ (another numeric token), $\boxed{\text{..}}$, $\boxed{\text{[[}}$, $\boxed{\text{a}}$, $\boxed{\text{+-}}$, $\boxed{\text{bc\_d}}$, $\boxed{\text{e}}$, $\boxed{\text{]}}$, $\boxed{\text{]}}$, $\boxed{\text{"a \%"}}$ (a string token), $\boxed{\text{<|>}}$, $\boxed{\text{(}}$ (see rule 5), $\boxed{\text{((}}$, $\boxed{\text{\$}}$, $\boxed{\text{1}}$ (a numeric token), $\boxed{\text{5}}$ (likewise numeric), $\boxed{\text{"+-"}}$ (a string token), and $\boxed{\text{""}}$ (a string token that denotes an empty sequence of characters). All of these tokens are symbolic unless otherwise mentioned. (Notice that four of the spaces and two of the periods were deleted by rule 1. One way to verify that METAFONT finds precisely these tokens is to prepare a test file that says 'isolated expression;' on its first line and that contains the stated text on its second line. Then respond to METAFONT's error message by repeatedly typing '1', so that one token is deleted at a time.)

6.3. The statement is basically true but potentially misleading. You can insert any number of spaces *between* tokens without changing the meaning of a program, but you cannot insert a space in the *middle* of any token without changing something. You can delete spaces between tokens *unless* that would "glue" two adjacent tokens together.

6.4. False. It may seem that this new sort of numeric token would be recognized only in cases where the period is not followed by a digit, hence the period would be dropped anyway by rule 1. However, the new rule would have disastrous consequences in a line like 'draw z1..z2'!

7.1. You can put a space between the subscripts, as in 'a1 5'. (We'll see later that a backslash acts as a null symbol, hence 'a1\5' is another solution.)

7.2. No; a[-1] can't be accessed without using [and]. The only other form of ⟨subscript⟩ is ⟨numeric token⟩, which can't be negative. (Well, strictly speaking, you could say 'let ?=[; let ??=]' and then refer to 'a?-1??'; but that's cheating.)

7.3. Assuming that '+' was still a spark when he said 'let plus=+', he can't refer to the variable 'a.plus1' unless he changes the meaning of plus again to make it a tag. (We will eventually learn a way to do this without permanently clobbering plus, as follows: 'begingroup save plus; a.plus1 endgroup'.)

7.4. True. (But a ⟨suffix⟩ is not always a ⟨variable⟩.)

7.5. Yes, because it removes any existing value that x may have had, of whatever type; otherwise you couldn't safely use x in a numeric equation. It's wise to declare numeric variables when you're not sure about their former status, and when you're sure that you don't care what their previous value was. A numeric declaration together with a comment also provides useful documentation. (Incidentally, 'numeric x' doesn't affect other variables like 'x2' or 'x.x' that might be present.)

7.6. (a) The '42' is illegal because subscripts must be collective. (b) The '24' is illegal because a ⟨declared variable⟩ must start with a ⟨symbolic token⟩, not a numeric token. (c) There's nothing wrong with the consecutive commas; the second comma begins a ⟨declared variable⟩, so it loses its former meaning and becomes a tag. Thus METAFONT tries to declare the variable ',t,path'. However, 'path' cannot appear in a suffix, since it's a spark. (Yes, this is admittedly tricky. Computers follow rules.)

8.1. ((z1+z2)..((z3/4)*5))..(z6-(7*(8z9))).

8.2. The fraction 100/3 is evaluated first (because such divisions take precedence); the rounding error in this fraction is then magnified by 100.

8.3. A `sqrt` takes precedence over any operation with two operands, hence the machine computes '(sqrt 2)**2'; METAFONT was somewhat lucky that the answer turned out to be exactly 2. (The `sqrt` operation computes the nearest multiple of $\frac{1}{65536}$, and the rounding error in this quantity is magnified when it is squared. If you try `sqrt 3**2`, you'll get 3.00002; also `sqrt 2**4` turns out to be 4.00002.) Incidentally, the `**` operation of plain METAFONT has the same precedence as `*` and `/`; hence 'x*y**2' means the same as '(x*y)**2', and '-x**2' means '(-x)**2', contrary to the conventions of FORTRAN.

8.4. Since '**or**' has stronger precedence than '<' or '>', METAFONT tries to evaluate this expression by putting things in parentheses as follows: '$(0 > (1 \text{ or } a)) < a$'. Now '1 **or** a' makes no sense, because '**or**' operates only on booleans; in such cases METAFONT uses the right operand 'a' as the result. Then '$0 > a$' is indeterminate because a is unknown; METAFONT treats this as false. Finally 'false $< a$' is another illegal combination of types.

8.5. The token '++-' is undefined, so it is a tag; therefore ++-7 is a subscripted variable, which was multiplied by zero.

8.6. The associative law is valid for exact computations, but not for rounded computations. For example, it fails even in the case of multiplication, since $(.1 * .1) * 10 = 0.09995$ while $.1 * (.1 * 10) = .1$ when products are rounded to the nearest multiples of $\frac{1}{65536}$. However, this observation doesn't quite explain the stated example, which would have yielded 7 in all cases if METAFONT had computed 2 ++ 4 with full accuracy! The closest approximation to $\sqrt{20}$ is $4\frac{30942}{65536}$, but 2 ++ 4 turns out to be $4\frac{30941}{65536}$ instead. METAFONT computes the absolutely best possible approximations to the true answers when it does multiplications, divisions, and square roots, but not when it does Pythagorean operations.

8.7. It's impossible to make an expression from '⟨numeric token⟩ ⟨numeric token⟩', because the rule for ⟨scalar multiplication operator⟩ specifically prohibits this. METAFONT will recognize the first '2' as a ⟨numeric primary⟩, which is ultimately regarded as a ⟨numeric expression⟩; the other '2' will probably be an extra token that is flushed away after an error message has been given.

8.8. If a numeric token is followed by '/⟨numeric token⟩' but not preceded by '⟨numeric token⟩/', the syntax allows it to become part of an expression only by using the first case of ⟨numeric token primary⟩. Therefore '1/2/3/4' must be treated as '(1/2)/(3/4)', and 'a/2/3/4' must be treated as 'a/(2/3)/4'.

8.9. ⟨string primary⟩ ⟶ ⟨string variable⟩
  | ⟨string token⟩
  | (⟨string expression⟩)
  | **substring** ⟨pair expression⟩ **of** ⟨string primary⟩
⟨string secondary⟩ ⟶ ⟨string primary⟩
⟨string tertiary⟩ ⟶ ⟨string secondary⟩
⟨string expression⟩ ⟶ ⟨string tertiary⟩
  | ⟨string expression⟩ **&** ⟨string tertiary⟩

(The full syntax in Chapter 25 includes several more varieties of ⟨string primary⟩ that haven't been hinted at yet.)

9.1. (a) Point 1 should lie nine pixels to the left of point 7, considering horizontal positions only; no information is given about the vertical positions y_1 or y_7. (b) Point 7 should sit directly above or below point 4, and its distance up from the baseline should be halfway between that of points 4 and 5. (c) The left edge of the currently-picked-up pen, when that pen is centered at point 21, should be one pixel to the right of its right edge when at point 20. (Thus there should be one clear pixel of white space between the images of the pen at points 20 and 21.)

9.2. (a) $y_{13} = -y_{11}$ (or $-y_{13} = y_{11}$, or $y_{13} + y_{11} = 0$). (b) $z_{10} = z_{12} + (mm, -1)$. (c) $z_{43} = \frac{1}{3}[(0, h), (w, -d)]$.

9.3. (a) $z_1 = z_2 = z_3 = (w, h)$; $z_4 = z_5 = z_6 = (0, 0)$. (b) $z_1 = z_6 = (.5w, .5h)$; $z_2 = (.75w, .75h)$; $z_3 = (w, h)$; $z_4 = (0, 0)$; $z_5 = (.25w, .25h)$.

9.4. $z = whatever[z_1, z_2]$; $z = whatever[z_3, z_4]$. (Incidentally, it's interesting to watch this computation in action. Run METAFONT with \tracingequations:= tracingonline:=1 and say, for example,

```
z=whatever[(1,5),(8,19)]; z=whatever[(0,17),(6,1)];
```

the solution appears as if by magic. If you use **alpha** and **beta** in place of the whatevers, the machine will also calculate values for *alpha* and *beta*.)

9.5. $z = whatever[z_1, z_2]$; $z - z_3 = whatever * (z_5 - z_4)$.

9.6. $z_{11} - z_{12} = whatever * (z_{13} - z_{14})$ rotated 90, assuming that $z_{13} - z_{14}$ is known. (It's also possible to say '$(z_{11} - z_{12}) \text{dotprod} (z_{13} - z_{14}) = 0$', although this risks overflow if the coordinates are large.)

9.7. One solution constructs the point z_4 on $z_2 \mathrel{..} z_3$ such that $z_4 \mathrel{..} z_1$ is perpendicular to $z_2 \mathrel{..} z_3$, using ideas like those in the previous two exercises: '$z_4 = whatever[z_2, z_3]$; $z_4 - z_1 = whatever * (z_3 - z_2)$ rotated 90'. Then the requested distance is $length(z_4 - z_1)$. But there's a slicker solution: Just calculate

$$\text{abs ypart}((z_1 - z_2) \text{ rotated } -angle(z_3 - z_2)).$$

9.8. It would be nice to say simply '$z = whatever[z_2, z_3]$' and then to be able to say either '$length(z - z_1) = l$' or '$z - z_1 = (l, 0)$ rotated *whatever*'; but neither of the second equations is legal. (Indeed, there couldn't possibly be a legal solution that has this general flavor, because any such solution would determine a unique z, while there are two points to be determined.) The best way seems to be to compute z_4 as in the previous exercise, and then to let $v = (l + - + length(z_4 - z_1)) * \text{unitvector}(z_3 - z_2)$; the desired points are then $z_4 + v$ and $z_4 - v$.

9.9. Such an equation tells us nothing new about a or b. Indeed, each use of *whatever* introduces a new independent variable, and each new independent variable "uses up" one equation, since we need n equations to determine the values of n unknowns. On the other hand an equation between pairs counts as two equations; so there's a net gain of one, when *whatever* appears in an equation between pairs.

10.1. Yes, but it must be done in two steps: '**numeric** *newcode*; *newcode* $=$ *code*$+1$; **numeric** *code*; *code* $=$ *newcode*'.

10.2. The assignment '$x_3 := $ *whatever*' does exactly what you want.

10.3. The result shows that $s_1 = s_3 = s_4$ and $s_2 = s_5 = s_6$ now:

```
s[]=unknown string
s1=unknown string s3
s2=unknown string s6
s3=unknown string s4
s4=unknown string s1
s5=unknown string s2
s6=unknown string s5
```

(The assignment $s_2 := s_5$ broke s_2's former relationship with s_1, s_3, and s_4.)

10.4. The results are

```
## a=1
## a=b+1                          (after the first assignment)
## b=0.5a-0.5                     (after the second assignment)
### -1.5a=-%CAPSULEnnnn-0.5       (after the third assignment)
## a=%CAPSULEnnnn                 (after the third, see below)
>> a                             (after 'show'; variable a is independent)
>> 0.33333a-0.33333              (this is the final value of b)
```

Let a_k denote the value of a after k assignments were made. Thus, $a_0 = 1$, and a_1 was dependent on the independent variable b. Then a_1 was discarded and b became dependent on the independent variable a_2. The right-hand side of the third assignment was therefore $a_2 + b$. At the time a_2 was about to be discarded, METAFONT had two dependencies $b = 0.5a_2 - 0.5$ and $\kappa = 1.5a_2 - 0.5$, where κ was a nameless "capsule" inside of the computer, representing the new value to be assigned. Since κ had a higher coefficient of dependency than b, METAFONT chose to make κ an independent variable, after which $-1.5a_2$ was replaced by $-\kappa - 0.5$ in all dependencies; hence b was equal to $0.33333\kappa - 0.33333$. After the third assignment was finished, κ disappeared and a_3 became independent in its place. (The line '`## a=%CAPSULEnnnn`' means that a was temporarily dependent on κ, before κ was discarded. If the equation $a = \kappa$ had happened to make κ dependent on a, rather than vice versa, no '`##`' line would have been printed; such lines are omitted when a capsule or part of a capsule has been made dependent, unless you have made *tracingcapsules* > 0.)

11.1. Almost, but not quite. The values of standard dimension variables like *pt* and *mm* will be identical in both setups, as will the values of ad hoc dimension variables like *em* and *x_height*. But pen-oriented dimensions that are defined via **define_blacker_pixels** will be slightly different, because *cheapo* mode has *blacker* $=$

0.65 while *luxo* mode has *blacker* = 0.1 (since the *luxo* printer has different physical characteristics). Similarly, **define_corrected_pixels** (which we are just about to discuss) will produce slightly different results in the two given modes.

11.2. Increasing $ht\#$ would make the letter shape and the bounding box taller; increasing $xgap\#$ would move point 5 to the left, thereby making the middle bar shorter; increasing $u\#$ would make the shape and its bounding box wider; increasing $s\#$ would widen the bounding box at both sides without changing the letter shape; increasing $o\#$ would move points 4, 5, and 6 to the right; increasing $px\#$ would make the pen thicker (preserving the top edge of the upper bar, the bottom edge of the lower bar, and the center of the middle bar and the stem).

11.3. The only possible surprise is the position of y_1, which should match similar details in the 'M' and the 'T' of Chapter 4:

```
beginchar("F",14*u#+2s#,ht#,0); pickup logo_pen;
x1=x2=x3=leftstemloc; x4=w-x1+o; x5=x4-xgap;
y2=y5; y3=y4; bot y1=-o; top y3=h; y2=barheight;
draw z1--z3--z4; draw z2--z5;
labels(1,2,3,4,5); endchar;
```

11.4. The quantity called *ss* in Chapter 4 is now *leftstemloc*.

```
beginchar("M",18*u#+2s#,ht#,0); pickup logo_pen;
x1=x2=leftstemloc; x4=x5=w-x1; x3=w-x3;
y1=y5; y2=y4; bot y1=-o; top y2=h+o; y3=y1+ygap;
draw z1--z2--z3--z4--z5;
labels(1,2,3,4,5); endchar;

beginchar("T",13*u#+2s#,ht#,0); pickup logo_pen;
lft x1=0; x2=w-x1; x3=x4=.5w;
y1=y2=y3; top y1=h; bot y4=-o;
draw z1--z2; draw z3--z4;
labels(1,2,3,4); endchar;
```

11.5. 'NONATONEMENT'; possibly also 'METAFOOTNOTE'; and Georgia Tobin suggests that 'ANTEENFEOFFMENT' might be a legal term.

11.6. Delete the line of `logo.mf` that defines `barheight#`, and insert that line into each of the parameter files `logo10.mf`, `logo9.mf`, `logo8.mf`. Then other bar-line heights are possible by providing new parameter files; another degree of "meta-ness" has therefore been added to the meta-font.

11.7. (This is tricky.) Insert the lines

```
if known pixmag: begingroup interim hppp:=pixmag*hppp;
 special "title cheapo simulation" endgroup;
 extra_endchar:="currentpicture:=currentpicture scaled pixmag;"
  & "w:=w*pixmag;" & extra_endchar; fi
```

right after 'mode_setup' in `logo.mf`, and also include the line

```
if known pixmag: hppp:=pixmag*hppp; vppp:=pixmag*vppp; fi
```

at the very end of that file. Then run METAFONT with

```
\mode="cheapo"; input cheaplogo10
```

where the file 'cheaplogo10.mf' says simply 'pixmag=10; input logo10'. (The interim *hppp* setting and the **special** command are used to fool METAFONT into giving the appropriate extension to the **gf** file name. Incidentally, you could print with this font on *cheapo* at ten-fold magnification if you told TEX to use the font 'cheaplogo10 scaled 10000'; but on *luxo* you would simply call this font 'cheaplogo10'.)

12.1. The changes are straightforward, except for the italic correction (for which a rough estimate like the one shown here is good enough):

```
"Right parenthesis";
numeric ht#, dp#;  ht# = body_height;  .5[ht#, −dp#] = axis#;
beginchar(")", 7u#, ht#, dp#);  italcorr axis# ∗ slant − .5u#;
pickup fine.nib;  penpos₁(hair − fine, 0);
penpos₂(.75[thin, thick] − fine, 0);  penpos₃(hair − fine, 0);
lft x₁ₗ = lft x₃ₗ = u;  rt x₂ᵣ = x₁ + 4u;  top y₁ = h;  y₂ = .5[y₁, y₃] = axis;
filldraw z₁ₗ{(z₂ₗ − z₁ₗ) xscaled 3} … z₂ₗ … {(z₃ₗ − z₂ₗ) xscaled 3}z₃ₗ
    -- z₃ᵣ{(z₂ᵣ − z₃ᵣ) xscaled 3} … z₂ᵣ … {(z₁ᵣ − z₂ᵣ) xscaled 3}z₁ᵣ -- cycle;
penlabels(1, 2, 3);  endchar;
```

We will see in Chapter 15 that it's possible to guarantee perfect symmetry between left and right parentheses by using picture transformations.

12.2. When horizontal lines are being typeset, TEX keeps track of the maximum height and maximum depth of all boxes on the line; this determines whether or not extra space is needed between baselines. The height and depth are also used to position an accent above or below a character, and to place symbols in mathematical formulas. Sometimes boxes are also stacked up vertically, in which case their heights and depths are just as important as their widths are for horizontal setting.

13.1. $(4, 4)$, $(4, 5)$, $(5, 5)$, $(5, 4)$. (Therefore the command

unfill $(4, 4)$ -- $(4, 5)$ -- $(5, 5)$ -- $(5, 4)$ -- cycle

will decrease the value of this pixel by 1.)

13.2. The result would be exactly the same; **fill** and **unfill** commands can be given in any order. (After an initial **unfill** command, some pixel values will be -1, the others will be zero.)

13.3. **unfill** $(4, 1)$ -- $(4, 8)$ -- $(5, 8)$ -- $(5, 1)$ -- cycle.

13.4. Here are two of the many solutions:

fill $(0, 3)$ -- $(9, 3)$ -- $(9, 6)$ -- $(6, 6)$ -- $(6, 9)$ --
        $(3, 9)$ -- $(3, 0)$ -- $(6, 0)$ -- $(6, 6)$ -- $(0, 6)$ -- cycle;
fill $(0, 3)$ -- $(9, 3)$ -- $(9, 6)$ -- $(0, 6)$ -- $(0, 3)$ --
        $(3, 3)$ -- $(3, 0)$ -- $(6, 0)$ -- $(6, 9)$ -- $(3, 9)$ -- $(3, 3)$ -- cycle.

(It turns out that *any* pixel pattern can be obtained by a single, sufficiently hairy **fill** command. But unnatural commands are usually also inefficient and unreadable.)

13.5. The value of the enclosed pixel is increased by 2. (We'll see later that there's a simpler way to do this.)

13.6. True; $j - k = l - m$, since $k + l = j + m$. (What comes up must go down.)

13.7. The tricky part is to remember that '**erase draw** z_i -- z_j' will erase pixels near z_i and z_j. Therefore if z_3 -- z_4 is drawn before z_4 -- z_2, we can't erase z_4 -- z_2 without losing some of z_3 -- z_4; it's necessary to erase only part of one line. One way to solve the problem is to do the following, after defining the points and picking up the pen as before:

> **draw** z_3 -- z_4; **draw** z_5 -- z_6;
> **cullit**; **pickup pencircle** scaled $1.6pt$;
> **undraw** z_7 -- $\frac{1}{2}[z_7, z_5]$; **undraw** z_2 -- $\frac{1}{2}[z_2, z_4]$;
> **cullit**; **pickup pencircle** scaled $.4pt$;
> **draw** z_3 -- z_1 -- z_2 -- z_4; **draw** z_5 -- z_7 -- z_8 -- z_6;
> **for** $k = 1$ **upto** 4: **draw** z_k -- z_{k+4}; **endfor**.

(Note that it would not be quite enough to erase only from z_7 to $\frac{1}{3}[z_7, z_5]$!) It's also possible to solve this problem without partial erasing, if we use additional features of METAFONT that haven't been explained yet. Let's consider only the job of drawing z_7 -- z_5 -- z_6 and z_3 -- z_4 -- z_2, since the other eight lines can easily be added later. Alternative Solution 1 uses picture operations:

> **pen** *eraser*; *eraser* = **pencircle** scaled $1.6pt$;
> **draw** z_3 -- z_4; **erase draw** z_7 -- z_5 **withpen** *eraser*; **draw** z_7 -- z_5;
> **picture** *savedpicture*; *savedpicture* = *currentpicture*; **clearit**;
> **draw** z_6 -- z_5; **erase draw** z_2 -- z_4 **withpen** *eraser*; **draw** z_2 -- z_4;
> **addto** *currentpicture* **also** *savedpicture*.

Alternative Solution 2 is trickier, but still instructive; it uses '**withweight**' options and the fact that **draw** does not increase any pixel values by more than the stated weight when the path is a straight line:

> **draw** z_3 -- z_4; **undraw** z_7 -- z_5 **withpen** *eraser*;
> **draw** z_7 -- z_5 **withweight** 2; **cullit withweight** 2;
> **draw** z_6 -- z_5; **undraw** z_2 -- z_4 **withpen** *eraser*;
> **draw** z_2 -- z_4 **withweight** 2;

(These alternative solutions were suggested by Bruce Leban.)

13.8. Here's an analog of the first solution to the previous exercise:

> **beginchar** ("*", $10pt\#, 7pt\#, 2pt\#$);
> **pair** *center*; ... ⟨as in the hint⟩
> **pickup pencircle** scaled $.4pt$; **draw** *star*;
> **cullit**; **pickup pencircle** scaled $1.6pt$;
> **for** $k = 0$ **upto** 4: **undraw** subpath$(k + .55, k + .7)$ **of** *star*; **endfor**
> **cullit**; **pickup pencircle** scaled $.4pt$;
> **for** $k = 0$ **upto** 4: **draw** subpath$(k + .47, k + .8)$ **of** *star*; **endfor**
> **labels**(0,1,2,3,4); **endchar**.

However, as in the previous case, there's an Alternate Solution 1 by Bruce Leban that is preferable because it doesn't depend on magic constants like .55 and .47:

> **beginchar** ... ⟨as above⟩ ... scaled *.4pt*;
> **picture** *savedpicture*; *savedpicture* = **nullpicture**;
> **pen** *eraser*; *eraser* := **pencircle** scaled *1.6pt*;
> **for** $k = 0$ **upto** 4:
> > **draw** subpath$(k, k + 1)$ **of** *star*; **cullit**;
> > **undraw** subpath$(k + 3, k + 4)$ **of** *star* **withpen** *eraser*; **cullit**;
> > **addto** *savedpicture* **also** *currentpicture*; **clearit**; **endfor**
>
> *currentpicture* := *savedpicture*; **labels**(0,1,2,3,4); **endchar**.

13.9. It increases pixel values by 1 in the five lobes of the star, and by 2 in the central pentagon-like region.

13.10. def overdraw expr c = **erase fill** c; **draw** c **enddef**.

13.11. First we need to generalize the **overdraw** macro of the previous exercise so that it applies to arbitrary cycles c, even those that are self-intersecting:

> **def overdraw expr** c = **begingroup**
> > **picture** *region*; *region* := **nullpicture**;
> > **interim** *turningcheck* := 0; **addto** *region* **contour** c;
> > **cull** *region* **dropping** $(0,0)$;
> > **cullit**; **addto** *currentpicture* **also** $-region$; **cullit**;
> > **draw** c **endgroup enddef**;

(This code uses operations defined later in this chapter; it erases the *region* of pixels that would be made nonzero by the command 'fill c'.) The watchband is now formed by overdrawing its links, one at a time, doing first the ones that are underneath:

> **beginchar**$(M, 1.25in^{\#}, .5in^{\#}, 0)$; **pickup pencircle** scaled *.4pt*;
> $z_1 = (20, -13)$; $z_2 = (30, -6)$; $z_3 = (20, 1)$; $z_4 = (4, -7)$;
> > $z_5 = (-12, -13)$; $z_6 = (-24, -4)$; $z_7 = (-15, 6)$;
>
> **path** M; $M = (origin \mathrel{..} z1 \mathrel{..} z2 \mathrel{..} z3 \mathrel{..} z4 \mathrel{..} z5 \mathrel{..} z6 \mathrel{..} z7 \mathrel{..}$
> > $origin \mathrel{..} -z7 \mathrel{..} -z6 \mathrel{..} -z5 \mathrel{..} -z4 \mathrel{..} -z3 \mathrel{..} -z2 \mathrel{..} -z1 \mathrel{..}$ cycle$)$
> > > scaled $(h/26)$ shifted $(.5w, .5h)$;
>
> **def link(expr** n) =
> > **overdraw** subpath $\frac{1}{3}(n, n + 1)$ of M --
> > > subpath $\frac{1}{3}(n + 25, n + 24)$ of M -- cycle **enddef**;
>
> **for** $k = 1$ **upto** 12: **link**$(k + 11)$; **link**$(12 - k)$; **endfor endchar**;

13.12. The pixel pattern $\begin{smallmatrix}1&1\\2&1\end{smallmatrix}$ is culled to $\begin{smallmatrix}1&1\\1&1\end{smallmatrix}$, and METAFONT needs to sort the edges as it does this; so the result is simply

```
row 1:  | 0+ 2-
row 0:  | 0+ 2-
```

13.13. The pixel pattern is $\begin{smallmatrix}1&1\\2&1\end{smallmatrix} + \begin{smallmatrix}1&1\\2&1\end{smallmatrix} + \begin{smallmatrix}1&1\\1&2\end{smallmatrix} - \begin{smallmatrix}2&1\\1&1\end{smallmatrix} = \begin{smallmatrix}1&2\\4&3\end{smallmatrix}$ before the final rotation, with the reference point at the lower left corner of the 4; after rotation it is $\begin{smallmatrix}2&3\\1&4\end{smallmatrix}$, with the reference point at the lower *right* corner of the 4. Rotation causes METAFONT to sort the edges, but the transition values per edge are never more than ±3. You weren't expected to know about this limit of ±3, but it accounts for what is actually reported:

```
row 1: | -2++ -1+ 0---
row 0: | -2+ -1+++ 0--- 0-
```

13.14. 'V scaled-1' should be the same as 'V rotated 180', because transformations apply to coordinates rather than to pixel values. (Note, incidentally, that the reflections 'V xscaled-1' and 'V yscaled-1' both work, and that 'V scaled-1' is the same as 'V xscaled-1 yscaled-1'.)

13.15. The result is the same as 'V shifted (2,3)'; the coordinates of a shift are rounded to the nearest integers when a picture is being shifted.

13.16.
```
row 3: 0+ 4- |
row 2: 0+ 4- |
row 1: 0+ 4- 0+ 2- |
row 0: 0+ 4- 0+ 2- |
```
(Scaling of pictures must be by an integer.)

13.17. METAFONT is currently executing instructions after having read as far as line 5 of the file expr.mf.

13.18. The pixel values of *currentpicture* become 1 if they were ±1, otherwise they become 0.

13.19. (a) **addto** V_1 **also** V_2; **cull** V_1 **keeping** $(2, 2)$.   (b) Same, but cull keeping $(1, 2)$.   (c) Same, but cull keeping $(1, 1)$.

13.20. Subtract one from the other, and cull the result dropping $(0, 0)$; then test to see if the total weight is zero.

13.21. (a) Same as '**draw** p', but using q instead of the currently-picked-up pen. (b) Same effect as '**draw** p; **draw** p; **draw** p' (but faster).   (c) Same as '**draw** p **withweight** w', because **undraw**'s '**withweight** -1' is overridden.   (d) Same as '**unfilldraw** c; **unfilldraw** c', but using q instead of *currentpen*.   (e) Same as '**erase filldraw** c', because the '**withweight** 2' is overridden.   [Since **erase** has culled all weights to 0 or 1, there's no need to "doubly erase."]   (f) Same effect as '**cullit**; **addto** *currentpicture* **also** *currentpicture*' (but faster).

13.22. **vardef safefill expr** c = **save** *region*;
      picture *region*; *region*=**nullpicture**;
      interim *turningcheck* := 0;
      addto *region* **contour** c; **cull** *region* **dropping** $(0, 0)$;
      addto *currentpicture* **also** *region* **enddef**.

13.23. **cull** *currentpicture* **keeping** $(1, \textit{infinity})$;
      picture v; $v := $ *currentpicture*;
      cull *currentpicture* **keeping** $(1, 1)$ **withweight** 3;
      addto *currentpicture* **also** $v - v$ shifted *right*
          $- v$ shifted *left* $- v$ shifted *up* $- v$ shifted *down*;
      cull *currentpicture* **keeping** $(1, 4)$.

13.24. (We assume that *currentpicture* initially has some configuration in which all pixel values are zero or one; one means "alive.")

> **picture** v; **def** $c = currentpicture$ **enddef**;
> **forever**: $v := c$; **showit**;
>   **addto** c **also** c shifted *left* + c shifted *right*;
>   **addto** c **also** c shifted *up* + c shifted *down*;
>   **addto** c **also** $c - v$; **cull** c **keeping** $(5,7)$; **endfor**.

(It is wise not to waste too much computer time watching this program.)

14.1. **beginchar**("b", $5pt\#, 5pt\#, 0$);
    fill $((0,0)$ -- *quartercircle* -- cycle$)$ scaled $10pt$; **endchar**.

14.2. A *quartercircle* corresponds to a circle whose diameter is 1; the radius is $\frac{1}{2}$.

14.3. **beginchar**("c", $5pt\#, 5pt\#, 0$);
pickup pencircle scaled $(.4pt + blacker)$;
draw *quartercircle* rotated 90 scaled $10pt$ shifted $(5pt, 0)$; **endchar**.

14.4. **beginchar**("d", $5pt\# * $ sqrt $2, 5pt\#, 0$);
pickup pencircle scaled $(.4pt + blacker)$;
draw $((0,0)$ -- *quartercircle* -- cycle$)$ rotated 45 scaled $10pt$ shifted $(.5w, 0)$;
endchar.

14.5. **beginchar**("e", $10pt\#, 7.5pt\#, 2.5pt\#$);
pickup pencircle scaled $(.4pt + blacker)$;
for $D = .2w, .6w, w$: **draw** *fullcircle* scaled D shifted $(.5w, .5[-d, h])$;
endfor endchar.

The program for '◈' is similar, but '*fullcircle* scaled D' is replaced by

unitsquare shifted $-(.5, .5)$ rotated 45 scaled $(D/$ sqrt $2)$.

14.6. There are inflection points, because there are no bounding triangles for the '...' operations in the *superellipse* macro of Appendix B, unless $.5 \leq s \leq 1$.

14.7. $(0,0)$ .. $(1,0)$ & $(1,0)$ .. $(1,1)$ & $(1,1)$ .. $(0,1)$ & $(0,1)$ .. $(0,0)$ & cycle. Incidentally, if each '&' in this path is changed to '..', we get a path that goes through the same points; but it is a path of length 8 that comes to a complete stop at each corner. In other words, the path remains motionless between times $1 \leq t \leq 2$, $3 \leq t \leq 4$, etc. This length-8 path therefore behaves somewhat strangely with respect to the 'directiontime' operation. It's better to use '&' than to repeat points of a path.

14.8. Let $\delta_1 = z_1 - z_0$, $\delta_2 = z_2 - z_1$, $\delta_3 = z_0 - z_2$; $l_1 = |\delta_1|$, $l_2 = |\delta_2|$, $l_3 = |\delta_3|$; $\psi_1 = \arg(\delta_2/\delta_1)$, $\psi_2 = \arg(\delta_3/\delta_2)$, $\psi_3 = \arg(\delta_1/\delta_3)$. The equations to be solved are $(*)$ and $(**)$ for $1 \leq k \leq 3$, where $\alpha_3 = \alpha_0$ and $\beta_4 = \beta_1$. These six equations determine $\theta_1, \theta_2, \theta_3$ and ϕ_1, ϕ_2, ϕ_3.

14.9. The path is of length 9, and it is equivalent to '$(0,1)$ -- $(1,1)$ -- $(1,2)$ -- $(0,2)$ -- $(0,1)\{down\}$ .. $\{right\}(1,0)$ -- $(2,0)$ -- $(2,1)$ -- $(1,1)$ -- $(1,0)$'. Although *unitsquare* is a cycle, the cycle is broken when it is used inside a larger path; the resulting non-cyclic square path goes *down* when it ends and *right* when it begins.

14.10. Yes; for example, '$z_0 \;..\; z_1 \;..\; z_2 \;\text{--}\; z_3$' would be equivalent to '$z_0 \;..\; z_1 \;..$
$\{\text{curl}\,2\}z_2\{\text{curl}\,2\} \;..\; \{\text{curl}\,2\}z_3$'. But a path like $z_0 \;\text{--}\; z_1 \;\text{--}\; z_2 \;\text{--}\; z_3$ would not be
affected, because all directions would turn out to be the same as before. (The path
'$z_0\{\text{curl}\,a\} \;..\; \{\text{curl}\,b\}z_1$' is a straight line regardless of the values of a and b, because
equations $(\ast\ast\ast)$ and $(\ast\ast\ast')$ always have the solution $\theta_0 = \phi_1 = 0$ when $n = 1$.)

14.11. It treats this as '$((0,0) \;..\; (3,3) \;..\; \text{cycle})\{\text{curl}\,1\}$'; i.e., the part up to and
including 'cycle' is treated as a subpath (cf. 'p2' in Chapter 8). The cycle is broken, after
which we have '$(0,0) \;..\; \text{controls}\,(2,-2)\,\text{and}\,(5,1) \;..\; (3,3) \;..\; \text{controls}\,(1,5)\,\text{and}\,(-2,2) \;..$
$(0,0)\{\text{curl}\,1\}$'. Finally the '$\{\text{curl}\,1\}$' is dropped, because all control points are known.
(The syntax by itself isn't really enough to answer this question, as you probably
realize. You also need to be told that the computation of directions and control points
is performed whenever METAFONT uses the second or third alternative in the definition
of ⟨path expression⟩.)

14.12. True. The length of a path is the number of '$z_k \;..\; \text{controls}\,u_k\,\text{and}\,v_{k+1} \;..\; z_{k+1}$'
segments that it contains, after all control points have been chosen.

14.13. True if $0 \le t \le 1$, except perhaps for rounding errors; otherwise false. The
path $z_0 \;\text{--}\; z_1$ expands into '$z_0 \;..\; \text{controls}\,1/3[z_0,z_1]\,\text{and}\,2/3[z_0,z_1] \;..\; z_1$', and the
Bernshteĭn polynomial simplifies because $t[w, w + \delta, w + 2\delta, w + 3\delta] = w + 3t\delta$. Incidentally, 'point t of $(z_0 \;\text{---}\; z_1)$' is usually quite different from $t[z_0, z_1]$.

14.14. If p is a cycle, or if p is a path of length ≥ 4, the stated subpath has length 2.
Otherwise the length is $\max(0, \text{length}\,p - 2)$.

14.15. **vardef** *posttension* **expr** t of $p =$
        save q; **path** q;
        $q = \text{point}\,t\,\text{of}\,p\,\{\text{direction}\,t\,\text{of}\,p\} \;..\; \{\text{direction}\,t+1\,\text{of}\,p\}\,\text{point}\,t+1\,\text{of}\,p$;
        $\text{length}(\text{postcontrol}\,0\,\text{of}\,q - \text{point}\,0\,\text{of}\,q)$
           $/\text{length}(\text{postcontrol}\,t\,\text{of}\,p - \text{point t of}\,p)$ **enddef**;
    vardef *pretension* **expr** t of $p =$
        save q; **path** q;
        $q = \text{point}\,t-1\,\text{of}\,p\,\{\text{direction}\,t-1\,\text{of}\,p\} \;..\; \{\text{direction}\,t\,\text{of}\,p\}\,\text{point}\,t\,\text{of}\,p$;
        $\text{length}(\text{precontrol}\,1\,\text{of}\,q - \text{point}\,1\,\text{of}\,q)$
           $/\text{length}(\text{precontrol}\,t\,\text{of}\,p - \text{point t of}\,p)$ **enddef**;
The stated posttension turns out to be 4.54019.

14.16. The '&' had to be changed to '..', because point t of p might not be exactly
equal to point u of q.

14.17. Since p intersects itself infinitely often at times (t, t), the task may seem impossible; but METAFONT's shuffled-binary search procedure provides a way. Namely,
p intersectiontimes reverse $p = (0.17227, 0.28339)$, from which we can deduce that
$t = 0.17227$ and $1 - u = 0.28339$.

15.1. $(\mathrm{x},\mathrm{-y})$.

15.2. (x, y) rotated 180, or (x, y) scaled -1.

15.3. True if and only if xpart $t =$ ypart $t = 0$. If the stated equation holds for
at least one pair (x, y), it holds for all (x, y). According to the syntax of Chapter 8,

METAFONT interprets '$-(x, y)$ transformed t' as $(-(x, y))$ transformed t. (Incidentally, mathematicians call METAFONT's transformers "affine transformations," and the special case in which the xpart and ypart are zero is called "homogeneous.")

15.4. $z_1 + z_2$.

15.5. beginchar$(126, 25u^\#, hheight^\# + border^\#, 0)$; `"Dangerous left bend"`; *currentpicture* := *dbend* reflectedabout $((.5w, 0), (.5w, h))$; **endchar**;

The same idea can be used to create right parentheses as perfect mirror images of left parentheses, etc., if the parentheses aren't slanted.

15.6. Change line 9 to

draw $(z_1 \ldots p)$ rotatedaround$((.5w, .5h), -45)$
   withpen pencircle scaled $3/4pt$ yscaled $1/3$ rotated -15;

15.7. Replace line 10 by

pickup pencircle scaled $3/4pt$ yscaled $1/3$ rotated -60;
draw $(z_1 \ldots p)$ transformed t;

16.1. If there are two points z_k and z_{k+1} with maximum y coordinate, the value of 'penoffset $(-infinity, epsilon)$ of p' will be z_k and 'penoffset $(-infinity, -epsilon)$ of p' will be z_{k+1}; 'penoffset *left* of p' will be one or the other. If there's only one top point, all three of these formulas will produce it. (Actually METAFONT also allows pens to be made with three or more vertices in a straight line. If there are more than two top vertices, you can use penoffset to discover the first and the last, as above; furthermore, if you really want to find them all, **makepath** will produce a path from which they can be deduced in a straightforward manner.)

16.2. 'pencircle scaled 1.016471' is the diamond but 'pencircle scaled 1.016472' is the square. (This assumes that *fillin* = 0. If, for example, *fillin* = .1, the change doesn't occur until the diameter is 1.19325.) The next change is at diameter 1.5, which gives a diamond twice the size of the first.

17.1. $(a + 1) + (2a + 2) = 3a + 3$ and $(2a) + (2a + 1) = 4a + 1$, respectively. The final value of x in the first case is $2a + 2$, hence $a = .5x - 1$; **expr** will report the answer as **1.5x** (in terms of x's new value), since it has not been told about 'a'. In the second case **expr** will, similarly, say **2x-1**.

This example shows that $\alpha + \beta$ is not necessarily equal to $\beta + \alpha$, when α and β involve group expressions. METAFONT evaluates expressions strictly from left to right, performing the statements within groups as they appear.

17.2. The save instruction gives '?' a fresh meaning, hence '?' is a numeric variable unconnected to any other variables. When the group ends and '?' is restored to its old meaning, the value of the group expression no longer has a name. (It's called a "capsule" if you try to **show** it.) Therefore the value of the group expression is a new, nameless variable, as desired.

17.3. It's a nameless pair whose xpart and ypart are equal; thus it is essentially equivalent to '*whatever* $* (1, 1)$'.

17.4. 'v_3 := **begingroup save** ?; **picture** ?; ? **endgroup**' refreshes the picture variable v_3 without changing other variables like v_2. This construction works also for pairs, pens, strings, etc.

18.1. Yes; the direction at z.j will be either *left* or *right*.

18.2.

```
beginlogochar("A",15);
  x1=.5w;
  x2=x4=leftstemloc;
  x3=x5=w-x2;
  top y1=h+o;
  y2=y3=barheight;
  bot y4=bot y5=-o;
  draw z4--z2--z3--z5;
  super_half(2,1,3);
  labels(1,2,3,4,5);
endchar;
```

Notice that all three calls of **super_half** in logo.mf are of the form '*super_half*(2, *j*, 3)'. But it would not be good style to eliminate parameters i and k, even though **super_half** is a special-purpose subroutine; that would make it too too special.

18.3. If *bracket* = 0 or *serif_darkness* = 0. (It's probably not a good idea to make *serif_darkness* = 0, because this would lead to an extreme case of the '...' triangle, which might not be numerically stable in the presence of rounding errors.)

18.4. That's a strange question. The *serif* routine includes a *penpos* that defines $z_{\$l}$, $z_{\$}$, and $z_{\$r}$ relative to each other, and it defines the other six points relative to them. Outside the routine the user ought to specify just one x coordinate and one y coordinate, in order to position all of the points. This can be done either before or after *serif* is called, but METAFONT has an easier job if it's done beforehand.

18.5. Yes; see the previous exercise. (But in the program for "A" it's necessary to define y_{4l} and y_{5r}, so that *theta*$_4$ and *theta*$_5$ can be calculated.)

18.6.
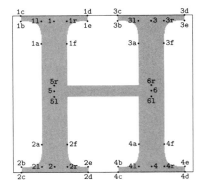
beginchar("H", $13u^\#$, $ht^\#$, 0);
$\quad x_1 = x_2 = x_5 = 3u$;
$\quad x_3 = x_4 = x_6 = w - x_1$;
$\quad y_{1c} = y_{3c} = h$; $\ y_{2c} = y_{4c} = 0$;
$\quad serif(1, thick, -90, jut, jut)$;
$\quad serif(2, thick, 90, jut, jut)$;
$\quad serif(3, thick, -90, jut, jut)$;
$\quad serif(4, thick, 90, jut, jut)$;
$\quad$**fill** *serif_edge*$_2$
$\qquad$ -- reverse *serif_edge*$_1$ -- cycle;
$\quad$**fill** *serif_edge*$_4$
$\qquad$ -- reverse *serif_edge*$_3$ -- cycle;
$\quad penpos_5(thin, 90)$; $\ penpos_6(thin, 90)$;
$\quad y_5 = y_6 = .52h$; **penstroke** z_{5e} -- z_{6e};
$\quad$**penlabels**(1, 2, 3, 4, 5, 6); **endchar**.

18.7. def *top_serif* (**suffix** $)(**expr** $xx, theta, left\_jut, right\_jut$) =
$penpos_\$(xx, 0)$; $z_{\$a} - z_{\$l} = z_{\$f} - z_{\$r} = (bracket/\text{abs sind } theta) * \text{dir } theta$;
$y_{\$c} = y_{\$d} = y_\$$; $x_{\$c} = x_{\$l} - left\_jut$; $x_{\$d} = x_{\$r} + right\_jut$;
$z_{\$b} = z_{\$l} + whatever * \text{dir } theta = z_{\$c} + whatever * \text{dir} - phi$;
$z_{\$e} = z_{\$r} + whatever * \text{dir } theta = z_{\$d} + whatever * \text{dir } phi$;
labels($\$a, \$b, \$c, \$d, \$e, \$f$) **enddef**;

      def *top_serif_edge* **suffix** $ =
        ($z_{\$a}$ .. controls $z_{\$b}$ .. $z_{\$c}$
          -- ($flex(z_{\$c}, .5[z_{\$c}, z_{\$d}] - dishing, z_{\$d}))$ shifted $(0, +epsilon)$
          -- $z_{\$d}$ .. controls $z_{\$e}$ .. $z_{\$f}$) **enddef**;

18.8. Assuming that $py = 0$, the effective right stroke weight would be $px \cdot \sin(\theta_5 - \phi)$ if it were drawn with one stroke of *broad_pen*, and $xxx \cdot \sin \theta_5$ is the additional weight corresponding to separate strokes xxx apart. The right-hand side of the equation is the same calculation in the case of vertical strokes ($\theta = 90°$), when the stroke weight of "I" is considered. (Since a similar calculation needs to be done for the letters K, V, W, X, Y, and Z, it would be a good idea to embed these details in another macro.)

18.9. **beginchar**("H", $13u^\#, ht^\#, 0$);
    $x_1 = x_2 = x_5 = 3u$;
    $x_3 = x_4 = x_6 = w - x_1$;
    $y_1 = y_3 = h$; $y_2 = y_4 = 0$;
    top_serif $(1, xx, -90, jut, jut)$;
    bot_serif $(2, xx, 90, jut, jut)$;
    top_serif $(3, xx, -90, jut, jut)$;
    bot_serif $(4, xx, 90, jut, jut)$;
    filldraw $bot\_serif\_edge_2$
      -- reverse $top\_serif\_edge_1$ -- cycle;
    fill $bot\_serif\_edge_4$
      -- reverse $top\_serif\_edge_3$ -- cycle;
    $y_5 = y_6 = .52h$; **draw** $z_5 -- z_6$;
    penlabels$(1, 2, 3, 4, 5, 6)$; **endchar**.

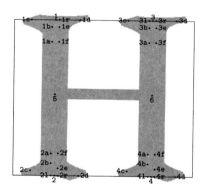

18.10. The replacement text contains ten tokens,

    `def` ⟨t⟩ `=` ⟨e⟩ `enddef` `;` `def` `t` `=` ⟨p⟩

where ⟨t⟩, ⟨e⟩, and ⟨p⟩ are placeholders for argument insertion. When this macro is expanded with *tracingmacros* > 0, METAFONT will type

    `foo(TEXT0)<expr>of<primary>->def(TEXT0)=(EXPR1)enddef;def.t=(EXPR2)`

followed by the arguments (TEXT0), (EXPR1), and (EXPR2).

18.11. According to the rule just stated, the first comma is an abbreviation for '}} {{'. Hence the first argument is a capsule containing the value of x; the second is the text '(,'; the third is the text '(}})'.

18.12. This snares future pens before they're converted to pens, because **pickup** wants to yscale by *aspect_ratio* before ellipses change to polygons.

18.13. The construction '*hide* (⟨statement list⟩)' expands into '*gobble* **begingroup** ⟨statement list⟩; **endgroup**', so the argument to *gobble* must be evaluated. The **begingroup** causes METAFONT to start executing statements. When that has been done, the final statement turns out to be ⟨empty⟩, so the argument to *gobble* turns out to be a vacuous expression (cf. Chapter 25). Finally, *gobble*'s replacement text is empty, so the hidden text has indeed disappeared. (The *hide* macro in Appendix B is actually a bit more efficient, but a bit trickier.)

19.1. Then METAFONT's "stomach" would see ';' if *mag* is known, but there would be no change if *mag* is unknown. An extra semicolon is harmless, since METAFONT statements can be ⟨empty⟩. But it's wise to get in the habit of putting ';' before **fi**, because it saves a wee bit of time and because ';' definitely belongs before **endfor**.

19.2. No; that would be shocking.

19.3. Yes, if and only if $n - \frac{1}{2}$ is an even integer. (Because ambiguous values are rounded up.)

19.4. No.

19.5. **def** even = not odd **enddef**.

19.6. The first is 5, because the pair is not considered to be a path. The second and third are 0, because the pair is forced to become a path.

19.7. (a) The loop text is never executed. (b) It's executed only once, for $x = 1$. (c) It's executed infinitely often, for $x = 1, 1, 1, \ldots$. (d) Since ten times META-FONT's internal representation of .1 is slightly larger than 1, the answer is not what you probably expect! The loop text is executed for $x = 0$, 0.1, 0.20001, 0.30002, 0.40002, 0.50003, 0.60004, 0.70004, 0.80005, and 0.90005 only. (If you want the values $(0, .1, .2, \ldots, 1)$, say '**for** $xx = 0$ **upto** 10: $x := xx/10$; ⟨text⟩ **endfor**' instead.)

19.8. $m = 1$, $n = 0$.

19.9. def exitunless expr b = **exitif** not b **enddef**. (The simpler alternative '**def exitunless** = **exitif** not **enddef**' wouldn't work, since 'not' applies only to the following ⟨primary⟩.)

19.10.
```
numeric p[]; boolean n_is_prime; p[1]=2; k:=1;
   for n=3 step 2 until infinity:
    n_is_prime:=true;
    for j=2 upto k: if n mod p[j]=0: n_is_prime:=false; fi
     exitif n/p[j]<p[j]; endfor
    if n_is_prime: p[incr k]:=n; exitif k=30; fi
    endfor fi
   show for k=1 upto 30: str p[k]&"="&decimal p[k], endfor "done" end.
```

19.11. '0; exitif true;'.

20.1. False; consider 'a1(2)'.

20.2. A value very close to z_2.

20.3. `vardef lo_cube(expr x)=x*x*x<10 enddef;`
`show solve lo_cube(0,10), 10**1/3; end.`

With the default *tolerance* of 0.1, this will show the respective values 2.14844 and 2.1544. A more general routine could also be written, with '10' as a parameter:

```
vardef lo_cube[](expr x)=x*x*x<@ enddef;
show solve lo_cube10(0,10);
```

if we ask for minimum tolerance (*tolerance* := *epsilon*), the result is 2.15445; the true value is ≈ 2.15443469.

20.4. `begingroup(p5dx,p5dy)endgroup.`

20.5. Say 'first#@' after defining 'vardef first.a[]@#=@ enddef'. (There are other solutions, e.g., using substrings of **str #@**, but this one is perhaps the most instructive.)

20.6. The machine answers thus:

```
incr=macro:<suffix>->
    begingroup(SUFFIX2):=(SUFFIX2)+1;(SUFFIX2)endgroup
z@#=macro:->begingroup(x(SUFFIX2),y(SUFFIX2))endgroup
```

Parameters to a macro are numbered sequentially, starting with zero, and classified as either (EXPR$_n$), (SUFFIX$_n$), or (TEXT$_n$). In a vardef, (SUFFIX0) and (SUFFIX1) are always reserved for the implicit parameters #@ and @; (SUFFIX2) will be @#, if it is used in the parameter heading, otherwise it will be the first explicit parameter, if it happens to be a suffix parameter.

20.7. `secondarydef t transum tt =`
`    begingroup save T; transform T;`
`    for z=origin,up,right:`
`     z transformed t + z transformed tt = z transformed T; endfor`
`    T endgroup enddef.`

21.1. False; about twice as often (2/3 versus 1/3).

21.2. `1+floor uniformdeviate n.`

21.3. A random point on the straight line segment from z_1 to z_2. (The point z_1 itself will occur with probability about $1/65536$; but point z_2 will never occur.)

21.4. A random "skyline" texture, 100 pt wide × 10 pt tall: The density decreases uniformly as you go up in altitude.

21.5. A more-or-less bell-shaped histogram: .

22.1. (a) Iff n is an integer between 0 and 255. (b) Iff s is a string of length 1.

22.2. Whoever says that there's no such primitive operation has forgotten about **scantokens**.

22.3.
```
vardef octal primary n =
   save m,s; m:=abs round n; string s; s=decimal(m mod 8);
   forever: m:=m div 8; exitif m=0;
    s:=decimal(m mod 8) & s; endfor
   s enddef;
```
'`str[m mod 8]`' could also be used instead of '`decimal(m mod 8)`'.

23.1. Point (x, y) is the upper left corner, $(x + c_1 - c_0, y)$ is the upper right corner, $(x, y - r_1 + r_0)$ is the lower left corner, and $(x + c_1 - c_0, y - r_1 + r_0)$ is the lower right corner. (Pixels outside this rectangle will not be displayed.)

23.2. Redefine **openit** so that it puts the top left at $(-50, 280)$.

23.3. (This routine is due to John Hobby.)
```
newinternal n_windows;    % the number of windows allocated so far
newinternal screen_bot;   % the first untouched screen row
pair screen_corner;       % the upper left corner of next window
def wipescreen =          % do this to initialize or reinitialize
 for i:=1 upto n_windows: display blankpicture inwindow i; endfor
 n_windows := screen_bot := 0; screen_corner := origin enddef;
wipescreen;
vardef new_window@#(expr u,v) = save r,c,up_lft; pair up_lft;
 if n_windows=15: errmessage "No more windows left"
 else: window@# := incr n_windows;
 up_lft = (min(xpart u,xpart v), max(ypart u, ypart v));
 (r,c) = (u+v-2up_lft) rotated 90;
 if ypart screen_corner + c > screen_cols:
  screen_corner:=(screen_bot,0); fi
 openwindow window@# from screen_corner
  to screen_corner+(r,c) at up_lft;
 screen_bot := max(screen_bot,xpart screen_corner + r);
 screen_corner := screen_corner + (0,c) fi; enddef;
```

24.1. The entire path now has negative y coordinates except at point $(0, 0)$, so the outline of the filled region is $(0, -1)$ -- $(10, -1)$ -- $(10, 0)$ -- $(0, 0)$ -- $(0, 1)$ -- cycle. (Notice that the digitized outline actually goes up to $(0, 1)$ before coming straight down again. This fills no pixels, but METAFONT correctly puts "cancelling" edges from $(0, 0)$ to $(0, 1)$ and back to $(0, 0)$ into its edge structure, because the point $(0, .5)$ is on the boundary and rounds to $(0, 1)$.)

24.2. The horizontal tangents are already taken care of by the equations $top\ y_1 = h + o$ and $bot\ y4 = -o$, so nothing needs to be done there. We should, however, say

$$x_2 = w - x_3 = good.x(1.5u + s)$$

so that vertical tangents will occur in good places. Since w is an integer, and since the *logo_pen* has left-right symmetry, $w - x_3$ will be good if and only if x_3 is.

24.3. Let b be the pen breadth. Then $.5w$ is a good x value if and only if *lft* $.5w$ is an integer; but *lft* $.5w = .5w - .5b$, and this is an integer if and only if $w - b$ is even.

24.4. There are no ambiguous points on the outlines of this stroke, except perhaps on the top and bottom edges; the latter can occur only if round py is odd. Hence there is always left-right symmetry, but top-bottom symmetry might fail because of a missing row at the bottom (e.g., when $px = py = 3$). In a case like the 'T' we do have both symmetries, because y_1 and x_4 are in good positions.

24.5. No matter where you place the octagon so that it isn't touching any ambiguous points, exactly seven ambiguous points are inside it; hence every one-point **draw** fills exactly seven pixels. (In fact, you always get one of the patterns ▞, ▚, ▛, or ▜.)

24.6. $f = .5(x_4 - x_3)$; the desired equation is '$x_1 - x_2 = \text{round}(x_1 - x_2 + .5(x_4 - x_3))$'.

24.7. Let $x_3 = n + \frac{1}{2} + \theta$, where n is an integer and $0 \le \theta < 1$. By drawing lines of slope 30° from the pixel centers, we find that there are three cases for the rightmost four columns:

> Case A, ▦⋯;   Case B, ▦⋯;   Case C, ▦.

Case A occurs for $0 \le \theta < 2\sqrt{3} - 3$; Case B occurs for $2\sqrt{3} - 3 \le \theta < \sqrt{3} - 1$; Case C occurs for $\sqrt{3} - 1 \le \theta < 1$. The tip in Case A looks a bit too sharp, and Case C looks too blunt, so Case B seems best. This case occurs when x_3 is near an integer, so it's OK to let x_3 be an integer.

24.8. Let $y_1 = n + \theta$. If θ lies between $\frac{1}{2}\sqrt{3} - \frac{1}{2}$ and $\frac{1}{6}\sqrt{3} + \frac{1}{2}$, the top row after digitization will contain two black pixels. If θ lies between $\frac{1}{6}\sqrt{3} + \frac{1}{2}$ and $\frac{5}{6}\sqrt{3} - \frac{1}{2}$, we get the desired shape. Otherwise we get '▦.'.

24.9. (We choose $\theta = \frac{1}{2}\sqrt{3}$ in the previous exercise, since this is the midpoint of the desirable interval.) The equations are changed to

$$x_1 = x_2 = w - x_3 = \text{round } s;$$
$$y_3 = .5 + \text{floor } .5h;$$
$$z_1 - z_2 = (z_3 - z_2) \text{ rotated } 60;$$
$$y_1 := .5 \, \text{sqrt } 3 + \text{round}(y_1 - .5 \, \text{sqrt } 3);$$
$$y_2 := h - y_1;$$

and then we **fill** $z_1 \text{ -- } z_2 \text{ -- } z_3 \text{ -- cycle}$ as before.

24.10. **vardef** *vround* **primary** $v =$
  floor$(v * aspect\_ratio + .5)/aspect\_ratio$ **enddef**;
vardef *good.y* **primary** $y =$
  vround$(y + pen\_top) - pen\_top$ **enddef**.

24.11. $(m + 1/2, (n + 1/2)/aspect\_ratio)$. These are the points that *currenttransform* maps into pixel centers.

25.1. By looking at the syntax rules, we find, for example,

⟨boolean expression⟩	`true`
⟨numeric expression⟩	`0`
⟨pair expression⟩	`(0,0)`
⟨path expression⟩	`makepath pencircle`
⟨pen expression⟩	`nullpen`

⟨picture expression⟩	`nullpicture`
⟨string expression⟩	`""`
⟨transform expression⟩	Impossible!
⟨vacuous expression⟩	`begingroup endgroup`

Every ⟨transform expression⟩ includes either a variable or a capsule. Incidentally, there are some amusing alternative 5-token solutions for ⟨pair expression⟩:

```
postcontrol 0 of makepath nullpen
makepath pencircle intersectiontimes makepath nullpen
```

26.1. The responses are

```
> a=left delimiter that matches ::
> b=(outer) a
> c=a
```

because: *a* has been redefined from internal quantity to delimiter; *b* is still an internal quantity (named *a*), and it has been stamped **outer**; *c* denotes the same internal quantity, but it hasn't got outerness.

27.1. We want to delete

from the sequence of tokens that METAFONT is about to read next, in order to get rid of the right bracket, which we can see is going to be just as erroneous as the left bracket was. However, there is another way to proceed (and indeed, this alternative would be preferable to counting tokens, if the bracketed expression were longer): We could simply delete 2 tokens, then 'I('. This would produce another error stop,

```
! Missing ')' has been inserted.
<to be read again>
                  ]
<*> show round[1 + sqrt43]
                         ;
? h
I found no right delimiter to match a left one. So I've
put one in, behind the scenes; this may fix the problem.
?
```

after which it's easy to delete the ']' and continue successfully.

27.2. METAFONT looked ahead, to see if the expression being evaluated was going to be something like 'round 0[1+sqrt43,x]'. But when it found no comma, it put back several tokens so that they could be read again. (The subexpression 1+sqrt43 had already been evaluated, so a "capsule" for its value, 7.55743, was inserted among the tokens to be reread.) The expression ended with '0', and 'round 0' was shown. Then METAFONT found extra tokens following the **show** command; a semicolon should have come next. To continue, the user should just plunge ahead recklessly once again, letting METAFONT delete those unwanted tokens.

27.3. The little program

```
path p,q; p=flex((-32,481),(-42,455),(-62,430));
q=flex((-62,430),(-20,452),(42,448));
show p intersectiontimes q, p intersectionpoint q,
 angle -direction 2 of p, angle direction 0 of q; end
```

gives the following results:

```
>> (1.88403,0.07692)
>> (-59.32149,432.59523)
>> 43.14589
>> 45.47263
```

(Actually, the paths would also cross if 452 were 451, but it's such a close call that METAFONT doesn't call the path strange; METAFONT prefers to turn counterclockwise when the amount of turn is close enough to 180°, even if it's slightly more.)

27.4. If this exercise isn't just a joke, the title of this appendix is a lie. (When you've solved this exercise you might also try to find all the lies and/or jokes that are the same in both this book and *The TEXbook.*)

> *Looke into this Businesse thorowly,*
> *And call these foule Offendors to their Answeres.*
> — WILLIAM SHAKESPEARE, *Second Part of Henry the Sixth* (1594)

> *If you can't solve a problem,*
> *you can always look up the answer.*
> *But please, try first to solve it by yourself;*
> *then you'll learn more and you'll learn faster.*
> — DONALD E. KNUTH, *The METAFONTbook* (1986)

B
Basic Operations

This appendix defines the macros of the plain METAFONT base. Let's begin with an informal inventory of all the features that are available.

- *Boolean things:* true, false; $\begin{Bmatrix} \texttt{known} \\ \texttt{unknown} \\ \texttt{cycle} \end{Bmatrix}$ ⟨expression⟩;

odd ⟨numeric⟩; charexists ⟨numeric⟩;

$\begin{Bmatrix} \texttt{boolean} \\ \texttt{numeric} \\ \texttt{pair} \\ \texttt{path} \\ \texttt{pen} \\ \texttt{picture} \\ \texttt{string} \\ \texttt{transform} \end{Bmatrix}$ ⟨expression⟩; $\begin{Bmatrix} \texttt{boolean} \\ \texttt{numeric} \\ \texttt{pair} \\ \texttt{string} \\ \texttt{transform} \end{Bmatrix} \begin{Bmatrix} \texttt{<} \\ \texttt{<=} \\ \texttt{=} \\ \texttt{<>} \\ \texttt{>=} \\ \texttt{>} \end{Bmatrix} \begin{Bmatrix} \texttt{boolean} \\ \texttt{numeric} \\ \texttt{pair} \\ \texttt{string} \\ \texttt{transform} \end{Bmatrix}$;

not ⟨boolean⟩; ⟨boolean⟩ and ⟨boolean⟩; ⟨boolean⟩ or ⟨boolean⟩.

- *Numeric things:* tracingtitles, ..., yoffset (see Chapter 25);

eps, epsilon, infinity; tolerance, join_radius, displaying; ⟨constant⟩;

$\begin{Bmatrix} \texttt{sqrt} \\ \texttt{sind} \\ \texttt{cosd} \\ \texttt{mlog} \\ \texttt{mexp} \end{Bmatrix}$ ⟨numeric⟩; $\begin{Bmatrix} \texttt{floor} \\ \texttt{round} \\ \texttt{hround} \\ \texttt{vround} \\ \texttt{ceiling} \end{Bmatrix}$ ⟨numeric⟩; $\begin{Bmatrix} \texttt{lft} \\ \texttt{rt} \\ \texttt{top} \\ \texttt{bot} \\ \texttt{good.x} \\ \texttt{good.y} \end{Bmatrix}$ ⟨numeric⟩;

$\begin{Bmatrix} \texttt{xpart} \\ \texttt{ypart} \end{Bmatrix} \begin{Bmatrix} \langle\text{pair}\rangle \\ \langle\text{transform}\rangle \end{Bmatrix}$; $\begin{Bmatrix} \texttt{xxpart} \\ \texttt{xypart} \\ \texttt{yxpart} \\ \texttt{yypart} \end{Bmatrix}$ ⟨transform⟩; $\begin{Bmatrix} \texttt{ASCII} \\ \texttt{oct} \\ \texttt{hex} \end{Bmatrix}$ ⟨string⟩;

normaldeviate; uniformdeviate ⟨numeric⟩; whatever;
angle ⟨pair⟩; turningnumber ⟨cycle⟩; totalweight ⟨picture⟩;

$\begin{Bmatrix} \texttt{+} \\ \texttt{-} \\ \langle\text{constant}\rangle \end{Bmatrix}$ ⟨numeric⟩; $\begin{Bmatrix} \texttt{incr} \\ \texttt{decr} \end{Bmatrix}$ ⟨variable⟩; byte $\begin{Bmatrix} \langle\text{numeric}\rangle \\ \langle\text{string}\rangle \end{Bmatrix}$;

⟨numeric⟩ $\begin{Bmatrix} \texttt{+} \\ \texttt{-} \end{Bmatrix}$ ⟨numeric⟩; ⟨numeric⟩ $\begin{Bmatrix} \texttt{++} \\ \texttt{+-+} \end{Bmatrix}$ ⟨numeric⟩;

⟨numeric⟩ $\begin{Bmatrix} \texttt{*} \\ \texttt{/} \\ \texttt{**} \end{Bmatrix}$ ⟨numeric⟩; ⟨numeric⟩ $\begin{Bmatrix} \texttt{mod} \\ \texttt{div} \end{Bmatrix}$ ⟨numeric⟩;

⟨pair⟩ dotprod ⟨pair⟩; $\begin{Bmatrix} \texttt{max} \\ \texttt{min} \end{Bmatrix}$ (⟨numerics⟩); $\begin{Bmatrix} \texttt{abs} \\ \texttt{length} \end{Bmatrix} \begin{Bmatrix} \langle\text{numeric}\rangle \\ \langle\text{pair}\rangle \\ \langle\text{path}\rangle \\ \langle\text{string}\rangle \end{Bmatrix}$;

⟨numeric⟩[⟨numeric⟩,⟨numeric⟩]; solve⟨function⟩(⟨numeric⟩,⟨numeric⟩);
directiontime ⟨pair⟩ of ⟨path⟩.

- *Pair things:* left, right, up, down, origin; ($\langle$numeric$\rangle$,$\langle$numeric$\rangle$); z$\langle$suffix$\rangle$; dir $\langle$numeric$\rangle$; unitvector $\langle$pair$\rangle$; round $\langle$pair$\rangle$;

$$\begin{Bmatrix} \texttt{lft} \\ \texttt{rt} \\ \texttt{top} \\ \texttt{bot} \end{Bmatrix} \langle\text{pair}\rangle; \quad \begin{Bmatrix} \texttt{good.lft} \\ \texttt{good.rt} \\ \texttt{good.top} \\ \texttt{good.bot} \end{Bmatrix} \langle\text{pair}\rangle; \quad \begin{Bmatrix} \texttt{point} \\ \texttt{precontrol} \\ \texttt{postcontrol} \\ \texttt{direction} \end{Bmatrix} \langle\text{numeric}\rangle \text{ of } \langle\text{path}\rangle;$$

$$\begin{Bmatrix} + \\ - \\ \langle\text{constant}\rangle \end{Bmatrix} \langle\text{pair}\rangle; \quad \langle\text{pair}\rangle \begin{Bmatrix} + \\ - \end{Bmatrix} \langle\text{pair}\rangle; \quad \langle\text{numeric}\rangle\texttt{[}\langle\text{pair}\rangle\texttt{,}\langle\text{pair}\rangle\texttt{]};$$

$\langle$numeric$\rangle$*$\langle$pair$\rangle$; $\langle$pair$\rangle$ $\begin{Bmatrix} * \\ / \end{Bmatrix}$ $\langle$numeric$\rangle$; $\langle$pair$\rangle\langle$transformer$\rangle$;

$\langle$path$\rangle$ $\begin{Bmatrix} \texttt{intersectionpoint} \\ \texttt{intersectiontimes} \end{Bmatrix}$ $\langle$path$\rangle$; $\begin{Bmatrix} \texttt{max} \\ \texttt{min} \end{Bmatrix}$ ($\langle$pairs$\rangle$);

penoffset $\langle$pair$\rangle$ of $\langle$pen$\rangle$; directionpoint $\langle$pair$\rangle$ of $\langle$path$\rangle$.

- *Path things:* quartercircle, halfcircle, fullcircle; unitsquare; flex($\langle$pairs$\rangle$); makepath $\langle$pen$\rangle$; superellipse($\langle$pair$\rangle$,$\langle$pair$\rangle$,$\langle$pair$\rangle$,$\langle$pair$\rangle$,$\langle$numeric$\rangle$); reverse $\langle$path$\rangle$; counterclockwise $\langle$path$\rangle$; tensepath $\langle$path$\rangle$; $\langle$path$\rangle\langle$transformer$\rangle$; interpath($\langle$numeric$\rangle$,$\langle$path$\rangle$,$\langle$path$\rangle$);

$$\begin{Bmatrix} \langle\text{pair}\rangle \\ \langle\text{path}\rangle \end{Bmatrix} \begin{Bmatrix} \texttt{\{}\langle\text{pair}\rangle\texttt{\}} \\ \texttt{\{}\langle\text{curl}\rangle\texttt{\}} \\ \langle\text{empty}\rangle \end{Bmatrix} \begin{Bmatrix} \texttt{..} \\ \texttt{...} \\ \texttt{..}\langle\text{tension}\rangle\texttt{..} \\ \texttt{..}\langle\text{controls}\rangle\texttt{..} \\ \texttt{--} \\ \texttt{---} \\ \texttt{\&} \\ \texttt{softjoin} \end{Bmatrix} \begin{Bmatrix} \texttt{\{}\langle\text{pair}\rangle\texttt{\}} \\ \texttt{\{}\langle\text{curl}\rangle\texttt{\}} \\ \langle\text{empty}\rangle \end{Bmatrix} \begin{Bmatrix} \langle\text{pair}\rangle \\ \langle\text{path}\rangle \\ \texttt{cycle} \end{Bmatrix};$$

subpath $\langle$pair$\rangle$ of $\langle$path$\rangle$.

- *Pen things:* pencircle, pensquare, penrazor, penspeck; nullpen; currentpen; makepen $\langle$path$\rangle$; $\langle$pen$\rangle\langle$transformer$\rangle$.

- *Picture things:* nullpicture, blankpicture; unitpixel; currentpicture; $\begin{Bmatrix} + \\ - \end{Bmatrix}$ $\langle$picture$\rangle$; $\langle$picture$\rangle$ $\begin{Bmatrix} + \\ - \end{Bmatrix}$ $\langle$picture$\rangle$; $\langle$picture$\rangle\langle$transformer$\rangle$.

- *String things:* "constant"; ditto; jobname; readstring; str$\langle$suffix$\rangle$; decimal $\langle$numeric$\rangle$; char $\langle$numeric$\rangle$; $\langle$string$\rangle$ & $\langle$string$\rangle$; $\begin{Bmatrix} \texttt{max} \\ \texttt{min} \end{Bmatrix}$ ($\langle$strings$\rangle$); substring $\langle$pair$\rangle$ of $\langle$string$\rangle$.

- *Transform things:* identity; currenttransform; inverse $\langle$transform$\rangle$; $\langle$transform$\rangle\langle$transformer$\rangle$.

- *Transformers:* `transformed` ⟨transform⟩;

$\left\{ \begin{matrix} \texttt{rotated} \\ \texttt{slanted} \end{matrix} \right\}$ ⟨numeric⟩; $\left\{ \begin{matrix} \texttt{scaled} \\ \texttt{xscaled} \\ \texttt{yscaled} \end{matrix} \right\}$ ⟨numeric⟩; $\left\{ \begin{matrix} \texttt{shifted} \\ \texttt{zscaled} \end{matrix} \right\}$ ⟨pair⟩;

`reflectedabout(`⟨pair⟩`,`⟨pair⟩`);` `rotatedaround(`⟨pair⟩`,`⟨numeric⟩`).`

- *Conditions:*

`if` ⟨boolean⟩`:` ⟨text⟩ `{elseif`⟨boolean⟩`:` ⟨text⟩`}`$^{\geq 0}$ $\left\{ \begin{matrix} \texttt{else:} \ \langle\text{text}\rangle \\ \langle\text{empty}\rangle \end{matrix} \right\}$ `fi.`

- *Loops:* `forever:`⟨text⟩ `endfor;`

`for` ν $\left\{ \begin{matrix} \texttt{=} \\ \texttt{:=} \end{matrix} \right\}$ $\left\{ \begin{matrix} \langle\text{numeric}\rangle \ \texttt{upto} \ \langle\text{numeric}\rangle \\ \langle\text{numeric}\rangle \ \texttt{downto} \ \langle\text{numeric}\rangle \\ \langle\text{numeric}\rangle \ \texttt{step} \ \langle\text{numeric}\rangle \ \texttt{until} \ \langle\text{numeric}\rangle \end{matrix} \right\}$ `:` ⟨text(ν)⟩ `endfor;`

`for` ϵ $\left\{ \begin{matrix} \texttt{=} \\ \texttt{:=} \end{matrix} \right\}$ ⟨expressions⟩`:` ⟨text(ϵ)⟩ `endfor;`

`forsuffixes` σ $\left\{ \begin{matrix} \texttt{=} \\ \texttt{:=} \end{matrix} \right\}$ ⟨suffixes⟩`:` ⟨text(σ)⟩ `endfor;`

`exitif` ⟨boolean⟩`; ;` `exitunless` ⟨boolean⟩`; .`

- *Diagnostic things:* `???;` `interact;` `hide(`⟨statements⟩`);`
`loggingall, tracingall, tracingnone.`

- *Starting a job:* `\mode=`⟨modename⟩`;` `mag=`$\left\{ \begin{matrix} \langle\text{numeric}\rangle \\ \texttt{magstep}\langle\text{numeric}\rangle \end{matrix} \right\}$`;`

`screenchars; screenstrokes; imagerules; gfboxes; nodisplays;`
`input` ⟨filename⟩`.`

- *Conversion to pixel units:* `mode_setup;` `fix_units;`
`pixels_per_inch, blacker, fillin, o_correction;`
`mm#, cm#, pt#, pc#, dd#, cc#, bp#, in#;`
`mm, cm, pt, pc, dd, cc, bp, in;`
`mode_def; extra_setup;`

$\left\{ \begin{matrix} \texttt{define\_pixels} \\ \texttt{define\_whole\_pixels} \\ \texttt{define\_whole\_vertical\_pixels} \\ \texttt{define\_good\_x\_pixels} \\ \texttt{define\_good\_y\_pixels} \\ \texttt{define\_blacker\_pixels} \\ \texttt{define\_whole\_blacker\_pixels} \\ \texttt{define\_whole\_vertical\_blacker\_pixels} \\ \texttt{define\_corrected\_pixels} \\ \texttt{define\_horizontal\_corrected\_pixels} \end{matrix} \right\}$ (⟨names⟩).

■ *Character and font administration:*

`beginchar(⟨code⟩,⟨width#⟩,⟨height#⟩,⟨depth#⟩);` `extra_beginchar;`
`italcorr ⟨numeric#⟩;` `change_width;` `endchar;` `extra_endchar;`

$$\left\{\begin{array}{c}\texttt{font\_size}\\\texttt{font\_slant}\\\texttt{font\_normal\_space}\\\texttt{font\_normal\_stretch}\\\texttt{font\_normal\_shrink}\\\texttt{font\_x\_height}\\\texttt{font\_quad}\\\texttt{font\_extra\_space}\end{array}\right\}\left\{\begin{array}{c}\texttt{=}\\\texttt{:=}\\\langle\text{empty}\rangle\end{array}\right\}\langle\text{numeric\#}\rangle;\quad\left\{\begin{array}{c}\texttt{ligtable}\langle\text{ligs/kerns}\rangle\\\texttt{charlist}\langle\text{codes}\rangle\\\texttt{extensible}\langle\text{codes}\rangle\\\texttt{fontdimen}\langle\text{info}\rangle\\\texttt{headerbytes}\langle\text{info}\rangle\end{array}\right\};$$

$$\left\{\begin{array}{c}\texttt{font\_identifier}\\\texttt{font\_coding\_scheme}\end{array}\right\}\left\{\begin{array}{c}\texttt{=}\\\texttt{:=}\\\langle\text{empty}\rangle\end{array}\right\}\langle\text{string}\rangle.$$

■ *Drawing:* `penpos⟨suffix⟩(⟨length⟩,⟨angle⟩);` `penstroke ⟨path(e)⟩;`

`pickup` $\left\{\begin{array}{c}\langle\text{pen}\rangle\\\langle\text{saved pen number}\rangle\end{array}\right\};$ `⟨pen number⟩:=savepen;` `clear_pen_memory;`

`pen_lft, pen_rt, pen_top, pen_bot;`

$$\left\{\begin{array}{c}\texttt{fill}\\\texttt{unfill}\\\texttt{filldraw}\\\texttt{unfilldraw}\end{array}\right\}\langle\text{cycle}\rangle;\quad\left\{\begin{array}{c}\texttt{draw}\\\texttt{undraw}\\\texttt{cutdraw}\end{array}\right\}\langle\text{path}\rangle;\quad\left\{\begin{array}{c}\texttt{drawdot}\\\texttt{undrawdot}\end{array}\right\}\langle\text{pair}\rangle;$$

`erase ⟨picture command⟩;` `cutoff(⟨pair⟩,⟨angle⟩);`
`addto ⟨picture variable⟩ also ⟨picture⟩;`

`addto ⟨picture variable⟩` $\left\{\begin{array}{c}\texttt{contour }\langle\text{cycle}\rangle\\\texttt{doublepath }\langle\text{path}\rangle\end{array}\right\}\left\{\begin{array}{c}\texttt{withpen}\langle\text{pen}\rangle\\\texttt{withweight}\langle\text{numeric}\rangle\end{array}\right\}^{\geq 0};$

`cull ⟨picture variable⟩` $\left\{\begin{array}{c}\texttt{keeping}\\\texttt{dropping}\end{array}\right\}\langle\text{pair}\rangle\left\{\begin{array}{c}\texttt{withweight}\langle\text{numeric}\rangle\\\langle\text{empty}\rangle\end{array}\right\}.$

■ *Screen display:* `currentwindow;` `screen_rows, screen_cols;`
`openwindow ⟨numeric⟩ from ⟨screen pair⟩ to ⟨screen pair⟩ at ⟨pair⟩;`
`display ⟨picture variable⟩ inwindow ⟨numeric⟩.`

■ *Statements:* `⟨empty⟩;` `⟨string⟩;` `begingroup ⟨statements⟩ endgroup;`

$$\left\{\begin{array}{c}\langle\text{boolean}\rangle\\\langle\text{numeric}\rangle\\\langle\text{pair}\rangle\\\langle\text{path}\rangle\\\langle\text{pen}\rangle\\\langle\text{picture}\rangle\\\langle\text{string}\rangle\\\langle\text{transform}\rangle\end{array}\right\}\left\{\begin{array}{c}\texttt{=}\\\texttt{:=}\end{array}\right\}\left\{\begin{array}{c}\langle\text{boolean}\rangle\\\langle\text{numeric}\rangle\\\langle\text{pair}\rangle\\\langle\text{path}\rangle\\\langle\text{pen}\rangle\\\langle\text{picture}\rangle\\\langle\text{string}\rangle\\\langle\text{transform}\rangle\end{array}\right\}^{\geq 1};\quad\left\{\begin{array}{c}\texttt{boolean}\\\texttt{numeric}\\\texttt{pair}\\\texttt{path}\\\texttt{pen}\\\texttt{picture}\\\texttt{string}\\\texttt{transform}\end{array}\right\}\langle\text{names}\rangle;$$

`save ⟨names⟩;` `interim ⟨internal⟩ := ⟨numeric⟩;` `let ⟨name⟩` $\left\{\begin{array}{c}\texttt{=}\\\texttt{:=}\end{array}\right\}$ `⟨name⟩;`

$$\left\{ \begin{array}{l} \texttt{def} \\ \texttt{vardef} \end{array} \right\} \langle\text{name}\rangle\langle\text{parameters}\rangle \left\{ \begin{array}{l} \texttt{=} \\ \texttt{:=} \end{array} \right\} \langle\text{text}\rangle \texttt{ enddef};$$

$$\left\{ \begin{array}{l} \texttt{primarydef} \\ \texttt{secondarydef} \\ \texttt{tertiarydef} \end{array} \right\} \alpha \ \langle\text{name}\rangle \ \beta \ \left\{ \begin{array}{l} \texttt{=} \\ \texttt{:=} \end{array} \right\} \langle\text{text}(\alpha,\beta)\rangle \texttt{ enddef};$$

`showit; shipit; cullit; openit; clearit; clearxy; clearpen;`

`stop` $\langle\text{string}\rangle$`;` `show` $\langle\text{expressions}\rangle$`;` $\left\{ \begin{array}{l} \texttt{message} \\ \texttt{errmessage} \\ \texttt{errhelp} \end{array} \right\}$ $\langle\text{string}\rangle$`;`

$\left\{ \begin{array}{l} \texttt{showvariable} \\ \texttt{showtoken} \end{array} \right\}$ $\langle\text{names}\rangle$`;` $\left\{ \begin{array}{l} \texttt{showdependencies} \\ \texttt{showstats} \end{array} \right\}$`;`

see also Chapter 26 for some more exotic commands.

- *Proofsheet information:*

$$\left\{ \begin{array}{l} \texttt{labels} \\ \texttt{penlabels} \end{array} \right\} \left\{ \begin{array}{l} \texttt{top} \\ \texttt{lft} \\ \texttt{rt} \\ \texttt{bot} \\ \langle\text{empty}\rangle \end{array} \right\} \left\{ \begin{array}{l} \texttt{nodot} \\ \langle\text{empty}\rangle \end{array} \right\} (\langle\text{suffixes}\rangle);$$

$$\texttt{makelabel} \left\{ \begin{array}{l} \texttt{top} \\ \texttt{lft} \\ \texttt{rt} \\ \texttt{bot} \\ \langle\text{empty}\rangle \end{array} \right\} \left\{ \begin{array}{l} \texttt{nodot} \\ \langle\text{empty}\rangle \end{array} \right\} (\langle\text{string}\rangle,\langle\text{pair}\rangle); \left\{ \begin{array}{l} \texttt{titlefont} \\ \texttt{labelfont} \\ \texttt{grayfont} \\ \texttt{slantfont} \end{array} \right\} \langle\text{name}\rangle;$$

$\left\{ \begin{array}{l} \texttt{proofrule} \\ \texttt{screenrule} \end{array} \right\} (\langle\text{pair}\rangle,\langle\text{pair}\rangle);$ `makegrid(`$\langle\text{pairs}\rangle$`)(`$\langle\text{pairs}\rangle$`);`

`proofrulethickness` $\langle\text{numeric}\rangle$`;` `proofoffset` $\langle\text{pair}\rangle$`.`

- *Hacks:* `gobble, gobbled; capsule_def; numtok`.

The remainder of this appendix contains an edited transcript of the "plain base file," which is a set of macros that come with normal implementations of METAFONT. These macros serve three basic purposes: (1) They make META-FONT usable, because METAFONT's primitive capabilities operate at a very low level. A "virgin" METAFONT system that has no macros is like a newborn baby that has an immense amount to learn about the real world; but it is capable of learning fast. (2) The plain METAFONT macros provide a basis for more elaborate and powerful bases tailored to individual tastes and applications. You can do a lot with plain METAFONT, but pretty soon you'll want to do even more. (3) The macros also serve to illustrate how additional bases can be designed.

Somewhere in your computer system you should be able to find a file called `plain.mf` that contains what has been preloaded into the running METAFONT system that you use. That file should match the code discussed below, except that it might do some things in an equivalent but slightly more efficient manner.

When we come to macros whose use has not yet been explained—for example, somehow **softjoin** and **stop** never made it into Chapters 1 through 27—we shall consider them from a user's viewpoint. But most of the comments that follow are addressed to a potential base-file designer.

A special program called INIMF is used to install METAFONT; INIMF is just like METAFONT except that it is able to 'dump' a base file suitable for preloading. This operation requires additional program space, so INIMF generally has less memory available than you would expect to find in a production version of METAFONT.

1. Getting started. A base file has to have a **delimiters** command near the beginning, since INIMF doesn't have any delimiters built in. The first few lines usually also give the base file a name and version number as shown here.

```
% This is the plain METAFONT base that's described in The METAFONTbook.
% N.B.: Please change "base_version" whenever this file is modified!
% And don't modify the file under any circumstances.
string base_name, base_version; base_name="plain"; base_version="2.7";

message "Preloading the plain base, version " & base_version;

delimiters (); % this makes parentheses behave like parentheses
```

Next we define some of the simplest macros, which provide "syntactic sugar" for commonly occurring idioms. For example, '**stop** "hello"' displays 'hello' on the terminal and waits until ⟨return⟩ is typed.

```
def upto = step 1 until enddef;   def downto = step -1 until enddef;
def exitunless expr c = exitif not c enddef;
let relax = \;                    % ignore the word 'relax', as in TeX
let \\ = \;                       % double relaxation is like single
def ]] = ] ] enddef;              % right brackets should be loners
def -- = {curl 1}..{curl 1} enddef;
def --- = .. tension infinity .. enddef;
def ... = .. tension atleast 1 .. enddef;

def gobble primary g = enddef;
primarydef g gobbled gg = enddef;
def hide(text t) = exitif numeric begingroup t; endgroup; enddef;
def ??? = hide(interim showstopping:=1; showdependencies) enddef;
def stop expr s = message s; gobble readstring enddef;
```

(Chapter 20 points out that '\' is an expandable token that expands into nothing. Plain METAFONT allows also '\\', because there's a formatting program called MFT that uses \\ to insert extra spacing in a pretty-printed listing.) The "clever" code for **hide** is based on the fact that a vacuous expression is not numeric; hence no loop is exited, and the computer doesn't mind the fact that we may not be in a loop at all.

The values of internal quantities are next on the agenda:

```
smoothing:=1; autorounding:=2;  % this adjusts curves to the raster
turningcheck:=2;                % this will warn about a "strange path"
granularity:=1;                 % this says that pixels are pixels

def interact =                  % prepares to make "show" commands stop
  hide(showstopping:=1; tracingonline:=1) enddef;
```

```
def loggingall =                    % puts tracing info into the log
 tracingcommands:=3; tracingedges:=2; tracingtitles:=1;
 tracingequations:=1; tracingcapsules:=1; tracingspecs:=1;
 tracingpens:=1; tracingchoices:=1; tracingstats:=1;
 tracingoutput:=1; tracingmacros:=1; tracingrestores:=1;
 enddef;
def tracingall =                    % turns on every form of tracing
 tracingonline:=1; showstopping:=1; loggingall enddef;
def tracingnone =                   % turns off every form of tracing
 tracingcommands:=0; tracingonline:=0; showstopping:=0;
 tracingedges:=0; tracingtitles:=0; tracingequations:=0;
 tracingcapsules:=0; tracingspecs:=0; tracingpens:=0;
 tracingchoices:=0; tracingstats:=0; tracingoutput:=0;
 tracingmacros:=0; tracingrestores:=0; enddef;
```

The user can say **interact** in the midst of a statement; but **loggingall**, **tracingall**, and **tracingnone** should come between statements. (You don't need a semicolon after them, because they come equipped with their own closing ';'.)

2. Math routines. The second major part of plain.mf contains the definitions of basic constants and mathematical macros that extend the primitive capabilities of META-FONT's expressions.

```
% numeric constants
newinternal eps,epsilon,infinity;
eps := .00049;                  % this is a pretty small positive number
epsilon := 1/256/256;           % but this is the smallest
infinity := 4095.99998;         % and this is the largest

% pair constants
pair right,left,up,down,origin;
origin=(0,0); up=-down=(0,1); right=-left=(1,0);

% path constants
path quartercircle,halfcircle,fullcircle,unitsquare;
quartercircle=(right{up}..(right+up)/sqrt2..up{left}) scaled .5;
halfcircle=quartercircle & quartercircle rotated 90;
fullcircle=halfcircle & halfcircle rotated 180 & cycle;
unitsquare=(0,0)--(1,0)--(1,1)--(0,1)--cycle;

% transform constants
transform identity;
for z=origin,right,up: z transformed identity = z; endfor

% picture constants
picture blankpicture,unitpixel;
blankpicture=nullpicture;       % 'display blankpicture...'
unitpixel=nullpicture; addto unitpixel contour unitsquare;

% string constants
string ditto; ditto = char 34;  % ASCII double-quote mark
```

```
% pen constants
def capsule_def(suffix s) primary u = def s = u enddef enddef;
capsule_def(pensquare) makepen(unitsquare shifted -(.5,.5));
capsule_def(penrazor) makepen((-.5,0)--(.5,0)--cycle);
pen penspeck; penspeck=pensquare scaled eps;
```

The **pensquare** and **penrazor** constants are defined here in a surprisingly roundabout way, just so that they can be future pens instead of pens. METAFONT can transform a future pen much faster than a pen, since pens have a complex internal data structure, so this trick saves time. But how does it work? Well, a variable cannot be a future pen, but a capsule can; hence **pensquare** and **penrazor** are defined, via **capsule_def**, to be macros that expand into single capsules. Incidentally, **penspeck** is an extremely tiny little pen that is used by the **drawdot** macro. Since it is not intended to be transformed, we are better off making it a pen; then it's immediately ready for use.

Now that the basic constants have been defined, we turn to mathematical operations. There's one operation that has no arguments:

```
% nullary operators
vardef whatever = save ?; ? enddef;
```

The reasoning behind this is discussed in exercise 17.2.

Operations that take one argument are introduced next.

```
% unary operators
let abs = length;

vardef round primary u =
 if numeric u: floor(u+.5)
 elseif pair u: (hround xpart u, vround ypart u)
 else: u fi enddef;

vardef hround primary x = floor(x+.5) enddef;
vardef vround primary y = floor(y.o_+.5)_o_ enddef;

vardef ceiling primary x = -floor(-x) enddef;

vardef byte primary s = if string s: ASCII fi s enddef;

vardef dir primary d = right rotated d enddef;

vardef unitvector primary z = z/abs z enddef;

vardef inverse primary T =
 transform T_; T_ transformed T = identity; T_ enddef;

vardef counterclockwise primary c =
 if turningcheck>0:
  interim autorounding:=0;
  if turningnumber c <= 0: reverse fi fi c enddef;

vardef tensepath expr r =
 for k=0 upto length r - 1: point k of r --- endfor
 if cycle r: cycle else: point infinity of r fi enddef;
```

Notice that the variable 'T_' was not saved by the *inverse* function. The plain base routines gain efficiency by using "private" tokens that are assumed to be distinct from any of the user's tokens; these private tokens always end with the underscore character, '_'. If ordinary user programs never contain such token names, no surprises will occur, provided that different macro designers who combine their routines are careful that their private names are not in conflict.

The private tokens 'o_' and '_o_' used in vround stand for '*aspect_ratio' and '/aspect_ratio', respectively, as we shall see shortly.

Now we define 'mod' and 'div', being careful to do this in such a way that the identities $a(x \bmod y) = (ax) \bmod (ay)$ and $(ax) \text{ div } (ay) = x \text{ div } y$ are valid.

```
% binary operators
primarydef x mod y = (x-y*floor(x/y)) enddef;
primarydef x div y = floor(x/y) enddef;
primarydef w dotprod z = (xpart w * xpart z + ypart w * ypart z) enddef;
```

The '**' operator is designed to be most efficient when it's used for squaring. A separate 'takepower' routine is used for exponents other than 2, so that METAFONT doesn't have to skip over lots of tokens in the common case. The takepower routine is careful to give the correct answer in expressions like '(-2)**(-3)' and '0**0'.

```
primarydef x ** y = if y=2: x*x else: takepower y of x fi enddef;
def takepower expr y of x =
 if x>0: mexp(y*mlog x)
 elseif (x=0) and (y>0): 0
 else: 1
  if y=floor y:
   if y>=0: for n=1 upto y: *x endfor
   else: for n=-1 downto y: /x endfor fi
  else: hide(errmessage "Undefined power: " & decimal x&"**"&decimal y)
 fi fi enddef;
```

METAFONT's primitive path operations have been defined in such a way that the following higher-level operations are easy:

```
vardef direction expr t of p =
 postcontrol t of p - precontrol t of p enddef;

vardef directionpoint expr z of p =
 a_:=directiontime z of p;
 if a_<0: errmessage("The direction doesn't occur"); fi
 point a_ of p enddef;

secondarydef p intersectionpoint q =
 begingroup save x_,y_; (x_,y_)=p intersectiontimes q;
 if x_<0: errmessage("The paths don't intersect"); (0,0)
 else: .5[point x_ of p, point y_ of q] fi endgroup
enddef;
```

The private token 'a_' will be declared as an internal quantity. Internal quantities are more efficient than ordinary numeric variables.

Plain METAFONT's 'softjoin' operation provides a way to hook paths together without the abrupt change of direction implied by '&'. Assuming that the final point of p is the first point of q, the path 'p softjoin q' begins on p until coming within *join_radius* of this common point; then it curves over and finishes q in essentially the same way. The internal quantity *join_radius* should be set to the desired value before softjoin is applied. (This routine is due to N. N. Billawala.)

```
tertiarydef p softjoin q =
 begingroup c_:=fullcircle scaled 2join_radius shifted point 0 of q;
 a_:=ypart(c_ intersectiontimes p); b_:=ypart(c_ intersectiontimes q);
 if a_<0:point 0 of p{direction 0 of p} else: subpath(0,a_) of p fi
   ... if b_<0:{direction infinity of q}point infinity of q
    else: subpath(b_,infinity) of q fi endgroup enddef;
newinternal join_radius,a_,b_; path c_;
```

The remaining math operators don't fall into the ordinary patterns; something is unusual about each of them. First we have 'incr' and 'decr', which apply only to variables; they have the side affect of changing the variable's value.

```
vardef incr suffix $ = $:=$+1; $ enddef;
vardef decr suffix $ = $:=$-1; $ enddef;
```

You can say either 'incr x' or 'incr (x)', within an expression; but 'incr x' by itself is not a valid statement.

To reflect about a line, we compute a transform on the fly:

```
def reflectedabout(expr w,z) =    % reflects about the line w..z
 transformed
  begingroup transform T_;
  w transformed T_ = w;  z transformed T_ = z;
  xxpart T_ = -yypart T_; xypart T_ = yxpart T_; % T_ is a reflection
  T_ endgroup enddef;
def rotatedaround(expr z, d) =    % rotates d degrees around z
 shifted -z rotated d shifted z enddef;
let rotatedabout = rotatedaround;   % for roundabout people
```

Now we come to an interesting trick: The user writes something like '$\min(a, b)$' or '$\max(a, b, c, d)$', and METAFONT's notation for macro calls makes it easy to separate the first argument from the rest—assuming that at least two arguments are present.

```
vardef max(expr u)(text t) = % t is a list of numerics, pairs, or strings
 save u_; setu_ u; for uu = t: if uu>u_: u_:=uu; fi endfor
 u_ enddef;
vardef min(expr u)(text t) = % t is a list of numerics, pairs, or strings
 save u_; setu_ u; for uu = t: if uu<u_: u_:=uu; fi endfor
 u_ enddef;
def setu_ primary u =
 if pair u: pair u_ elseif string u: string u_ fi;
 u_=u enddef;
```

Appendix D discusses some variations on this theme.

The flex routine defines part of a path whose directions at the endpoints will depend on the environment, because this path is not enclosed in parentheses.

```
def flex(text t) =              % t is a list of pairs
 hide(n_:=0; for z=t: z_[incr n_]:=z; endfor
  dz_:=z_[n_]-z_1)
 z_1 for k=2 upto n_-1: ...z_[k]{dz_} endfor ...z_[n_] enddef;
newinternal n_; pair z_[],dz_;
```

The five parameters to 'superellipse' are the right, the top, the left, the bottom, and the superness.

```
def superellipse(expr r,t,l,b,s)=
r{up}...(s[xpart t,xpart r],s[ypart r,ypart t]){t-r}...
t{left}...(s[xpart t,xpart l],s[ypart l,ypart t]){l-t}...
l{down}...(s[xpart b,xpart l],s[ypart l,ypart b]){b-l}...
b{right}...(s[xpart b,xpart r],s[ypart r,ypart b]){r-b}...cycle enddef;
```

Chapter 14 illustrates the 'interpath' routine, which interpolates between paths to find a path that would be written '$a[p,q]$' if METAFONT's macro notation were more general.

```
vardef interpath(expr a,p,q) =
 for t=0 upto length p-1: a[point t of p, point t of q]
  ..controls a[postcontrol t of p, postcontrol t of q]
   and a[precontrol t+1 of p, precontrol t+1 of q] .. endfor
 if cycle p: cycle
 else: a[point infinity of p, point infinity of q] fi enddef;
```

Finally we come to the *solve* macro, which has already been presented in Chapter 20. Appendix D gives further illustrations of its use.

```
vardef solve@#(expr true_x,false_x)= % @#(true_x)=true, @#(false_x)=false
 tx_:=true_x; fx_:=false_x;
 forever: x_:=.5[tx_,fx_]; exitif abs(tx_-fx_)<=tolerance;
 if @#(x_): tx_ else: fx_ fi :=x_; endfor
 x_ enddef; % now x_ is near where @# changes from true to false
newinternal tolerance, tx_,fx_,x_; tolerance:=.1;
```

3. Conversion to pixels. The next main subdivision of plain.mf contains macros and constants that help convert dimensions from device-independent "sharped" or "true" units into the pixel units corresponding to a particular device. First comes a subroutine that computes eight basic units, assuming that the number of *pixels_per_inch* is known:

```
def fix_units =   % define the conversion factors, given pixels_per_inch
 mm:=pixels_per_inch/25.4;      cm:=pixels_per_inch/2.54;
 pt:=pixels_per_inch/72.27;     pc:=pixels_per_inch/6.0225;
 dd:=1238/1157pt;               cc:=12dd;
 bp:=pixels_per_inch/72;        in:=pixels_per_inch;
 hppp:=pt;                      % horizontal pixels per point
 vppp:=aspect_ratio*hppp;       % vertical pixels per point
 enddef;
```

Sharped units are actually expressed in terms of points, but a virtuous user will not write programs that exploit this fact.

mm#=2.84528;	pt#=1;	dd#=1.07001;	bp#:=1.00375;
cm#=28.45276;	pc#=12;	cc#=12.84010;	in#:=72.27;

A particular device is supposed to be modeled by four parameters, called *pixels_per_inch*, *blacker*, *o_correction*, and *fillin*, as discussed in Chapter 11. Appropriate values will be assigned to these internal quantities by **mode_setup**.

```
newinternal pixels_per_inch;        % the given resolution
newinternal blacker, o_correction;  % device-oriented corrections
```

(The fourth parameter, *fillin*, is already an internal quantity of METAFONT.)

Here are the ten principal ways to convert from sharped units to pixels:

```
def define_pixels(text t) =
 forsuffixes $=t: $:=$.#*hppp; endfor enddef;
def define_whole_pixels(text t) =
 forsuffixes $=t: $:=hround($.#*hppp); endfor enddef;
def define_whole_vertical_pixels(text t) =
 forsuffixes $=t: $:=vround($.#*hppp); endfor enddef;
def define_good_x_pixels(text t) =
 forsuffixes $=t: $:=good.x($.#*hppp); endfor enddef;
def define_good_y_pixels(text t) =
 forsuffixes $=t: $:=good.y($.#*hppp); endfor enddef;
def define_blacker_pixels(text t) =
 forsuffixes $=t: $:=$.#*hppp+blacker; endfor enddef;
def define_whole_blacker_pixels(text t) =
 forsuffixes $=t: $:=hround($.#*hppp+blacker);
   if $<=0: $:=1; fi endfor enddef;
def define_whole_vertical_blacker_pixels(text t) =
 forsuffixes $=t: $:=vround($.#*hppp+blacker);
   if $<=0: $:=1_o_; fi endfor enddef;
def define_corrected_pixels(text t) =
 forsuffixes $=t: $:=vround($.#*hppp*o_correction)+eps; endfor enddef;
def define_horizontal_corrected_pixels(text t) =
 forsuffixes $=t: $:=hround($.#*hppp*o_correction)+eps; endfor enddef;
```

Chapter 24 discusses the **lowres_fix** routine, which helps to correct anomalies that may have occurred when sharped dimensions were rounded to whole pixels.

```
def lowres_fix(text t) expr ratio =
 begingroup save min,max,first;
 forsuffixes $=t:
  if unknown min: min=max=first=$; min#=max#=$.#;
  elseif $.#<min#: min:=$; min#:=$.#;
  elseif $.#>max#: max:=$; max#:=$.#; fi endfor
 if max/min>ratio*max#/min#: forsuffixes $=t: $:=first; endfor fi
 endgroup enddef;
```

4. Modes of operation. The standard way to create a font with plain METAFONT is to start up the program by saying

> \mode=⟨mode name⟩; mag=⟨magnification⟩; input ⟨font file name⟩

in response to METAFONT's initial '******'. The mag is omitted if the magnification is 1, and the mode is omitted if mode=proof. Additional commands like 'screenchars' might be given before the 'input'; we shall discuss them later. If you are using another base file, called say the '**super**' base, this whole command line should be preceded by '**&super**'. The mode name should have been predeclared in your base file, by the mode_def routine below. If, however, you need a special mode that isn't in the base, you can put its commands into a file (e.g., '**specmode.mf**') and invoke it by saying

> \smode="specmode"; mag= ⋯

instead of giving a predeclared mode name.

Here is the **mode_setup** routine, which is usually one of the first macros to be called in a METAFONT program:

```
def mode_setup =
 warningcheck:=0;
 if unknown mode: mode=proof; fi
 numeric aspect_ratio; transform currenttransform;
 scantokens if string mode:("input "&mode) else: mode_name[mode] fi;
 if unknown mag: mag=1; fi
 if unknown aspect_ratio: aspect_ratio=1; fi
 displaying:=proofing;
 pixels_per_inch:=pixels_per_inch*mag;
 if aspect_ratio=1: let o_=\; let _o_=\
 else: def o_=*aspect_ratio enddef; def _o_=/aspect_ratio enddef fi;
 fix_units;
 scantokens extra_setup; % the user's special last-minute adjustments
 currenttransform:=
  if unknown currenttransform: identity else: currenttransform fi
   yscaled aspect_ratio;
 clearit;
 pickup pencircle scaled (.4pt+blacker);
 warningcheck:=1; enddef;
def smode = string mode; mode enddef;
string extra_setup, mode_name[];
extra_setup="";              % usually there's nothing special to do
newinternal displaying;   % if positive, endchar will 'showit'
```

The first '**scantokens**' in **mode_setup** either reads a special file or calls a macro that expands into commands defining the mode. Notice that *aspect_ratio* is always cleared to an undefined value when these commands are performed; you can't simply give a value to *aspect_ratio* when you set *mode* and *mag*. If the aspect ratio isn't assigned a definite value by the mode routine, it will become unity, and the 'o_' and '_o_' operations will be omitted from subsequent calculations. Notice also that the mode commands might do something special to *mag*, since *mag* isn't examined until after the mode routine has acted. The *currenttransform* might also be given a special value. METAFONT's *warningcheck* is temporarily disabled during these computations, since there might be more than 4096 pixels per inch. After **mode_setup** is finished, the *currentpicture* will be null, the *currenttransform* will take the *aspect_ratio* into account, and the *currentpen* will be a circular nib with the standard default thickness of 0.4 pt. (You should save this pen if you want to use it in a character, because **beginchar** will clear it away.)

Plain TₑX has a convention for magnifying fonts in terms of "magsteps," where magstep $m = 1.2^m$. A geometric progression of font sizes is convenient, because scaling by magstep m followed by magstep n is equivalent to scaling by magstep $m + n$.

```
vardef magstep primary m = mexp(46.67432m) enddef;
```

When a mode is defined (e.g., 'proof'), a numeric variable of that name is created and assigned a unique number (e.g., 1). Then an underscore character is appended, and a macro is defined for the resulting name (e.g., 'proof_'). The *mode_name* array is used to convert between number and name (e.g., $mode_name_1 = $ "proof_").

```
def mode_def suffix $ =
 $:=incr number_of_modes;
 mode_name[$]:=str$ & "_";
 expandafter quote def scantokens mode_name[$] enddef;
newinternal number_of_modes;
```

(This **mode_def** strategy was suggested by Bruce Leban.)

Three basic modes are now defined, starting with two for proofing:

```
% proof mode: for initial design of characters
mode_def proof =
 proofing:=2;              % yes, we're making full proofs
 fontmaking:=0;            % no, we're not making a font
 tracingtitles:=1;         % yes, show titles online
 pixels_per_inch:=2601.72; % that's 36 pixels per pt
 blacker:=0;               % no additional blackness
 fillin:=0;                % no compensation for fillin
 o_correction:=1;          % no reduction in overshoot
 enddef;
% smoke mode: for label-free proofs to mount on the wall
mode_def smoke =
 proof_;                   % same as proof mode, except:
 proofing:=1;              % yes, we're making unlabeled proofs
 extra_setup:=extra_setup&"grayfont black"; % with solid black pixels
 let makebox=maketicks;    % make the boxes less obtrusive
 enddef;
```

Notice that *smoke* mode saves a lot of fuss by calling on 'proof_'; this is the macro that was defined by the first **mode_def**.

A typical mode for font generation appears next.

```
% lowres mode: for certain devices that print 200 pixels per inch
mode_def lowres =
 proofing:=0;              % no, we're not making proofs
 fontmaking:=1;            % yes, we are making a font
```

```
tracingtitles:=0;          % no, don't show titles at all
pixels_per_inch:=200;      % that's pretty low resolution
blacker:=.65;              % make pens a bit blacker
fillin:=.2;                % compensate for diagonal fillin
o_correction:=.4;          % but don't overshoot as much
enddef;
localfont:=lowres;     % the mode most commonly used to make fonts
```

Installations of METAFONT typically have several more predefined modes, and they generally set *localfont* to something else. Such alterations should not be made in the master file `plain.mf`; they should appear in a separate file, as discussed below.

5. Drawing and filling. Now we come to the macros that provide an interface between the user on METAFONT's primitive picture commands. First, some important program variables are introduced:

```
pen currentpen;
path currentpen_path;
picture currentpicture;
transform currenttransform;
def t_ = transformed currenttransform enddef;
```

The key macros are **fill**, **draw**, **filldraw**, and **drawdot**.

```
def fill expr c = addto_currentpicture contour c.t_ enddef;
def addto_currentpicture = addto currentpicture enddef;
def draw expr p =
 addto_currentpicture doublepath p.t_ withpen currentpen enddef;
def filldraw expr c = fill counterclockwise c withpen currentpen enddef;
def drawdot expr z = if unknown currentpen_path: def_pen_path_ fi
 addto_currentpicture contour
   currentpen_path shifted (z.t_) withpen penspeck enddef;
def def_pen_path_ =
hide(currentpen_path=tensepath makepath currentpen) enddef;
```

And they have negative counterparts:

```
def unfill expr c = fill c withweight -1 enddef;
def undraw expr p = draw p withweight -1 enddef;
def unfilldraw expr c = filldraw c withweight -1 enddef;
def undrawdot expr z = drawdot z withweight -1 enddef;
def erase text t = begingroup interim default_wt_:=-1;
 cullit; t withweight -1; cullit; endgroup enddef;
newinternal default_wt_; default_wt_:=1;
```

It's more difficult to cut off the ends of a stroke, but the following macros (discussed near the end of Chapter 16) do the job:

```
def cutdraw expr p = % caution: you may need autorounding=0
 cutoff(point 0 of p, 180+angle direction 0 of p);
 cutoff(point infinity of p, angle direction infinity of p);
 draw p enddef;
```

```
vardef cutoff(expr z,theta) =
 interim autorounding := 0; interim smoothing := 0;
 addto pic_ doublepath z.t_ withpen currentpen;
 addto pic_ contour
   (cut_ scaled (1+max(pen_lft,pen_rt,pen_top,pen_bot))t_
    rotated theta shifted z);
 cull pic_ keeping (2,2) withweight -default_wt_;
 addto currentpicture also pic_;
 pic_:=nullpicture enddef;
picture pic_; pic_:=nullpicture;
path cut_; cut_ = ((0,-1)--(1,-1)--(1,1)--(0,1)--cycle) scaled 1.42;
```

The use of *default_wt_* here makes '**erase cutdraw**' work. The private variable *pic_* is usually kept equal to **nullpicture** in order to conserve memory space.

Picking up a pen not only sets *currentpen*, it also establishes the values of *pen_lft*, *pen_rt*, *pen_top*, and *pen_bot*, which are used by *lft*, *rt*, *top*, and *bot*.

```
def pickup secondary q =
 if numeric q: numeric_pickup_ else: pen_pickup_ fi q enddef;
def numeric_pickup_ primary q =
 if unknown pen_[q]: errmessage "Unknown pen"; clearpen
 else: currentpen:=pen_[q];
  pen_lft:=pen_lft_[q];
  pen_rt:=pen_rt_[q];
  pen_top:=pen_top_[q];
  pen_bot:=pen_bot_[q];
  currentpen_path:=pen_path_[q] fi; enddef;
def pen_pickup_ primary q =
  currentpen:=q yscaled aspect_ratio;
  pen_lft:=xpart penoffset down of currentpen;
  pen_rt:=xpart penoffset up of currentpen;
  pen_top:=(ypart penoffset left of currentpen)_o_;
  pen_bot:=(ypart penoffset right of currentpen)_o_;
  path currentpen_path; enddef;
newinternal pen_lft,pen_rt,pen_top,pen_bot,pen_count_;
```

And saving a pen saves all the relevant values for later retrieval.

```
vardef savepen = pen_[incr pen_count_]=currentpen;
 pen_lft_[pen_count_]=pen_lft;
 pen_rt_[pen_count_]=pen_rt;
 pen_top_[pen_count_]=pen_top;
 pen_bot_[pen_count_]=pen_bot;
 pen_path_[pen_count_]=currentpen_path;
 pen_count_ enddef;

def clearpen = currentpen:=nullpen;
 pen_lft:=pen_rt:=pen_top:=pen_bot:=0;
 path currentpen_path; enddef;
```

```
def clear_pen_memory =
 pen_count_:=0;
 numeric pen_lft_[],pen_rt_[],pen_top_[],pen_bot_[];
 pen currentpen,pen_[];
 path currentpen_path, pen_path_[];
 enddef;
```

The four basic pen-edge functions offer no surprises:

```
vardef lft primary x = x + if pair x: (pen_lft,0) else: pen_lft fi enddef;
vardef rt primary x = x + if pair x: (pen_rt,0) else: pen_rt fi enddef;
vardef top primary y = y + if pair y: (0,pen_top) else: pen_top fi enddef;
vardef bot primary y = y + if pair y: (0,pen_bot) else: pen_bot fi enddef;
```

There are six functions that round to good positions for pen placement.

```
vardef good.x primary x = hround(x+pen_lft)-pen_lft enddef;
vardef good.y primary y = vround(y+pen_top)-pen_top enddef;
vardef good.lft primary z = save z_; pair z_;
  (z_+(pen_lft,0))t_=round((z+(pen_lft,0))t_); z_ enddef;
vardef good.rt primary z = save z_; pair z_;
  (z_+(pen_rt,0))t_=round((z+(pen_rt,0))t_); z_ enddef;
vardef good.top primary z = save z_; pair z_;
  (z_+(pen_top,0))t_=round((z+(pen_top,0))t_); z_ enddef;
vardef good.bot primary z = save z_; pair z_;
  (z_+(pen_bot,0))t_=round((z+(pen_bot,0))t_); z_ enddef;
```

So much for fixed pens. When pen-like strokes are defined by outlines, the *penpos* macro is of primary importance. Since *penpos* may be used quite frequently, we might as well write out the x and y coordinates explicitly instead of using the (somewhat slower) z convention:

```
vardef penpos@#(expr b,d) =
 (x@#r-x@#l,y@#r-y@#l)=(b,0) rotated d;
 x@#=.5(x@#l+x@#r); y@#=.5(y@#l+y@#r) enddef;
```

Simulated pen strokes are provided by the convenient **penstroke** command.

```
def penstroke text t =
 forsuffixes e = l,r: path_.e:=t; endfor
 if cycle path_.l: cyclestroke_
 else: fill path_.l -- reverse path_.r -- cycle fi enddef;
def cyclestroke_ =
 begingroup interim turningcheck:=0;
 addto pic_ contour path_.l.t_ withweight 1;
 addto pic_ contour path_.r.t_ withweight -1;
 cull pic_ dropping origin withweight default_wt_;
 addto_currentpicture also pic_;
 pic_:=nullpicture endgroup enddef;
path path_.l,path_.r;
```

6. Proof labels and rules. The next main section of `plain.mf` is devoted to macros for the annotations on proofsheets. These macros are discussed in Appendix H, and they use the **special** and **numspecial** commands discussed in Appendix G.

Labels are generated at the lowest level by **makelabel**:

```
vardef makelabel@#(expr s,z) =                    % puts string s at point z
 if known z: special lcode_@# & s;
  numspecial xpart(z.t_); numspecial ypart(z.t_) fi enddef;
string lcode_,lcode_.top,lcode_.lft,lcode_.rt,lcode_.bot,
  lcode_.top.nodot,lcode_.lft.nodot,lcode_.rt.nodot,lcode_.bot.nodot;
lcode_.top=" 1"; lcode_.lft=" 2"; lcode_.rt=" 3"; lcode_.bot=" 4";
lcode_=" 0"; % change to " /" to avoid listing in overflow column
lcode_.top.nodot=" 5"; lcode_.lft.nodot=" 6";
lcode_.rt.nodot=" 7"; lcode_.bot.nodot=" 8";
```

Users generally don't invoke **makelabel** directly, because there's a convenient shorthand. For example, '**labels**$(1, 2, 3)$' expands into '**makelabel**$("1", z_1)$; **makelabel**$("2", z_2)$; **makelabel**$("3", z_3)$'. (But nothing happens if *proofing* ≤ 1.)

```
vardef labels@#(text t) =
 if proofing>1: forsuffixes $=t: makelabel@#(str$,z$); endfor fi enddef;
vardef penlabels@#(text t) =
 if proofing>1: forsuffixes $$=l,,r: forsuffixes $=t:
  makelabel@#(str$.$$,z$.$$); endfor endfor fi enddef;
```

When there are lots of purely numeric labels, you can say, e.g.,

labels$(1,$ **range** 5 **thru** $9,$ **range** 100 **thru** $124, 223)$

which is equivalent to '**labels**$(1, 5, 6, 7, 8, 9, 100, 101, \ldots, 124, 223)$'. Labels are omitted from the proofsheets if the corresponding z value isn't known, so it doesn't hurt (much) to include unused subscript numbers in a range.

```
def range expr x = numtok[x] enddef;
def numtok suffix x=x enddef;
tertiarydef m thru n =
 m for x=m+1 step 1 until n: , numtok[x] endfor enddef;
```

(This **range** abbreviation will work in any **forsuffixes** list; and in a '**for**' list you can even omit the word '**range**'. But you might fill up METAFONT's main memory if too many values are involved.)

A straight line will be drawn on the proofsheet by **proofrule**. Although **makelabel** takes the current transform into account, **proofrule** does not. There's also a corresponding routine '**screenrule**' that puts a straight line in the current picture, so that design guidelines will be visible on your screen:

```
def proofrule(expr w,z) =
 special "rule"; numspecial xpart w; numspecial ypart w;
 numspecial xpart z; numspecial ypart z enddef;
def screenrule(expr w,z) =
 addto currentpicture doublepath w--z withpen rulepen enddef;
pen rulepen; rulepen = pensquare scaled 2;
```

(The *rulepen* is two pixels wide, because screen rules are usually drawn exactly over raster lines. A two-pixel-wide pen straddles the pixel edges so that you can "see" the correct line position. If a two-pixel-wide line proves to be too dark, you can redefine *rulepen* to be simply **pensquare**; then METAFONT will draw the thinnest possible screen rule, but it will be a half-pixel too high and a half-pixel too far to the right.)

You can produce lots of proof rules with **makegrid**, which connects an arbitrary list of x coordinates with an arbitrary list of y coordinates:

```
def makegrid(text xlist,ylist) =
 xmin_ := min(xlist); xmax_ := max(xlist);
 ymin_ := min(ylist); ymax_ := max(ylist);
 for x=xlist: proofrule((x,ymin_), (x,ymax_)); endfor
 for y=ylist: proofrule((xmin_,y), (xmax_,y)); endfor
 enddef;
```

Finally we have a few macros that allow further communication with the hardcopy proof-drawing routine of Appendix H. You can change the fonts, the thickness of proof rules, and the position of the image on its page.

```
vardef titlefont suffix $ = special "titlefont "&str$ enddef;
vardef labelfont suffix $ = special "labelfont "&str$ enddef;
vardef grayfont suffix $ = special "grayfont "&str$ enddef;
vardef slantfont suffix $ = special "slantfont "&str$ enddef;
def proofoffset primary z =   % shift proof output by z
 special "offset"; numspecial xpart z; numspecial ypart z enddef;
vardef proofrulethickness expr x =
 special "rulethickness"; numspecial x enddef;
```

7. Character and font administration. After this elaborate preparation, we're finally ready to consider the **beginchar** . . . **endchar** framework for the individual characters of a font. Each **beginchar** begins a group, which should end at the next **endchar**. Then **beginchar** stores the given character code and device-independent box dimensions in METAFONT's internal variables *charcode*, *charwd*, *charht*, and *chardp*. Then it computes the device-dependent box dimensions w, h, and d. Finally it clears the z variables, the current picture, and the current pen.

```
def beginchar(expr c,w_sharp,h_sharp,d_sharp) =
 begingroup
 charcode:=if known c: byte c else: 0 fi;
 charwd:=w_sharp;      charht:=h_sharp;       chardp:=d_sharp;
 w:=hround(charwd*hppp); h:=vround(charht*hppp); d:=vround(chardp*hppp);
 charic:=0; clearxy; clearit; clearpen; scantokens extra_beginchar;
 enddef;
```

The italic correction is normally zero, unless the user gives an '**italcorr**' command; even then, the correction stays zero unless the given value is positive:

```
def italcorr expr x_sharp = if x_sharp>0: charic:=x_sharp fi enddef;
```

When we want to change the pixel width w from even to odd or vice versa, the **change_width** macro does the right thing.

```
def change_width =
 w:=w if w>charwd*hppp:- else:+ fi 1 enddef;
```

(The user might also decide to change w in some other way.) The current value of w at the time of **endchar** will be the "official" pixel width of the character, *chardx*, that is shipped to the **gf** output file.

```
def endchar =
 scantokens extra_endchar;
 if proofing>0: makebox(proofrule); fi
 chardx:=w;    % desired width of the character in pixels
 shipit;
 if displaying>0: makebox(screenrule); showit; fi
 endgroup enddef;
```

Extensions to these routines can be provided by putting commands in the string variables *extra_beginchar* and *extra_endchar*.

```
string extra_beginchar, extra_endchar;
extra_beginchar=extra_endchar="";
```

A "bounding box" that surrounds the character according to the specifications given in **beginchar** is produced by **makebox**, which takes into account the possibility that pixels might not be square. An extra line is drawn to mark the width of the character with its italic correction included, if this correction is nonzero.

```
def makebox(text r) =
 for y=0,h.o_,-d.o_: r((0,y),(w,y)); endfor % horizontals
 for x=0,w:   r((x,-d.o_),(x,h.o_)); endfor % verticals
 if charic<>0: r((w+charic*hppp,h.o_),(w+charic*hppp,.5h.o_));
 enddef;
```

The **maketicks** routine is an alternative to **makebox** that draws less conspicuous lines. This makes it easier to visualize a character's appearance near the edges of its bounding box.

```
def maketicks(text r) =
 for y=0,h.o_,-d.o_: r((0,y),(10,y)); r((w-10,y),(w,y)); endfor
 for x=0,w: r((x,10-d.o_),(x,-d.o_)); r((x,h.o_-10),(x,h.o_)); endfor
 if charic<>0: r((w+charic*hppp,h.o_-10),(w+charic*hppp,h.o_)); fi
 enddef;
```

Overall information about the font as a whole is generally supplied by the following commands, which are explained in Appendix F.

```
def font_size expr x = designsize:=x enddef;
def font_slant expr x = fontdimen 1: x enddef;
def font_normal_space expr x = fontdimen 2: x enddef;
def font_normal_stretch expr x = fontdimen 3: x enddef;
def font_normal_shrink expr x = fontdimen 4: x enddef;
```

```
def font_x_height expr x = fontdimen 5: x enddef;
def font_quad expr x = fontdimen 6: x enddef;
def font_extra_space expr x = fontdimen 7: x enddef;

def font_identifier expr x = font_identifier_:=x enddef;
def font_coding_scheme expr x = font_coding_scheme_:=x enddef;
string font_identifier_, font_coding_scheme_;
font_identifier_=font_coding_scheme_="UNSPECIFIED";
```

8. The endgame. What have we left out? A few miscellaneous things still need to be handled. First, we almost forgot to define the *z* convention for points:

```
vardef z@#=(x@#,y@#) enddef;
```

Then we need to do something rudimentary about METAFONT's "windows."

```
newinternal screen_rows, screen_cols, currentwindow;
screen_rows:=400;      % these values should be corrected,
screen_cols:=500;      % by reading in a separate file after plain.mf
def openit = openwindow currentwindow
 from origin to (screen_rows,screen_cols) at (-50,300) enddef;
def showit = openit; let showit=showit_; showit enddef; % first time only
def showit_ = display currentpicture inwindow currentwindow enddef;
```

Plain METAFONT has several other terse commands like 'openit' and 'showit':

```
def clearxy = save x,y enddef;
def clearit = currentpicture:=nullpicture enddef;
def shipit = shipout currentpicture enddef;
def cullit = cull currentpicture dropping (-infinity,0) enddef;
```

The next several macros are handy things to put on your command line when you are starting a METAFONT job (i.e., just before 'input ⟨font file name⟩'):

- **screenchars**. Say this when you're making a font but want the characters to be displayed just before they are shipped out.
- **screenstrokes**. Say this when you're in *proof* mode and want to see each stroke as it's added to the current picture.
- **imagerules**. Say this when you want to include the bounding box in the current character, before you begin to draw it.
- **gfcorners**. Say this when you expect to make proofsheets with large pixels, from a low-resolution font.
- **nodisplays**. Say this to save computer time when you don't want *proof* mode to display each character automatically.
- **notransforms**. Say this to save computer time when you know that the current transform is the identity.

```
def screenchars =      % endchar should 'showit'
 extra_endchar:=extra_endchar&"showit;" enddef;

def screenstrokes =    % every stroke should 'showit'
 def addto_currentpicture text t=
  addto currentpicture t; showit enddef; enddef;
```

```
def imagerules =       % a box should be part of the character image
 extra_beginchar:=extra_beginchar & "makebox(screenrule);" enddef;
def gfcorners =        % 'maketicks' should send rules to the gf file
 extra_setup:=extra_setup & "let makebox=maketicks;proofing:=1;" enddef;
def nodisplays =       % endchar shouldn't 'showit'
 extra_setup:=extra_setup & "displaying:=0;" enddef;
def notransforms =     % currenttransform should not be used
 let t_ = \ enddef;
```

We make 'bye' synonymous with 'end', just in case TeX users expect META-
FONT programs to end like TeX documents do.

```
let bye = end; outer end,bye;
```

And finally, we provide the default environment that a user gets when simple
experiments like those at the beginning of Chapter 5 are desired.

```
clear_pen_memory;    % initialize the 'savepen' mechanism
mode_setup;          % establish proof mode as the default
numeric mode,mag;    % but leave mode and mag undefined
```

Whew! That's the end of the `plain.mf` file.

9. Adapting to local conditions. In order to make plain METAFONT programs interchangeable between different computers, everybody should use the same `plain.mf` base.
But there are some things that clearly should be customized at each installation:

- Additional modes should be defined, so that fonts can be made for whatever
  output devices are of interest.
- The proper *localfont* mode should be established.
- The correct numbers should be assigned to *screen_rows* and *screen_cols*.

Here's an example of a supplementary file 'local.mf' that would be appropriate for
a computer center with the hypothetical *cheapo* and *luxo* printers described in Chapter 11. We assume that *cheapo* mode is to be identical to *lowres* mode, except that
the *cheapo* fonts should be generated with a *negative* value of *fillin* (because *cheapo*
tends to make diagonal lines lighter than normal, not heavier). The terminal screens
are assumed to be 768 pixels wide and 512 pixels high.

```
% A file to be loaded after "plain.mf".
base_version:=base_version&"/drofnats";

screen_rows:=512; screen_cols:=768;

mode_def cheapo =      % cheapo mode: to generate fonts for cheapo
 lowres_;              % do as in lowres mode, except:
 fillin:=-.1;          % compensate for lighter diagonals
 enddef;

mode_def luxo =        % luxo mode: to generate fonts for luxo
 proofing:=0;          % no, we're not making proofs
 fontmaking:=1;        % yes, we are making a font
 tracingtitles:=1;     % yes, show titles online
 pixels_per_inch:=2000; % almost 30 pixels per pt
```

```
blacker:=.2;              % make pens a teeny bit blacker
fillin:=.1;               % but compensate for heavy diagonals
o_correction:=1;          % and keep the full overshoot
enddef;
localfont:=cheapo;
```

The macro '**bye**' might also be redefined, as suggested at the close of Appendix F.

To prepare a preloaded base file at this installation, a suitably privileged person should run INIMF in the following way:

```
This is METAFONT, Version 2.0 (INIMF)  8 NOV 1989 10:09
**plain
(plain.mf
Preloading the plain base, version 2.0)
*input local
(local.mf)
*dump
Beginning to dump on file plain.base
```

(The stuff after '**' or '*' is typed by the user; everything else is typed by the system. A few more messages actually come out.)

Notice that `local.mf` does not include any new macros or features that a programmer could use in a special way. Therefore it doesn't make plain METAFONT incompatible with implementations at other computing centers.

Changes and/or extensions to the `plain.mf` macros should never be made, unless the resulting base file is clearly distinguished from the standard plain base. But new, differently named bases are welcome. For example, the author prepared a special base for the Computer Modern fonts, so that they could be generated without first reading the same 700 lines of macro definitions each time. To load this base at high speed, he can type '**&cm**' after METAFONT's initial '******'. (Or, on some machines, he has a special version called '**cmmf**' in which the new base is already present.)

None but the Base, in baseness doth delight.
— MICHAEL DRAYTON, *Robert, Duke of Normandy* (1605)

So far all was plain sailing, as the saying is;
but Mr. Till knew that his main difficulties were yet to come.
— FRANCIS E. PAGET, *Milford Malvoisin* (1842)

C
Character
Codes

Different computers tend to have different ways of representing the characters in files of text, but METAFONT gives the same results on all machines, because it converts everything to a standard internal code when it reads a file. METAFONT also converts back from its internal representation to the appropriate external code, when it writes a file of text; therefore most users need not be aware of the fact that the codes have actually switched back and forth inside the machine.

The purpose of this appendix is to define METAFONT's internal code, which has the same characteristics on all implementations of METAFONT. The existence of such a code is important, because it makes METAFONT programs portable. METAFONT's scheme is based on the American Standard Code for Information Interchange, known popularly as "ASCII." There are 128 codes, numbered 0 to 127; we conventionally express the numbers in octal notation, from oct"000" to oct"177", or in hexadecimal notation, from hex"00" to hex"7F". Thus, the value of ASCII"b" is normally called oct"142" or hex"62", not 98. In the ASCII scheme, codes oct"000" through oct"037" and code oct"177" are assigned to special functions; for example, code oct"007" is called BEL, and it means "Ring the bell." The other 95 codes are assigned to visible symbols and to the blank space character. Here is a chart that shows ASCII codes in such a way that octal and hexadecimal equivalents can easily be read off:

	´0	´1	´2	´3	´4	´5	´6	´7	
´00x	NUL	SOH	STX	ETX	EOT	ENQ	ACK	BEL	˝0x
´01x	BS	HT	LF	VT	FF	CR	SO	SI	
´02x	DLE	DC1	DC2	DC3	DC4	NAK	SYN	ETB	˝1x
´03x	CAN	EM	SUB	ESC	FS	GS	RS	US	
´04x		!	"	#	$	%	&	'	˝2x
´05x	(	)	*	+	,	-	.	/	
´06x	0	1	2	3	4	5	6	7	˝3x
´07x	8	9	:	;	<	=	>	?	
´10x	@	A	B	C	D	E	F	G	˝4x
´11x	H	I	J	K	L	M	N	O	
´12x	P	Q	R	S	T	U	V	W	˝5x
´13x	X	Y	Z	[	\	]	^	_	
´14x	`	a	b	c	d	e	f	g	˝6x
´15x	h	i	j	k	l	m	n	o	
´16x	p	q	r	s	t	u	v	w	˝7x
´17x	x	y	z	{	|	}	~	DEL	
	˝8	˝9	˝A	˝B	˝C	˝D	˝E	˝F	

Ever since ASCII was established in the early 1960s, people have had different ideas about what to do with positions oct"000" thru oct"037" and oct"177", because most of the functions assigned to those codes are appropriate only for special purposes like file transmission, not for applications to printing or to interactive computing. Manufacturers soon started producing line printers that were capable of generating 128 characters, 33 of which were tailored to the special needs of particular customers; part of the advantage of a standard code was therefore lost. An extended ASCII code intended for text editing and interactive computing was developed at several universities about 1965, and for many years there have been terminals in use at Stanford, MIT, Carnegie-Mellon, and elsewhere that have 120 or 121 symbols, not just 95. For example, the author developed METAFONT on a keyboard that includes the symbols '≠', '≤', '≥', and '←', which are easier to use than the character pairs '<>', '<=', '>=', and ':='. The full character set looks like this:

	'0	'1	'2	'3	'4	'5	'6	'7	
'00x	·	↓	α	β	∧	¬	∈	π	"0x
'01x	λ	γ	δ	↑	±	⊕	∞	∂	
'02x	⊂	⊃	∩	∪	∀	∃	⊗	↔	"1x
'03x	←	→	≠	◇	≤	≥	≡	∨	
'04x		!	"	#	$	%	&	'	"2x
'05x	(	)	*	+	,	−	.	/	
'06x	0	1	2	3	4	5	6	7	"3x
'07x	8	9	:	;	<	=	>	?	
'10x	@	A	B	C	D	E	F	G	"4x
'11x	H	I	J	K	L	M	N	O	
'12x	P	Q	R	S	T	U	V	W	"5x
'13x	X	Y	Z	[	\	]	^	_	
'14x	`	a	b	c	d	e	f	g	"6x
'15x	h	i	j	k	l	m	n	o	
'16x	p	q	r	s	t	u	v	w	"7x
'17x	x	y	z	{	|	}	~	∫	
	"8	"9	"A	"B	"C	"D	"E	"F	

METAFONT can also be configured to accept any or all of the character codes 128–255. However, METAFONT programs that make use of anything in addition to the 95 standard ASCII characters cannot be expected to run on other systems, so the use of extended character sets is discouraged.

A possible middle ground has been suggested, based on the fact that it's easy to write a program that converts extended-character files into standard files by substituting '<>' for '≠', etc. In the author's implementation at Stanford, the symbols '≠', '≤', '≥', and '←' are considered to be in the same class as '<', '=', ':', and '>' when tokens are formed (see Chapter 6). Tokens like '≠=' and '<≥' are therefore distinct, although they both become '<>=' after conversion. As long as such tokens are avoided, the author's programs can easily be expurgated into a portable form for general distribution. (Another feasible approach would have been to convert nonstandard codes to character pairs during METAFONT's input process; that would have been slightly less efficient.)

Computers with non-ASCII character sets should specify a correspondence between 95 distinct characters and the standard ASCII codes oct"040" thru oct"176". METAFONT programs written on any such machines will be completely interchangeable with each other.

If any shall suggest, that some of the Enquiries here insisted upon
(as particularly those about the Letters of the Alphabet)
do seem too minute and trivial, for any prudent Man
to bestow his serious thoughts and time about.
Such Persons may know, that the discovery
of the true nature and Cause of any the most minute thing,
doth promote real Knowledge,
and therefore cannot be unfit for any Mans endeauours,
who is willing to contribute to the advancement of Learning.
— JOHN WILKINS, *Towards a Real Character* (1668)

Clearly even the simple A.B.C. is a thing of mystery.
Like all codes, it should not be trifled with,
but it is to be feared that in modern times
it has not always been respected.
— STANLEY MORISON, *On Type Faces* (1923)

D

Dirty Tricks

Any powerful computer language can be used in ways that go considerably beyond what the language designer originally had in mind, especially when macro expansion is possible. Sometimes the unexpected constructions are just amusing; sometimes they are disgustingly arcane. But sometimes they turn out to be quite useful, and they graduate from "tricks" to the status of "techniques." (For example, several of the macros now in Appendix B started out as suggestions for Appendix D.) In any case, gurus of a language always like to explore its limits. The depths of METAFONT have hardly been plumbed, but this appendix probably reached a new low at the time it was written.

Acknowledgment: More than half of the ideas in this appendix are due to John Hobby, who has been a tireless and inspiring co-worker during the entire development of the new METAFONT system.

Please don't read this material until you've had plenty of experience with plain METAFONT. After you have read and understood the secrets below, you'll know all sorts of devious combinations of METAFONT commands, and you will often be tempted to write inscrutable macros. Always remember, however, that there's usually a simpler and better way to do something than the first way that pops into your head. You may not have to resort to any subterfuge at all, since METAFONT is able to do lots of things in a straightforward way. Try for simple solutions first.

1. Macro madness. If you need to write complicated macros, you'll need to be familiar with the fine points in Chapter 20. METAFONT's symbolic tokens are divided into two main categories, "expandable" and "unexpandable"; the former category includes all macros and **if** ... **fi** tests and **for** ... **endfor** loops, as well as special operations like **input**, while the latter category includes the primitive operators and commands listed in Chapters 25 and 26. The expansion of expandable tokens takes place in METAFONT's "mouth," but primitive statements (including equations, declarations, and the various types of commands) are done in METAFONT's "stomach." There's a communication between the two, since the stomach evaluates expressions that are needed as arguments to the mouth's macros; any statement can be embedded in a group expression, so arbitrarily complicated things can be done as part of the expansion process.

Let's begin by considering a toy problem that is treated at the beginning of Appendix D in *The TEXbook*, in case some readers are interested in comparing TEX to METAFONT. Given a numeric variable $n \geq 0$, we wish to define a macro **asts** whose replacement text consists of precisely n asterisks. This task is somewhat tricky because expansion is suppressed when a replacement text is being read; we want to use a **for** loop, but loops are special cases of expansion. In other words,

```
def asts = for x=1 upto n: * endfor enddef
```

defines **asts** to be a macro with a **for** loop in its replacement text; in practice, **asts** would behave as if it contained n asterisks (using possibly different values of n), but we have not solved the stated problem. The alternative

```
def makedef primary n =
  def asts = for x=1 upto n: * endfor enddef enddef;
makedef n
```

"freezes" the present value of n; but this doesn't solve the problem either.

One solution is to build up the definition by adding one asterisk at a time, using **expandafter** as follows:

```
def asts = enddef;
for x=1 upto n:
 expandafter def expandafter asts expandafter = asts * enddef;
endfor.
```

The three expandafters provide a "finger" into the replacement text, before **def** suppresses expansion; without them the replacement text would turn out to be 'asts *', causing infinite recursion.

This solution involves a running time proportional to n^2, so the reader might wonder why a simpler approach like

```
expandafter def expandafter asts expandafter =
  for x = 1 upto n: * endfor enddef
```

wasn't suggested? The reason is that this doesn't work, unless $n = 0$! A **for** loop isn't entirely expanded by expandafter, only METAFONT's first step in loop expansion is carried out. Namely, the loop text is read, and a special inaccessible token 'ENDFOR' is placed at its end. Later on when METAFONT's mouth encounters 'ENDFOR' (which incidentally is an expandable token, but it wasn't listed in Chapter 20), the loop text is re-inserted into the input stream, unless of course the loop has finished. The special ENDFOR is an 'outer' token, hence it should not appear in replacement texts; META-FONT will therefore stop with a "forbidden token" error if you try the above with $n \geq 1$. You might try to defeat the outerness by saying

```
for x=1: inner endfor;
```

but METAFONT won't let you. And even if this had worked, it wouldn't have have solved the problem; it would simply have put ENDFOR into the replacement text of ast, because expansion is inhibited when the replacement text is being read.

There's another way to solve the problem that seems to have running time proportional to n rather than n^2:

```
scantokens("def asts=" for x=1 upto n: & "* " endfor) enddef;
```

but actually METAFONT's string concatenation operation takes time proportional to the length of the strings it deals with, so the running time is still order n^2. Furthermore, the string operations in METAFONT are rather primitive, because this isn't a major aspect of the language; so it turns out that this approach uses order n^2 storage cells in the string pool, although they are recycled later. Even if the pool size were infinite, METAFONT's "buffer size" would be exceeded for large n, because **scantokens** puts the string into the input buffer before scanning it.

Is there a solution of order n? Yes, of course. For example,

```
def a=a* enddef;
for x=0 upto n:
 if x=n: def a=quote quote def asts = enddef; fi
 expandafter endfor a enddef;
showtoken asts.
```

(The first 'quote' is removed by the **for**, hence one will survive until a is redefined. If you don't understand this program, try running it with $n = 3$; insert an isolated expression '0;' just before the 'if', and look at the lines of context that are shown when METAFONT gives you four error messages.) The only flaw in this method is that it uses up n cells of stack space; METAFONT's input stack size may have to be increased, if n is bigger than 25 or so.

The asterisk problem is just a puzzle; let's turn now to a genuine application. Suppose we want to define a macro called '*ten*' whose replacement text is the contents of the parameter file `logo10.mf` in Chapter 11, up to but *not* including the last two lines of that file. Those last two lines say

```
input logo        % now generate the font
end               % and stop.
```

The *ten* macro will make it possible to set up the 10-point parameters repeatedly (perhaps alternating with 9-point parameters in a *nine* macro); Appendix E explains how to create a meta-design tool via such macros.

One idea would be to try to input the entire file `logo10.mf` as the replacement text for *ten*. We could nullify the effect of the last three unwanted tokens by saying

```
save input,logo,end;
forsuffixes s=input,logo,end: let s=\; endfor
```

just before *ten* is used. To get the entire file as a replacement text, we can try one of the approaches that worked in the asterisk problem, say

```
expandafter def expandafter ten expandafter = input logo10 enddef.
```

But this first attempt runs awry if we haven't already redefined '**end**'; Appendix B makes '**end**' an '**outer**' token, preventing its appearance in replacement texts. So we say '**inner end**' and try again, only to discover an unwritten law that somehow never came up in Chapters 20 or 26:

```
Runaway definition?
font_size10pt#;ht#:=6pt#;xgap#:=0.6pt#;u#:=4/9pt#;s#:=0;o#:=1/ ETC.
! File ended while scanning the definition of ten.
<inserted text>
                    enddef
1.2 ...fter ten expandafter = input logo10
                                                enddef;
```

The end of a file is invisible; but it's treated like an '**outer**' token, in the sense that a file should never end when METAFONT is passing rapidly over text.

Therefore this whole approach is doomed to failure. We'll have to find a way to stop the replacement text before the file ends. OK, we'll redefine '**input**' so that it means '**enddef**', and redefine *logo* so that it means '**endinput**'.

```
let INPUT = input; let input = enddef; let logo = endinput;
expandafter def expandafter ten expandafter = INPUT logo10;
showtoken ten.
```

It works! By the way, the line with three expandafters can be replaced by a more elegant construction that uses **scantokens** as follows:

```
scantokens "def ten=" INPUT logo10;
```

This does the job because METAFONT always looks ahead and expands the token immediately following an expression that is being evaluated. (The expression in this case is the string `"def ten="`, which is an argument to **scantokens**. The token that immediately follows an expression almost always needs to be examined in order to be sure that the expression has ended, so METAFONT always examines it.) Curiously, the **expandafter** alternative causes *ten*'s replacement text to begin with the tokens '`font_size10pt#;ht#:=...`', while the **scantokens** way makes it start with '`designsize:=(10);ht#:=...`'. Do you see why? In the second case, expansion continued until an unexpandable token ('`designsize`') was found, so the `font_size` macro was changed into its replacement text; but **expandafter** just expanded '`INPUT`'.

Now let's make the problem a bit harder. Suppose we know that '`input`' comes at the end of where we want to read, but we don't know that '`logo`' will follow. We know that some program file name will be there, but it might not be for the logo font. Furthermore, let's assume that '`end`' might not be present; therefore we can't simply redefine it to be **enddef**. In this case we can make '`input`' into a right delimiter, and read the file as a *delimited text argument*; that will give us enough time to insert other tokens, which will terminate the input and flush the unwanted file name. But the construction is more complex:

```
let INPUT = input; delimiters begintext input;
def makedef(expr name)(text t) =
  expandafter def scantokens name = t enddef;
  endinput flushfilename enddef;
def flushfilename suffix s = enddef;
makedef("ten") expandafter begintext INPUT logo10;
showtoken ten.
```

This example merits careful study, perhaps with '**tracingall**' to show exactly how METAFONT proceeds. We have assumed that the unknown file name can be parsed as a suffix; this solves the problem that a file cannot end inside of a **text** parameter or a false condition. (If we knew that '**end**' were present, we could have replaced '`endinput flushfilename`' by '`if false:`' and redefined '`end`' to be '`fi`'.)

Let's turn now to a simpler problem. METAFONT allows you to consider the '`and`' of two Boolean expressions, but it always evaluates both expressions. This is problematical in situations like

```
if pair x and (x>(0,0)): A else: B fi
```

because the expression '`x>(0,0)`' will stop with an error message unless x is of type **pair**. The obvious way to avoid this error,

```
if pair x:  if x>(0,0): A else: B fi  else: B fi
```

is cumbersome and requires B to appear twice. What we want is a "conditional and" operation in which the second Boolean expression is evaluated only if the first one turns out to be true; then we can safely write

```
if pair x cand (x>(0,0)): A else: B fi.
```

Similarly we might want "conditional or" in which the second operand is evaluated only if the first is false, for situations like

```
if unknown x cor (x<0): A else: B fi.
```

Such `cand` and `cor` macros can be defined as follows:

```
def cand(text q) = startif true q else: false fi enddef;
def cor(text q) = startif true true else: q fi enddef;
tertiarydef p startif true = if p: enddef;
```

the text arguments are now evaluated only when necessary. We have essentially replaced the original line by

```
if if pair x: x<(0,0) else: false fi: A else: B fi.
```

This construction has one catch; namely, the right-hand operands of `cand` and `cor` must be explicitly enclosed in delimiters. But delimiters are only a minor nuisance, because the operands to 'and' and 'or' usually need them anyway. It would be impossible to make `cand` and `cor` obey the normal expression hierarchy; when macros make primary/secondary/tertiary distinctions, they evaluate their arguments, and such evaluation is precisely what `cand` and `cor` want to avoid.

If these `cand` and `cor` macros were changed so that they took *undelimited* text arguments, the text argument wouldn't stop at a colon. We could, however, use such modified macros with group delimiters instead. For example, after

```
let {{ = begingroup; let }} = endgroup;
def cand text q = startif true q else: false fi enddef
```

we could write things like

```
if {{pair x cand x>(0,0)}}: A else: B fi.
```

(Not that this buys us anything; it just illustrates a property of undelimited text arguments.) Group delimiters are not valid delimiters of *delimited* text arguments.

Speaking of group delimiters, the gratuitous **begingroup** and **endgroup** tokens added by **vardef** are usually helpful, but they can be a nuisance. For example, suppose we want to write a `zz` macro such that '`zz1..zz2..zz3`' expands into

```
z1{dz1}..z2{dz2}..z3{dz3}
```

It would be trivial to do this with **def**:

```
def zz suffix $ = z${dz$} enddef;
```

but this makes `zz` a "spark." Let's suppose that we want to use **vardef**, so that `zz` will be usable in suffixes of variable names. Additional **begingroup** and **endgroup** delimiters will mess up the syntax for paths, so we need to get rid of them. Here's one way to finesse the problem:

```
vardef zz@# =
  endgroup gobbled true z@#{dz@#} gobble begingroup enddef.
```

The **gobbled** and **gobble** functions of Appendix B will remove the vacuous expressions '**begingroup endgroup**' at the beginning and end of the replacement text.

(The initial **begingroup endgroup** won't be gobbled if the vardef is being read as a primary instead of as a secondary, tertiary, or expression. But in such cases you probably don't mind having **begingroup** present.)

2. Fortuituous loops. The 'max' and 'min' macros in Appendix B make use of the fact that commas are like ')(' in argument lists. Although the definition heading is

```
def max(expr x)(text t)
```

we can write 'max(a, b, c)' and this makes $x = a$ and $t = $ 'b, c'. Of course, a person isn't supposed to say 'max(a)(b)(c)'.

Here are two more applications of the idea: We want 'inorder(a, b, c)' to be true if and only if $a \leq b \leq c$; and we want '**equally_spaced**(x_1, x_2, x_3) dx' to produce the equations '$x_2 - x_1 = x_3 - x_2 = dx$'.

```
def inorder(expr x)(text t) =
  ((x for u=t: <= u)
   and (u endfor gobbled true true)) enddef;
def equally_spaced(expr x)(text t) expr dx =
  x for u=t: - u = u endfor gobbled true
  - dx enddef.
```

Isn't this fun? (Look closely.)

There is a problem, however, if we try to use these macros with loops in the arguments. Consider the expressions

```
inorder(for n=1 upto 10: a[n], endfor infinity),
inorder(a[1] for n=2 upto 10: ,a[n] endfor),
inorder(a[1],a[2] for n=3 upto 10: ,a[n] endfor);
```

the first two give error messages, but the third one works! The reason is that, in the first two cases, the **for** loop begins to be expanded before METAFONT begins to read the text argument, hence ENDFOR rears its ugly head again. We can avoid this problem by rewriting the macros in a more complicated way that doesn't try to single out the first argument x:

```
def inorder(text t) =
  expandafter startinorder for u=t:
   <= u endgroup and begingroup u endfor
  gobbled true true endgroup) enddef;
def startinorder text t =
  (begingroup true enddef;
def equally_spaced(text t) expr dx =
  if pair dx: (whatever,whatever) else: whatever fi
  for u=t: - u = u endfor gobbled true
  - dx enddef;
```

Two separate tricks have been used here: (1) The '**endgroup**' within 'inorder' will stop an undelimited text argument; this gets rid of the unwanted '<= u' at the beginning. (2) A throwaway variable, '*whatever*', nullifes an unwanted equation at the beginning of '**equally_spaced**'. With the new definitions, all three of the expressions above will be understood, and so will things like

```
equally_spaced(for n=1 upto 10: x[n], endfor whatever) dx.
```

Furthermore the single-argument cases now work: 'inorder(a)' will always be true, and '**equally_spaced**(x) dx' will produce no new equations.

If we want to improve max and min in the same way, so that a person can specify loop arguments like

```
max(a[1] for n=2 upto 10: ,a[n] endfor)
```

and so that 'max(a) $= a$' in the case of a single argument, we have to work harder, because max and min treat their first argument in quite a special way; they need to apply the special macro *setu_*, which defines the type of the auxiliary variable u_-. The fastest way to solve this problem is probably to use a token whose meaning changes during the first time through the loop:

```
vardef max(text t) =
 let switch_ = firstset_;
 for u=t: switch_ u>u_: u_ := u ;fi endfor
 u_ enddef;
vardef min(text t) =
 let switch_ = firstset_;
 for u=t: switch_ u<u_: u_ := u ;fi endfor
 u_ enddef;
def firstset_ primary u =
 setu_ u; let switch_ = if; if false: enddef.
```

Incidentally, the author's first programs for max and min contained an interesting bug. They started with '**save** u_-', and they tried to recognize the first time through the loop by testing if u_- was unknown. This failed because u_- could be constantly unknown in well-defined cases like max($x, x + 1, x + 2$).

3. Types. Our programs for **inorder**, **equally_spaced**, and **max** are careful not to make unnecessary assumptions about the type of an expression. The 'round' and 'byte' functions in Appendix B are further examples of macros that change behavior based on the types of their **expr** arguments. Let's look more closely at applications of type testing.

When the author was developing macros for plain METAFONT, his first "correct" solution for **max** had the following form:

```
vardef max(text t) =
 save u_; boolean u_;
 for u=t: if boolean u_: setu_ u
   elseif u_<u: u_ := u fi; endfor
 u_ enddef.
```

This was interesting because it showed that there was no need to set u_- to true or false; the simple fact that it was boolean was enough to indicate the first time through the loop. (A slightly different *setu_* macro was used at that time.)

We might want to generalize the 'scaled' operation of METAFONT so that 'scaled (x, y)' is shorthand for 'xscaled x yscaled y'. That's pretty easy:

```
let SCALED = scaled;
def scaled primary z =
 if pair z: xscaled xpart z yscaled ypart z
 else: SCALED z fi enddef;
```

It's better to keep the primitive operation '**SCALED** z' here than to replace it by the slower variant '**xscaled z yscaled z**'.

METAFONT allows you to compare booleans, numerics, pairs, strings, and transforms for equality; but it doesn't allow the expression '$p = q$' where p and q are paths or pens or pictures. Let's write a general equality test macro such that '$p == q$' will be true if and only if p and q are known and equal, whatever their type.

```
tertiarydef p == q =
 if unknown p or unknown q: false
 elseif boolean p and boolean q: p=q
 elseif numeric p and numeric q: p=q
 elseif pair p and pair q: p=q
 elseif string p and string q: p=q
 elseif transform p and transform q: p=q
 elseif path p and path q:
  if (cycle p = cycle q) and (length p = length q)
   and (point 0 of p = point 0 of q): patheq p of q
  else: false fi
 elseif pen p and pen q: (makepath p == makepath q)
 elseif picture p and picture q: piceq p of q
 elseif vacuous p and vacuous q: true
 else: false fi enddef;
vardef vacuous primary p =
 not(boolean p or numeric p or pair p or path p
  or pen p or picture p or string p or transform p) enddef;
vardef patheq expr p of q =
 save t; boolean t; t=true;
 for k=1 upto length p:
  t := (postcontrol k-1 of p = postcontrol k-1 of q)
   and (precontrol k of p = precontrol k of q)
   and (point k of p = point k of q);
  exitunless t; endfor
 t enddef;
vardef piceq expr p of q =
 save t; picture t;
 t=p; addto t also -q;
 cull t dropping origin;
 (totalweight t=0) enddef;
```

If p and q are numeric or pair expressions, we could relax the condition that they both be known by saying 'if known $p - q$: $p = q$ else false fi'; transforms could be handled similarly by testing each of their six parts. But there's no way to tell if booleans, paths, etc., have been equated when they're both unknown, without the risk of irrevocably changing the values of other variables.

4. Nonlinear equations. METAFONT has a built-in solution mechanism for linear equations, but it balks at nonlinear ones. You might be able to solve a set of nonlinear equations yourself by means of algebra or calculus, but in difficult cases it is probably simplest to use the '*solve*' macro of plain METAFONT. This makes it possible to solve n equations in n unknowns, provided that at most one of the equations is nonlinear when one of the unknowns is fixed.

The general technique will be illustrated here in the case $n = 3$. Let us try to find numbers a, b, and c such that

$$-2a + 3b/c = c - 3;$$
$$ac + 2b = c^3 - 20;$$
$$a^3 + b^3 = c^2.$$

When c is fixed, the first two equations are linear in a and b. We make an inequality out of the remaining equation by changing '$=$' to '$<$', then we embed the system in a boolean-valued function:

```
vardef f(expr c) = save a,b;
 -2a + 3b/c = c - 3;
 a*c + 2b = c*c*c - 20;
 a*a*a + b*b*b < c*c enddef;
c = solve f(1,7);
-2a + 3b/c = c - 3;
a*c + 2b = c*c*c - 20;
show a, b, c.
```

If we set *tolerance* = *epsilon* (which is the minimum value that avoids infinite looping in the *solve* routine), the values $a = 1$, $b = 2$, and $c = 3$ are shown (so it is obvious that the example was rigged). If *tolerance* has its default value 0.1, we get $a = 1.05061$, $b = 2.1279$, $c = 3.01563$; this would probably be close enough for practical purposes, assuming that the numbers represent pixels. (Increasing the tolerance saves time because it decreases the number of iterations within *solve*; you have to balance time versus necessary accuracy.)

The only tricky thing about this use of solve was the choice of the numbers 1 and 7 in '$f(1,7)$'. In typical applications we'll usually have obvious values of the unknown where f will be true and false, but a bit of experimentation was necessary for the problem considered here. In fact, it turns out that $f(-3)$ is true and $f(-1)$ is false, in this particular system; setting $c = $ *solve* $f(-3,-1)$ leads to another solution: $a = 7.51442$, $b = -7.48274$, $c = -2.3097$. Furthermore, it's interesting to observe that this system has no solution with c between -1 and $+1$, even though $f(+1)$ is true and $f(-1)$ is false! When $c \to 0$, the quantity $a^3 + b^3$ approaches $-\infty$ when c is negative, $+\infty$ when c is positive. An attempt to '*solve* $f(1,-1)$' will divide by zero and come up with several arithmetic overflows.

Let's consider now a real application instead of a contrived example. We wish to find the vertices of a parallelogram z_{1l}, z_{1r}, z_{0l}, z_{0r}, such that

$$x_{1l} = a; \quad y_{1r} = b; \quad z_{0r} = (c,d);$$
$$\text{length}(z_{1r} - z_{1l}) = \text{length}(z_{0r} - z_{0l}) = stem,$$

and such that the lines z_{1r} -- z_{1l} and z_{1r} -- z_{0r} meet at a given angle *phi*. We can consider the common angle θ of $z_{1r} - z_{1l}$ and $z_{0r} - z_{0l}$ to be the "nonlinear" unknown, so the equations to be solved can be written

$$penpos_1(stem, \theta); \quad penpos_0(stem, \theta);$$
$$x_{1l} = a; \quad y_{1r} = b; \quad z_{0r} = (c,d);$$
$$\text{angle}(z_{1r} - z_{0r}) = \theta + \phi.$$

When θ has a given value, all but the last of these equations are linear; hence we can solve them by turning the crank in our general method:

```
vardef f(expr theta) = save x,y;
 penpos1(stem,theta); penpos0(stem,theta);
 x1l=a; y1r=b; z0r=(c,d);
 angle(z1r-z0r)<theta+phi enddef;
theta=solve f(90,0);
penpos1(stem,theta); penpos0(stem,theta);
x1l=a; y1r=b; z0r=(c,d);
show z1l,z1r,z0l,z0r,theta,angle(z1r-z0r).
```

For example, if $a = 1$, $b = 28$, $c = 14$, $d = 19$, *stem* $= 5$, and $\phi = 80$, we get

$$(1, 23.703) \quad (3.557, 28) \quad (11.443, 14.703) \quad (1\overset{?}{4}, 19) \quad 59.25 \quad 139.25$$

as answers when *tolerance* $=$ *epsilon*, and

$$(1, 23.702) \quad (3.554, 28) \quad (11.446, 14.702) \quad (14, 19) \quad 59.28 \quad 139.25$$

when *tolerance* $= 0.1$. The function f prescribed by the general method can often be simplified; for example, in this case we can remove redundancies and get just

```
vardef f(expr theta) = save x,y;
 penpos1(stem,theta); x1l=a; y1r=b;
 angle(z1r-(c,d))<theta+phi enddef.
```

The problem just solved can be called the "d problem," because it arose in connection with N. N. Billawala's meta-design of a black-letter '𝖉', and because it appears in Appendix D.

5. Nonlinear interpolation. Suppose a designer has empirically determined good values of some quantity $f(x)$ for several values of x; for example, $f(x)$ might be a stroke weight or a serif length or an amount of overshoot, etc. These empirical values can be generalized and incorporated into a meta-design if we are able to interpolate between the original x's, obtaining $f(x)$ at intermediate points.

Suppose the data points are known for $x = x_1 < x_2 < \cdots < x_n$. We can represent $f(x)$ by its graph, which we can assume is well approximated by the META-FONT path defined by

$$F = (x_1, f(x_1)) \ldots (x_2, f(x_2)) \ldots \langle \text{etc.} \rangle \ldots (x_n, f(x_n))$$

if $f(x)$ is a reasonable function. Therefore interpolation can be done by using path intersection (!):

```
vardef interpolate expr F of x = save t; t =
 if x < xpart point 0 of F: extrap_error 0
 elseif x > xpart point infinity of F: extrap_error infinity
 else: xpart(F intersectiontimes verticalline x) fi;
 ypart point t of F enddef;
def extrap_error = hide(errhelp "The extreme value will be used.";
 errmessage "'interpolate' has been asked to extrapolate";
 errhelp "") enddef;
vardef verticalline primary x =
 (x,-infinity)--(x,infinity) enddef;
```

For example, if $f(1) = 1$, $f(3) = 2$, and $f(15) = 4$, this interpolation scheme gives 'interpolate $(1, 1) \mathbin{..} (3, 2) \mathbin{..} (15, 4)$ of 7' the value 3.37.

6. *Drawing with overlays.* Let's leave numerical computations now and go back into the realm of pictures. Bruce Leban has suggested an extension of plain METAFONT's '**clearit**/**showit**/**shipit**' commands by which '**fill**' and '**draw**' essentially operate on imaginary sheets of clear plastic. A new command '**keepit**' places a fresh sheet of plastic on top of whatever has already been drawn, thereby preserving the covered image against subsequent erasures.

We can implement **keepit** by introducing a new picture variable *totalpicture*, and new boolean variables *totalnull*, *currentnull*, then defining macros as follows:

```
def clearit = currentpicture:=totalpicture:=nullpicture;
 currentnull:=totalnull:=true; enddef;
def keepit = cull currentpicture keeping (1,infinity);
 addto totalpicture also currentpicture;
 currentpicture:=nullpicture;
 totalnull:=currentnull; currentnull:=true; enddef;
def addto_currentpicture =
 currentnull:=false; addto currentpicture enddef;
def mergeit (text do) =
 if totalnull: do currentpicture
 elseif currentnull: do totalpicture
 else: begingroup save v; picture v; v:=currentpicture;
  cull v keeping (1,infinity); addto v also totalpicture;
  do v endgroup fi enddef;
def shipit = mergeit(shipout) enddef;
def showit_ = mergeit(show_) enddef;
def show_ suffix v = display v inwindow currentwindow enddef;
```

The *totalnull* and *currentnull* bookkeeping isn't strictly necessary, but it contributes greatly to the efficiency of this scheme if the extra generality of **keepit** is not actually being used. The '*v*' computations in **mergeit** involve copying the accumulated picture before displaying it or shipping it out; this takes time, and it almost doubles the amount of memory needed, so we try to avoid it when possible.

7. *Filing pictures.* If you want to store a picture in a file and read it in to some other METAFONT job, you face two problems: (1) METAFONT's **shipout** command implicitly culls the picture, so that only binary data is left. Pixel values > 0 are distinguished from pixel values ≤ 0, but no other information about those values will survive. (2) The result of **shipout** can be used in another METAFONT job only if you have an auxiliary program that converts from binary **gf** format to a METAFONT source program; METAFONT can write **gf** files, but it can't read them.

These problems can be resolved by using METAFONT's transcript or log file as the output medium, instead of using the **gf** file. For example, let's consider first the use of *tracingedges*. Suppose we say

> *tracingedges* := 1;
> ⟨any sequence of **fill**, **draw**, or **filldraw** commands⟩
> **message** "Tracing edges completed."; *tracingedges* := 0;

then the log file will contain lines such as the following:

```
Tracing edges at line 15: (weight 1)
(1,5)(1,2)(2,2)(2,1)(3,1)(3,0)(8,0)(8,1)(9,1)(9,2)(10,2)(10,8)(9,8)
(9,9)(8,9)(8,10)(3,10)(3,9)(2,9)(2,8)(1,8)(1,5).
Tracing edges at line 15: (weight -1)
(3,5)(3,2)(4,2)(4,1)(7,1)(7,2)(8,2)(8,8)(7,8)(7,9)(4,9)(4,8)(3,8)(3,5).
Tracing edges at line 18: (weight -1)
(No new edges added.)
Tracing edges completed.
```

Let us write macros so that these lines are acceptable input to METAFONT.

```
def Tracing=begingroup save :,[,],Tracing,edges,at,weight,w;
 delimiters []; let Tracing = endfill; interim turningcheck := 0;
 vardef at@#(expr wt) = save (,); w := wt;
 let ( = lp; let ) = rp; fill[gobble begingroup enddef;
 let edges = \; let weight = \; let : = \; enddef;
def lp = [ enddef;
def rp = ] -- enddef;
vardef No@# = origin enddef;
def endfill = cycle] withweight w endgroup; enddef;
def completed = endgroup; enddef;
```

The precise form of edge-traced output, with its limited vocabulary and its restricted use of parentheses and commas, has been exploited here.

With slight changes to this code, you can get weird effects. For example, if the definition of **rp** is changed to ']..tension 4..', , and if 'scaled 5pt' is inserted before 'withweight', the image will be an "almost digitized" character:

(The bumps at the left here are due to the repeated points '(1,5)' and '(3,5)' in the original data. You can remove them by adding an extra pass, first tracing the edges that are output by the *unmodified* Tracing macros.)

Although the effects of **fill** and **draw** can be captured by *tracingedges*, other operations like culling are not traced. Let us therefore consider the more general picture representation that METAFONT produces when *tracingoutput* is positive, or when you ask it to **show** a picture (see Chapter 13). The macros on the next page will recreate a picture from input of the form

```
beginpicture
row 1: 1+ -2- | 0+ 2-
row 0: | 0+ 2++ 5---
row -2: 0- -2+ |
endpicture
```

where the middle three lines have been copied verbatim from a transcript file. (The task would be easier if the token '-' didn't have to perform two different functions!)

```
let neg_ = -; let colon_ = :;
def beginpicture =
 begingroup save row, |, :, ---, --, +, ++, +++, v, xx, yy, done;
 picture v; v := nullpicture; interim turningcheck := 0;
 let --- = mmm_; let -- = mm_;
 let + = p_; let ++ = pp_; let +++ = ppp_;
 let row = pic_row; let | = relax; let : = pic_colon; : enddef;
def pic_row primary y = done; yy := y; enddef;
def pic_colon primary x =
 if known x colon_ ; xx := x; pic_edge fi enddef;
def pic_edge =
 let - = m_;
 addto v contour unitsquare xscaled xx shifted(0,yy) enddef;
def mmm_ = withweight 3; let - = neg_; : enddef;
def mm_ = withweight 2; let - = neg_; : enddef;
def m_ = withweight 1; let - = neg_; : enddef;
def p_ = withweight neg_1; let - = neg_; : enddef;
def pp_ = withweight neg_2; let - = neg_; : enddef;
def ppp_ = withweight neg_3; let - = neg_; : enddef;
transform xy_swap; xy_swap = identity rotated 90 xscaled -1;
def endpicture = done;
 v transformed xy_swap transformed xy_swap endgroup enddef;
```

The reader will find it instructive to study these macros closely. When 'done' appears, it is an unknown primary, so pic_colon will not attempt to generate another edge. Each new edge also inserts a cancelling edge at $x = 0$. The two applications of xy_swap at the end will clear away all redundant edges. (Double swapping is a bit faster than the operation 'rotated-90 rotated 90' that was used for this purpose in Chapter 13.)

8. Fattening a pen. Let's move on to another aspect of METAFONT by considering an operation on pen polygons: Given a **pen** value p, the task is to construct a pen '**taller** p' that is one pixel taller. For example, if p is the diamond nib '$(0.5, 0)$ -- $(0, 0.5)$ -- $(-0.5, 0)$ -- $(0, -0.5)$ -- cycle', the taller nib will be

$$(0.5, 0.5) \text{ -- } (0, 1) \text{ -- } (-0.5, 0.5) \text{ -- } (-0.5, -0.5) \text{ -- } (0, -1) \text{ -- } (0.5, -0.5) \text{ -- cycle};$$

if p is a tilted penrazor '$(-x, -y)$ -- (x, y) -- cycle', the taller nib will be

$$(-x, -y - 0.5) \text{ -- } (x, y - 0.5) \text{ -- } (x, y + 0.5) \text{ -- } (-x, -y + 0.5) \text{ -- cycle},$$

assuming that $x > 0$. The macro itself turns out to be fairly simple, but it makes instructive use of path and pen operations.

We want to split the pen into two parts, a "bottom" half and a "top" half; the bottom half should be shifted down by .5 pixels, and the top half should be shifted up. The dividing points between halves occur at the leftmost and rightmost vertices of the pen. Hmmm; a potential problem arises if there are two or more leftmost or rightmost points; for example, what if we try to make '**taller taller** p'? Fortunately METAFONT doesn't mind if a pen polygon has three or more consecutive vertices that lie on a line, hence we can safely choose *any* leftmost point and any rightmost point.

The next question is, "How should we find leftmost and rightmost points?" We will, of course, use **makepath** to find the set of all vertices; so we could simply traverse the path and find the minimum and maximum x coordinates. However, it will be faster (and more fun) to use either directiontime or penoffset for this purpose. Let's try directiontime first:

```
vardef taller primary p =
  save r, n, t, T; path r;
  r = tensepath makepath p; n = length r;
  t = round directiontime up of r;
  T = round directiontime down of r;
  if t>T: t := t-n; fi
  makepen(subpath(T-n,t) of r shifted .5down
    --subpath(t,T) of r shifted .5up -- cycle) enddef;
```

The result of **makepath** has control points equal to their adjacent vertices, so it could not be used with **directiontime**. (If any key point is equal to its precontrol or postcontrol, the "velocity" of the path is zero at that point; **directiontime** assumes that all directions occur whenever the velocity drops to zero.) Therefore we have used 'tensepath'. This almost works, once we realize that the values of t and T sometimes need to be rounded to integers. But it fails for pens like **penspeck** that have points very close together, since **tensepath** is no better than an unadulterated **makepath** in such cases. Furthermore, even if we could define a nice path from p (for example by scaling it up), we would run into problems of numerical instability, in cases like **penrazor** where the pen polygon takes a 180° turn. Razor-thin pens cannot be recognized easily, because they might have more than two vertices; for example, rotations of future pens such as '**makepen**(*left* .. *origin* .. *right* .. *cycle*)' are problematical.

We can obtain a more robust result by using penoffset, because this operation makes use of the convexity of the polygon. The "fastest" solution looks like this:

```
vardef taller primary p =
  save q, r, n, t, T; pen q; q = p;
  path r; r = makepath q; n = length r;
  t = round xpart(r intersectiontimes penoffset up of q);
  T = round xpart(r intersectiontimes penoffset down of q);
  if t>T: t := t-n; fi
  makepen(subpath(T-n,t) of r shifted .5down
    --subpath(t,T) of r shifted .5up -- cycle) enddef;
```

(The argument p is copied into q, in case it's a future pen; this means that the conversion of future pen to pen need be done only once instead of three times.)

9. Bernshteĭn polynomials. And now, for our last trick, let's try to extend METAFONT's syntax so that it will accept generalized mediation formulas of the form '$t[u_1,\ldots,u_n]$' for all $n \geq 2$. (This notation was introduced for $n = 3$ and 4 in Chapter 14, when we were considering fractional subpaths.) If $n > 2$, the identity

$$t[u_1,\ldots,u_n] = t[t[u_1,\ldots,u_{n_1}], t[u_2,\ldots,u_n]]$$

defines $t[u_1,\ldots,u_n]$ recursively, and it can be shown that the alternative definition

$$t[u_1,\ldots,u_n] = t[t[u_1,u_2],\ldots,t[u_{n-1},u_n]]$$

gives the same result. (Indeed, we have

$$t[u_1, \ldots, u_n] \;=\; \sum_{k=1}^{n} \binom{n-1}{k-1} (1-t)^{n-k} t^{k-1} u_k,$$

a Bernstein polynomial of order $n - 1$.)

Our problem is to change the meaning of METAFONT's brackets so that expressions like '$1/2[a, b, c, d]$' will evaluate to '$.125a + .375b + .375c + .125d$' in accordance with the formulas just given, but we don't want to mess up the other primitive uses of brackets in contexts like '`x[n]`' and '`path p[][]a`'. We also want to be able to use brackets inside of brackets.

The reader is challenged to try solving this problem before looking at the weird solution that follows. Perhaps there is a simpler way?

```
let [[[ = [; let ]]] = ]; let [ = lbrack;
def lbrack = hide(delimiters []) lookahead [ enddef;
def lookahead(text t) =
 hide(let [ = lbrack;
   for u=t, hide(n_ := 0; let switch_ = first_): switch_ u; endfor)
 if n_<3: [[[t]]] else: Bernshtein n_ fi enddef;
def first_ primary u =
   if numeric u: numeric u_[[[]]]; store_ u
   elseif pair u: pair u_[[[]]]; store_ u fi;
   let switch_ = store_ enddef;
def store_ primary u = u_[[[incr n_]]] := u enddef;
primarydef t Bernshtein nn =
 begingroup for n=nn downto 2:
   for k=1 upto n-1: u_[[[k]]]:=t[[[u_[[[k]]],u_[[[k+1]]] ]]];
   endfor endfor u_[[[1]]] endgroup enddef;
```

The most subtle thing about this code is the way it uses the 'empty' option of a ⟨for list⟩ to dispense with empty text arguments. Since METAFONT evaluates all the expressions of a **for** loop before reading the loop text, and since '`n_`' and '`u_`' are used here only when no recursion is taking place, it is unnecessary to save their values even when brackets are nested inside of brackets.

Of course this trick slows METAFONT down tremendously, whenever brackets appear, so it is just of academic interest. But it seems to work in all cases except with respect to formulas that involve '`]]`' (two consecutive brackets); the latter token, which plain METAFONT expands to '`] ]`', is not expanded when `lookahead` reads its text argument, hence the user must remember to insert a space between consecutive brackets.

> *Their tricks an' craft hae put me daft,*
> *They've taen me in, an' a' that.*
> — ROBERT BURNS, *The Jolly Beggar* (1799)

> *Ebery house hab him dutty carner.*
> — ANDERSON and CUNDALL, *Jamaica Proverbs and Sayings* (1927)

E

Examples

We've seen lots of examples of individual letters or parts of letters; let's concentrate now on the problem of getting things all together. The next two pages contain the entire contents of an example file 'logo.mf', which generates the letters of the METAFONT logo. The file is short, because only seven letters are involved, and because those letters were intentionally done in a style that would be easy for the system they name. But the file is complete, and it illustrates in simplified form all the essential aspects of larger fonts: Ad hoc dimensions are converted to pixels; subroutines are defined; programs for individual letters appear; intercharacter and interword spacing conventions are nailed down. Furthermore, the character programs are careful to draw letters that will be well adapted to the raster, even if pixels on the output device are not square.

We've been studying the 'METAFONT' letters off and on since Chapter 4, making our examples slightly more complex as more of the language has been encountered. Finally we're ready to pull out all the stops and look at the real, professional-quality logo.mf, which incorporates all the best suggestions that have appeared in the text and in answers to the exercises.

It's easy to generate a font with logo.mf, by proceeding as explained in Chapter 11. For example, the logo10 font that produces 'METAFONT' in 10-point size can be created for a low-resolution printer by running METAFONT with the command line

```
\mode=lowres; input logo10
```

where the parameter file logo10.mf appears in that chapter. Furthermore the slanted version '*METAFONT*' can be created by inputting the parameter file logosl10.mf, which says simply

```
% 10-point slanted METAFONT logo
slant := 1/4;
input logo10
```

The *slant* parameter affects *currenttransform* as explained in Chapter 15.

There isn't a great deal of "meta-ness" in the logo.mf design, because only a few forms of the METAFONT logo are needed. However, some interesting variations are possible; for example, if we use the parameter files

```
font_size 30pt#;          font_size 10pt#;
ht#:=25pt#;               ht#:=6pt#;
xgap#:=1.5pt#;            xgap#:=2pt#;
u#:=3/9pt#;               u#:=4/3pt#;
s#:=1/3pt#;               s#:=-2/3pt#;
o#:=2/9pt#;               o#:=1/9pt#;
px#:=1pt#;                px#:=1/3pt#;
slant:=-1/9;
```

we get METAFONT and METAFONT, respectively.

```
% Routines for the METAFONT logo, as found in The METAFONTbook
% (logo10.mf is a typical parameter file)

mode_setup;
if unknown slant: slant:=0 else: currenttransform:=
  identity slanted slant yscaled aspect_ratio fi;
```

```
ygap#:=(ht#/13.5u#)*xgap#;          % vertical adjustment
ho#:=o#;                            % horizontal overshoot
leftstemloc#:=2.5u#+s#;             % position of left stem
barheight#:=.45ht#;                 % height of bar lines
py#:=.9px#;                         % vertical pen thickness
```

```
define_pixels(s,u);
define_whole_pixels(xgap);
define_whole_vertical_pixels(ygap);
define_blacker_pixels(px,py);
pickup pencircle xscaled px yscaled py;
logo_pen:=savepen;
define_good_x_pixels(leftstemloc);
define_good_y_pixels(barheight);
define_corrected_pixels(o);
define_horizontal_corrected_pixels(ho);
```

```
def beginlogochar(expr code, unit_width) =
  beginchar(code,unit_width*u#+2s#,ht#,0);
  pickup logo_pen enddef;
```

```
def super_half(suffix i,j,k) =
  draw z.i{0,y.j-y.i}
  ... (.8[x.j,x.i],.8[y.i,y.j]){z.j-z.i}
  ... z.j{x.k-x.i,0}
  ... (.8[x.j,x.k],.8[y.k,y.j]){z.k-z.j}
  ... z.k{0,y.k-y.j} enddef;
```

```
beginlogochar("M",18);
x1=x2=leftstemloc; x4=x5=w-x1; x3=w-x3;
y1=y5; y2=y4; bot y1=-o;
top y2=h+o; y3=y1+ygap;
draw z1--z2--z3--z4--z5;
labels(1,2,3,4,5); endchar;
```

```
beginlogochar("E",14);
x1=x2=x3=leftstemloc;
x4=x6=w-x1+ho; x5=x4-xgap;
y1=y6; y2=y5; y3=y4;
bot y1=0; top y3=h; y2=barheight;
```

```
draw z6--z1--z3--z4; draw z2--z5;
labels(1,2,3,4,5,6); endchar;

beginlogochar("T",13);
italcorr ht#*slant + .5u#;
if .5w<>good.x .5w: change_width; fi
lft x1=-eps; x2=w-x1; x3=x4=.5w;
y1=y2=y3; top y1=h; bot y4=-o;
draw z1--z2; draw z3--z4;
labels(1,2,3,4); endchar;

beginlogochar("A",15);
x1=.5w; x2=x4=leftstemloc; x3=x5=w-x2;
top y1=h+o; y2=y3=barheight;
bot y4=bot y5=-o;
draw z4--z2--z3--z5; super_half(2,1,3);
labels(1,2,3,4,5); endchar;

beginlogochar("F",14);
x1=x2=x3=leftstemloc;
x4=w-x1+ho; x5=x4-xgap;
y2=y5; y3=y4; bot y1=-o;
top y3=h; y2=barheight;
draw z1--z3--z4; draw z2--z5;
labels(1,2,3,4,5); endchar;

beginlogochar("O",15);
x1=x4=.5w; top y1=h+o; bot y4=-o;
x2=w-x3=good.x(1.5u+s); y2=y3=barheight;
super_half(2,1,3); super_half(2,4,3);
labels(1,2,3,4); endchar;

beginlogochar("N",15);
x1=x2=leftstemloc; x3=x4=x5=w-x1;
bot y1=bot y4=-o;
top y2=top y5=h+o; y3=y4+ygap;
draw z1--z2--z3; draw z4--z5;
labels(1,2,3,4,5); endchar;

ligtable "T": "A" kern -.5u#;
ligtable "F": "O" kern -u#;

font_quad:=18u#+2s#;
font_normal_space:=6u#+2s#;
font_normal_stretch:=3u#;
font_normal_shrink:=2u#;
font_identifier:="MFLOGO" if slant<>0: & "SL" fi;
font_coding_scheme:="AEFMNOT only";
```

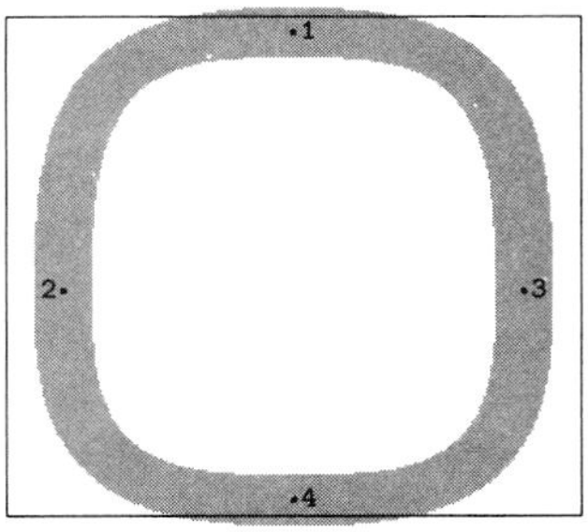

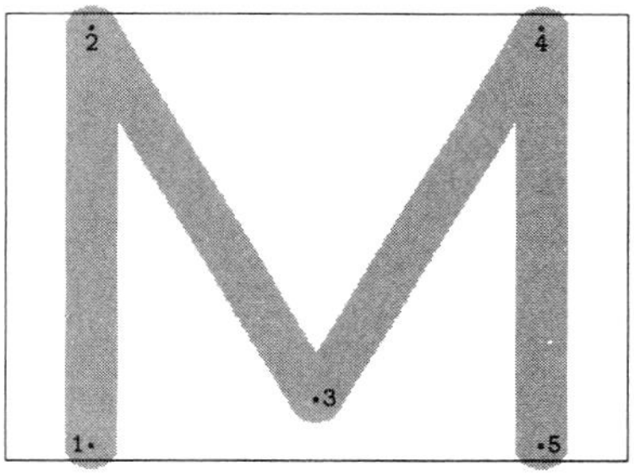

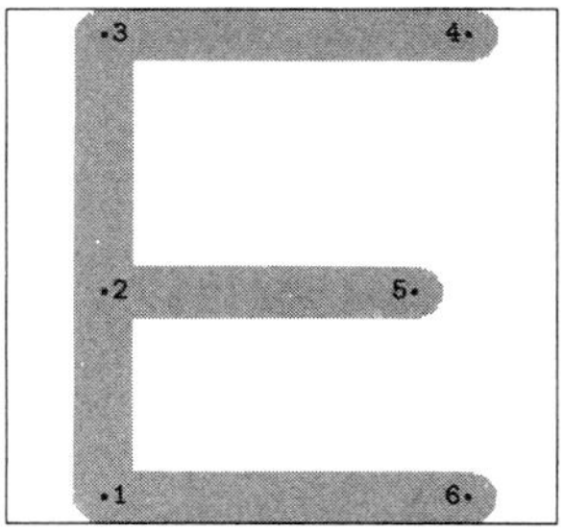

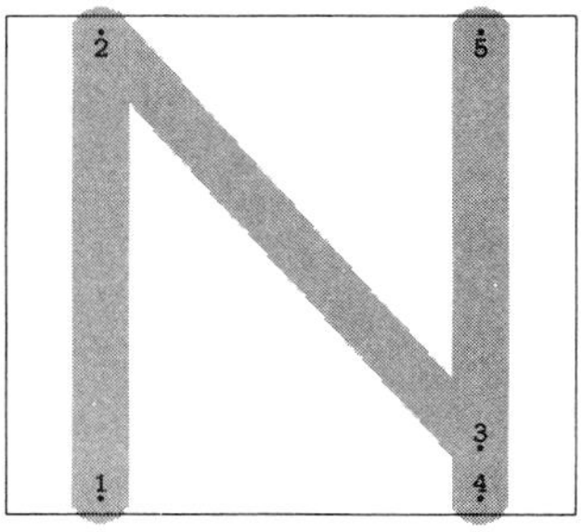

Everything in `logo.mf` has already been explained previously in this book except for the very last two lines, which define a '**font_identifier**' and a '**font_coding_scheme**'. These are optional bits of information that are discussed in Appendix F. Furthermore an italic correction has been specified for the letter 'T', since it's the final letter of '*METAFONT*'.

The program for a complete typeface will differ from the program for this simple logo font primarily in degree; there will be lots more parameters, lots more subroutines, lots more characters, lots more ligatures and kerns and whatnot. But there will probably also be more administrative machinery, designed to facilitate the creation, testing, and modification of characters, since a large enterprise requires good organization. The remainder of this appendix is devoted to an example of how this might be done: We shall discuss the additional kinds of routines that the author found helpful while he was developing the Computer Modern family of typefaces.

The complete, unexpurgated programs for Computer Modern appear in *Computers & Typesetting*, Volume E; but since they have evolved over a long period of time, they are rather complex. We shall simplify the details so that it will be easier to grasp the important issues without being distracted by irrelevant technicalities.

The simple logo fonts discussed above are generated by two types of files: There are parameter files like `logo10.mf`, and there is a program file `logo.mf`. The Computer Modern fonts, being more extensive, are generated by four types of files: There are *parameter files* like '`cmr10.mf`', which specify the ad hoc dimensions for particular sizes and styles of type; there are *driver files* like '`roman.mf`', which serve as chief executives of the font-generation process; there are *program files* like '`punct.mf`', which contain programs for individual characters; and there's a *base file* called '`cmbase.mf`', which contains the subroutines and other macros used throughout the system.

Our logo example could have been cast in this more general mold by moving the character programs into a program file '`METAFON.mf`', and by moving most of the opening material into a base file '`logobase.mf`' that looks like this:

```
% Base file for the METAFONT logo
logobase:=1;            % when logobase is known, this file has been input
\smallskip
def font_setup =
 if unknown slant: slant:=0 else: currenttransform:=
    ⋮    (the previous code is unchanged)
 define_corrected_pixels(o);
 define_horizontal_corrected_pixels(ho); enddef;
```

followed by the definitions of `beginlogochar` and `super_half`. Then we're left with a driver file `logo.mf` that looks like this:

```
% Driver file for the METAFONT logo
if unknown logobase: input logobase fi

mode_setup; font_setup;                  % establish pixel-oriented units
input METAFON                            % generate the characters

ligtable "T": "A" kern -.5u#;
```

and so on, concluding as before.

In general, a parameter file calls on a driver file, which calls on one or more program files; the base file contains predefined macros shared by all. There may be several driver files, each using a different combination of program files; for example, Computer Modern has 'roman.mf' and 'italic.mf', both of which call on punct.mf to generate punctuation marks, although they use different program files to generate the lowercase alphabets. Characters are partitioned into program files so that they can be shared by different drivers.

Parameter files in Computer Modern don't quite follow the conventions of logo10.mf. Here, for example, are the opening and closing lines of cmr10.mf:

```
% Computer Modern Roman 10 point
if unknown cmbase: input cmbase fi

font_identifier "CMR"; font_size 10pt#;

u#:=20/36pt#;                    % unit width
serif_fit:=0pt#;                 % extra sidebar near serifs
letter_fit:=0pt#;                % extra space added to all sidebars
   ⋮
serifs:=true;                    % should serifs and bulbs be attached?
monospace:=false;                % should all characters have the same width?

generate roman                   % switch to the driver file
```

The main differences are: (1) There's special code at the beginning, to make sure that cmbase.mf has been loaded. The base file includes several things that are needed right away; for example, **cmbase** declares the variables '*serifs*' and '*monospace*' to be of type **boolean**, so that boolean-valued parameter assignments like '*serifs* := **true**' will be legal. (2) The **font_identifier** is defined in the parameter file, not in the driver file. (3) The last line says '**generate**' instead of '**input**'; the base file defines **generate** to be the same as **input**, but other meanings are assigned by utility routines that we'll study later. (4) The final '**end**' is no longer present in the parameter file.

The roman.mf driver looks like this (vastly simplified):

```
% The Computer Modern Roman family of fonts
mode_setup; font_setup;

input romanu;                    % upper case (majuscules)
input romanl;                    % lower case (minuscules)
input romand;                    % numerals
input punct;                     % punctuation marks

font_slant slant;
if monospace: font_quad 18u#;
 font_normal_space 9u#;          % no stretching or shrinking
else: font_quad 18u#+4letter_fit#;
 font_normal_space 6u#+2letter_fit#;  % interword spacing
 font_normal_stretch 3u#;        % with ''glue''
 font_normal_shrink 2u#;
 input romlig;                   % f ligatures
 ligtable "f": "i" =: oct"014", "f" =: oct"013", "l" =: oct"015",
          "'" kern u#, "?" kern u#, "!" kern u#;
```

```
ligtable oct"013": "i" =: oct"016", "l" =: oct"016",      % ffi and ffl
           "'" kern u#, "?" kern u#, "!" kern u#;
ligtable "-": "-" =: oct"173";                            % en dash
ligtable oct"173": "-" =: oct"174";                       % em dash
ligtable "`": "`" =: oct"134";                            % open quotes
ligtable "'": "'" =: oct"042",                            % close quotes
           "?" kern 2u#, "!" kern 2u#;
fi; bye.
```

In a monospaced font like `cmtt10`, all characters will be exactly $9u\#$ wide. Both `cmr10` and `cmtt10` use the `roman` driver, but `roman` omits the ligatures and changes the interword spacing when it is producing monospaced fonts.

The program files of Computer Modern have slightly different conventions from those of plain METAFONT. Here, for example, are the programs for two of the simplest punctuation marks:

```
cmchar "Period";
numeric dot_diam#; dot_diam# = if monospace: 5/4 fi dot_size#;
define_whole_blacker_pixels(dot_diam);
beginchar(".",5u#,dot_diam#,0);
adjust_fit(0,0); pickup fine.nib;
pos1(dot_diam,0); pos2(dot_diam,90);
x1l=good.x(x1l+.5w-x1); bot y2l=0; z1=z2; dot(1,2);        % dot
penlabels(1,2); endchar;
```

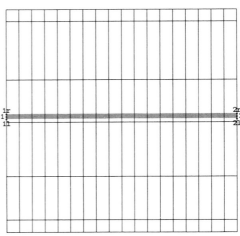

```
iff not monospace: cmchar "Em dash";
beginchar(oct"174",18u#,x_height#,0);
italcorr .61803x_height#*slant + .5u#;
adjust_fit(letter_fit#,letter_fit#);
pickup crisp.nib; pos1(vair,90); pos2(vair,90);
y1r=y2r=good.y(y1r+.61803h-y1); lft x1=-eps; rt x2=w+eps;
filldraw stroke z1e--z2e;                                 % crossbar
penlabels(1,2); endchar;
```

The new structural features in these programs are: (1) '**cmchar**', which appears at the very beginning of each character program; (2) '**iff** ⟨boolean expression⟩:', which precedes **cmchar** if the character is to be generated only when the boolean expression is true; (3) '**adjust_fit**', which can change the amount of white space at the character's left and/or right; (4) pens called '*fine.nib*' and '*crisp.nib*'; (5) new macros '*pos*', '*dot*', and '*stroke*', discussed further below.

The base file `cmbase.mf` begins as follows:

```
% The base file for Computer Modern (a supplement to plain.mf)

cmbase:=1;                % when cmbase is known, this file has been input

let cmchar = relax;       % 'cmchar' should precede each character
let generate = input;     % 'generate' should follow the parameters

newinternal slant, superness, ···   % purely numeric parameters
boolean serifs, monospace, ···      % boolean parameters
```

These few lines are straightforward enough. Although `cmchar` is defined to be the same as **relax**, which does nothing, the definition of `cmchar` will be changed by certain utility programs below; this will prove to be a convenience when characters are designed, tested, and maintained.

The next few lines of `cmbase` are trickier. They implement the '**iff**' feature, which bypasses unwanted characters at high speed.

```
let semi_ = ;; let colon_ = :; let endchar_ = endchar;
def iff expr b =
 if b: let next_ = use_it else: let next_ = lose_it fi;
 next_ enddef;
def use_it = let : = restore_colon; enddef;
def restore_colon = let : = colon_; enddef;
def lose_it = let endchar = fi; inner cmchar; let ; = fix_ semi_
 if false enddef;
def fix_ = let ; = semi_; let endchar = endchar_; outer cmchar; enddef;
def always_iff = let : = endgroup; killboolean enddef;
def killboolean text t = use_it enddef;
outer cmchar;
```

(The `lose_it` routine assumes that every character program will end with '`endchar;`'.)

The most interesting part of `cmbase` is probably the way it allows the "sidebearings" of each character to be fine-tuned. The amount of space at the left and right edges of the character's "bounding box" can be adjusted without actually shifting the picture, and without changing the width that was specified in **beginchar**. Here's how it works: After a **beginchar** command and an optional **italcorr**, each Computer Modern character program is supposed to say

adjust_fit(⟨left sidebearing adjustment⟩, (⟨right sidebearing adjustment⟩);

sidebearing adjustments are given in true, "sharped" units. The **adjust_fit** routine essentially adds extra space at the left and right, corresponding to the sidebearing adjustments. An ad-hoc dimension called "*letter_fit#*" is also added to all sidebearings, behind the scenes.

Our example program for the "." says simply '**adjust_fit**$(0,0)$'; this means that only *letter_fit* is added. The program for em-dash says '**adjust_fit**(*letter_fit*#, *letter_fit*#)', hence the sidebearings are increased by 2*letter_fit* at each side. The total character width of the em-dash comes to $18u$# + 4*letter_fit*# (which is indeed one em, the value of **font_quad** specified in the **roman** driver file).

The program for lowercase 'b' in file **roman1.mf** says '**adjust_fit**(*serif_fit*#, 0)'; this adds the *serif_fit* parameter at the left, to compensate for the possible appearance of a serif at the left of this character. The *serif_fit* is zero in **cmr10**, but it has a negative value in a sans-serif font, and a positive value when serifs are extralong.

The nice thing about **adjust_fit** is that it's an "add-on" specification that doesn't affect the rest of the character design. The program can still be written as if 0 were the left edge and w were the right edge; afterwards the fit can be adjusted without changing the program or the shapes.

There are two versions of **adjust_fit**, one for normal fonts and one for mono-space fonts. Both of them are slightly complicated by something called *shrink_fit*, which will be explained later; for the moment, let's just imagine that *shrink_fit* = 0. Here is the routine for the normal case:

```
def normal_adjust_fit(expr left_adjustment,right_adjustment) =
 l := -hround(left_adjustment*hppp)-letter_fit;
 interim xoffset := -l;
 charwd := charwd+2letter_fit#+left_adjustment+right_adjustment;
 r := l+hround(charwd*hppp)-shrink_fit;
 w := r-hround(right_adjustment*hppp)-letter_fit;
 enddef;
```

Variables l and r are set to the actual pixel boundaries of the character; thus, plain METAFONT's bounding box has $0 \le x \le w$, but Computer Modern's has $l \le x \le r$. Rounding has been done very carefully so that the sidebearings will have consistent relationships across an entire font. Notice that w has been recalculated; this means that **adjust_fit** can affect the digitization, but—we hope—in a beneficial way.

In a monospaced font, the **adjust_fit** routine changes the unit-width parameter, u, so that the total width after adjustment comes out to be constant. Similar adjustments are made to parameters like *jut*, the nominal serif length. The width of all characters in a monospaced font will be *mono_charwd*# in true units, *mono_charwd* in pixels. The italic correction of all characters will be *mono_charic*#.

```
def mono_adjust_fit(expr left_adjustment,right_adjustment) =
 numeric expansion_factor; mono_charwd# = 2letter_fit#
   + expansion_factor*(charwd+left_adjustment+right_adjustment);
 forsuffixes $=u,jut, ··· :
  $ := $.#*expansion_factor*hppp; endfor
 l := -hround(left_adjustment*expansion_factor*hppp)-letter_fit;
 interim xoffset := -l;
 r := l+mono_charwd-shrink_fit;
 w := r-hround(right_adjustment*expansion_factor*hppp)-letter_fit;
 charwd := mono_charwd#; charic := mono_charic#;
 enddef;
```

It took the author umpteen trials to get this routine right.

The *xoffset* calculations in **adjust_fit** are enough to shift the character by the proper amount when it's being shipped out. We just have to take care of getting the correct character width in pixels, and cmbase does this by setting

```
extra_endchar := extra_endchar&"r:=r+shrink_fit;w:=r-1;";
```

No other changes to plain METAFONT's **endchar** routine are needed; but we do need to redefine **makebox** and **maketicks**, in order to show the adjusted bounding box. It's convenient to change **makebox** so that it also slants the box, in a slanted font, and so that it draws vertical lines one unit apart as aids to the designer; several more horizontal lines are also drawn:

```
def makebox(text rule) =
 for y=0,asc_height,body_height,x_height,bar_height,
    -desc_depth,-body_depth: rule((l,y)t_,(r,y)t_); endfor % horizontals
 for x=l,r: rule((x,-body_depth)t_,(x,body_height)t_); endfor % verticals
 for x=u*(1+floor(l/u)) step u until r-1:
  rule((x,-body_depth)t_,(x,body_height)t_); endfor       % more verticals
 if charic<>0:
  rule((r+charic*pt,h.o_),(r+charic*pt,.5h.o_)); fi   % italic correction
 enddef;
def maketicks(text rule) =
 for y=0,h.o_,-d.o_:
  rule((l,y),(l+10,y)); rule((r-10,y),(r,y)); endfor       % horizontals
 for x=l,r: rule((x,10-d.o_),(x,-d.o_));
            rule((x,h.o_-10),(x,h.o_)); endfor             % verticals
 if charic<>0:
  rule((r+charic*pt,h.o_-10),(r+charic*pt,h.o_)); fi % italic correction
 enddef;
```

(Examples of the new **makebox** routine appear in the illustrations for period and em-dash earlier in this appendix, and also in Chapter 23.)

Plain METAFONT's **change_width** routine must also be generalized:

```
def change_width = if not monospace:           % change width by +1 or -1
 if r+shrink_fit-l = floor(charwd*hppp): w := w+1; r := r+1;
 else: w := w-1; r := r-1; fi fi enddef;
```

The Computer Modern **font_setup** routine is invoked at the beginning of each driver file. This is what converts sharped units to pixels; **font_setup** also computes additional quantities that are important to the font as a whole. It's a long macro, but here are its important features:

```
def font_setup =
 define_pixels(u,jut, ··· );
 define_whole_pixels(letter_fit,fine,crisp, ··· );
 define_whole_vertical_pixels(body_height,cap_height, ··· );
 define_whole_blacker_pixels(hair,stem,curve, ··· );
 define_whole_vertical_blacker_pixels(vair,slab, ··· );
 define_corrected_pixels(o, ··· );
```

```
if monospace: mono_charwd# := 9u#; define_whole_pixels(mono_charwd);
 mono_charic# := max(0,body_height#*slant);
 let adjust_fit = mono_adjust_fit;
else: let adjust_fit = normal_adjust_fit; fi
lowres_fix(stem,curve) 1.2;
⟨Initialize pen nibs, see below⟩
currenttransform:=identity slanted slant
 yscaled aspect_ratio scaled granularity;
shrink_fit := 1+hround(2letter_fit#*hppp)-2letter_fit;
if not string mode: if mode <= smoke: shrink_fit := 0; fi fi
enddef;
```

If *letter_fit#* $= 0$, the '*shrink_fit*' is set to 1; otherwise *shrink_fit* is 0, 1, or 2, depending on how *letter_fit* has rounded to an integer. This amount is essentially subtracted from w before each character in the font has been drawn. Experience shows that this trick greatly improves the readability of fonts at medium and low resolutions.

Many of the Computer Modern characters are drawn with **filldraw**, which is a mixture of outline-filling and fixed-pen drawing. Several macros are included in cmbase to facilitate filldrawing, especially '*pos*' and '*stroke*':

```
vardef pos@#(expr b,d) =
 (x@#r-x@#l,y@#r-y@#l)=(b-currentbreadth,0) rotated d;
 x@#=.5(x@#l+x@#r); y@#=.5(y@#l+y@#r) enddef;

vardef stroke text t =
 forsuffixes e=l,r: path_.e:=t; endfor
 path_.l -- reverse path_.r -- cycle enddef;
```

Thus *pos* is like *penpos*, except that it subtracts *currentbreadth* from the overall breadth. (Cf. the program for left parentheses in Chapter 12.) The *stroke* routine is a simplified alternative to **penstroke**, such that **penstroke** is equivalent to '**fill** *stroke*' if the specified path isn't a cycle.

The value of *currentbreadth* is maintained by redefining plain METAFONT's '*numeric_pickup_*' macro so that it includes the new line

```
    if known breadth_[q]: currentbreadth:=breadth_[q]; fi
```

The **clear_pen_memory** macro is redefined so that its second line now says

```
    numeric pen_lft_[],pen_rt_[],pen_top_[],pen_bot_[],breadth_[];
```

relevant entries of the *breadth_* array will be defined by **font_setup**, as we'll see soon.

The example programs for period and em-dash say '**pickup** *fine.nib*' and '**pickup** *crisp.nib*'. These nibs are initialized by **font_setup** in the following way:

```
clear_pen_memory;
forsuffixes $ = fine,crisp, ··· :
 $.breadth := $;
 pickup if $=0: nullpen else: pencircle scaled $; $ := $-eps fi;
 $.nib := savepen; breadth_[$.nib] := $;
 forsuffixes $$ = lft,rt,top,bot: shiftdef($.$$,$$ 0); endfor endfor
```

If, for example, we have *fine* = 4, this code sets *fine.breadth* := 4, *fine.nib* := 1, *fine* := 4 − *eps*, and *breadth_*[4] := 4 − *eps*. (A small amount *eps* has been subtracted so that *pos* will usually find *b* − *currentbreadth* > 0.) Furthermore, four subroutines *fine.lft*, *fine.rt*, *fine.top*, and *fine.bot* are defined, so that it's easy to refer to the edges of *fine.nib* when it has not been picked up. These four subroutines are created by a slightly tricky `shiftdef` macro:

```
def shiftdef(suffix $)(expr delta) =
 vardef $ primary x = x+delta enddef enddef;
```

OK, we've just about covered everything in `cmbase` that handles the extra administrative complexity inherent in a large-scale design. The rest of the base file simply contains subroutines like *serif* and *dot*, for recurring features of the characters themselves. Such subroutines needn't be shown here.

To make a binary file called `cm.base`, there's a trivial file 'cm.mf':

```
% This file creates 'cm.base', assuming that plain.base is preloaded
input cmbase; dump.
```

Besides parameter files, driver files, program files, and the base file, the Computer Modern routines also include a number of *utility files* that provide a convenient environment for designing new characters and improving old ones. We'll conclude this appendix by studying the contents of those utility files.

Let's suppose, for example, that test proofs have revealed problems with the characters 'k' and 'S', so we want to fix them. Instead of working with the font as a whole, we can copy the programs for those two characters (and only those two) into a temporary file called 'test.mf'. Then we can run METAFONT on the file 'rtest.mf', which says the following:

```
% try all characters on 'test.mf' using the parameters of cmr10
if unknown cmbase: input cmbase fi
mode_setup;
def generate suffix t = enddef;
input cmr10; font_setup;
let echar = endchar;
def endchar = echar; stop "done with char "&decimal charcode&". " enddef;
let iff = always_iff;
input test; bye
```

This will produce proofs of 'k' and 'S', using the cmr10 parameters. Notice the simple trick by which `rtest` is able to stay in charge after inputting `cmr10`, without letting the `roman` driver come into action: 'generate' is redefined so that it becomes innocuous. Furthermore `rtest` changes `endchar` so that METAFONT will stop and display each character before moving on to the next. The 'iff' convention is changed to 'always_iff', so that every test character will be tested even if the boolean expression is undefined; this makes it easier to copy from program files into the test file and back again, since the `iff` indications do not have to be touched.

If you invoke METAFONT with '\mode=lowres; input rtest', you'll generate a low-resolution font called `rtest` with the parameters of cmr10, but containing only the characters in the test file. If you leave out the mode, you get proof mode as usual.

There are similar pseudo-drivers ttest.mf (for cmtt10 instead of cmr10), btest.mf (for cmbx10), etc.; these make it possible to try the test characters with many different parameter settings. There's also ztest.mf, which inputs parameters from a temporary file 'z.mf' that contains special parameters of interest at the moment. (If file z.mf does not exist, you'll get a chance to specify another parameter file, online.)

A more elaborate pseudo-driver file called '6test.mf' allows you to test up to six parameter settings simultaneously, and to see the results all at once on your screen, as illustrated in Chapter 23. Here is the program that does the necessary magic:

```
% try all characters on 'test.mf' using six different sets of parameters
if unknown cmbase: input cmbase fi
mag=.5; % the user can override this equation
mode_setup; let mode_setup=\;

boolean running;
def abort = hide(scrollmode; running := false) enddef;
def pause = stop "done with char "&decimal charcode&". " enddef;
let iff = always_iff;
def ligtable text t=enddef;
def charlist text t=enddef;
def extensible text t=enddef;

string currenttitle;
let semi = ;; let echar = endchar; let endchar = enddef;
def cmchar expr s = currenttitle := s;
 let ; = testchar semi quote def chartext = enddef;
def testchar = semi let ; = semi;
 running := true; errorstopmode;
 for k=1 upto 6:
  if running: if known params[k]: scantokens params[k]; font_setup;
   currentwindow:=k;
   currenttitle & ", " & fontname[k];
   chartext echar; fi fi endfor
 pause; enddef;

string params[],fontname[];
params[1] = "roman_params";      fontname[1] = "cmr10";
params[2] = "sans_params";       fontname[2] = "cmsx10";
params[3] = "ital_params";       fontname[3] = "cmti10";
params[4] = "tt_params";         fontname[4] = "cmtt10";
params[5] = "bold_params";       fontname[5] = "cmb10";
params[6] = "quote_params";      fontname[6] = "cmssqi8";

w_rows = floor 1/2 screen_rows; w_cols = floor 1/3 screen_cols;
def open(expr k,i,j)=
 openwindow k from ((i-1)*w_rows,(j-1)*w_cols) to (i*w_rows,j*w_cols)
 at (-10,140) enddef;
def openit =
 open(1,1,1); open(2,1,2); open(3,1,3);
 open(4,2,1); open(5,2,2); open(6,2,3); enddef;
```

```
begingroup delimiters begintext generate;
 def makedef(expr s)(text t) =
  expandafter def scantokens s = t enddef; flushtext enddef;
 def flushtext suffix t = enddef;
 for k=1 upto 6: if known params[k]:
 makedef(params[k])
  expandafter expandafter expandafter begintext
  scantokens ("input "&fontname[k]); fi endfor
endgroup;
```

```
input test; bye
```

Parameters are moved from parameter files into macros, using a trick discussed near
the beginning of Appendix D. Then **cmchar** is redefined so that the entire text of
each character-to-be-tested will be embedded in another macro called *chartext*. Each
instance of *chartext* is repeatedly applied to each of the six font setups.

An error that occurs with the first or second set of parameters may be so bad
that you won't want to see what happens with the third, fourth, fifth, and sixth sets.
For example, when `test.mf` contains characters that are being newly designed, some
equations might have been omitted or mistyped, so the results will be ludicrous. In
this case you can interrupt the program and type 'I abort'. The 6test routine has an
abort macro that will stop at the end of the current font setup and move directly to
the next character, without trying any of the remaining parameter combinations.

It's possible to include material in `test.mf` that isn't part of a character
program. For example, you might want to redefine a subroutine in the base file. Only
the character programs themselves (i.e., the sequences of tokens between '**cmchar**' and
'**endchar**;') are subject to six-fold repetition.

Some large characters may not appear in full, because there might not be
room for them on the screen at the stated magnification. You can make everything
smaller by running METAFONT with, say, '\mag=1/3; input 6test'. The computer
will stop with an error message, saying that the equation 'mag=.5' is inconsistent; but
you can safely proceed, because you will have the magnification you want.

An ensampull yn doyng ys more commendabull
þen ys techyng oþer prechyng.
— JOHN MIRK, *The Festyuall* (c. 1400)

Old people love to give good advice,
to console themselves for no longer being able to give bad examples.
— LA ROCHEFOUCALD, *Maximes* (1665)

F
Font Metric Information

The TEX typesetting system assumes that some "intelligence" has been built into the fonts it uses. In other words, information stored with TEX's fonts will have important effects on TEX's behavior. This has two consequences: (a) Typesetting is quite flexible, since few conventions are frozen into TEX itself. (b) Font designers must work a little harder, since they have to tell TEX what to do. The purpose of this appendix is to explain how you, as a font designer, can cope with (b) in order to achieve spectacular successes with (a).

The information used by TEX is embedded in compact binary files called TEX Font Metric (`tfm`) files. Although the 't' in '`tfm`' stands for TEX, this is an artifact of history, because other formatting systems can work with `tfm` files too. The files should have been called just '`fm`', but it's too late now.

METAFONT is able to produce two different kinds of binary output files. One, a '`gf`' file, contains digitized character shapes and some additional information needed by programs that drive printing devices; such files are discussed in Appendix G. The other type of output is a `tfm` file, which contains font information used by formatting routines like TEX; such files are our present concern. You get a `tfm` file if and only if METAFONT's internal quantity '*fontmaking*' is positive at the end of your job. (Plain METAFONT's **mode_setup** routine usually sets *fontmaking* to an appropriate value automatically.)

The `tfm` file contains some information about each character, some information about combinations of characters, and some information about the font as a whole. We shall consider these three kinds of information in turn. All of the font metric data that refers to physical dimensions should be expressed in device-independent, "sharp" units; when a particular font is produced with different modes or magnifications, all its `tfm` files should be identical.

A formatting program like TEX needs to know the size of each character's "bounding box." For example, when TEX typesets a word like 'box', it places the first letter 'b' into a little box in such a way that the METAFONT pixel whose lower left corner is at $(0,0)$ will appear on the baseline of the current line being typeset, at the left edge of the box. (We assume for simplicity that *xoffset* and *yoffset* were zero when 'b' was shipped out). The second letter, 'o', is placed in a second little box adjacent to the first one, so we obviously must tell TEX how wide to make the 'b'.

In fact, TEX also wants to know the height and depth of each letter. This affects the placing of accents, if you wish to typeset 'b̄ōx̃ỹ', and it also avoids overlap when adjacent lines contain boxes that go unusually far above or below the baselines. A total of four dimensions is given for each character, in sharp units (i.e., in units of printer's points):

- *charwd*, the width of the bounding box.
- *charht*, the height (above the baseline) of the bounding box.
- *chardp*, the depth (below the baseline) of the bounding box. This is a *positive* number if the character descends below the baseline, even though the corresponding y values are negative.
- *charic*, the character's "italic correction." TEX adds this amount to the width of the box (at the right-hand side) in two cases: (a) When the user specifies an italic correction explicitly, by typing \/ immediately after the character.

(b) When an isolated character is used in math mode, unless it has a subscript but no superscript. For example, the italic correction is applied to 'P' in the formulas '$P(x)$' and 'P^2', but not in the formula 'P_n'; it is applied to position the superscript but not the subscript in 'P_n^2'.

In plain METAFONT programs, you specify *charwd*, *charht*, and *chardp* in a **beginchar** command, and you specify *charic* (if it's positive) in an **italcorr** command. But **beginchar** and **italcorr** are macros, not primitives of METAFONT. What really happens is that METAFONT records the value of its internal quantities *charwd*, *charht*, *chardp*, and *charic* at the time of a **shipout** command. These values (and all other dimensions to be mentioned below) must be less than $2048pt\#$ in absolute value.

A font contains at most 256 character codes; the charexists operator can be used to tell which codes have already appeared. If two or more characters are shipped out with the same code number (possibly with different *charext* values), the *charwd*, *charht*, *chardp*, and *charic* of the final one are assumed to apply to them all.

At most 15 different nonzero heights, 15 different nonzero depths, and 63 different nonzero italic corrections may appear in a single font. If these limits are exceeded, METAFONT will change one or more values, by as little as possible, until the restriction holds. A warning message is issued if such changes are necessary; for example, '(some charht values had to be adjusted by as much as 0.12pt)' means that you had too many different nonzero heights, but METAFONT found a way to reduce the number to at most 15 by changing some of them; none of them had to be changed by more than 0.12 points. No warning is actually given unless the maximum amount of perturbation exceeds $\frac{1}{16}$ pt.

The next kind of information that TEX wants is concerned with pairs of adjacent characters that are typeset from the same font. For example, TEX moves the 'x' slightly closer to the 'o' in the word 'box', and it moves the 'o' slightly away from the 'b', because of information stored in the **tfm** file for the font you're now reading. This space adjustment is called *kerning*. Otherwise (if the three characters had simply been placed next to each other according to their *charwd* values) the word would have been 'box', which looks slightly worse. Similarly, there's a difference between 'difference' and 'difference', because the **tfm** file tells TEX to substitute the ligature 'ff' when there are two f's in a row.

Ligature information and kerning information is specified in short "ligtable programs" of a particularly simple form. Here's an example that illustrates most of the features (although it is not a serious example of typographic practice):

```
ligtable "f": "f" =: oct"013", "i" |=: oct"020", skipto 1;
ligtable "o": "b": "p": "e" kern .5u#, "o" kern .5u#, "x" kern-.5u#,
          1:: "!" kern u#;
```

This sequence of instructions can be paraphrased as follows:

Dear TEX, when you're typesetting an 'f' with this font, and when the following character also belongs to this font, look at it closely because you might need to do something special: If that following character is another 'f', replace the two f's by character code oct"013" [namely 'ff']; if it's an 'i', retain the 'f' but replace the 'i' by character code oct"020" [a dotless 'ı']; otherwise skip down to label '1::' for further instructions. When you're typesetting an 'o' or 'b' or 'p', if the next input to TEX is 'e' or 'o', add a half unit of space between the letters; if it's an 'x', subtract a half unit; if it's an exclamation point, add a full unit. The last instruction applies also to exclamation points following 'f' (because of the label '1::').

When a character code appears in front of a colon, the colon "labels" the starting place for that character's ligature and kerning program, which continues to the end of the ligtable statement. A double colon denotes a "local label"; a `skipto` instruction advances to the next matching local label, which must appear before 128 ligtable steps intervene. The special label ||: can be used to initiate ligtable instructions for an invisible "left boundary character" that is implicitly present just before every word; an invisible "right boundary character" equal to *boundarychar* is also implicitly present just after every word, if *boundarychar* lies between 0 and 255.

The general syntax for ligtable programs is pretty easy to guess from these examples, but we ought to exhibit it for completeness:

⟨ligtable command⟩ ⟶ **ligtable** ⟨ligtable program⟩⟨optional skip⟩
⟨ligtable program⟩ ⟶ ⟨ligtable step⟩ | ⟨ligtable program⟩ , ⟨ligtable step⟩
⟨optional skip⟩ ⟶ , **skipto** ⟨code⟩ | ⟨empty⟩
⟨ligtable step⟩ ⟶ ⟨code⟩⟨ligature op⟩⟨code⟩
    | ⟨code⟩ **kern** ⟨numeric expression⟩
    | ⟨label⟩⟨ligtable step⟩
⟨ligature op⟩ ⟶ =: | |=: | |=:> | =:| | =:|> | |=:| | |=:|> | |=:|>>
⟨label⟩ ⟶ ⟨code⟩ : | ⟨code⟩ :: | ||:
⟨code⟩ ⟶ ⟨numeric expression⟩ | ⟨string expression⟩

A ⟨code⟩ should have a numeric value between 0 and 255, inclusive, after having been rounded to the nearest integer; or it should be a string of length 1, in which case it denotes the corresponding ASCII code (Appendix C). For example, `"A"` and `64.61` both specify the code value 65. Vertical bars to the left or right of '=:' tell TeX to retain the original left and/or right character that invoked a ligature. Additional '>' signs tell TeX to advance its focus of attention instead of doing any further ligtable operations at the current character position.

Caution: Novices often go overboard on kerning. Things usually work out best if you kern by at most half of what looks right to you at first, since kerning should not be noticeable by its presence (only by its absence). Kerning that looks right in a logo or in a headline display often interrupts the rhythm of reading when it appears in ordinary textual material.

You can improve TeX's efficiency by ordering the steps of a ligtable program so that the most frequent alternatives come first. TeX will stop reading the program when it finds the first "hit."

Several characters of a font can be linked together in a series by means of a **charlist** command. For example,

```
charlist oct"000": oct"020": oct"022": oct"040": oct"060"
```

is used in the font `cmex10` to specify the left parentheses that TeX uses in displayed math formulas, in increasing order of size. TeX follows charlists to make variable-size delimiters and variable-width accents, as well as to link text-size operators like '$\sum$' to the display-size '$\sum$'.

TₑX builds up large delimiters by using "extensible" characters, which are specified by giving top, middle, bottom, and repeatable characters in an **extensible** command. For example, the extensible left parentheses in `cmex10` are defined by

<code>extensible oct"060": oct"060", 0, oct"100", oct"102";</code>

this says that character code `oct"060"` specifies an extensible delimiter constructed from itself as the top piece, from character number `oct"100"` as the bottom piece, and from character number `oct"102"` as the piece that should be repeated as often as necessary to reach a desired size. In this particular example there is no middle piece, but characters like curly braces have a middle piece as well. A zero value in the top, middle, or bottom position means that no character should be used in that part of the construction; but a zero value in the final position means that character number zero is the repeater. The width of an extensible character is taken to be the width of the repeater.

The first eight different sizes of parentheses available to TₑX in `cmex10`, when the user asks for '`\left(`', look like this:

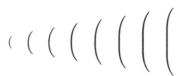

According to what we know from the examples of **charlist** and **extensible** above, the first four of these are the characters in positions `oct"000"`, `oct"020"`, `oct"022"`, and `oct"040"`. The other four have character `oct"060"` on top; character `oct"100"` is at the bottom; and there are respectively zero, one, two, and three occurrences of character `oct"102"` in the middle.

Here is the formal syntax:

⟨charlist command⟩ ⟶ `charlist` ⟨labeled code⟩
⟨labeled code⟩ ⟶ ⟨code⟩
    | ⟨label⟩⟨labeled code⟩
⟨extensible command⟩ ⟶ `extensible` ⟨label⟩⟨four codes⟩
⟨four codes⟩ ⟶ ⟨code⟩ , ⟨code⟩ , ⟨code⟩ , ⟨code⟩

Notice that a ⟨label⟩ can appear in a ligtable, charlist, or extensible command. These appearances are mutually exclusive: No code may be used more than once as a label. Thus, for example, a character with a ligature/kerning program cannot also be extensible, nor can it be in a charlist (except as the final item).

The last type of information that appears in a `tfm` file applies to the font as a whole. Two kinds of data are involved, bytes and numerics; and they are specified in "headerbyte" and "fontdimen" commands, according to the following general syntax:

⟨headerbyte command⟩ ⟶ `headerbyte` ⟨numeric expression⟩ : ⟨byte list⟩
⟨fontdimen command⟩ ⟶ `fontdimen` ⟨numeric expression⟩ : ⟨numeric list⟩
⟨byte list⟩ ⟶ ⟨code⟩
    | ⟨byte list⟩ , ⟨code⟩
⟨numeric list⟩ ⟶ ⟨numeric expression⟩
    | ⟨numeric list⟩ , ⟨numeric expression⟩

We shall defer discussion of header bytes until later, because they are usually unnecessary. But **fontdimen** commands are important. Numeric parameters of a font can be specifed by saying, e.g.,

fontdimen 3: 2.5, 6.5, 0, 4x

which means that parameters 3–6 are to be 2.5, 6.5, 0, and $4x$, respectively. These are the parameters that TEX calls \fontdimen3 thru \fontdimen6. (Parameter numbering is old-fashioned: There is no \fontdimen0.)

The first seven fontdimen parameters have special significance, so plain METAFONT has seven macros to specify them symbolically, one at a time:

- **font_slant** (\fontdimen1) is the amount of slant per point; TEX uses this information when raising or lowering an accent character.
- **font_normal_space** (\fontdimen2) is the interword spacing. If the value is zero, all characters of this font will be considered to be "isolated" in math mode, so the italic correction will be added more often than otherwise.
- **font_normal_stretch** (\fontdimen3) is the stretchability of interword spacing, as explained in *The TEXbook*.
- **font_normal_shrink** (\fontdimen4) is the shrinkability of interword spacing, as explained in *The TEXbook*.
- **font_x_height** (\fontdimen5) is the height of characters for which accents are correctly positioned. An accent over a character will be raised by the difference between the character's *charht* and this value. The x-height is also the unit of height that TEX calls one 'ex'.
- **font_quad** (\fontdimen6) is the unit of width that TEX calls one 'em'.
- **font_extra_space** (\fontdimen7) is the additional amount added to the normal interword space between sentences, depending on the "spacefactor" as defined in *The TEXbook*.

Parameters are zero unless otherwise specified.

Math symbol fonts for TEX are required to have at least 22 fontdimen parameters, instead of the usual seven; math extension fonts need at least 13. Appendix G of *The TEXbook* explains the precise significance of these additional parameters, which control such things as the placement of superscripts and subscripts.

The *design size* of a font is not one of the fontdimen parameters; it's an internal quantity of METAFONT that is actually output among the header bytes as explained below. When a TEX user asks for a font 'at' a certain size, the font is scaled by the ratio between the "at size" and the design size. For example, cmr10 has a design size of 10 pt; if a TEX user requests 'cmr10 at 15pt', the result is the same as 'cmr10 scaled 1500' (or, in plain METAFONT terms, cmr10 with mag=1.5).

What does the design size really mean? It's an imprecise notion, because there need be no connection between the design size and any specific measurement in a font. Typographers have always been vague when they speak about "10 point" fonts, because some fonts look larger than others even though the horizontal and vertical dimensions are the same. It's something like dress sizes or shoe sizes.

In general, the design size is a statement about the approximate size of the type. Type with a larger design size generally looks bigger than type with a smaller design size. Two fonts with the same design size are supposed to work well together;

for example, cmr9 and cmtt9 both have 9 pt design size, although the uppercase letters of cmtt9 are quite a bit smaller ('A' versus 'A').

The *designsize* must be at least $1pt\#$. And, as with all tfm dimensions, it must be less than $2048pt\#$. Any other value is changed to $128pt\#$.

METAFONT looks at the value of *designsize* only when the job ends, so you needn't set it before characters are shipped out. At the end of a job, when the tfm file is being written, METAFONT checks to make sure that every dimension of the font is less than 16 times the design size in absolute value, because this limitation is imposed by the tfm file format. Thus, for example, if the design size is 10 pt, you cannot have a character whose width or height is 160 pt or more. If one or more dimensions prove to be too big, METAFONT will tell you how many of them had to be changed.

The **headerbyte** command is similar to **fontdimen**, but it gives 8-bit ⟨code⟩ data instead of numeric information. For example,

```
headerbyte 33: 0, 214, 0, "c"
```

says that bytes 33–36 of the tfm file header will be 0, 214, 0, and 99. The first four header bytes (numbers 1–4) are automatically set to a check sum, unless you have specified other values for at least one of those bytes. (This check sum will match a similar value in the gf file, so that other typesetting software can check the consistency of the different files they use.) Similarly, the next four header bytes (numbers 5–8) are set automatically to the design size times 2^{20}, unless you have specified something else.

TeX looks only at the first eight header bytes, so you needn't use the header-byte command if you are simply producing a font for standard TeX. But other software that reads tfm files may have a need for more header information. For example, the original tfm format (developed by Lyle Ramshaw at Xerox Palo Alto Research Center) included **font_coding_scheme** information in bytes 9–48 of the header, and **font_identifier** information in bytes 49–68. The design size of certain fonts was also packed into byte 72. Each font in the "Xerox world" is uniquely identified by its font identifier and its design size, rather than by its font file name.

The "font coding scheme" is merely a comment that can be used to help understand large collections of fonts; it's usually a nice thing to know. Some of the coding scheme names in common use are

TeX text	TeX math italic
TeX typewriter text	TeX math symbols
XEROX text	TeX math extension
ASCII	TeX extended ASCII
PI	GRAPHIC

The coding-scheme string should not include parentheses.

Here are macros that can be used, if desired, to convert plain METAFONT's **font_identifier** and **font_coding_scheme** into the format required by Ramshaw's original tfm files:

```
def BCPL_string(expr s,n) = % string s becomes an n-byte BCPL string
 for l:=if length(s)>=n: n-1 else: length(s) fi: l
  for k:=1 upto l: , substring (k-1,k) of s endfor
  for k:=l+2 upto n: , 0 endfor endfor enddef;
```

```
inner end;
def bye = if fontmaking>0:
  headerbyte 9: BCPL_string(font_coding_scheme_,40);
  special "codingscheme " & font_coding_scheme_;
  headerbyte 49: BCPL_string(font_identifier_,20);
  special "identifier " & font_identifier;
  headerbyte 72: max(0, 254 - round 2designsize); fi
 end enddef;
outer bye,end;
```

These macros could be included among the `local.mf` extensions to `plain.mf` at particular installations. When a user says '**bye**' instead of '**end**', the additional headerbyte
documentation will then be automatically inserted into the `tfm` file.

Let us now conclude this appendix by summarizing what we've learned. A
METAFONT programmer can provide various types of information about how to typeset
with a font, by using font metric commands. Simple versions of these commands,
sufficient for simple fonts, are standard operations in plain METAFONT; examples have
appeared in Chapter 11 and the beginning of Appendix E. The general cases are
handled by five types of font metric commands:

⟨font metric command⟩ ⟶ ⟨ligtable command⟩
  | ⟨charlist command⟩
  | ⟨extensible command⟩
  | ⟨fontdimen command⟩
  | ⟨headerbyte command⟩

This completes the syntax of METAFONT that was left slightly unfinished in Chapter 26.

> *Such things induced me to untangle the chaos*
> *by introducing order where it had never been before:*
> *I think I may say I have had the good fortune to succeed*
> *with an exactness & a precision leaving nothing more to be desired,*
> *by the invention of* Typographic points.
> — PIERRE FOURNIER, *Manuel Typographique* (1764)

> *One should absorb the color of life,*
> *but one should never remember its details.*
> *Details are always vulgar.*
> — OSCAR WILDE, *The Picture of Dorian Gray* (1890)

G

Generic Font Files

METAFONT's main output goes into a `gf` or "Generic Font" file, so-called because it can easily be translated into any other digital font format, although it does not match the specifications of any "name brand" manufacturer. The purpose of this appendix is to explain exactly what kinds of information go into the `gf` file, and under what circumstances METAFONT puts things there.

A `gf` file is a compact binary representation of a digitized font, containing all the information needed by "device driver" software that produces printed documents from TEX's `dvi` files. The exact internal representation scheme of `gf` files doesn't concern us here, but we ought to know what type of data is encoded.

The first thing in a `gf` file is a string that explains its origin. METAFONT writes strings of the form

> `METAFONT output 1986.06.24:1635`

based on the values of the internal quantities *day*, *month*, *year*, and *time* when the `gf` file was started. (In this case *day* = 24, *month* = 6, *year* = 1986, and *time* = $16 \times 60 + 35 = 995$.)

After the opening string, the `gf` file contains a sequence of "special" commands interspersed with shipped-out character images. Special commands are intended to provide a loophole for future extensions to METAFONT's set of primitives, so that METAFONT itself will not have to change. Some specials are predefined, but others will undoubtedly be created in years to come. (TEX has an analogous \special command, which puts an arbitrary string into a `dvi` file.)

A special command gets into the `gf` file when you say '**special** ⟨string⟩' or '**numspecial** ⟨numeric⟩' at a time when *proofing* ≥ 0. A **special** string should come before **numspecial**, and it should either be a keyword all by itself or it should consist of a keyword followed by a space followed by additional information. Keywords that specify operations requiring numeric arguments should be followed by numbers produced by **numspecial**. For example, the '**proofrule**' macro in Appendix B expands into a sequence of five special commands,

> **special** "rule";
> **numspecial** x_1; **numspecial** y_1;
> **numspecial** x_2; **numspecial** y_2;

this represents a rule on the proofsheet that runs from point (x_1, y_1) to point (x_2, y_2). If you say '**grayfont grray5**', the **grayfont** macro in Appendix B expands to '**special** "grayfont gray5"'. Software that reads `gf` files will examine all of the special strings, until coming to a space or to the end of the string. If the resulting keyword isn't known to the program, the special string will be ignored, together with all numspecials that immediately follow. But when the keyword is known, the program will be able to determine the corresponding arguments. For example, the `GFtoDVI` program described in Appendix H knows about the plain METAFONT keywords '**rule**' and '**grayfont**'.

METAFONT might also create **special** commands on its own initiative, but only when *proofing* is strictly greater than zero. There are two cases: (1) When a ⟨title⟩ statement occurs, the special string '"title " & ⟨string⟩' is output. (This is how the phrase '`The letter O`' got onto your proofsheets in the experiments of Chapter 5.) (2) Just before a character image is shipped out, METAFONT implicitly executes the following sequence of instructions:

> **if** round *xoffset* $\neq$ 0: **special** "xoffset"; **numspecial** round *xoffset*; **fi**
> **if** round *yoffset* $\neq$ 0: **special** "yoffset"; **numspecial** round *yoffset*; **fi**

A **shipout** command sends a digitized picture to the **gf** file, if *proofing* $\geq$ 0, but nothing is output if *proofing* < 0. Furthermore the current values of *charwd*, *charht*, *chardp*, *charic*, *chardx*, and *chardy* are stored away for the current *charcode*; these values are stored in all cases, regardless of the value of *proofing*. The current character code is henceforth said to "exist."

When a picture is shipped out, its pixels of positive value are considered to be "black," and all other pixels are considered to be "white." The pattern of blacks and whites is encoded in such a way that doubling the resolution approximately doubles the length of the **gf** output, in most cases.

METAFONT reports its progress by typing '[*c*]' on the terminal when character code *c* is being shipped out. (The '[' is typed before output conversion begins, and the ']' is typed after; hence you can see how much time output takes.) If *charext* is nonzero, after being rounded to an integer, the typed message is '[*c.x*]' instead; for example, '[65.3]' refers to character 65 with extension code 3.

TEX allows only 256 characters per font, but extensions of TEX intended for oriental languages will presumably use the *charext* feature. All characters with the same code share the same width, height, and depth, but they can correspond to distinct graphics if they have different extension codes.

A **special** command generally refers to the picture that follows it, rather than the picture that precedes it. Special commands before the first digitized picture might, however, give instructions about the font as a whole. Special commands that follow the final picture invariably refer to the font as a whole. (For example, the '**bye**' macro at the end of Appendix F creates two special strings that will appear after the final character of a font.)

No **gf** file will be written unless a character is shipped out or a special command is performed at a time when *proofing* $\geq$ 0, or unless a title statement is encountered at a time when *proofing* > 0. When one of these things first happens, the **gf** file receives its name. If no **input** commands have yet occurred, METAFONT will set the job name to '**mfput**'; otherwise the job name will already have been determined. The full name of the **gf** file will be '⟨jobname⟩.⟨resolution⟩gf', where the ⟨resolution⟩ is based on the current value of *hppp*. (If *hppp* $\leq$ 0, the resolution will be omitted; otherwise it will be converted to an equivalent number of pixels per inch, in the horizontal dimension.) Subsequent **input** operations or changes to *hppp* will not change the name of the **gf** file.

The end of a **gf** file contains a bunch of numeric data needed for typesetting. First come the design size and the check sum; these match precisely the data in the **tfm** file, unless the header bytes of the **tfm** have explicitly been set to something else. Then come the values of *hppp* and *vppp*. (These are the values at the end of the job, so *hppp* might not agree with the ⟨resolution⟩ value in the **gf** file name.)

Finally, the **gf** file gets the *charwd*, *chardx*, and *chardy* of each existing character code. The values of *chardx* and *chardy* represent desired "escapements" when characters are typeset on a particular device (cf. Chapter 12). The *charwd* values are identical to the widths in the **tfm** file.

The check sum is based entirely on the *charwd* data; two fonts with the same character widths will have the same check sum, but two fonts with different character widths will almost never have the same check sum.

The purpose of check sums can be understood by considering the following scenario: A font named `cmr10` might be generated by METAFONT at any time, producing a `tfm` file called `cmr10.tfm` and a `gf` file called, say, `cmr10.300gf`. A document named `doc`, which uses `cmr10`, might be generated by TeX at any time, producing a `dvi` file called `doc.dvi`; TeX had to read `cmr10.tfm` in order to produce this `dvi` file. Now on some future date, a "device driver" program will be used to print `doc.dvi`, using the font `cmr10.300gf`. Meanwhile, the font may have changed. If the current `gf` file doesn't match the `tfm` file that was assumed by TeX, mysterious glitches will probably occur in the printed document, because `dvi` information is kept concise by the assumption that the device driver knows the `tfm` widths of all characters. Potential problems are kept to a minimum if TeX puts the assumed design size and check sum of each font into the `dvi` files it produces; a device driver can then issue a warning message when it finds a `gf` file that is inconsistent with TeX's assumptions.

> But if our Letter-Cutter *will have no Forge,*
> *yet he must of necessity accommodate*
> *himself with a* Vice, Hand-Vice, Hammers,
> Files, Small *and* Fine Files *(commonly called* Watch-makers Files*)*
> *of these he saves all, as they wear out.*
> — JOSEPH MOXON, *Mechanick Exercises* (1683)

> *The natural definition lists all possible generic characters.*
> — LINNÆUS, *Philosophia Botanica* (1751)

H

Hardcopy Proofs

A font cannot be proved correct like a mathematical theorem; a font must be seen to be believed. Moreover, if some characters of a font are faulty, the best way to fix them is to look at diagrams that indicate what went wrong. Therefore METAFONT is incomplete by itself; additional programs are needed to convert the output of METAFONT into graphic form.

The purpose of this appendix is to discuss two such auxiliary programs, which serve as examples of many others that could be devised. The first of these, called GFtoDVI, takes gf files and converts them into dvi files, which can be printed just like the output of TEX. Each character image in the gf file will have a printed page to itself, with labelled points and with bounding boxes just as in the illustrations we have seen throughout this book. (Indeed, the illustrations in this book were produced by GFtoDVI.) The second auxiliary program to be discussed below is TEX itself; we shall look at a set of TEX macros designed to facilitate font testing.

1. Large scale proofs. The gf files produced by plain METAFONT when it is in *proof* mode or *smoke* mode can be converted to annotated diagrams by running them through GFtoDVI, as we know from the experiments in Chapter 5. It's also possible to study low-resolution characters with GFtoDVI, especially if plain METAFONT's 'gfcorners' feature has been used. We shall now take a thorough look at what GFtoDVI can do.

All communication from METAFONT to GFtoDVI comes through the gf file and from options that you might type when you run GFtoDVI. If there are no "special" commands in the gf file (cf. Appendix G), each page of GFtoDVI's output will show just the "black" pixels of a character; furthermore there will be a title line at the top of the page, showing the date and time of the METAFONT run, together with the character code number and extension code (if they are nonzero). The black pixels are typeset via characters of a so-called "gray font," described in detail below; by changing the gray font you can produce a variety of different outputs from a single gf file.

To get other things on your proof sheets, "special" commands must appear in the gf file. For example, METAFONT will automatically output a `title` command, if *proofing* > 0, as explained in Appendix G; GFtoDVI will typeset this title on the title line of the next character image that follows the command. If there are several title statements, they all will appear; they are supposed to fit on a single line.

The most important special commands tell GFtoDVI to create labeled points on the character diagram. When you say, for example, '**labels**$(1, 2)$' in a plain META-FONT program, at a time when *proofing* > 1, the macros of Appendix B will convert this to the special commands

> **special** " 01"; **numspecial** x_1; **numspecial** y_1;
> **special** " 02"; **numspecial** x_2; **numspecial** y_2;

GFtoDVI will then put a dot labeled '1' at point (x_1, y_1) and a dot labeled '2' at (x_2, y_2).

Labels are placed in one of four positions relative to their dots—either at the top, the left, the right, or the bottom. GFtoDVI will ordinarily try to place all labels so that they don't interfere with each other, and so that they stay clear of other dots. But if you want to exercise fine control over the placement yourself, you can say, for example, '**labels**.*top*$(1a, 2a)$'; in this case the specified labels will appear above their dots, regardless of whether or not other labels and/or dots are thereby overprinted.

The **gf** file in this case will contain

$$\text{special } " \text{ 11a"}; \quad \text{numspecial } x_{1a}; \quad \text{numspecial } y_{1a};$$
$$\text{special } " \text{ 12a"}; \quad \text{numspecial } x_{2a}; \quad \text{numspecial } y_{2a}.$$

GFtoDVI looks at the character following a leading blank space to determine what sort of labeling convention is desired; the subsequent characters are the text of the label.

The command '**labels**.$top(1a, 2a)$' in plain METAFONT is just an abbreviation for '**makelabel**.$top("1a", z_{1a})$; **makelabel**.$top("2a", z_{2a})$', when $proofing > 1$; the **makelabel** macro is really the fundamental one, and you should use it directly if you want more unusual effects. Suppose, for example, you just want to put a dot but no label at point z_5; then you can say '**makelabel**$("", z_5)$'. And suppose you want to put a label to the left of point z_5 but with no dot; you can say '**makelabel**.$lft.nodot("5", z_5)$'. Furthermore you could say '**makelabel**.$lft.nodot("5", z_5 - (2,3))$' to move that label left by 2 pixels and down by 3 pixels, thereby getting the effect of a label that is diagonally adjacent to its dot. Labels without dots can also be used to put words on a diagram.

GFtoDVI recognizes nine varieties of labels in all, based on the first two characters of the special string command:

- **makelabel** (special " 0"): choose the label position automatically.
- **makelabel**.*top* (special " 1"): center the label just above the dot.
- **makelabel**.*lft* (special " 2"): place the label just left of the dot.
- **makelabel**.*rt* (special " 3"): place the label just right of the dot.
- **makelabel**.*bot* (special " 4"): center the label just below the dot.
- **makelabel**.*top*.*nodot* (special " 5"): like *top*, but omit the dot.
- **makelabel**.*lft*.*nodot* (special " 6"): like *lft*, but omit the dot.
- **makelabel**.*rt*.*nodot* (special " 7"): like *rt*, but omit the dot.
- **makelabel**.*bot*.*nodot* (special " 8"): like *bot*, but omit the dot.

The first case is called *autolabeling*; this is the normal command. Autolabeling always places a dot, whether or not that dot overlaps other dots, but you don't always get a label. Autolabels are typeset only after all explicit labels have been established; then GFtoDVI tries to place as many of the remaining labels as possible.

If there's no place to put an autolabel, an "overflow equation" is put in the upper right corner of the proofsheet. For example, the overflow equation '5 = 5r + (-4.9,0)' means that there was no room for label 5, whose dot is 4.9 pixels to the left of the dot for 5r (which is labeled).

You can avoid overflow equations by sending GFtoDVI the special command " /" instead of " 0"; this is a variant of autolabeling that does everything as usual except that the label will simply be forgotten if it can't be placed. To do this with plain METAFONT, set '*lcode_* := " /"' near the beginning of your program; *lcode_* is the string that **makelabel** uses to specify autolabeling.

The next most important kind of annotation for proofs is a straight line or "rule." Plain METAFONT's command for this is '**proofrule**(z_1, z_2)', which expands to

$$\text{special "rule"}; \quad \text{numspecial } x_1; \quad \text{numspecial } y_1;$$
$$\text{numspecial } x_2; \quad \text{numspecial } y_2.$$

GFtoDVI has trouble drawing diagonal rules, because standard **dvi** format includes no provision for drawing straight lines unless they are vertical or horizontal. Therefore you might get an error message unless $x_1 = x_2$ (vertical rule) or $y_1 = y_2$ (horizontal rule). However, a limited escape from this restriction is available via a "slant font," by which GFtoDVI is able to typeset diagonal lines as sequences of characters. Only one slope is permitted per job, but this is better than nothing (see below).

To control the weight of proof rules, you say, e.g., '**proofrulethickness** $1.5mm^{\#}$' in a plain METAFONT program; this expands to

> **special "rulethickness"**; **numspecial** $1.5mm^{\#}$.

Each horizontal or vertical rule is drawn as if by a pen of the current rulethickness, hence you can get different weights of lines in a single diagram. If the current rulethickness is negative, no rule will appear; if it is zero, a default rulethickness based on a parameter of the gray font will be used; if it is positive, the stated thickness will be increased if necessary until it equals an integer number of pixels, and that value will be used to draw the rule. At the beginning of each character the current rulethickness is zero.

You can reposition an entire diagram on its page by saying '**proofoffset** (x, y)'; this expands to

> **special "offset"**; **numspecial** x; **numspecial** y

and it tells GFtoDVI to shift everything except the title line on the next character image, x pixels to the right and y pixels upward.

GFtoDVI uses four fonts to typeset its output: (1) The *title font* is used for the top line on each page. (2) The *label font* is used for all labels. (3) The *gray font* is used for dots and for black pixels. (4) The *slant font* is used for diagonal rules. Appropriate default fonts will be used at each installation unless you substitute specific fonts yourself, by using the **special** commands **titlefont**, **labelfont**, **grayfont**, or **slantfont**. GFtoDVI also understands special strings like '**"grayfontarea /usr/dek"**', which can be used to specify a nonstandard file area or directory name for the gray font. Furthermore the **gf** file might say, e.g.,

> **special "labelfontat"**; **numspecial** 20

if you want the label font to be loaded at 20 pt instead of its design size. The area name and the at size must be given after the font name itself; in other words, '**"grayfont"**' cancels a previous '**"grayfontarea"**'.

The four fonts used by GFtoDVI must be established before the first character bitmap appears in the **gf** file. This means that the special font commands must be given before the first **shipout** or **endchar** in your program; but they shouldn't appear until after **mode_setup**, so that your **gf** file will have the correct name. If it's inconvenient to specify the fonts that way, you can change them at run time when you use GFtoDVI: Just type '/' following the name of the **gf** file that's being input, and you will be asked to type special strings online. For example, the run-time dialog might look like this:

```
This is GFtoDVI, Version 2.0
GF file name: io.2602gf/
Special font substitution: labelfont cmbx10
OK; any more?          grayfont black
OK; any more?
```

After the final carriage return, GFtoDVI does its normal thing, ignoring font specifications in the file that conflict with those just given.

2. Gray fonts. A proof diagram constructed by GFtoDVI can be regarded as an array of rectangles, where each rectangle is either blank or filled with a special symbol that we shall call '⋆'. A blank rectangle represents a white pixel, while ⋆ represents a black pixel. Additional labels and reference lines are often superimposed on this array of rectangles; hence it is usually best to choose a symbol ⋆ that has a somewhat gray appearance, although any symbol can actually be used.

In order to construct such proofs, GFtoDVI needs to work with a special type of font known as a "gray font"; it's possible to obtain a wide variety of different sorts of proofs by using different sorts of gray fonts. The next few paragraphs explain exactly what gray fonts are supposed to contain, in case you want to design your own.

The simplest gray font contains only two characters, namely ⋆ and another symbol that is used for dots that identify key points. If proofs with relatively large pixels are desired, a two-character gray font is all that's needed. However, if the pixel size is to be relatively small, practical considerations make a two-character font too inefficient, since it requires the typesetting of tens of thousands of tiny little characters; printing-device drivers rarely work very well when they are presented with data that is so different from ordinary text. Therefore a gray font with small pixels usually has a number of characters that replicate ⋆ in such a way that comparatively few characters actually need to be typeset.

Since many printing devices are not able to cope with arbitrarily large or complex characters, it is not possible for a single gray font to work well on all machines. In fact, ⋆ must have a width that is an integer multiple of the printing device's units of horizontal and vertical positioning, since rounding the positions of grey characters would otherwise produce unsightly streaks on proof output. Thus, there is no way to make the gray font as device-independent as normal fonts of type can be.

This understood, we can now take a look at what GFtoDVI expects to see in a gray font. The character ⋆ always appears in position 1. It must have positive height h and positive width w; its depth and italic correction are ignored.

Positions 2–120 of a gray font are reserved for special combinations of ⋆'s and blanks, stacked on top of each other. None of these character codes need be present in the font; but if they are, the slots must be occupied by characters of width w that have certain configurations of ⋆'s and blanks, prescribed for each character position. For example, position 3 of the font should either contain no character at all, or it should contain a character consisting of two ⋆'s, one above the other; one of these ⋆'s should rest on the baseline, and the other should appear immediately below.

It will be convenient to use a horizontal notation like '⋆ ⋆⋆' to stand for a vertical stack of ⋆'s and blanks. The convention will be that the stack is built from bottom to top, and the topmost rectangle should sit on the baseline. Thus, '⋆ ⋆⋆' stands actually for a character of height h and depth $4h$ that looks like this:

⋆⟵ baseline
⋆

We use a horizontal notation in this discussion instead of a vertical one because column vectors take too much space, and because the horizontal notation corresponds to binary numbers in a convenient way.

Positions 1–63 of a gray font are reserved for the patterns ⋆, ⋆ , ⋆⋆, ⋆ , ⋆⋆, and so on up to ⋆⋆⋆⋆⋆⋆, just as in the normal binary notation of the numbers 1–63, with ⋆'s substituted for 1's and blanks for 0's. Positions 64–70 are reserved for the special patterns ▪▪▪▪▪▪, ▪▪▪▪▪▪, ▪▪▪▪▪▪, ▪▪▪▪▪▪, ▪▪▪▪▪▪, ▪▪▪▪▪▪, ▪▪▪▪▪▪ of length seven; positions 71–78 are, similarly, reserved for the length-eight patterns ▪▪▪▪▪▪ through ▪▪▪▪▪▪. The length-nine patterns ▪▪▪▪▪▪ through ▪▪▪▪▪▪ are assigned to positions 79–87, the length-ten patterns to positions 88–97, the length-eleven patterns to positions 98–108, and the length-twelve patterns to positions 109–120.

Position 0 of a gray font is reserved for the "dot" character, which should have positive height h' and positive width w'. When GFtoDVI wants to put a dot at some place (x, y) on the figure, it positions the dot character so that its reference point is at (x, y). The dot will be considered to occupy a rectangle whose corners are at $(x \pm w', y \pm h')$; the rectangular box for a label will butt up against the rectangle enclosing the dot.

All other character positions of a gray font (namely, positions 121–255) are unreserved, in the sense that they have no predefined meaning. But GFtoDVI may access them via the **charlist** feature of **tfm** files, starting with any of the characters in positions 1–120. In such a case each succeeding character in a list should be equivalent to two of its predecessors, horizontally adjacent to each other. For example, in

charlist 53: 121: 122: 123

character 121 will stand for two 53's, character 122 for two 121's (i.e., four 53's), and character 123 for two 122's (i.e., eight 53's). Since position 53 contains the pattern ▪▪ ▪ ▪, character 123 in this example would have height h, depth $5h$, and width $8w$, and it would stand for the pattern

▪▪▪▪▪▪▪▪ ◄— baseline
▪▪▪▪▪▪▪▪
▪▪▪▪▪▪▪▪

Such a pattern is, of course, rather unlikely to occur in a **gf** file, but GFtoDVI would be able to use if it were present. Designers of gray fonts should provide characters only for patterns that they think will occur often enough to make the doubling worthwhile. For example, the character in position 120 (▪▪▪▪▪▪▪▪▪▪▪▪), or whatever is the tallest stack of ▪'s present in the font, is a natural candidate for repeated doubling.

Here's how GFtoDVI decides what characters of the gray font will be used, given a configuration of black and white pixels: If there are no black pixels, stop. Otherwise look at the top row that contains at least one black pixel, and the eleven rows that follow. For each such column, find the largest k such that $1 \leq k \leq 120$ and the gray font contains character k and the pattern assigned to position k appears in the given column. Typeset character k (unless no such character exists) and erase the corresponding black pixels; use doubled characters, if they are present in the gray font, if two or more consecutive equal characters need to be typeset. Repeat the same process on the remaining configuration, until all the black pixels have been erased.

If all characters in positions 1–63 are present, this process is guaranteed to take care of at least six rows each time; and with characters 64–120 as well, it usually takes care of twelve, since all patterns that contain at most one "run" of ▪'s are present.

Some of the **fontdimen** parameters discussed in Appendix F are important in gray fonts. The **font_slant** value s, if nonzero, will cause GFtoDVI to skew its output; in this case the character ▪ will presumably be a parallelogram with a corresponding slant, rather than the usual rectangle. METAFONT's coordinate (x, y) will appear in physical position $(xw + yhs, yh)$ on the proofsheets. (This is appropriate for proofing unslanted fonts whose pixels will become slanted by mechanical obliquing.)

Parameter **fontdimen** 8 of a gray font specifies the thickness of rules that go on the proofs. If this parameter is zero, TEX's default rule thickness (0.4 pt) will be used. The other parameters of a gray font are ignored by GFtoDVI, but it is conventional to set **font_normal_space** and **font_quad** to w, **font_x_height** to h.

For best results the designer of a gray font should choose w and h so that the user's dvi-to-hardcopy software will not make any rounding errors. Furthermore, the dot should be an even number $2m$ of pixels in diameter, and the rule thickness should work out to an even number $2n$ of pixels; then the dots and rules will be centered on the correct positions, in the common case of integer coordinates. Gray fonts are almost always intended for particular output devices, even though 'dvi' stands for "device independent"; we use dvi files for METAFONT proofs chiefly because software to print dvi files is already in place.

The METAFONT program for a fairly versatile gray font generator, called 'grayf.mf', appears on the next few pages. It should be invoked by a parameter file that establishes values of several quantities:

- If *large_pixels* is of type **boolean**, only 15 characters will be generated; otherwise there will be 123.
- If *pix_picture* is of type **picture**, it should be the desired pixel image '.', and in this case *pix_wd* and *pix_ht* should be the width and height in pixels. Otherwise a default gray pixel pattern will be used.
- If *rep* is known, it should be a positive integer; the default pixel pattern will be magnified *rep* times so that the final proofs will be this much bigger than usual, and the pattern will be clipped slightly at the edges so that discrete pixels can be seen plainly.
- If *lightweight* is of type **boolean**, the default pixel pattern will be only half as dark as usual.
- If *dotsize* is known, it should be the diameter of the special dot character, in pixel units.
- The **font_identifier** should be specified.

(The *rep* and *lightweight* options are ignored if *pix_picture* is explicitly given.) Since gray fonts are inherently device-dependent, we do not start with "sharp" dimensions as in normal fonts; we go backwards and compute the sharp units from pixel units.

The name of each gray font should include the name of the device for which it is intended. (A "favorite" proof device can also be chosen at each installation, for which the alternate font names 'gray' and 'black' are valid; these installation-dependent fonts are the defaults for *proof* mode and *smoke* mode.)

Here, for example, is a suitable parameter file 'graycheap.mf', which generates a vanilla-flavored gray font for the hypothetical *cheapo* printer:

```
% Gray font for Cheapo with proofsheet resolution 50 pixels per inch
if mode<>cheapo: errmessage "This file is for cheapo only"; fi
font_identifier "GRAYCHEAP";
input grayf
```

(The proofsheet resolution will be 50 per inch, because *cheapo* has 200 pixels per inch, and the default *pix_picture* in grayf will be four pixels square in this case.) If the default pixel pattern turns out to be such a dark gray that the labels and rules are obscured, the statement 'boolean lightweight' should be added. A solid black font with slightly higher-resolution images can be generated by the following file 'blackcheap.mf':

```
% Black font for Cheapo with proofsheet resolution 66.7 pixels per inch
if mode<>cheapo: errmessage "This file is for cheapo only"; fi
picture pix_picture; pix_wd := pix_ht := 3;
pix_picture := unitpixel scaled 3;
font_identifier "BLACKCHEAP";
input grayf
```

And here is a file 'graycheap5.mf' that generates a gray font suitable for studying large proofs of low-resolution characters:

```
% Gray font for Cheapo with proofsheet resolution 10 pixels per inch
if mode<>cheapo: errmessage "This file is for cheapo only"; fi
rep=5; boolean large_pixels;
font_identifier "GRAYCHEAP";
input grayf
```

Now let's look at the program file 'grayf.mf' itself. It begins with a simple test to ensure that *mag* and *rep* are positive integers, if they're known; then comes some less obvious code that handles magnification in a nonstandard way:

```
% More-or-less general gray font generator
% See Appendix H of The METAFONTbook for how to use it
forsuffixes m = mag,rep:
 if unknown m: m := 1;
 elseif (m<1) or (m<>floor m):
  errmessage "Sorry, " & str m & " must be a positive integer";
  m := 1; fi endfor
mg := mag; mag := 1; mode_setup;
if mg>1: hppp := hppp*mg; vppp := vppp*mg;
 extra_endchar:=
  "if charcode>0:currentpicture:=currentpicture scaled mg;fi"
  & extra_endchar; fi;
```

This circumlocution is the easiest way to guarantee that the **tfm** file will be completely unaffected by magnification.

The next part of **grayf** computes the pixel representation, *pix_picture*.

```
if picture pix_picture: rep := 1;
 cull pix_picture keeping (1,infinity);
else: for z=(0,2),(1,0),(2,3),(3,1):
  fill unitsquare shifted z; endfor
 if not boolean lightweight:
  addto currentpicture also
  currentpicture rotated 90 xscaled -1; fi
 if unknown scale: scale := max(1,round(pixels_per_inch/300)); fi
 pix_wd := pix_ht := 4scale;
```

```
if rep>1: picture pix;
 currentpicture := pix_picture shifted-(1,1); pix := currentpicture;
 for r=1 upto rep-1: addto currentpicture also pix shifted(4r,0); endfor
 cullit; pix := currentpicture;
 for r=1 upto rep-1: addto currentpicture also pix shifted(0,4r); endfor
 unfill unitsquare xscaled 4rep yscaled 2 shifted-(1,1);
 unfill unitsquare yscaled 4rep xscaled 2 shifted-(1,1); cullit; fi
picture pix_picture; pix_picture := currentpicture scaled scale;
 pix_wd := pix_ht := 4scale*rep; fi
```

The lightweight pattern has 4 of every 16 pixels turned on; the normal pattern has twice as many.

Character 0 is the dot, which is quite simple:

```
def # = *72.27/pixels_per_inch enddef;
if unknown dotsize: dotsize := 2.5pix_wd/rep; fi

beginchar(0,1.2dotsize#,1.2dotsize#,0);
fill fullcircle scaled dotsize scaled mg; endchar;
```

The special coding scheme of gray fonts is implemented next:

```
numeric a[]; newinternal b,k;
def next_binary =
 k := 0; forever: if k>b: a[incr b] := 0; fi
  exitif a[k]=0; a[k] := 0; k := k+1; endfor
 a[k] := 1 enddef;
def next_special_binary =
 if a[0]=1: for k=0 upto b: a[k] := 0; endfor a[incr b]
 else: k := 0; forever: exitif a[incr k]=1; endfor
  a[k-1] fi := 1 enddef;

def make_char =
 clearit; next_binary;
 for k=0 upto b: if a[k]=1:
  addto currentpicture also pix_picture shifted(0,-k*pix_ht); fi endfor
 charcode := charcode+1; chardp := b*charht;
 scantokens extra_endchar; shipout currentpicture enddef;
```

Now we are ready to generate all the pixel characters.

```
charwd := pix_wd#; charht := pix_ht#; chardx := pix_wd*mg;
b := -1;

if boolean large_pixels:
 for k=1 upto 7: make_char; charlist k:k+120; endfor
 charcode := 120; b := -1;
 addto pix_picture also pix_picture shifted (chardx,0);
 charwd := 2charwd; chardx := 2chardx;
 for k=1 upto 7: make_char; endfor
else: for k=1 upto 63: make_char; endfor
 let next_binary = next_special_binary;
 for k=64 upto 120: make_char; endfor
```

```
for k=121,122: charcode := k;
  addto currentpicture also currentpicture shifted (chardx,0);
  charwd := 2charwd; chardx := 2chardx;
  scantokens extra_endchar; shipout currentpicture; endfor
charlist 120:121:122; fi
```

The program closes by establishing fontwide parameters:

```
font_coding_scheme "GFGRAY";
font_size 8(pix_wd#);
font_normal_space pix_wd#;
font_x_height pix_ht#;
font_quad pix_wd#;
fontdimen 8: if known rulethickness: rulethickness
  else: pix_wd#/(2rep) fi;
bye.
```

(The extra complications of an *aspect_ratio* or a slant have not been addressed.)

3. Slant fonts. GFtoDVI also makes use of another special type of font, if it is necessary to typeset slanted rules. The format of such so-called "slant fonts" is quite a bit simpler than the format of gray fonts.

A slant font contains exactly n characters, in positions 1 to n, for some positive integer n. The character in position k represents a slanted line k units tall, starting at the baseline. These lines all have a fixed slant ratio s. The vertical "unit" is usually chosen to be an integral number of pixels, small enough so that it suffices to draw rules that are an integer number of units high; in fact, it should probably be no larger than the thickness of the rules being drawn.

The following simple algorithm is used to typeset a rule that is m units high: Compute $q = \lceil m/n \rceil$; then typeset q characters of approximately equal size, namely $(m \bmod q)$ copies of character number $\lceil m/q \rceil$ and $q - (m \bmod q)$ copies of character number $\lfloor m/q \rfloor$. For example, if $n = 15$ and $m = 100$, we have $q = 7$; a 100-unit-high rule will be composed of 7 pieces, using characters 14, 14, 14, 14, 14, 15, 15.

GFtoDVI looks at the *charht* of character n only, so the **tfm** file need not be accurate about the heights of the other characters. (This is fortunate, since **tfm** format allows at most 15 different nonzero heights per font.)

The *charwd* of character k should be k/n times s times the *charht* of n.

The **font_slant** parameter should be s. It is customary to set the parameter **fontdimen** 8 to the thickness of the slanted rules, but GFtoDVI doesn't look at it.

Here's an example of a slant-font parameter file, 'slantcheap6', for the *cheapo* printer and a slant of $1/6$:

```
% Slant font for Cheapo with slope 1/6
if mode<>cheapo: errmessage "This file is for cheapo only"; fi
s=1/6;              % the slant ratio
n=30;               % the number of characters
r#=.4pt#;           % thickness of the rules
u=1;                % vertical unit
font_identifier "SLANTCHEAP6";
input slant
```

The corresponding program file 'slant.mf' looks like this:

```
% More-or-less general slant font generator for GFtoDVI
% The calling file should set the font_identifier and
%    n = number of characters
%    s = slant ratio
%    r# = rule thickness (in sharp units)
%    u = vertical unit   (in pixels)
if unknown mag: mag := 1;
elseif (mag<1) or (mag<>floor mag):
 errmessage "Sorry, mag must be a positive integer"; mag := 1; fi
mg := mag; mag := 1; mode_setup; u# := u*72.27/pixels_per_inch;
pixels_per_inch := pixels_per_inch*mg; fix_units;
define_whole_pixels(u); define_blacker_pixels(r);
pickup pencircle scaled r; ruler := savepen;
for k=1 upto n:
 beginchar(k,k*u#*s,n*u#,0);
 pickup ruler; draw origin--(k*u*s,k*u);   % draw the line
 unfill (lft-1,bot -1)--(rt 1,bot -1)
   --(rt 1,0)--(lft-1,0)--cycle;           % clip the ends
 unfill ((lft -1,0)--(rt 1,0)
   --(rt 1,top 1)--(lft -1,top 1)--cycle) shifted (k*u*s,k*u);
 endchar; endfor
font_size 16pt#;
font_slant s;
fontdimen 8: r#;
font_coding_scheme "GFSLANT";
bye.
```

4. Font samples. The real test of a font is its appearance at the final size, after it has actually been typeset. The TEX typesetting system can be used with the following example macro file 'testfont.tex' (in addition to plain TEX format) to put a new font through its paces.

We shall comment on typical uses of **testfont** as we examine its parts. At the beginning, **testfont.tex** turns off several of TEX's normal features.

```
% A testbed for font evaluation
\tracinglostchars=0               % missing characters are OK
\tolerance=1000                   % and so are loose lines
\raggedbottom                     % pages can be short
\nopagenumbers                    % and they won't be numbered
\parindent=0pt                    % nor will paragraphs be indented
\hyphenpenalty=200                % hyphens are discouraged
\doublehyphendemerits=30000       % and two in a row are terrible
\newlinechar='@                   % we want to type multiline messages
\chardef\other=12                 % and redefine "catcodes"
\newcount\m \newcount\n \newcount\p \newdimen\dim   % temporary variables
```

Then there are macros to print the time and date—an extremely valuable thing to have on any proofsheet.

```
\def\today{\ifcase\month\or
  January\or February\or March\or April\or May\or June\or
  July\or August\or September\or October\or November\or December\fi
  \space\number\day, \number\year}
\def\hours{\n=\time \divide\n 60
  \m=-\n \multiply\m 60 \advance\m \time
  \twodigits\n\twodigits\m}
\def\twodigits#1{\ifnum #1<10 0\fi \number#1}
```

An online "menu" of the available test routines will be typed at your terminal if you request \help.

```
{\catcode`\|=0 \catcode`\\=\other    % use | as the escape, temporarily
|gdef|help{|message{%
\init switches to another font;@%
\end or \bye finishes the run;@%
\table prints the font layout in tabular format;@%
\text prints a sample text, assuming TeX text font conventions;@%
\sample combines \table and \text;@%
\mixture mixes a background character with a series of others;@%
\alternation interleaves a background character with a series;@%
\alphabet prints all lowercase letters within a given background;@%
\ALPHABET prints all uppercase letters within a given background;@%
\series prints a series of letters within a given background;@%
\lowers prints a comprehensive test of lowercase;@%
\uppers prints a comprehensive test of uppercase;@%
\digits prints a comprehensive test of numerals;@%
\math prints a comprehensive test of TeX math italic;@%
\names prints a text that mixes upper and lower case;@%
\punct prints a punctuation test;@%
\bigtest combines many of the above routines;@%
\help repeats this message;@%
and you can use ordinary TeX commands (e.g., to \input a file).}}}
```

The program prompts you for a font name. If the font is in your local directory instead of a system directory, you might have to specify the directory name as part of the font name. You should also specify scaling if the font has been magnified, as in the example of Chapter 5. Several fonts can be tested during a single run, if you say '\init' before '\end'.

```
\def\init{\message{@Name of the font to test = }
  \read-1 to\fontname \startfont
  \message{Now type a test command (\string\help\space for help):}}
\def\startfont{\font\testfont=\fontname \spaceskip=0pt
  \leftline{\sevenrm Test of \fontname\unskip\ on \today\ at \hours}
  \medskip
  \testfont \setbaselineskip
```

```
\ifdim\fontdimen6\testfont<10pt \rightskip=0pt plus 20pt
\else\rightskip=0pt plus 2em \fi
\spaceskip=\fontdimen2\testfont % space between words (\raggedright)
\xspaceskip=\fontdimen2\testfont
\advance\xspaceskip by\fontdimen7\testfont}
```

The specified font will be called \testfont. As soon as you have specified it, \init calls on \startfont, which puts a title line on the page; then it chooses what it hopes will be a good distance between baselines, and gets ready to typeset text with "ragged right" margins. (The code above improves on plain TEX's \raggedright.)

The baselineskip distance is taken to be 6 pt plus the height of the tallest character plus the depth of the deepest character. This is the distance between baselines for "series" tests, but it is decreased by 4 pt when the sample text is set. If you want to change the baseline distance chosen by testfont, you can just say, e.g., '\baselineskip=11pt'.

```
\def\setbaselineskip{\setbox0=\hbox{\n=0
\loop\char\n \ifnum \n<255 \advance\n 1 \repeat} % 256 chars in \box0
\baselineskip=6pt \advance\baselineskip\ht0 \advance\baselineskip\dp0 }
```

When testfont prompts you for a "background character" or a "starting character" or an "ending character," you can type the character you want (assuming ASCII code); or you can say, e.g., '#35' to get character code number 35. Codes 0–32 and 127–255 have to be specified with the '#' option, on non-fancy installations of TEX, and so does code 35 (which is the ASCII code of '#' itself).

```
\def\setchar#1{{\escapechar-1\message{\string#1 character = }%
  \def\do##1{\catcode'##1=\other}\dospecials
  \read-1 to\next
  \expandafter\finsetchar\next\next#1}}
\def\finsetchar#1#2\next#3{\global\chardef#3='#1
  \ifnum #3='\# \global\chardef#3=#2 \fi}
\def\promptthree{\setchar\background
  \setchar\starting \setchar\ending}
```

(The TEX hackery here is a bit subtle, because special characters like '\' and '$' must temporarily lose their special significance.)

Suppose the background character is 'o' and the starting and ending characters are respectively 'p' and 'q'. Then the \mixture operation will typeset 'opooppoooopppop' and 'oqooqqooooqqqoq'; the \alternation operation will typeset 'opopopopopopopopo' and 'oqoqoqoqoqoqoqoqo'. Other patterns could be added in a similar way.

```
\def\mixture{\promptthree \domix\mixpattern}
\def\alternation{\promptthree \domix\altpattern}
\def\mixpattern{\0\1\0\0\1\1\0\0\0\1\1\1\0\1}
\def\altpattern{\0\1\0\1\0\1\0\1\0\1\0\1\0\1\0}
\def\domix#1{\par\chardef\0=\background \n=\starting
  \loop \chardef\1=\n #1\endgraf
  \ifnum \n<\ending \advance\n 1 \repeat}
```

The `\series` operation puts the background character between all the others (e.g., 'opoqo'). Special series containing the lowercase letters of TEX text fonts (including 'ß', 'æ', 'œ', and ø') and the uppercase letters (including 'Æ', 'Œ', and 'Ø') are provided. Although `\mixture` and `\alternation` show you the effects of ligatures and kerning, `\series` does not.

```
\def\!{\discretionary{\background}{\background}{\background}}
\def\series{\promptthree \!\doseries\starting\ending\par}
\def\doseries#1#2{\n=#1\loop\char\n\!\ifnum\n<#2\advance\n 1 \repeat}
\def\complower{\!\doseries{`a}{`z}\doseries{'31}{'34}\par}
\def\compupper{\!\doseries{`A}{`Z}\doseries{'35}{'37}\par}
\def\compdigs{\!\doseries{`0}{`9}\par}
\def\alphabet{\setchar\background\complower}
\def\ALPHABET{\setchar\background\compupper}
```

(A long series might fill more than one line; TEX's `\discretionary` break operation is used here so that the background character will end the line and be repeated at the beginning of the next.)

A "comprehensive" test uses a series of background characters against a series of others. The series will consist of lowercase letters ('`\lowers`'), uppercase letters ('`\uppers`'), or numerals ('`\digits`').

```
\def\lowers{\docomprehensive\complower{`a}{`z}{'31}{'34}}
\def\uppers{\docomprehensive\compupper{`A}{`Z}{'35}{'37}}
\def\digits{\docomprehensive\compdigs{`0}{`4}{`5}{`9}}
\def\docomprehensive#1#2#3#4#5{\par\chardef\background=#2
  \loop{#1} \ifnum\background<#3\m=\background\advance\m 1
  \chardef\background=\m \repeat \chardef\background=#4
  \loop{#1} \ifnum\background<#5\m=\background\advance\m 1
  \chardef\background=\m \repeat}
```

The `\names` test puts uppercase letters and accents together with lowercase letters. The accents will look funny if the test font doesn't have them in plain TEX's favorite positions.

```
\def\names{ {\AA}ngel\aa\ Beatrice Claire
  Diana \'Erica Fran\c{c}oise Ginette H\'el\`ene Iris
  Jackie K\=aren {\L}au\.ra Mar{\'\i}a N\H{a}ta{\l}{\u\i}e Octave
  Pauline Qu\^eneau Roxanne Sabine T\~a{\'\j}a Ur\v{s}ula
  Vivian Wendy Xanthippe Yv{\o}nne Z\"azilie\par}
```

Punctuation marks are tested in juxtaposition with different sorts of letters, by the '`\punct`' macro:

```
\def\punct{\par\dopunct{min}\dopunct{pig}\dopunct{hid}
  \dopunct{HIE}\dopunct{TIP}\dopunct{fluff}
  \$1,234.56 + 7/8 = 9\% @ \#0\par}
\def\dopunct#1{#1,\ #1:\ #1;\ `#1'\
  ?`#1?\ !`#1!\ (#1)\ [#1]\ #1*\ #1.\par}
```

Mixtures and alternations and series are excellent ways to discover that letters are too dark, too light, or too tightly spaced. But a font also has to be readable; in fact, this is the number one objective. So `testfont` provides a sample '\text'. One of the sentences is optional, because it contains lots of accents and unusual letters; you can omit it from the text by saying '\omitaccents'. Furthermore, you can type your own text, online, or you can input one from a file, instead of using this canned example.

```
\def\text{{\advance\baselineskip-4pt
\setbox0=\hbox{abcdefghijklmnopqrstuvwxyz}
\ifdim\hsize>2\wd0 \ifdim 15pc>2\wd0 \hsize=15pc \else\hsize=2\wd0 \fi\fi
On November 14, 1885, Senator \& Mrs.~Leland Stanford called together at
their San Francisco mansion the 24~prominent men who had been chosen as
the first trustees of The Leland Stanford Junior University.  They
handed to the board the Founding Grant of the University, which they had
executed three days before. This document---with various amendments,
legislative acts, and court decrees---remains as the University's
charter.  In bold, sweeping language it stipulates that the objectives of
the University are ``to qualify students for personal success and direct
usefulness in life; and to promote the publick welfare by exercising an
influence in behalf of humanity and civilization, teaching the blessings
of liberty regulated by law, and inculcating love and reverence for the
great principles of government as derived from the inalienable rights of
man to life, liberty, and the pursuit of happiness.'' \moretext
(!`THE DAZED BROWN FOX QUICKLY GAVE 12345--67890 JUMPS!)\par}}
\def\moretext{?`But aren't Kafka's Schlo{\ss} and {\AE}sop's {\OE}uvres
often na{\"\i}ve  vis-\`a-vis the d{\ae}monic ph{\oe}nix's official
r\^ole in fluffy souffl\'es? }
\def\omitaccents{\let\moretext=\relax}
```

Now comes one of the hardest parts of the file, from the TeX standpoint: The \table macro prints a font diagram, omitting groups of sixteen characters that are entirely absent from the font. The format of this table is the same as that used in Appendix F of *The TeXbook*. When the font contains unusually large characters that ought to be vertically centered, you should say '\centerlargechars' before '\table'. (A TeX math symbol font or math extension font would use this feature.)

```
\def\oct#1{\hbox{\rm\'{}\kern-.2em\it#1\/\kern.05em}} % octal constant
\def\hex#1{\hbox{\rm\H{}\tt#1}} % hexadecimal constant
\def\setdigs#1"#2{\gdef\h{#2}% \h=hex prefix; \0\1=corresponding octal
 \m=\n \divide\m by 64 \xdef\0{\the\m}%
 \multiply\m by-64 \advance\m by\n \divide\m by 8 \xdef\1{\the\m}}
\def\testrow{\setbox0=\hbox{\penalty 1\def\\{\char"\h}%
 \\0\\1\\2\\3\\4\\5\\6\\7\\8\\9\\A\\B\\C\\D\\E\\F%
\global\p=\lastpenalty}} % \p=1 if none of the characters exist
\def\oddline{\cr
 \noalign{\nointerlineskip}
 \multispan{19}\hrulefill&
 \setbox0=\hbox{\lower 2.3pt\hbox{\hex{\h x}}}\smash{\box0}\cr
 \noalign{\nointerlineskip}}
```

```
\newif\ifskipping
\def\evenline{\loop\skippingfalse
 \ifnum\n<256 \m=\n \divide\m 16 \chardef\next=\m
 \expandafter\setdigs\meaning\next \testrow
 \ifnum\p=1 \skippingtrue \fi\fi
 \ifskipping \global\advance\n 16 \repeat
 \ifnum\n=256 \let\next=\endchart\else\let\next=\morechart\fi
 \next}
\def\morechart{\cr\noalign{\hrule\penalty5000}
 \chartline \oddline \m=\1 \advance\m 1 \xdef\1{\the\m}
 \chartline \evenline}
\def\chartline{&\oct{\0\1x}&&\:&&\:&&\:&&\:&&\:&&\:&&\:&&\:&&}
\def\chartstrut{\lower4.5pt\vbox to14pt{}}
\def\table{$$\global\n=0
  \halign to\hsize\bgroup
    \chartstrut##\tabskip0pt plus10pt&
    &\hfil##\hfil&\vrule##\cr
    \lower6.5pt\null
    &&&\oct0&&\oct1&&\oct2&&\oct3&&\oct4&&\oct5&&\oct6&&\oct7&\evenline}
\def\endchart{\cr\noalign{\hrule}
  \raise11.5pt\null&&&\hex 8&&\hex 9&&\hex A&&\hex B&
  &\hex C&&\hex D&&\hex E&&\hex F&\cr\egroup$$\par}
\def\:{\setbox0=\hbox{\char\n}%
  \ifdim\ht0>7.5pt\reposition
  \else\ifdim\dp0>2.5pt\reposition\fi\fi
  \box0\global\advance\n 1 }
\def\reposition{\setbox0=\vbox{\kern2pt\box0}\dim=\dp0
  \advance\dim 2pt \dp0=\dim}
\def\centerlargechars{
  \def\reposition{\setbox0=\hbox{$\vcenter{\kern2pt\box0\kern2pt}$}}}
```

Two of the most important combinations of tests are treated now: `\sample` prints the `\table` and the **text**; `\bigtest` gives you the works, plus a mysterious word that is traditional in type specimens:

```
\def\sample{\table\text}
```

```
\def\bigtest{\sample
  hamburgefonstiv HAMBURGEFONSTIV\par
  \names \punct \lowers \uppers \digits}
```

Finally, there's a `\math` routine useful for checking out the spacing in the math italic fonts used by plain TeX; `\mathsy` does a similar thing for the uppercase letters in a math symbols font.

```
\def\math{\textfont1=\testfont \skewchar\testfont=\skewtrial
  \mathchardef\Gamma="100 \mathchardef\Delta="101
  \mathchardef\Theta="102 \mathchardef\Lambda="103 \mathchardef\Xi="104
  \mathchardef\Pi="105 \mathchardef\Sigma="106 \mathchardef\Upsilon="107
  \mathchardef\Phi="108 \mathchardef\Psi="109 \mathchardef\Omega="10A
```

```
\def\ii{i} \def\jj{j}
\def\\##1{|##1|+}\mathtrial
\def\\##1{##1_2+}\mathtrial
\def\\##1{##1^2+}\mathtrial
\def\\##1{##1/2+}\mathtrial
\def\\##1{2/##1+}\mathtrial
\def\\##1{##1,{}+}\mathtrial
\def\\##1{d##1+}\mathtrial
\let\ii=\imath \let\jj=\jmath \def\\##1{\hat##1+}\mathtrial}
\newcount\skewtrial \skewtrial='177
\def\mathtrial{$\\A \\B \\C \\D \\E \\F \\G \\H \\I \\J \\K \\L \\M \\N
  \\O \\P \\Q \\R \\S \\T \\U \\V \\W \\X \\Y \\Z \\a \\b \\c \\d \\e \\f
  \\g \\h \\\ii \\\jj \\k \\l \\m \\n \\o \\p \\q \\r \\s \\t \\u \\v \\w
  \\x \\y \\z \\\alpha \\\beta \\\gamma \\\delta \\\epsilon \\\zeta
  \\\eta \\\theta \\\iota \\\kappa \\\lambda \\\mu \\\nu \\\xi \\\pi
  \\\rho \\\sigma \\\tau \\\upsilon \\\phi \\\chi \\\psi \\\omega
  \\\vartheta \\\varpi \\\varphi \\\Gamma \\\Delta \\\Theta \\\Lambda
  \\\Xi \\\Pi \\\Sigma \\\Upsilon \\\Phi \\\Psi \\\Omega
  \\\partial \\\ell \\\wp$\par}
\def\mathsy{\begingroup\skewtrial='060 % for math symbol font tests
  \def\mathtrial{$\\A \\B \\C \\D \\E \\F \\G \\H \\I \\J \\K \\L
  \\M \\N \\O \\P \\Q \\R \\S \\T \\U \\V \\W \\X \\Y \\Z$\par}
  \math\endgroup}
```

The last line of `testfont` is

```
\ifx\noinit!\else\init\fi
```

and it means "automatically call '\init' unless '\noinit' is an exclamation point." Why this? Well, you might have your own test file from which you'd like to use the facilities of `testfont`, without typing commands online. If your file says '\let\noinit! \input testfont' TeX will read in `testfont` but the routine will not prompt you for a file name. The file can then continue to test one or more fonts by saying, e.g.,

```
\def\fontname{cmbx10 }\startfont\sample\vfill\eject
\def\fontname{cmti10 scaled \magstep3}\startfont\sample\vfill\eject
```

thereby defining \fontname directly, and using \startfont to do the initialization instead of \init.

To conclude this appendix, let's look at the listing of a file that can be used to test special constructions in math fonts with the conventions of plain TeX:

```
\raggedright \rightskip=2em plus 5em minus 2em
$\hbar \not\equiv B$, but $\sqrt C \mapsto \sqrt x$,
$Z \hookrightarrow W$,         $Z \hookleftarrow W$,
$Z \longmapsto W$,    $Z \bowtie W$,  $Z \models W$,
$Z \Longrightarrow W$,         $Z \longrightarrow W$,
$Z \longleftarrow W$,          $Z \Longleftarrow W$,
$Z \longleftrightarrow W$,    $Z \Longleftrightarrow W$,
$\overbrace{\hbox{very long things for testing}}$,
```

```
$\underbrace{\hbox{very long things for testing}}$,
$Z \choose W$, $Z \brack W$, $Z \brace W$, $Z \sqrt W$,
$Z \cong W$,   $Z \notin W$, $Z \rightleftharpoons W$,
$\widehat Z$,     $\widehat{ZW}$,     $\widehat{Z+W}$,
$\widetilde Z$,   $\widetilde{ZW}$,   $\widetilde{Z+W}$.
\def\sizetest#1#2{$$
  \Bigggl{#1}\bigggl{#1}\Biggl{#1}\biggl{#1}\Bigl{#1}\bigl{#1}\left#1
  \bullet
  \right#2\bigr{#2}\Bigr{#2}\biggr{#2}\Biggr{#2}\bigggr{#2}\Bigggr{#2}$$}
\def\biggg#1{{\hbox{$\left#1\vbox to20.5pt{}\right.$}}}
\def\bigggl{\mathopen\biggg}  \def\bigggr{\mathclose\biggg}
\def\Biggg#1{{\hbox{$\left#1\vbox to23.5pt{}\right.$}}}
\def\Bigggl{\mathopen\Biggg}  \def\Bigggr{\mathclose\Biggg}

\sizetest ()        \sizetest []            \sizetest \lgroup\rgroup
\sizetest \lmoustache\rmoustache            \sizetest \vert\Vert
\sizetest \arrowvert\Arrowvert              \sizetest \uparrow\downarrow
\sizetest \updownarrow\Updownarrow          \sizetest \Uparrow\Downarrow
\sizetest \bracevert{\delimiter"342} \sizetest \backslash/
\sizetest \langle\rangle                    \sizetest \lbrace\rbrace
\sizetest \lceil\rceil                      \sizetest \lfloor\rfloor

$$\sqrt{\sqrt{\sqrt{\sqrt{\sqrt{\sqrt{\sqrt{\sqrt{-1}}}}}}}}$$

\def\dobig{\do\bigvee \do\bigwedge \do\bigotimes \do\bigoplus \do\bigodot
 \do\bigcap \do\bigcup \do\biguplus \do\bigsqcup
 \do\int \do\ointop \do\smallint \do\prod \do\coprod \do\sum}
\def\do#1{#1_a^b A} $\dobig$ $$\dobig$$
\bye
```

Be sure of it: Giue me the Occular proofe.
— WILLIAM SHAKESPEARE, *Othello* (1604)

*The figure itself appears here
as a very necessary adjunct to the verbalization.
In Euclid's presentation we cannot wholly follow the argumentation
without the figure, and unless we are strong enough
to imagine the figure in our mind's eye, we would also be reduced
to supplying our own figure if the author had not done it for us.
Notice also that the language of the proof has a
formal and severely restricted quality about it.
This is not the language of history, nor of drama,
nor of day to day life;
this is language that has been sharpened and refined so as to serve
the precise needs of a precise but limited inellectual goal.*
— P. J. DAVIS and R. HERSH, *Proof* (1981)

Index

The author has tried to provide as complete an index as possible, so that people will be able to find things that are tucked away in obscure corners of this long book. Therefore the index itself is rather long. A short summary of the simpler aspects of METAFONT appears at the beginning of Appendix B; a summary of the standard character classes for tokens can be found at the end of Chapter 6; a summary of other special things appears under 'tables' below.

Page numbers are <u>underlined</u> in the index when they represent the definition or the main source of information about whatever is being indexed. (Underlined entries are the most definitive, but not necessarily the easiest for a beginner to understand.) A page number is given in italics (e.g., '*123*') when that page contains an instructive example of how the concept in question might be used. Sometimes both underlining and italics are appropriate. When an index entry refers to a page containing a relevant exercise, the answer to that exercise (in Appendix A) might divulge further information; an answer page is not indexed here unless it refers to a topic that isn't included in the statement of the relevant exercise.

Index entries for quoted symbols like 'T' refer to example programs that draw the symbols in question.

Symbolic tokens that are preceded by an asterisk (*) in this index are primitives of METAFONT; i.e., they are built in. It may be dangerous to redefine them.

The more we search,
the More are we Deceived.

— MERCY OTIS WARREN, *To Mr. Adams* (1773)

A heavy weight is now to be removed from my conscience.
So essential did I consider an Index to be to every book,
that I proposed to bring a Bill into Parliament
to deprive an author who publishes a book without an Index
of the privilege of copyright; and, moreover,
to subject him, for his offence, to a pecuniary penalty.
Yet, from difficulties started by my printers,
my own books have hitherto been without an Index.

— LORD CAMPBELL, *Lives of the Chief Justices of England*, vol. 3 (1857)

J

Joining the
T_EX Community

This appendix is about grouping of another kind: T_EX and METAFONT users from around the world have banded together to form the T_EX Users Group (TUG), in order to exchange information about common problems and solutions.

A newsletter/journal called *TUGboat* has been published since 1980, featuring articles about all aspects of T_EX and METAFONT. TUG has a network of "site coordinators" who serve as focal points of communication for people with the same computer configurations. Occasional short courses are given, to provide concentrated training in special topics; videotapes of these courses are available for rental. Meetings of the entire TUG membership are held at least once a year. You can buy METAFONT T-shirts at these meetings.

Information about membership in TUG and subscription to *TUGboat* is available from

> T_EX Users Group
> P.O. Box 9506
> Providence RI 02940-9506, USA.

TUG is established to serve members having a common interest in T_EX, a system for typesetting technical text, and in METAFONT, a system for font design.
— T_EX USERS GROUP, *Bylaws, Article II* (1983)

Don't delay, write today! That number again is T_EX Users Group P.O. Box 9506 Providence RI 02940-9506, USA.
— DONALD E. KNUTH, *The T_EXbook* (1985)